YOU HAVE KILLED ME

An Oni Press Production

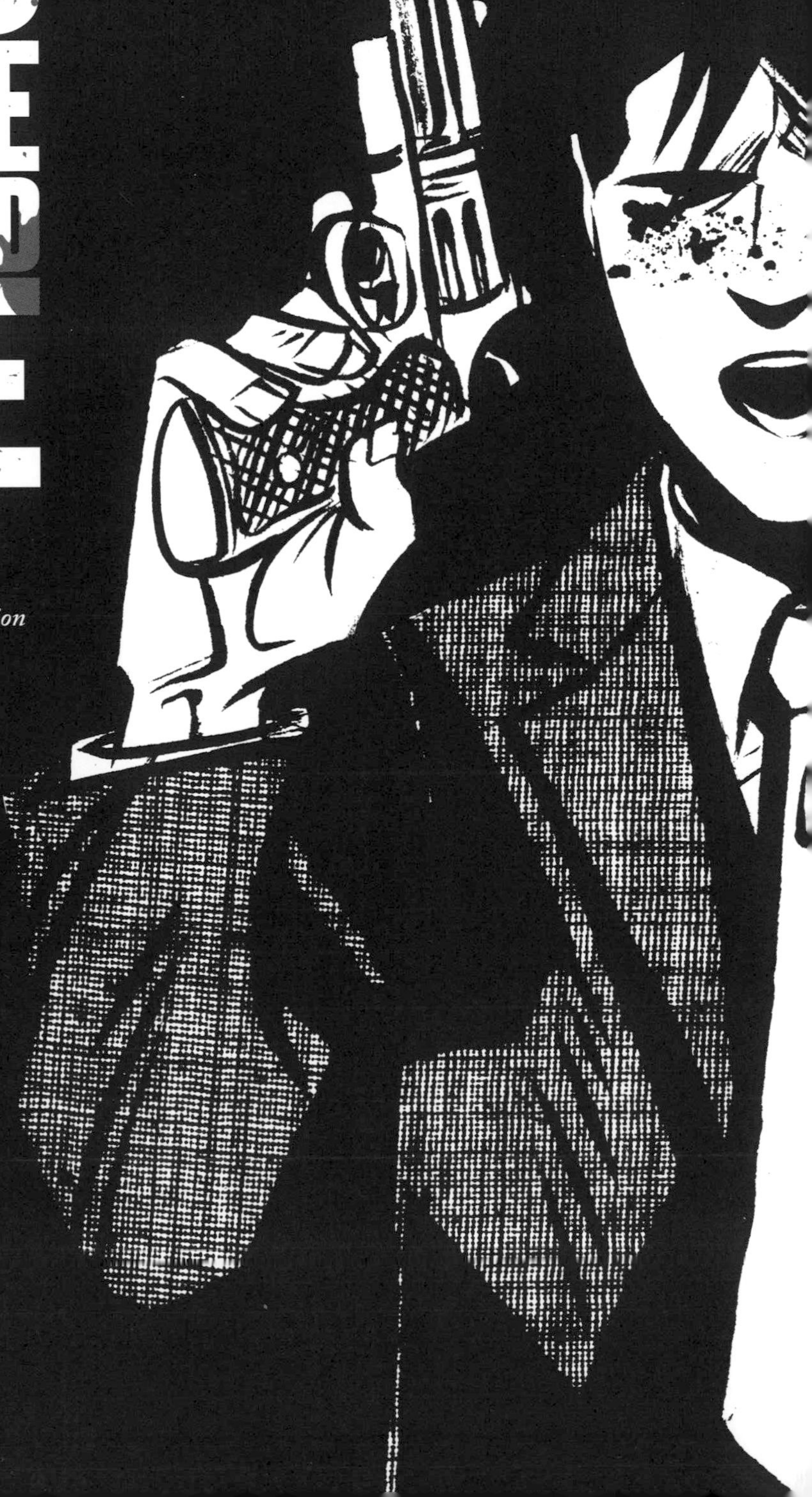

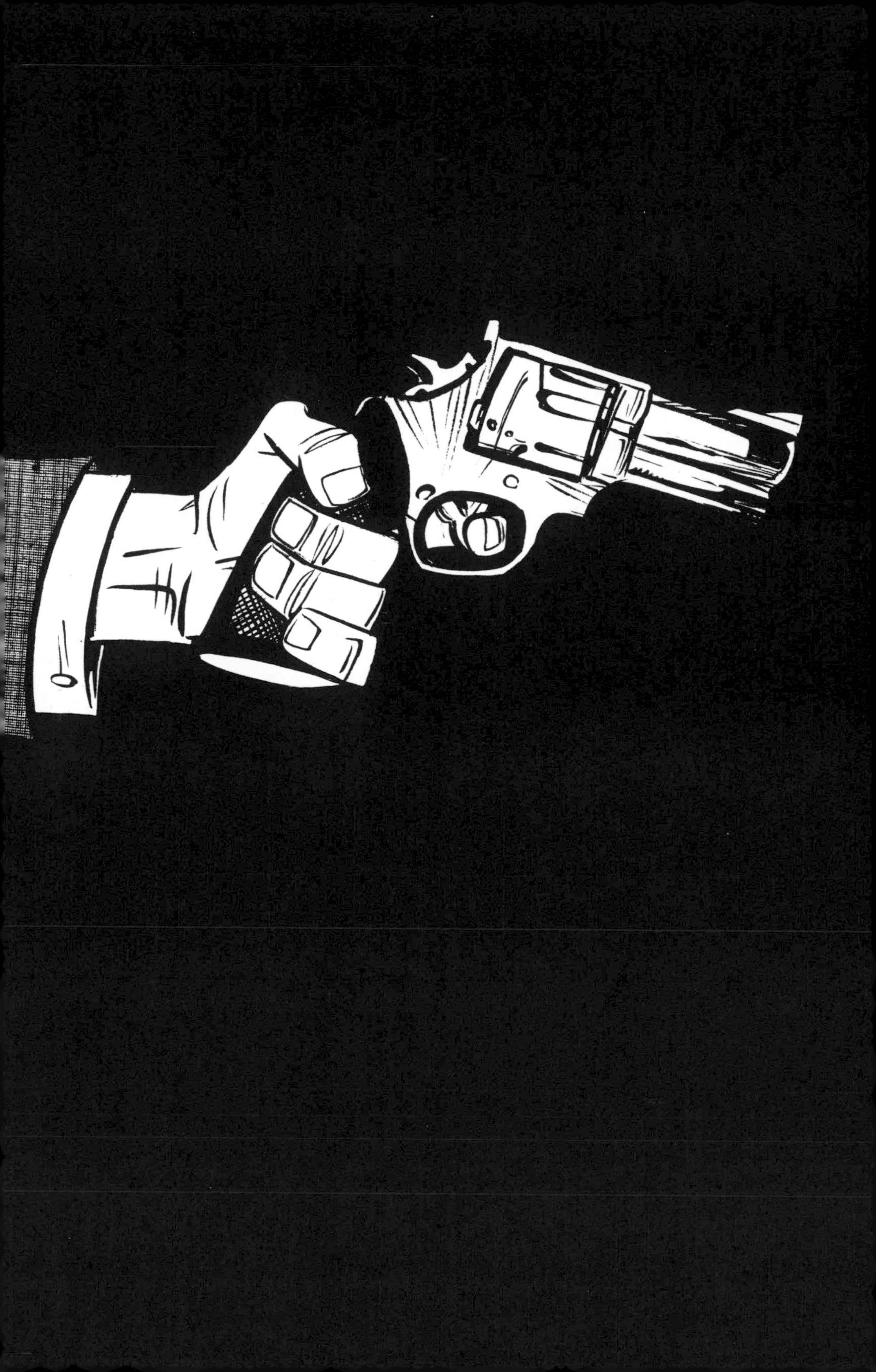

YOU HAVE KILLED ME

by JAMIE S. RICH & JOËLLE JONES

lettered by DOUGLAS E. SHERWOOD

designed by KEITH WOOD

edited by JAMES LUCAS JONES & JILL BEATON

PUBLISHED BY ONI PRESS, INC.

JOE NOZEMACK *publisher*

JAMES LUCAS JONES *editor in chief*

RANDAL C. JARRELL *managing editor*

CORY CASONI *marketing director*

KEITH WOOD *art director*

JILL BEATON *assistant editor*

DOUGLAS E. SHERWOOD *production assistant*

*Special thanks to Terry and Satoka for their
assistance with the tones, which were all
applied by hand. Their aid was a big help in
completing the process.*

ONI PRESS, INC.
1305 SE Martin Luther King Jr. Blvd.
Suite A
Portland, OR 97214
USA

www.onipress.com
www.confessions123.com
www.joellejones.com

First edition: June 2009
ISBN: 978-1-932664-88-1

10 9 8 7 6 5 4 3 2 1
PRINTED IN CHINA

CHAPTER 1

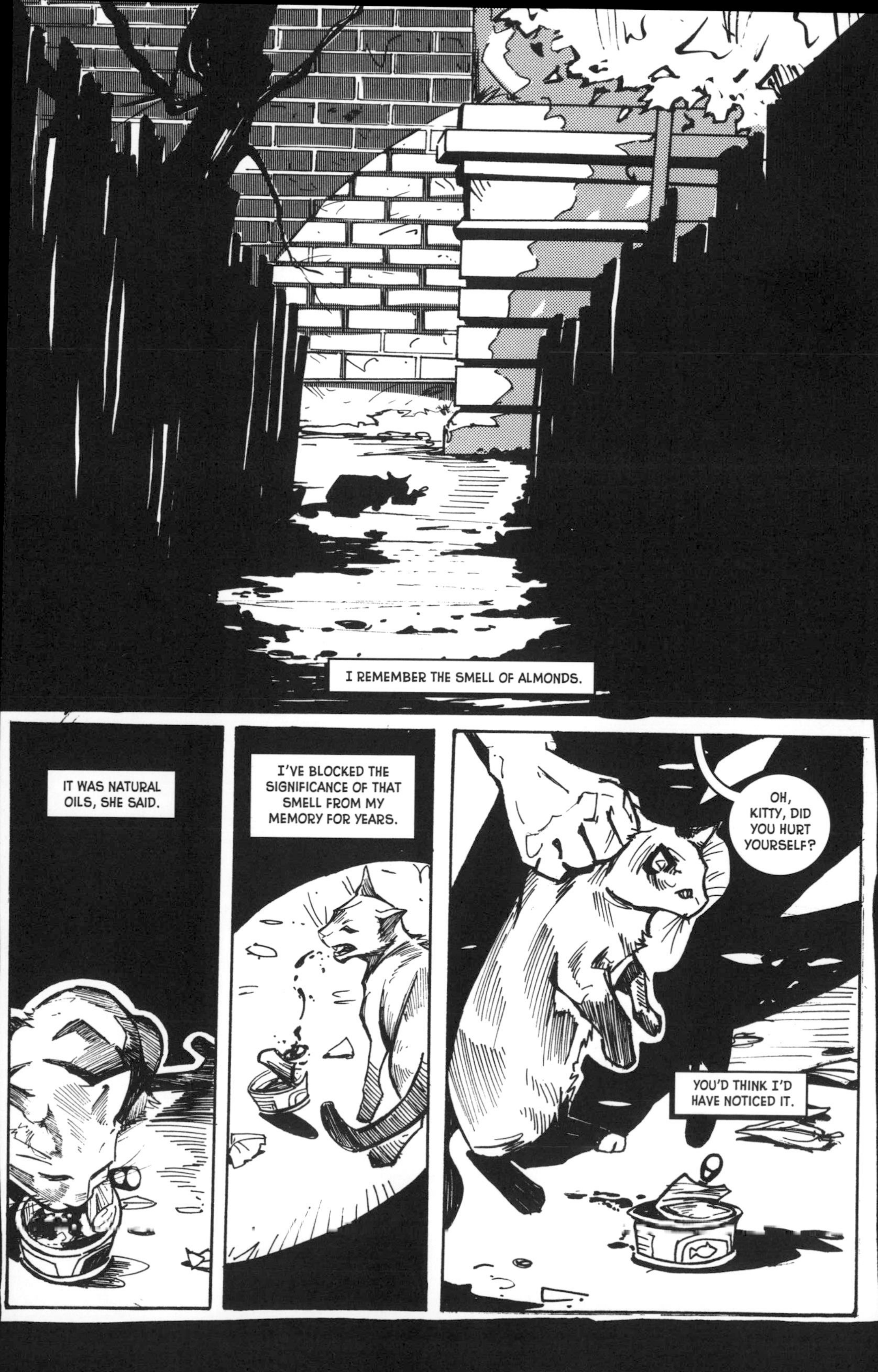
I REMEMBER THE SMELL OF ALMONDS.
IT WAS NATURAL OILS, SHE SAID.
I'VE BLOCKED THE SIGNIFICANCE OF THAT SMELL FROM MY MEMORY FOR YEARS.
OH, KITTY, DID YOU HURT YOURSELF?
YOU'D THINK I'D HAVE NOTICED IT.

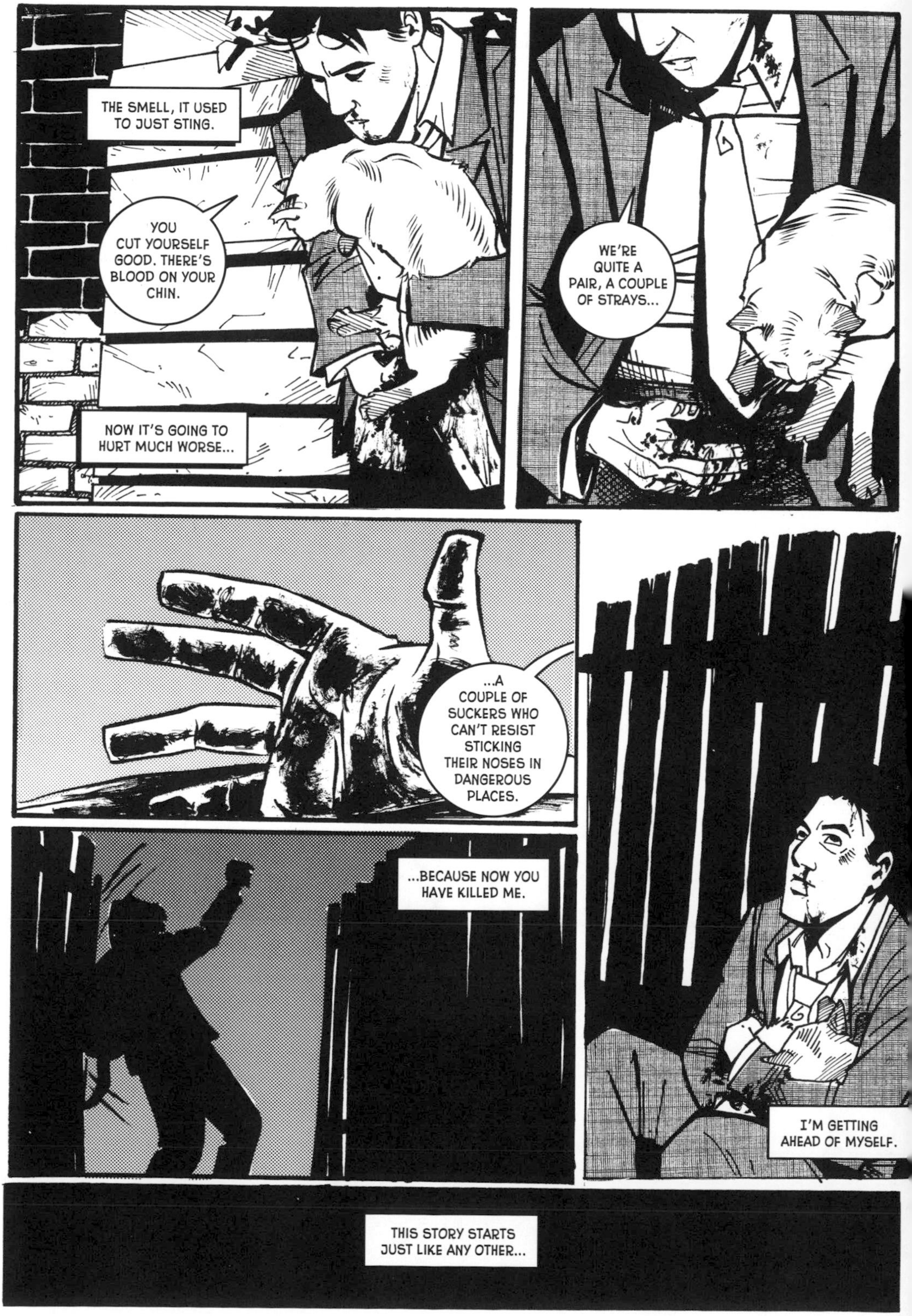
THE SMELL, IT USED TO JUST STING.
YOU CUT YOURSELF GOOD. THERE'S BLOOD ON YOUR CHIN.
NOW IT'S GOING TO HURT MUCH WORSE...
WE'RE QUITE A PAIR, A COUPLE OF STRAYS...
...A COUPLE OF SUCKERS WHO CAN'T RESIST STICKING THEIR NOSES IN DANGEROUS PLACES.
...BECAUSE NOW YOU HAVE KILLED ME.
I'M GETTING AHEAD OF MYSELF.
THIS STORY STARTS JUST LIKE ANY OTHER...

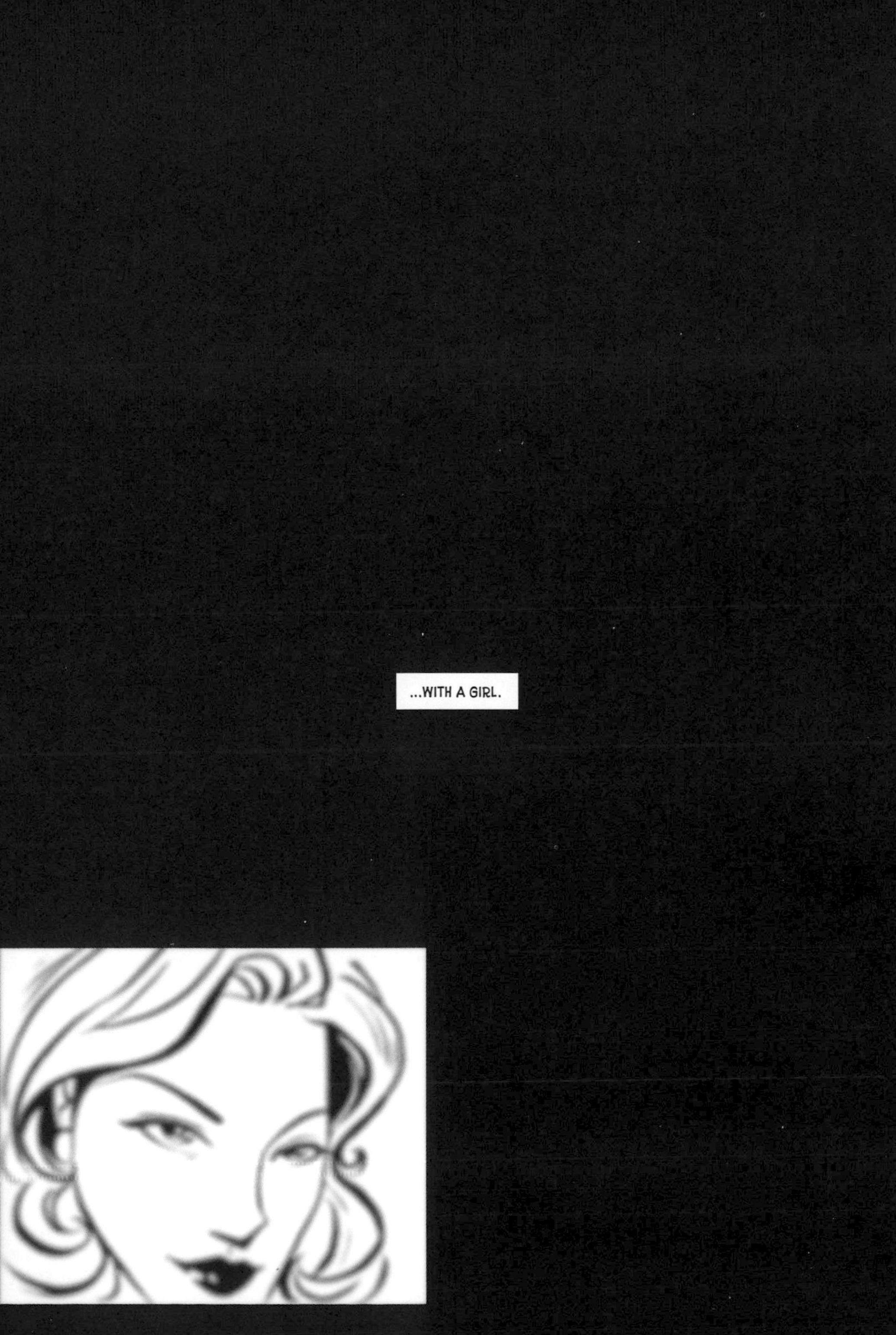
...WITH A GIRL.

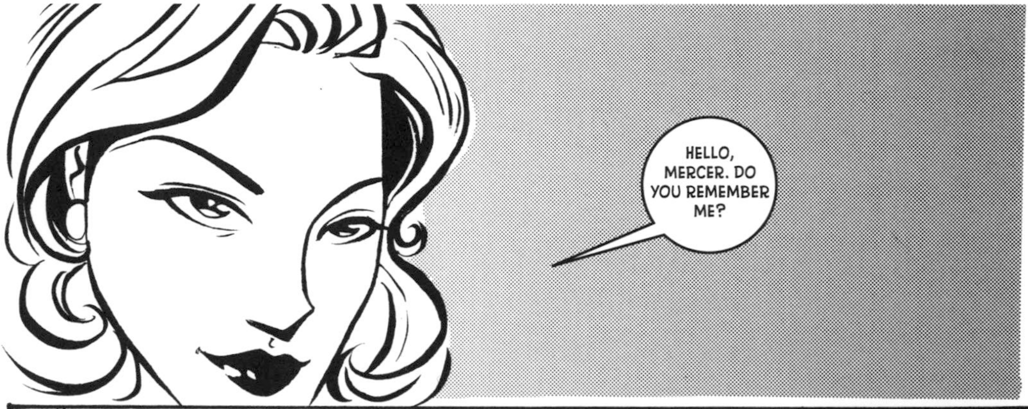
HELLO, MERCER. DO YOU REMEMBER ME?

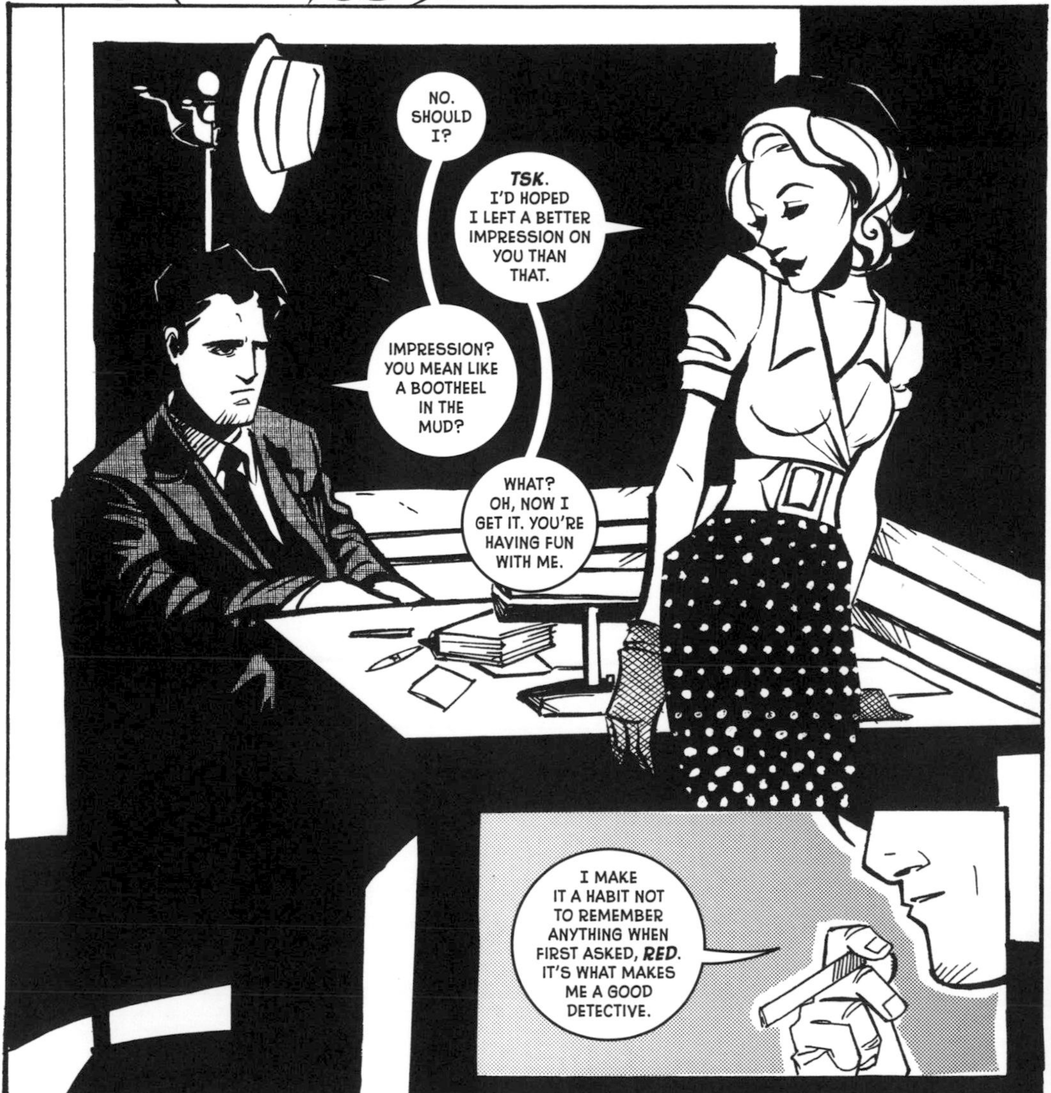
NO. SHOULD I?
TSK. I'D HOPED I LEFT A BETTER IMPRESSION ON YOU THAN THAT.
IMPRESSION? YOU MEAN LIKE A BOOTHEEL IN THE MUD?
WHAT? OH, NOW I GET IT. YOU'RE HAVING FUN WITH ME.
I MAKE IT A HABIT NOT TO REMEMBER ANYTHING WHEN FIRST ASKED, RED. IT'S WHAT MAKES ME A GOOD DETECTIVE.

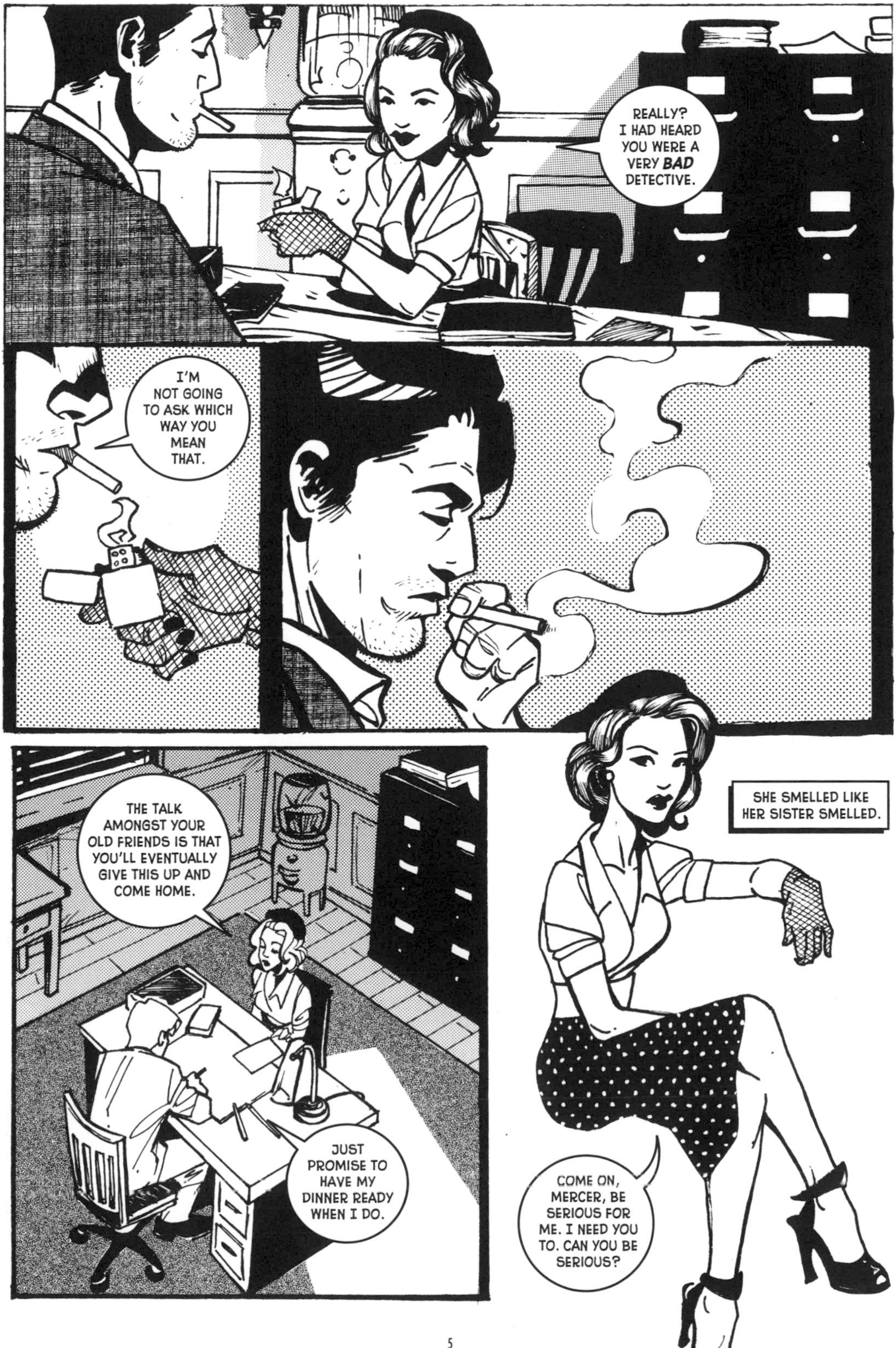
REALLY? I HAD HEARD YOU WERE A VERY BAD DETECTIVE.
I'M NOT GOING TO ASK WHICH WAY YOU MEAN THAT.
THE TALK AMONGST YOUR OLD FRIENDS IS THAT YOU'LL EVENTUALLY GIVE THIS UP AND COME HOME.
JUST PROMISE TO HAVE MY DINNER READY WHEN I DO.
SHE SMELLED LIKE HER SISTER SMELLED.
COME ON, MERCER, BE SERIOUS FOR ME. I NEED YOU TO. CAN YOU BE SERIOUS?

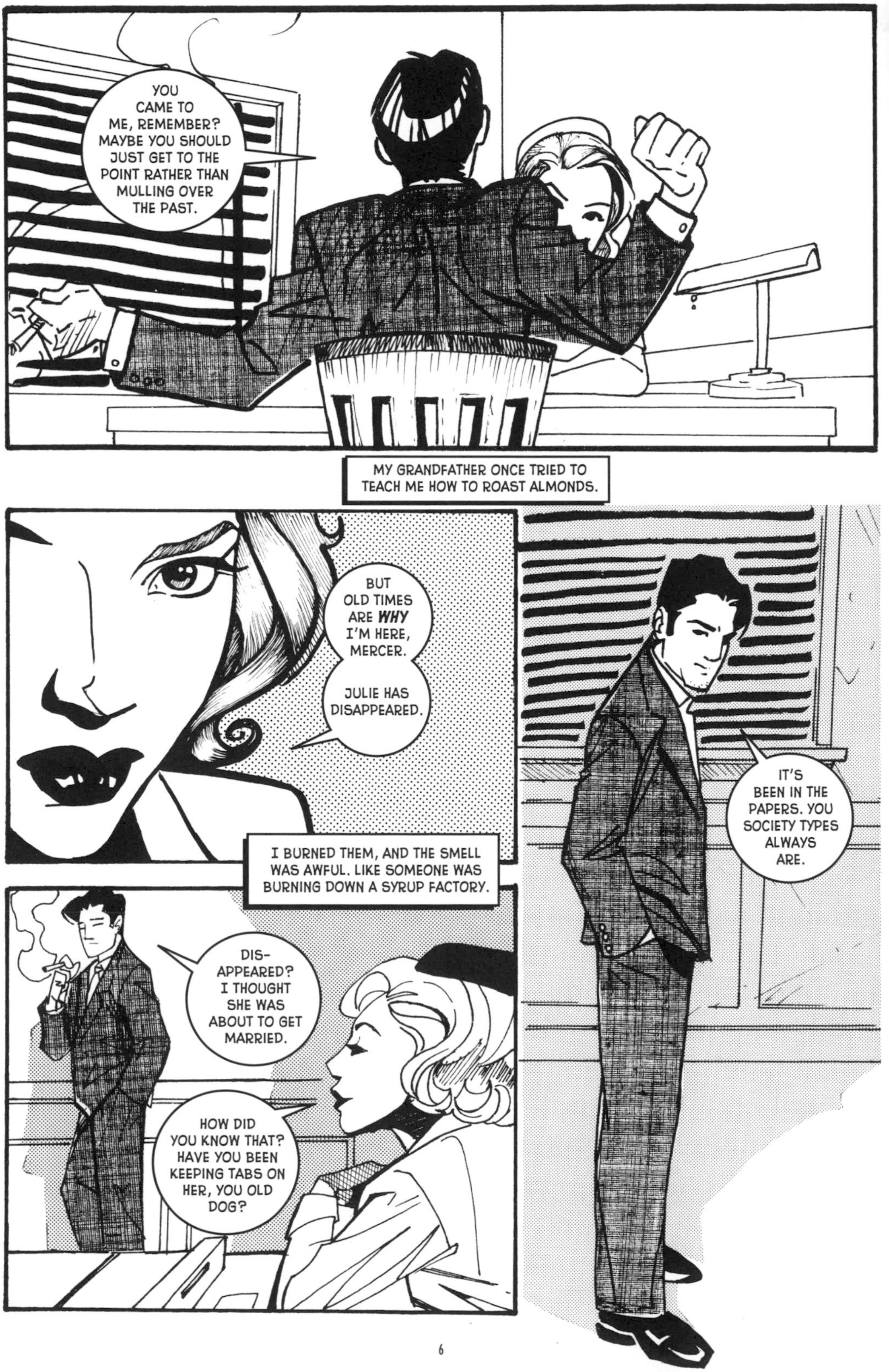
YOU CAME TO ME, REMEMBER? MAYBE YOU SHOULD JUST GET TO THE POINT RATHER THAN MULLING OVER THE PAST.
MY GRANDFATHER ONCE TRIED TO TEACH ME HOW TO ROAST ALMONDS.
BUT OLD TIMES ARE *WHY* I'M HERE, MERCER.
JULIE HAS DISAPPEARED.
I BURNED THEM, AND THE SMELL WAS AWFUL. LIKE SOMEONE WAS BURNING DOWN A SYRUP FACTORY.
DIS-APPEARED? I THOUGHT SHE WAS ABOUT TO GET MARRIED.
HOW DID YOU KNOW THAT? HAVE YOU BEEN KEEPING TABS ON HER, YOU OLD DOG?
IT'S BEEN IN THE PAPERS. YOU SOCIETY TYPES ALWAYS ARE.

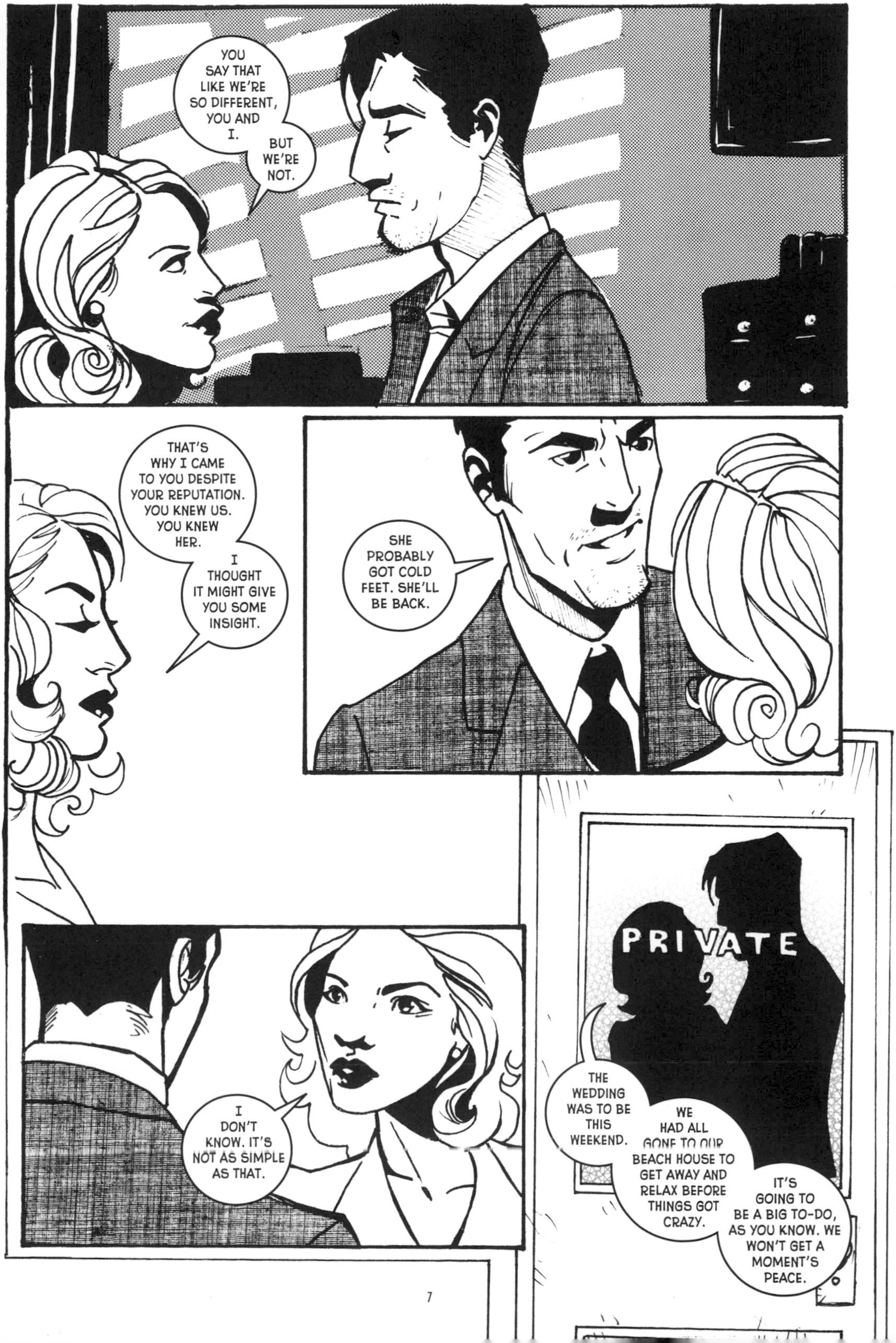
YOU SAY THAT LIKE WE'RE SO DIFFERENT, YOU AND I.
BUT WE'RE NOT.
THAT'S WHY I CAME TO YOU DESPITE YOUR REPUTATION. YOU KNEW US. YOU KNEW HER.
I THOUGHT IT MIGHT GIVE YOU SOME INSIGHT.
SHE PROBABLY GOT COLD FEET. SHE'LL BE BACK.
I DON'T KNOW. IT'S NOT AS SIMPLE AS THAT.
PRIVATE
THE WEDDING WAS TO BE THIS WEEKEND.
WE HAD ALL GONE TO OUR BEACH HOUSE TO GET AWAY AND RELAX BEFORE THINGS GOT CRAZY.
IT'S GOING TO BE A BIG TO-DO, AS YOU KNOW. WE WON'T GET A MOMENT'S PEACE.

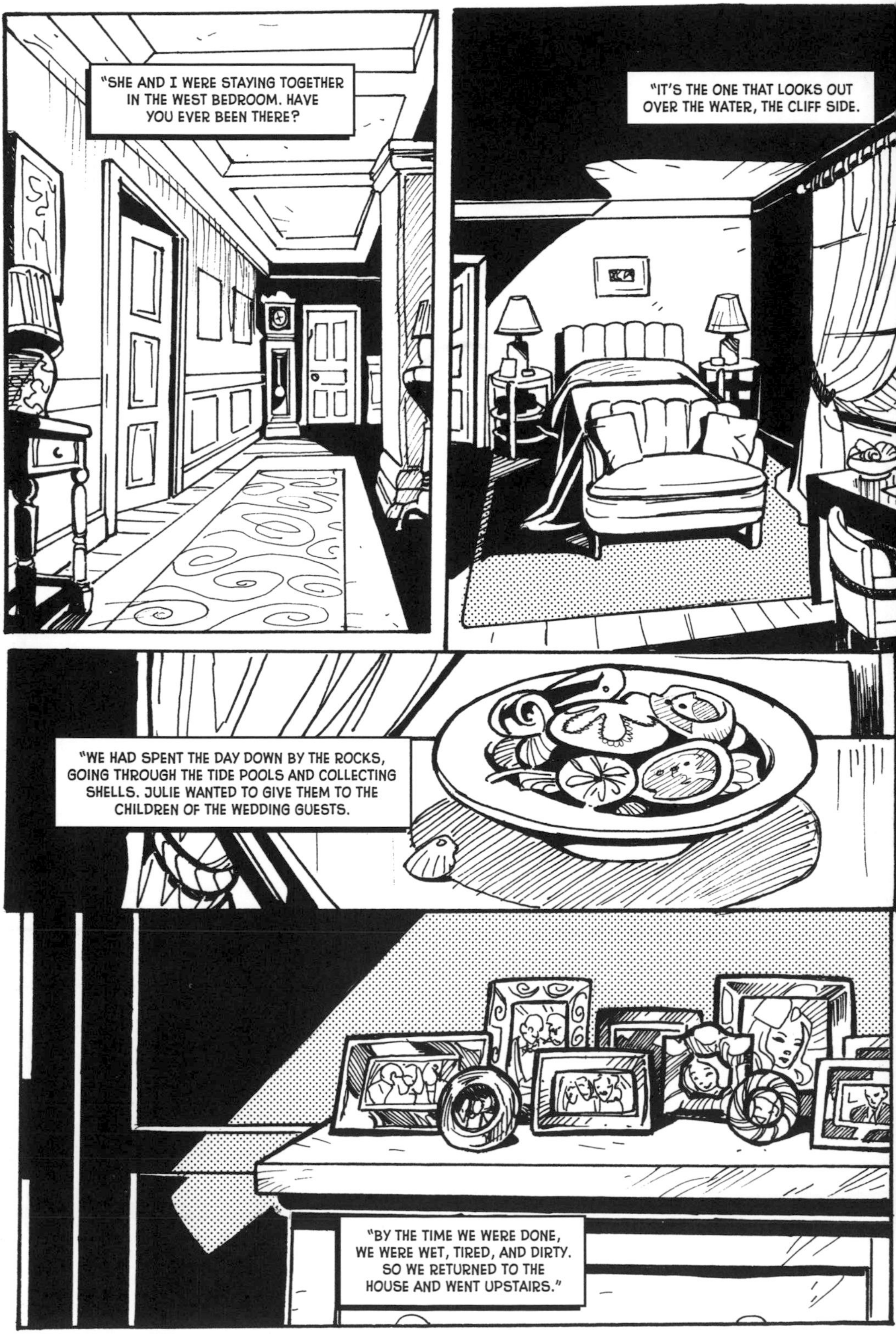
"SHE AND I WERE STAYING TOGETHER IN THE WEST BEDROOM. HAVE YOU EVER BEEN THERE?
"IT'S THE ONE THAT LOOKS OUT OVER THE WATER, THE CLIFF SIDE.
"WE HAD SPENT THE DAY DOWN BY THE ROCKS, GOING THROUGH THE TIDE POOLS AND COLLECTING SHELLS. JULIE WANTED TO GIVE THEM TO THE CHILDREN OF THE WEDDING GUESTS.
"BY THE TIME WE WERE DONE, WE WERE WET, TIRED, AND DIRTY. SO WE RETURNED TO THE HOUSE AND WENT UPSTAIRS."

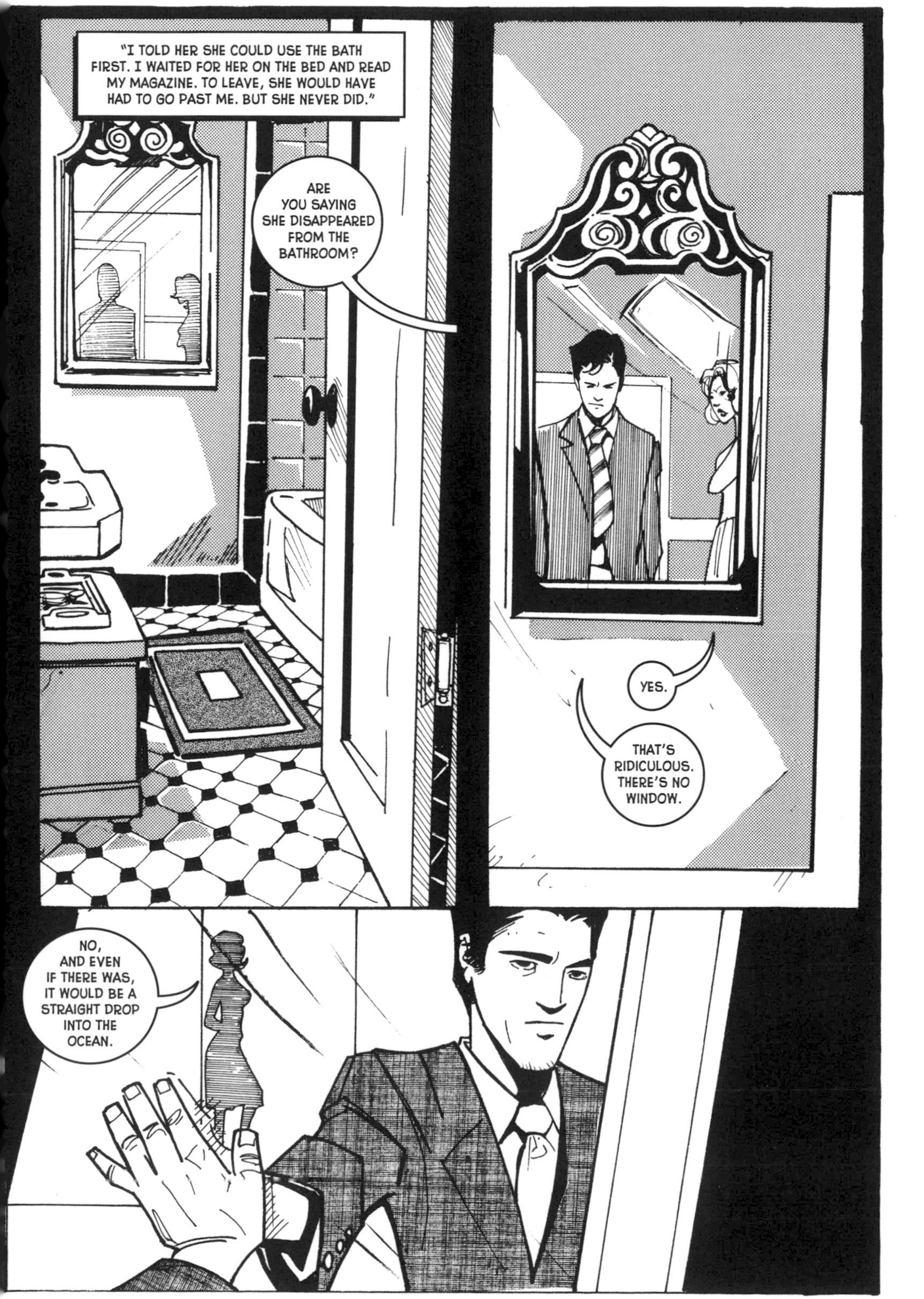
"I TOLD HER SHE COULD USE THE BATH FIRST. I WAITED FOR HER ON THE BED AND READ MY MAGAZINE. TO LEAVE, SHE WOULD HAVE HAD TO GO PAST ME. BUT SHE NEVER DID."
ARE YOU SAYING SHE DISAPPEARED FROM THE BATHROOM?
YES.
THAT'S RIDICULOUS. THERE'S NO WINDOW.
NO, AND EVEN IF THERE WAS, IT WOULD BE A STRAIGHT DROP INTO THE OCEAN.

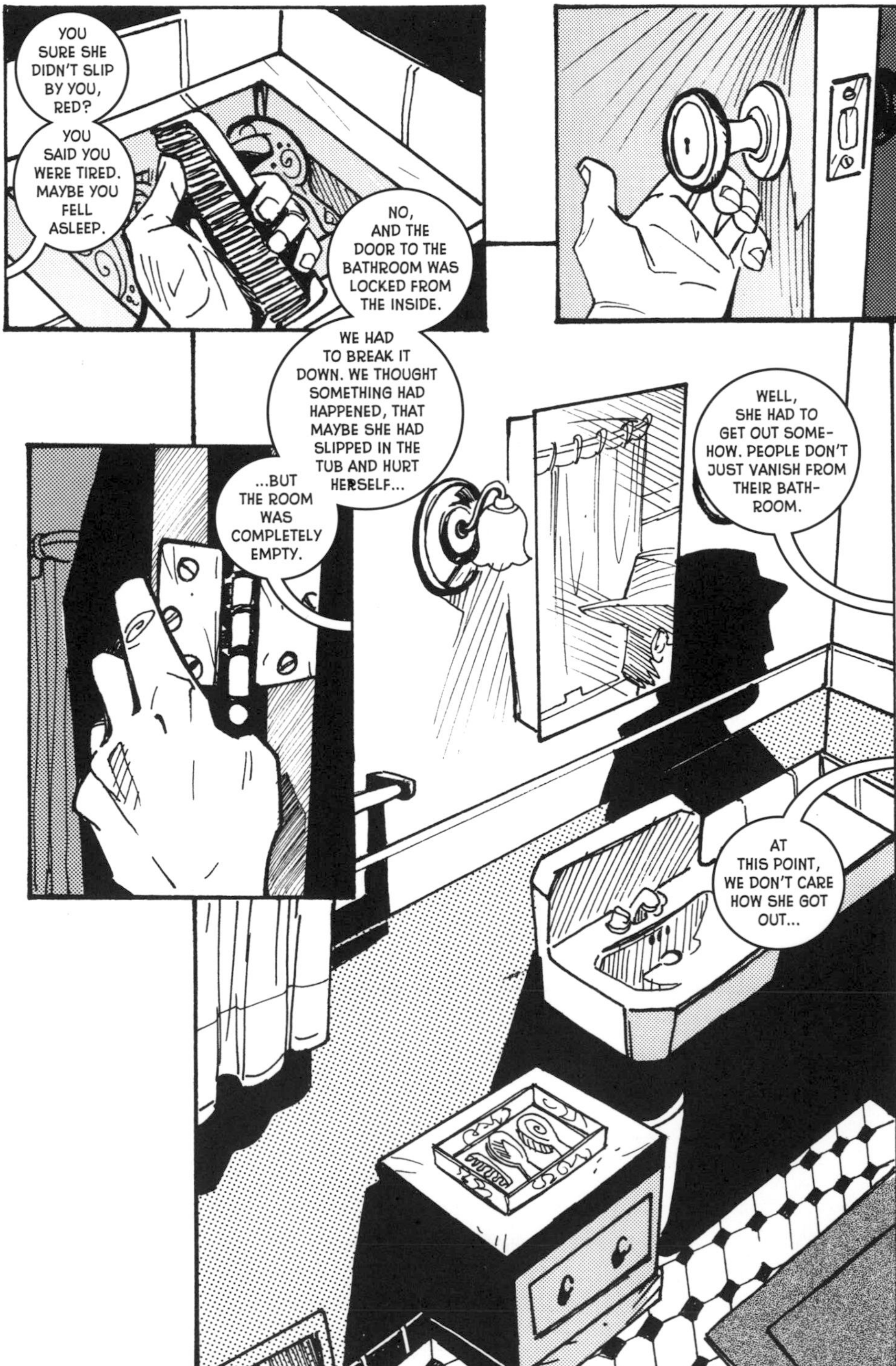
YOU SURE SHE DIDN'T SLIP BY YOU, RED?
YOU SAID YOU WERE TIRED. MAYBE YOU FELL ASLEEP.
NO, AND THE DOOR TO THE BATHROOM WAS LOCKED FROM THE INSIDE.
WE HAD TO BREAK IT DOWN. WE THOUGHT SOMETHING HAD HAPPENED, THAT MAYBE SHE HAD SLIPPED IN THE TUB AND HURT HERSELF...
...BUT THE ROOM WAS COMPLETELY EMPTY.
WELL, SHE HAD TO GET OUT SOME-HOW. PEOPLE DON'T JUST VANISH FROM THEIR BATH-ROOM.
AT THIS POINT, WE DON'T CARE HOW SHE GOT OUT...

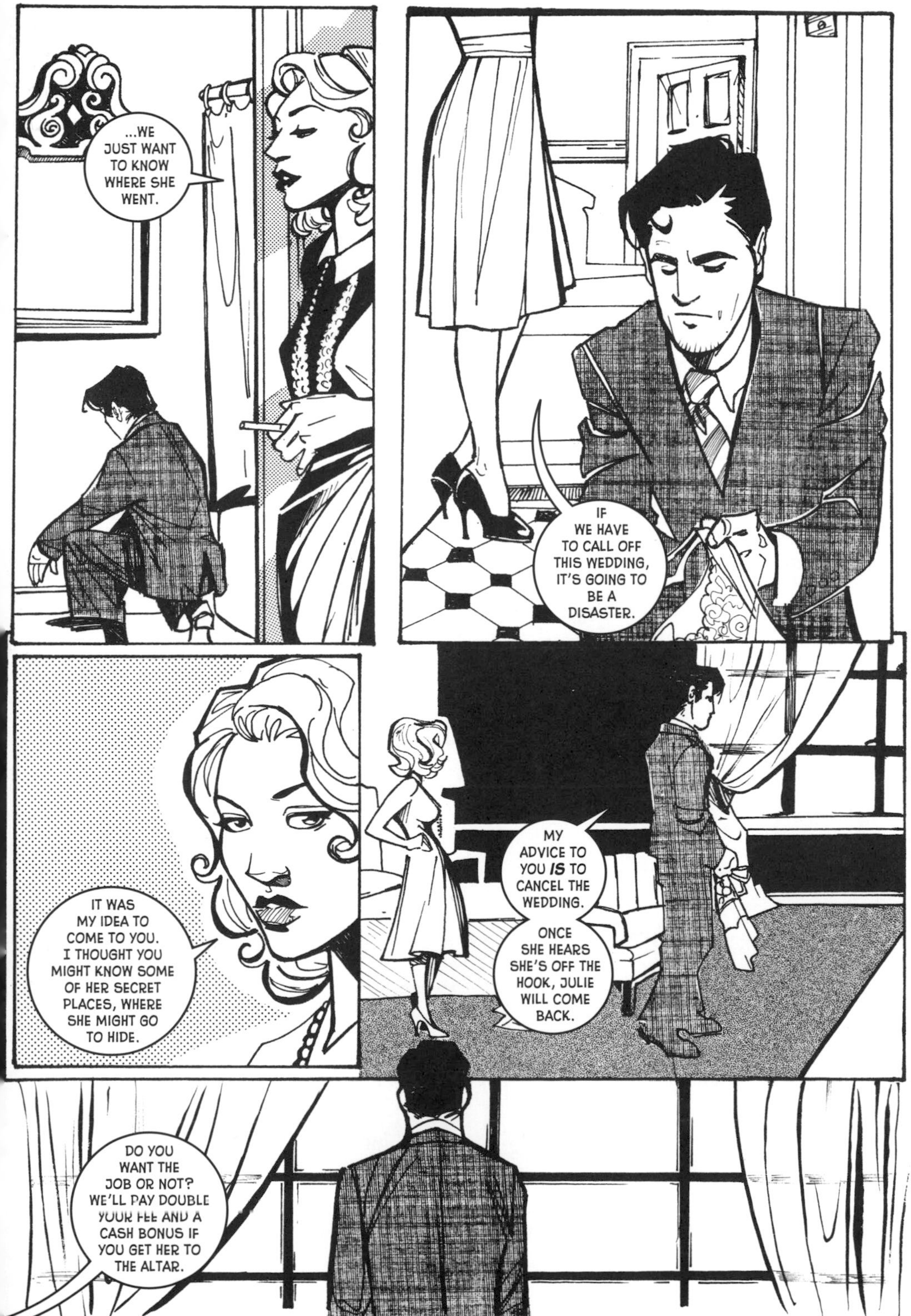
...WE JUST WANT TO KNOW WHERE SHE WENT.
IF WE HAVE TO CALL OFF THIS WEDDING, IT'S GOING TO BE A DISASTER.
IT WAS MY IDEA TO COME TO YOU. I THOUGHT YOU MIGHT KNOW SOME OF HER SECRET PLACES, WHERE SHE MIGHT GO TO HIDE.
MY ADVICE TO YOU *IS* TO CANCEL THE WEDDING.
ONCE SHE HEARS SHE'S OFF THE HOOK, JULIE WILL COME BACK.
DO YOU WANT THE JOB OR NOT? WE'LL PAY DOUBLE YOUR FEE AND A CASH BONUS IF YOU GET HER TO THE ALTAR.

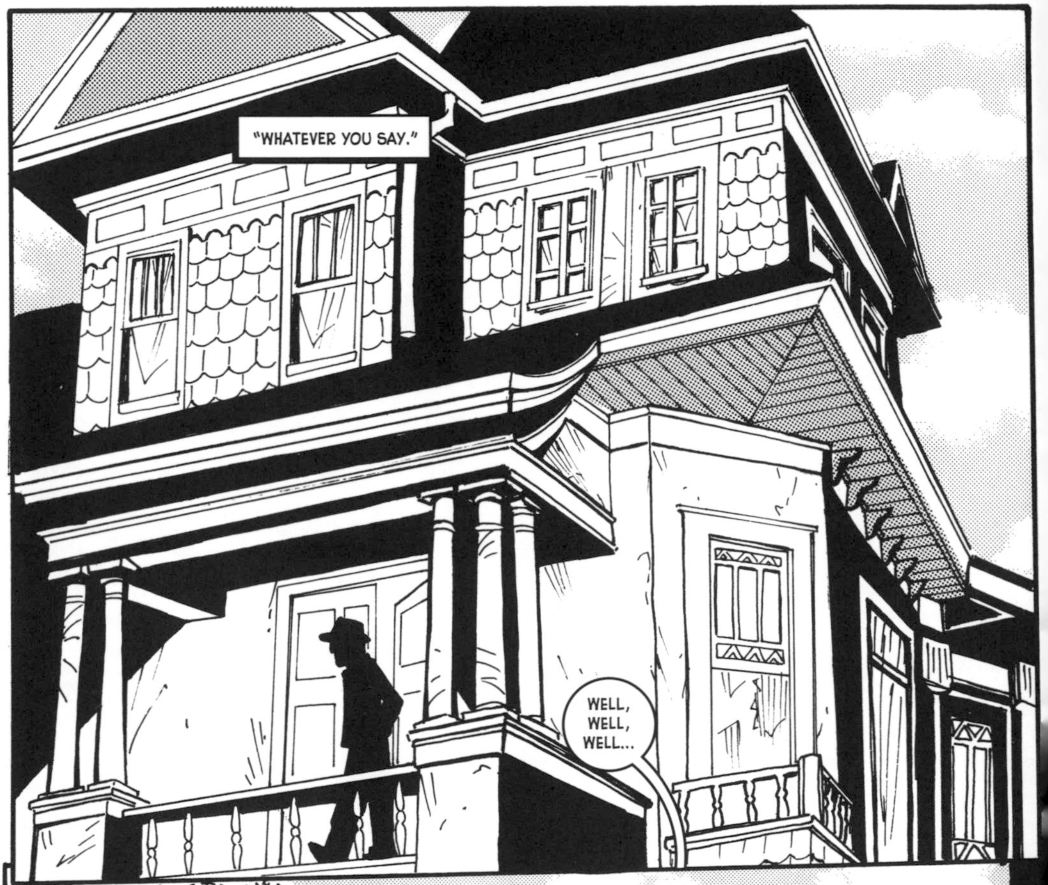
"WHATEVER YOU SAY."
WELL, WELL, WELL...

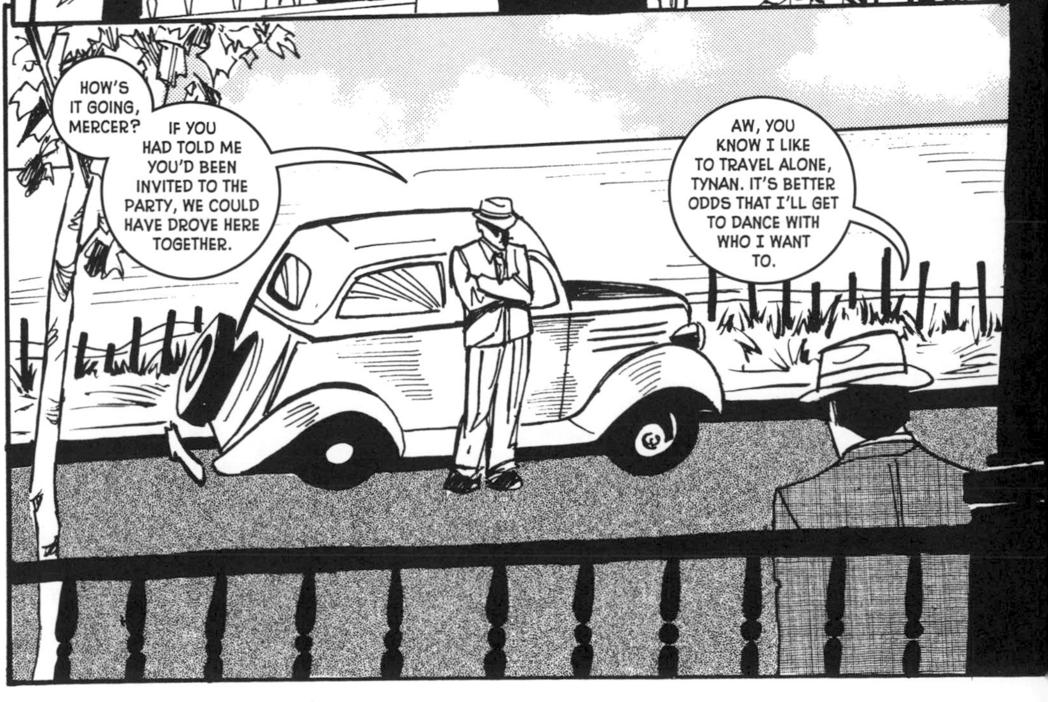
HOW'S IT GOING, MERCER?
IF YOU HAD TOLD ME YOU'D BEEN INVITED TO THE PARTY, WE COULD HAVE DROVE HERE TOGETHER.
AW, YOU KNOW I LIKE TO TRAVEL ALONE, TYNAN. IT'S BETTER ODDS THAT I'LL GET TO DANCE WITH WHO I WANT TO.

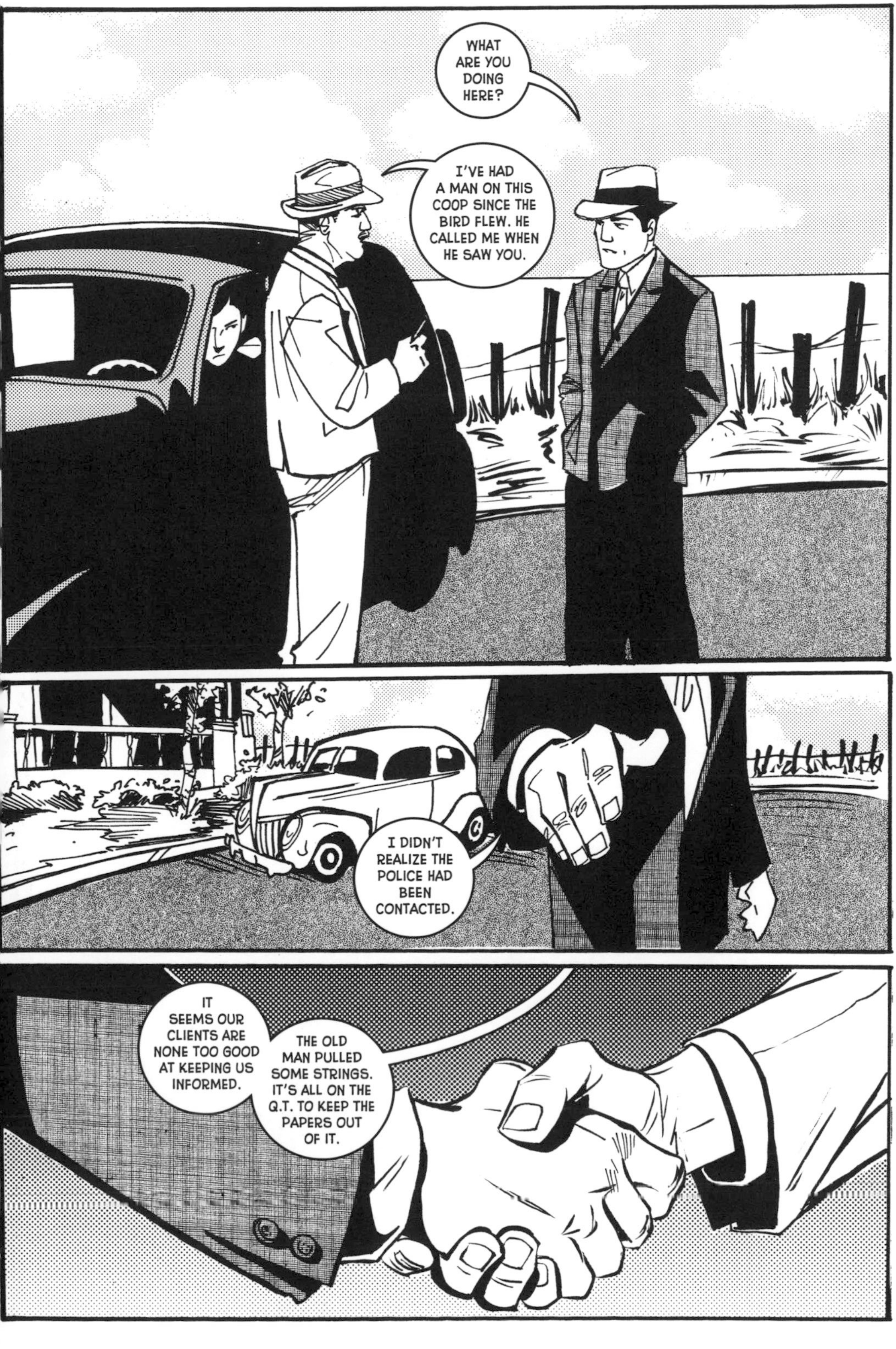
WHAT ARE YOU DOING HERE?
I'VE HAD A MAN ON THIS COOP SINCE THE BIRD FLEW. HE CALLED ME WHEN HE SAW YOU.
I DIDN'T REALIZE THE POLICE HAD BEEN CONTACTED.
IT SEEMS OUR CLIENTS ARE NONE TOO GOOD AT KEEPING US INFORMED.
THE OLD MAN PULLED SOME STRINGS. IT'S ALL ON THE Q.T. TO KEEP THE PAPERS OUT OF IT.

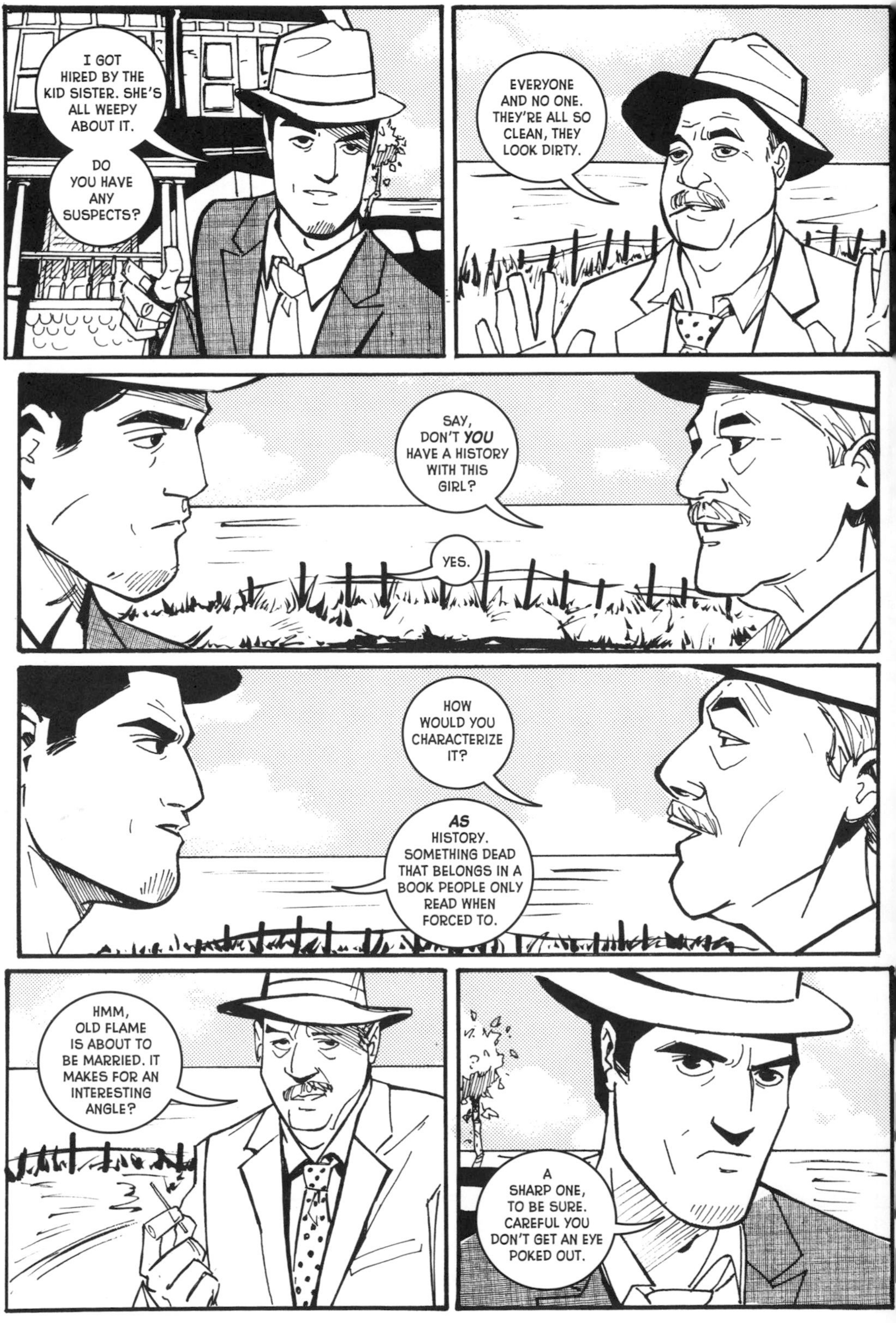
I GOT HIRED BY THE KID SISTER. SHE'S ALL WEEPY ABOUT IT.
DO YOU HAVE ANY SUSPECTS?
EVERYONE AND NO ONE. THEY'RE ALL SO CLEAN, THEY LOOK DIRTY.
SAY, DON'T *YOU* HAVE A HISTORY WITH THIS GIRL?
YES.
HOW WOULD YOU CHARACTERIZE IT?
AS HISTORY. SOMETHING DEAD THAT BELONGS IN A BOOK PEOPLE ONLY READ WHEN FORCED TO.
HMM, OLD FLAME IS ABOUT TO BE MARRIED. IT MAKES FOR AN INTERESTING ANGLE?
A SHARP ONE, TO BE SURE. CAREFUL YOU DON'T GET AN EYE POKED OUT.

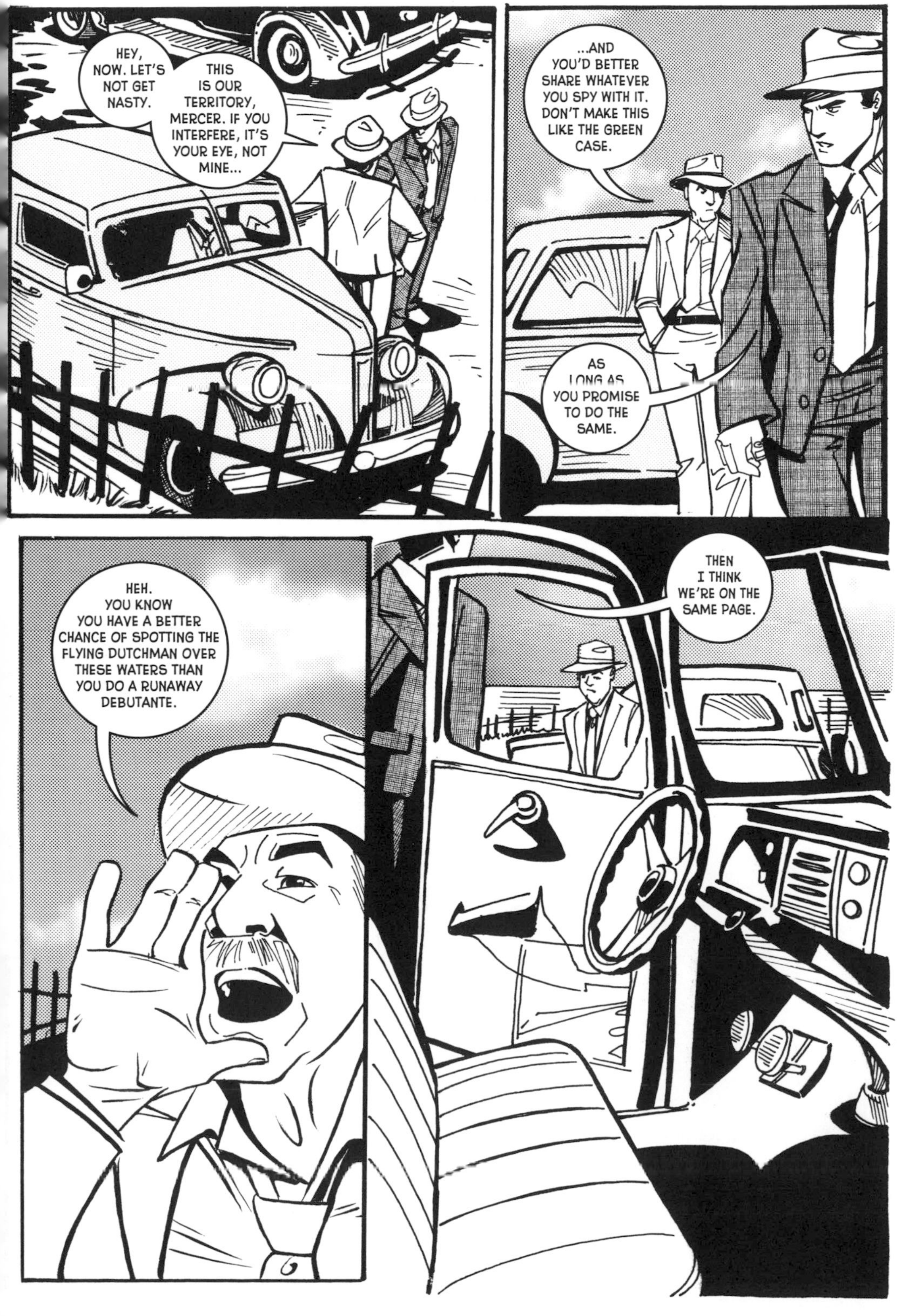
HEY, NOW. LET'S NOT GET NASTY.
THIS IS OUR TERRITORY, MERCER. IF YOU INTERFERE, IT'S YOUR EYE, NOT MINE...
...AND YOU'D BETTER SHARE WHATEVER YOU SPY WITH IT. DON'T MAKE THIS LIKE THE GREEN CASE.
AS LONG AS YOU PROMISE TO DO THE SAME.
HEH. YOU KNOW YOU HAVE A BETTER CHANCE OF SPOTTING THE FLYING DUTCHMAN OVER THESE WATERS THAN YOU DO A RUNAWAY DEBUTANTE.
THEN I THINK WE'RE ON THE SAME PAGE.

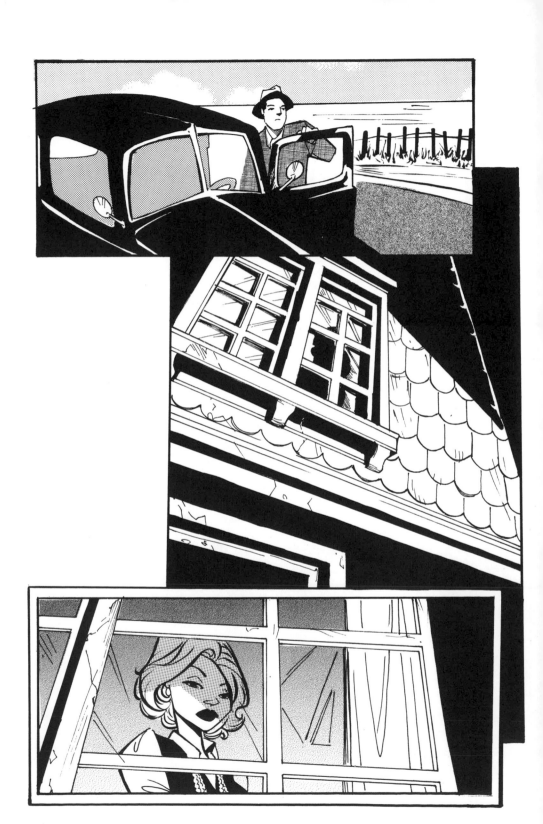

CHAPTER 2

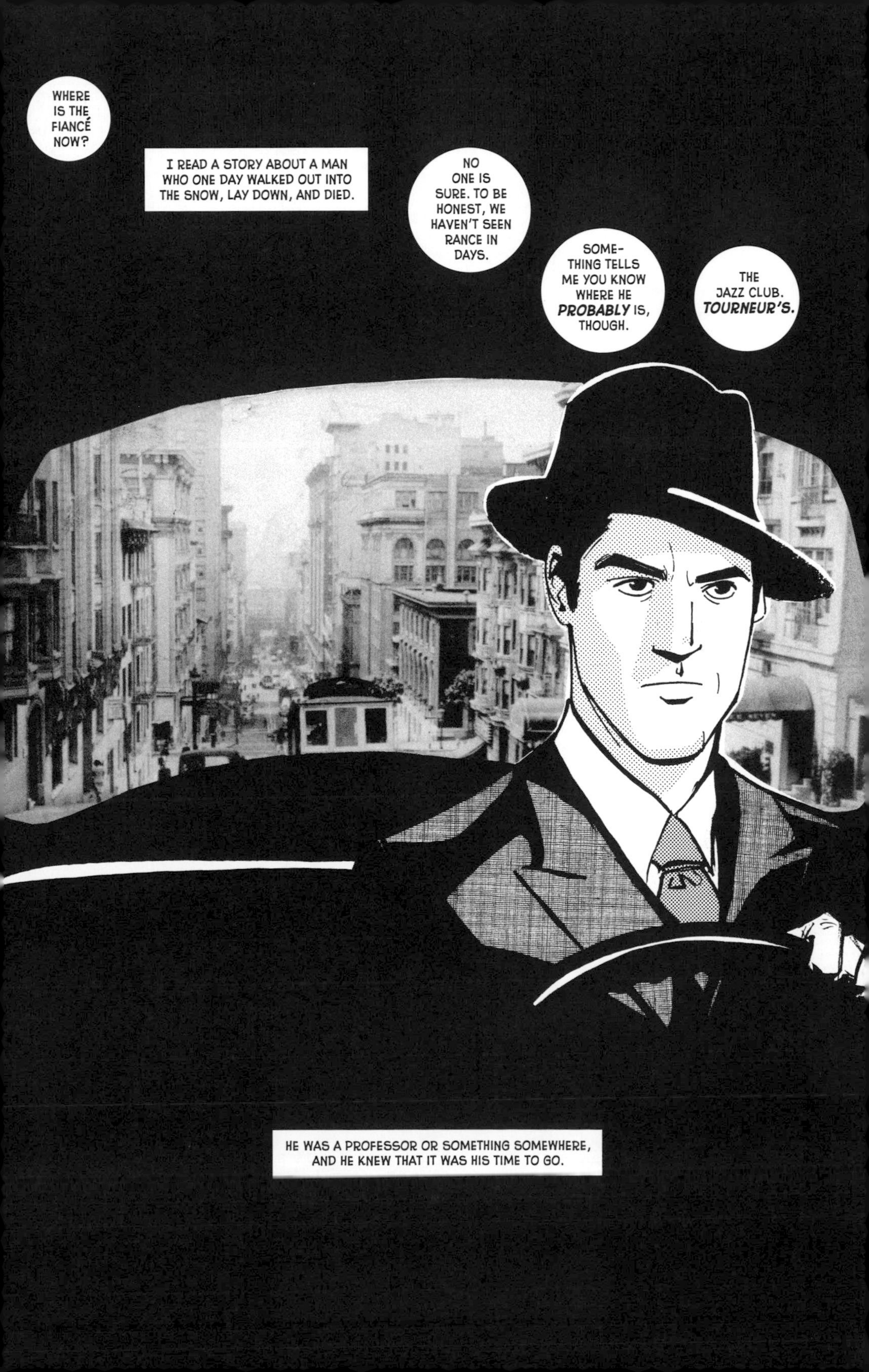
WHERE IS THE FIANCÉ NOW?
I READ A STORY ABOUT A MAN WHO ONE DAY WALKED OUT INTO THE SNOW, LAY DOWN, AND DIED.
NO ONE IS SURE. TO BE HONEST, WE HAVEN'T SEEN RANCE IN DAYS.
SOME-THING TELLS ME YOU KNOW WHERE HE PROBABLY IS, THOUGH.
THE JAZZ CLUB. TOURNEUR'S.
HE WAS A PROFESSOR OR SOMETHING SOMEWHERE, AND HE KNEW THAT IT WAS HIS TIME TO GO.

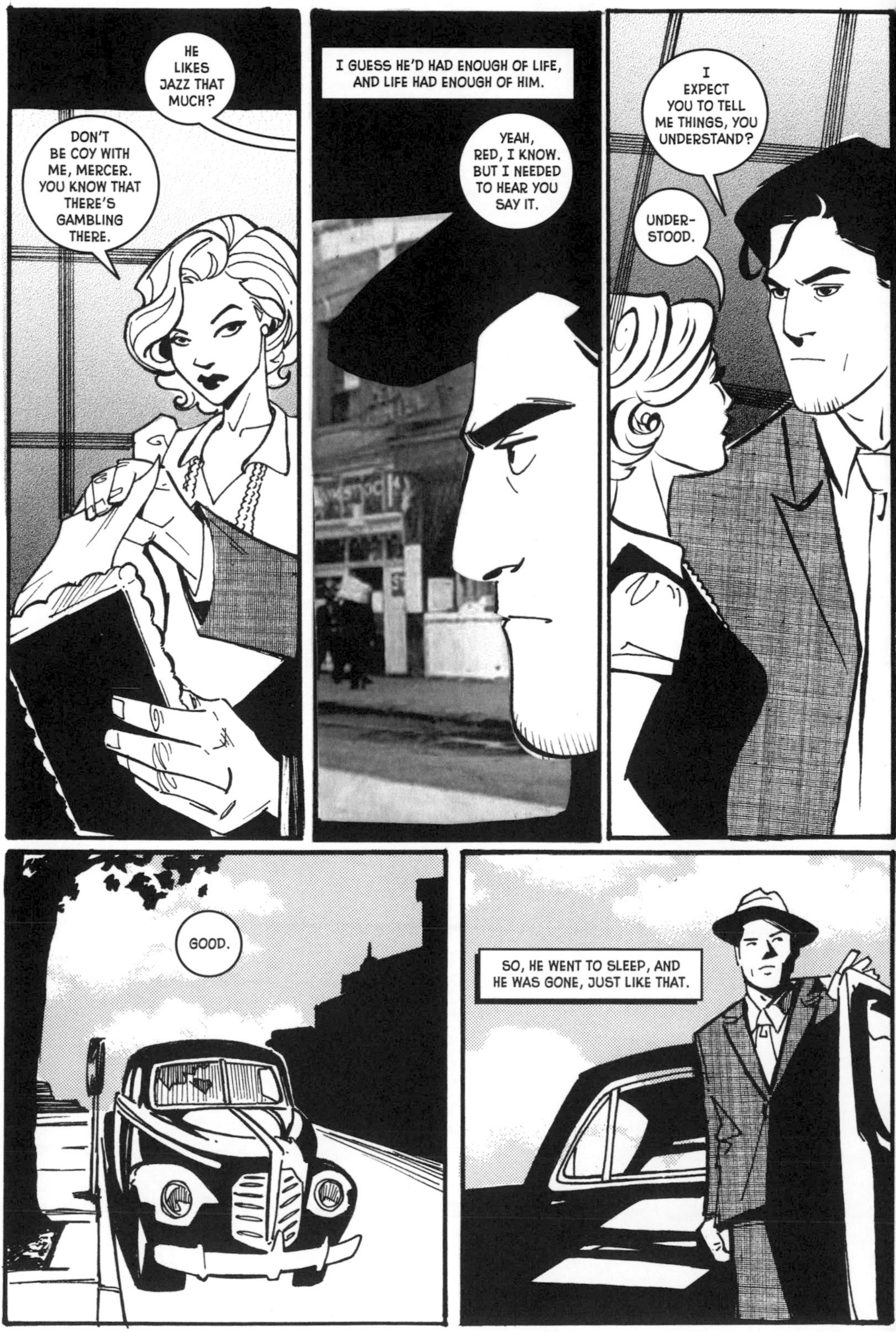
HE LIKES JAZZ THAT MUCH?
DON'T BE COY WITH ME, MERCER. YOU KNOW THAT THERE'S GAMBLING THERE.
I GUESS HE'D HAD ENOUGH OF LIFE, AND LIFE HAD ENOUGH OF HIM.
YEAH, RED, I KNOW. BUT I NEEDED TO HEAR YOU SAY IT.
I EXPECT YOU TO TELL ME THINGS, YOU UNDERSTAND?
UNDER-STOOD.
GOOD.
SO, HE WENT TO SLEEP, AND HE WAS GONE, JUST LIKE THAT.

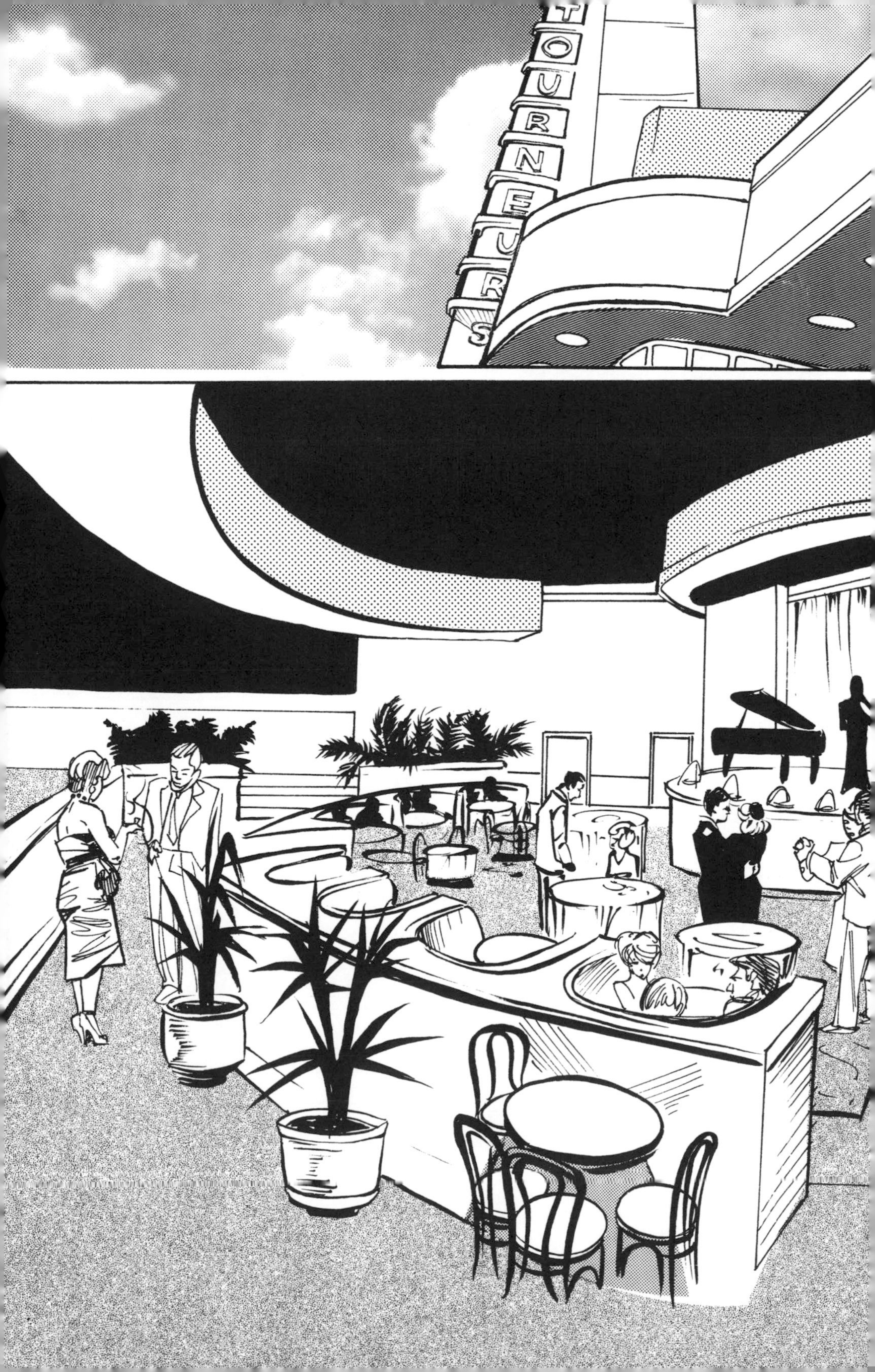
TOURNEURS

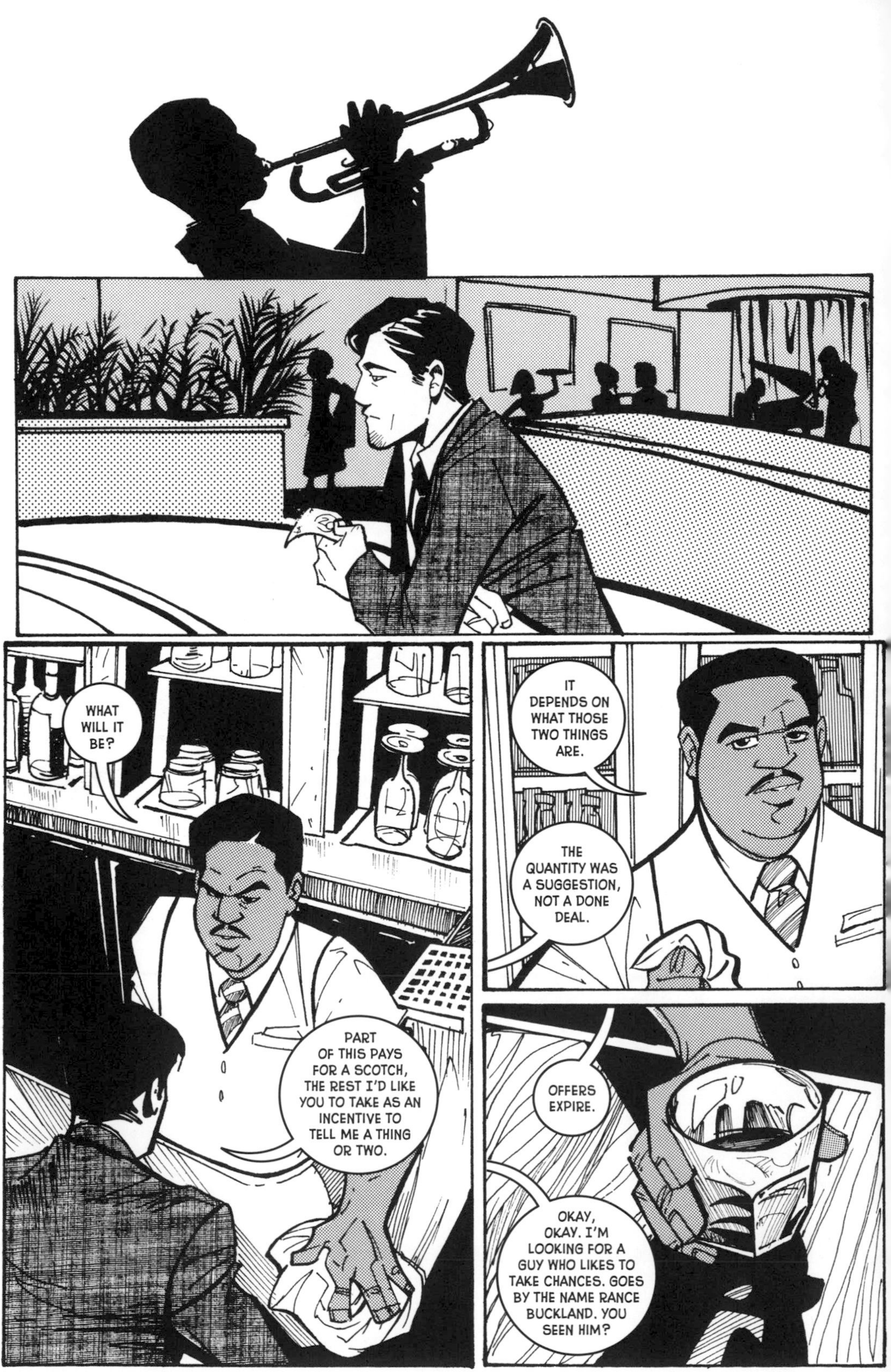
WHAT WILL IT BE?
PART OF THIS PAYS FOR A SCOTCH, THE REST I'D LIKE YOU TO TAKE AS AN INCENTIVE TO TELL ME A THING OR TWO.
IT DEPENDS ON WHAT THOSE TWO THINGS ARE.
THE QUANTITY WAS A SUGGESTION, NOT A DONE DEAL.
OFFERS EXPIRE.
OKAY, OKAY. I'M LOOKING FOR A GUY WHO LIKES TO TAKE CHANCES. GOES BY THE NAME RANCE BUCKLAND. YOU SEEN HIM?

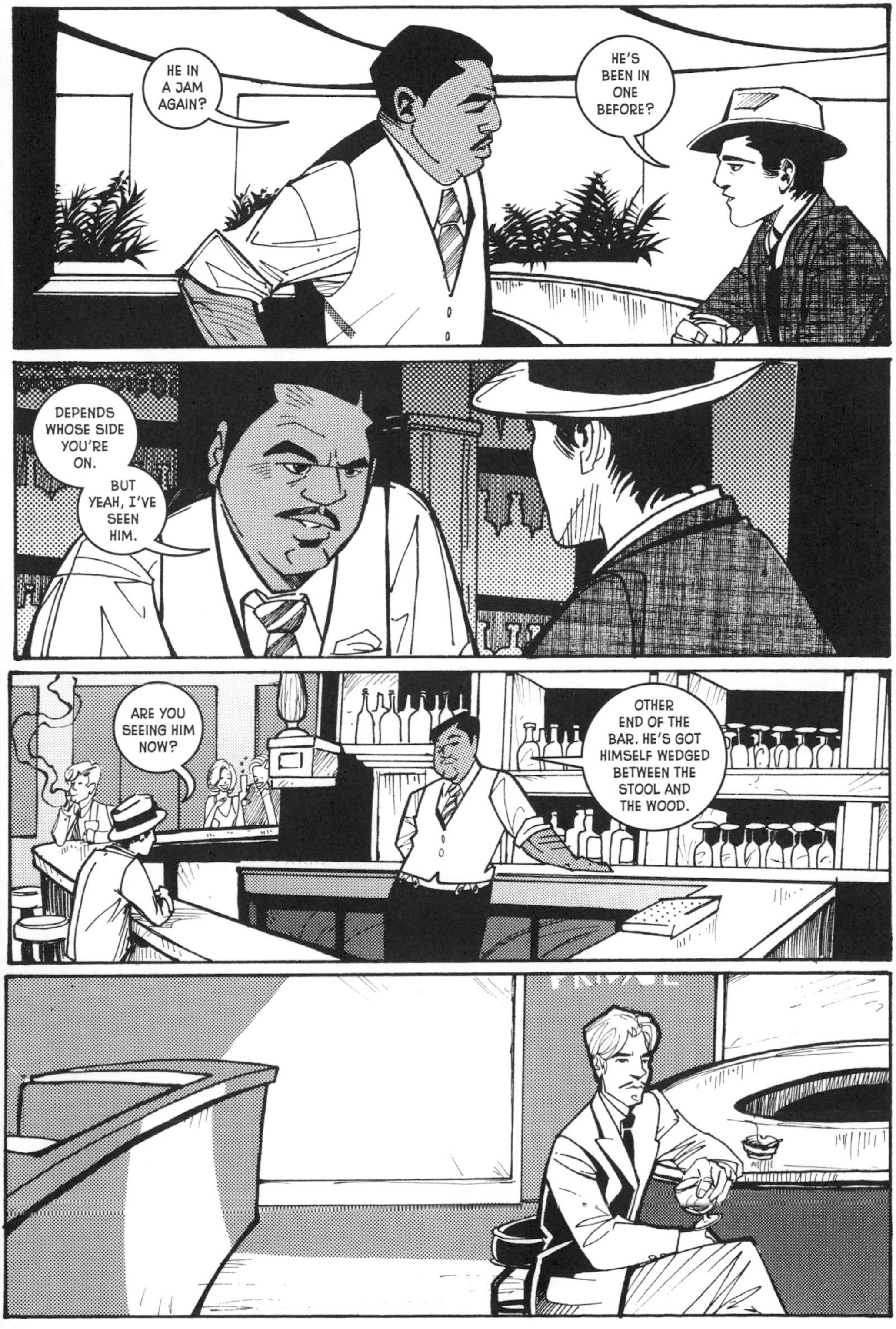
HE IN A JAM AGAIN?
HE'S BEEN IN ONE BEFORE?
DEPENDS WHOSE SIDE YOU'RE ON.
BUT YEAH, I'VE SEEN HIM.
ARE YOU SEEING HIM NOW?
OTHER END OF THE BAR. HE'S GOT HIMSELF WEDGED BETWEEN THE STOOL AND THE WOOD.

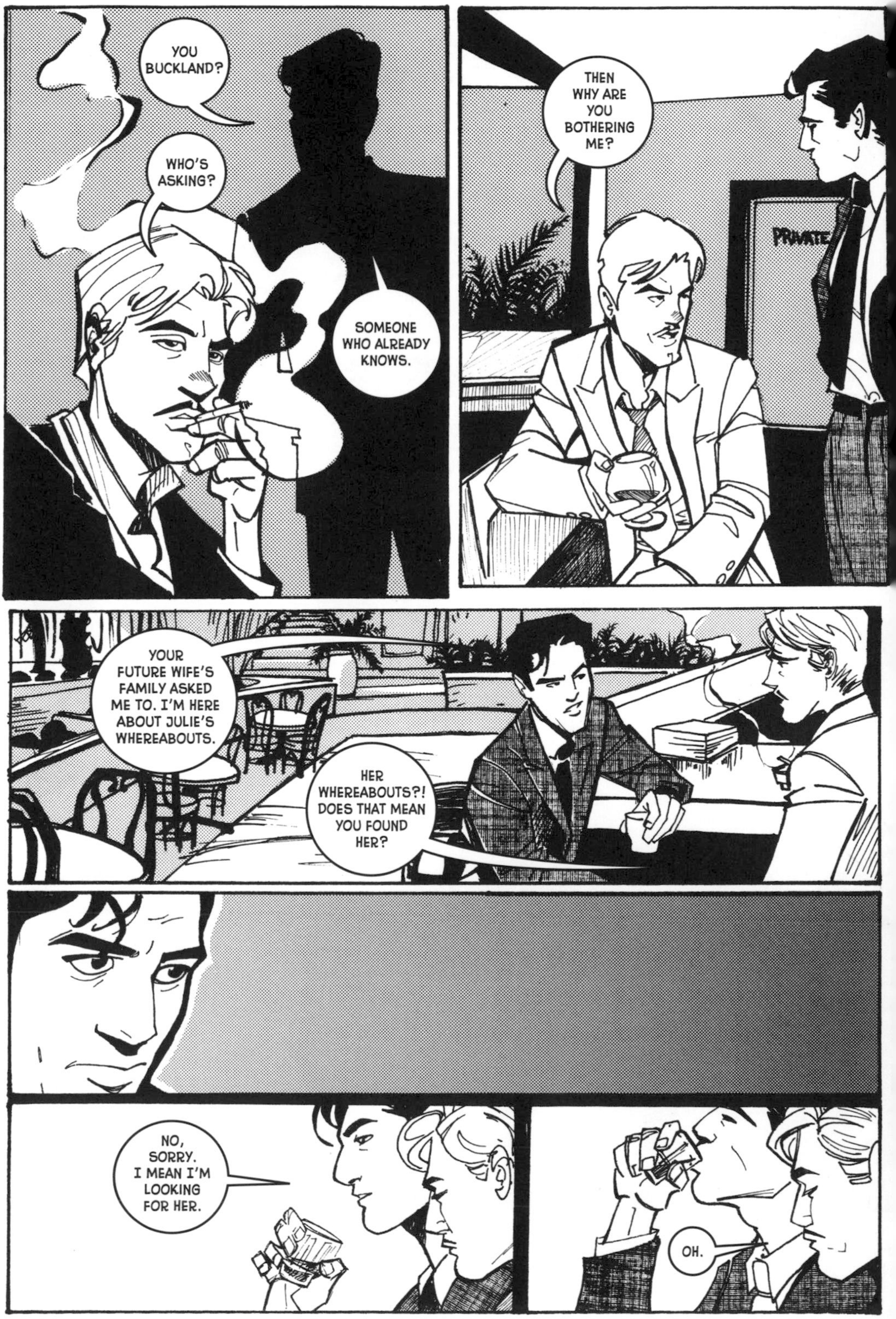
YOU BUCKLAND?
WHO'S ASKING?
SOMEONE WHO ALREADY KNOWS.
THEN WHY ARE YOU BOTHERING ME?
PRIVATE
YOUR FUTURE WIFE'S FAMILY ASKED ME TO. I'M HERE ABOUT JULIE'S WHEREABOUTS.
HER WHEREABOUTS?! DOES THAT MEAN YOU FOUND HER?
NO, SORRY. I MEAN I'M LOOKING FOR HER.
OH.

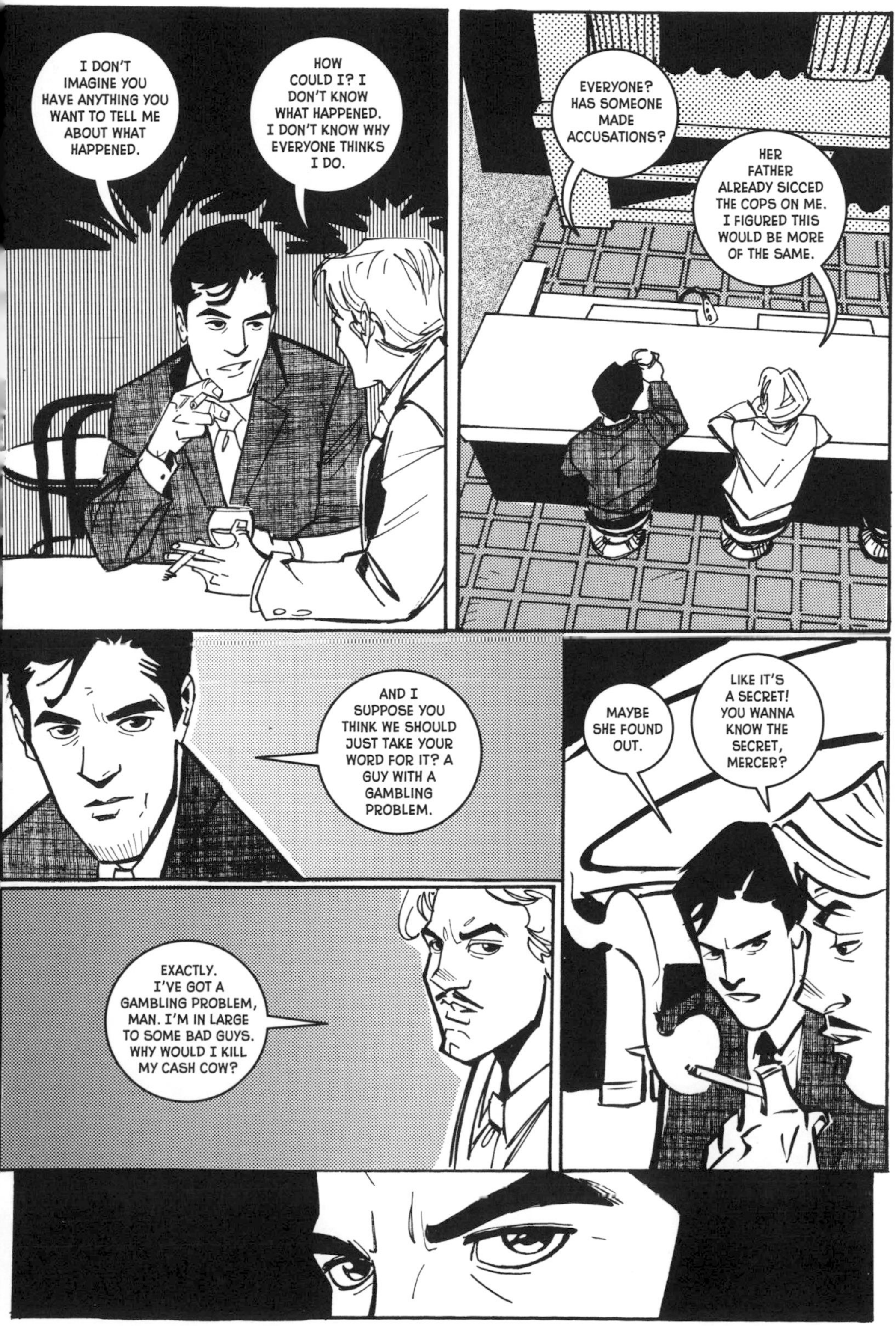
I DON'T IMAGINE YOU HAVE ANYTHING YOU WANT TO TELL ME ABOUT WHAT HAPPENED.
HOW COULD I? I DON'T KNOW WHAT HAPPENED. I DON'T KNOW WHY EVERYONE THINKS I DO.
EVERYONE? HAS SOMEONE MADE ACCUSATIONS?
HER FATHER ALREADY SICCED THE COPS ON ME. I FIGURED THIS WOULD BE MORE OF THE SAME.
AND I SUPPOSE YOU THINK WE SHOULD JUST TAKE YOUR WORD FOR IT? A GUY WITH A GAMBLING PROBLEM.
EXACTLY. I'VE GOT A GAMBLING PROBLEM, MAN. I'M IN LARGE TO SOME BAD GUYS. WHY WOULD I KILL MY CASH COW?
MAYBE SHE FOUND OUT.
LIKE IT'S A SECRET! YOU WANNA KNOW THE SECRET, MERCER?

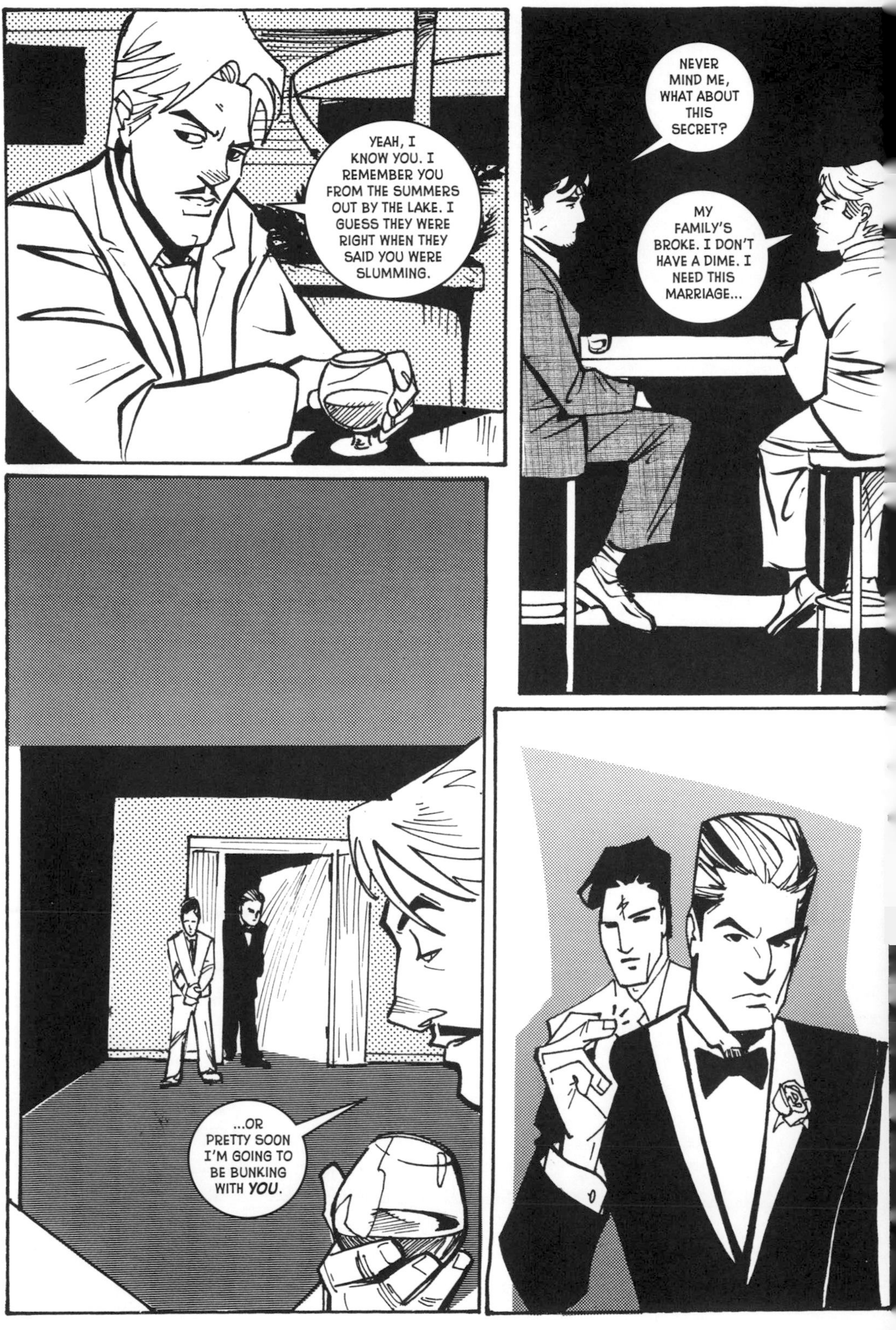
YEAH, I KNOW YOU. I REMEMBER YOU FROM THE SUMMERS OUT BY THE LAKE. I GUESS THEY WERE RIGHT WHEN THEY SAID YOU WERE SLUMMING.
NEVER MIND ME, WHAT ABOUT THIS SECRET?
MY FAMILY'S BROKE. I DON'T HAVE A DIME. I NEED THIS MARRIAGE...
...OR PRETTY SOON I'M GOING TO BE BUNKING WITH *YOU*.

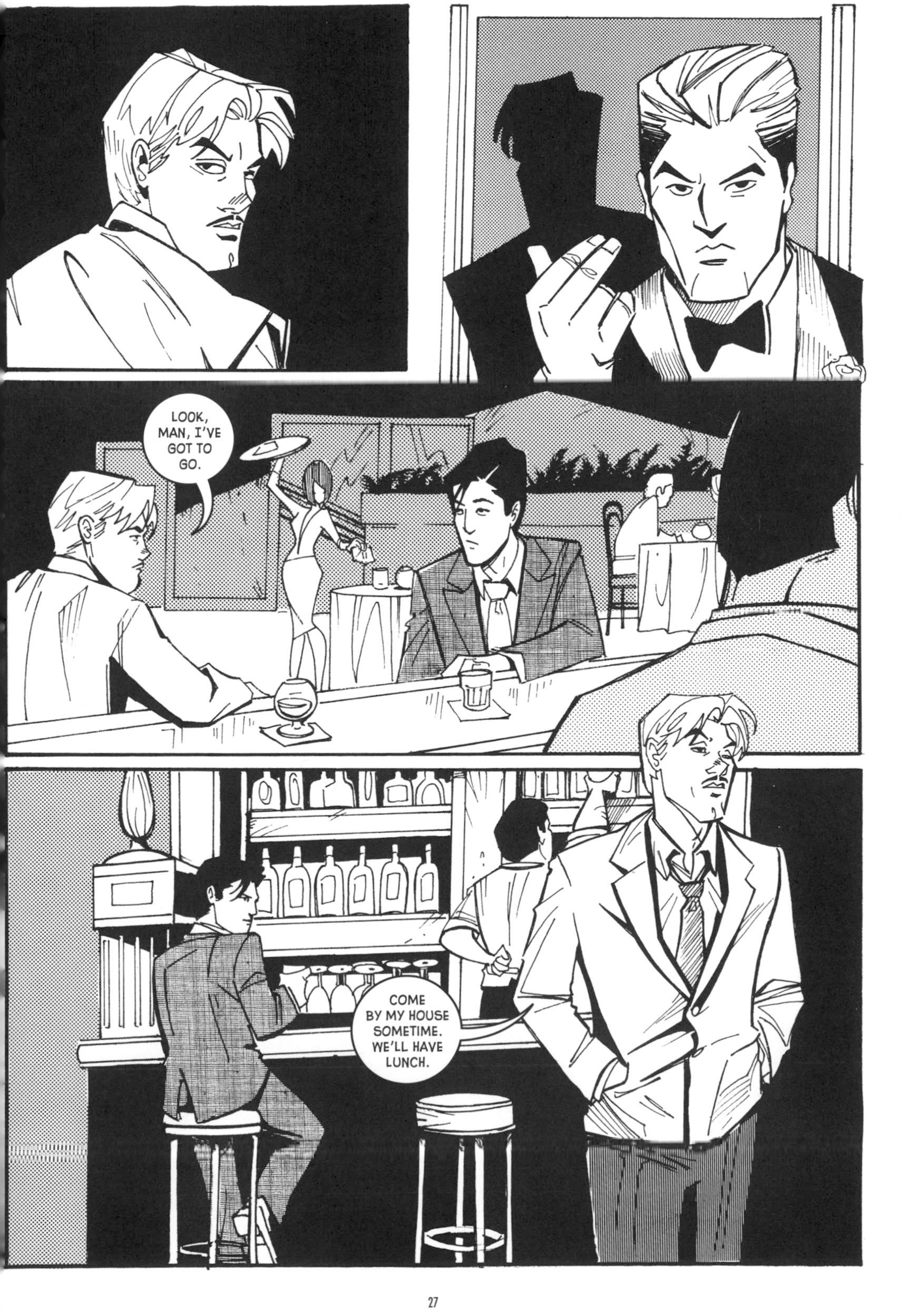
LOOK, MAN, I'VE GOT TO GO.
COME BY MY HOUSE SOMETIME. WE'LL HAVE LUNCH.

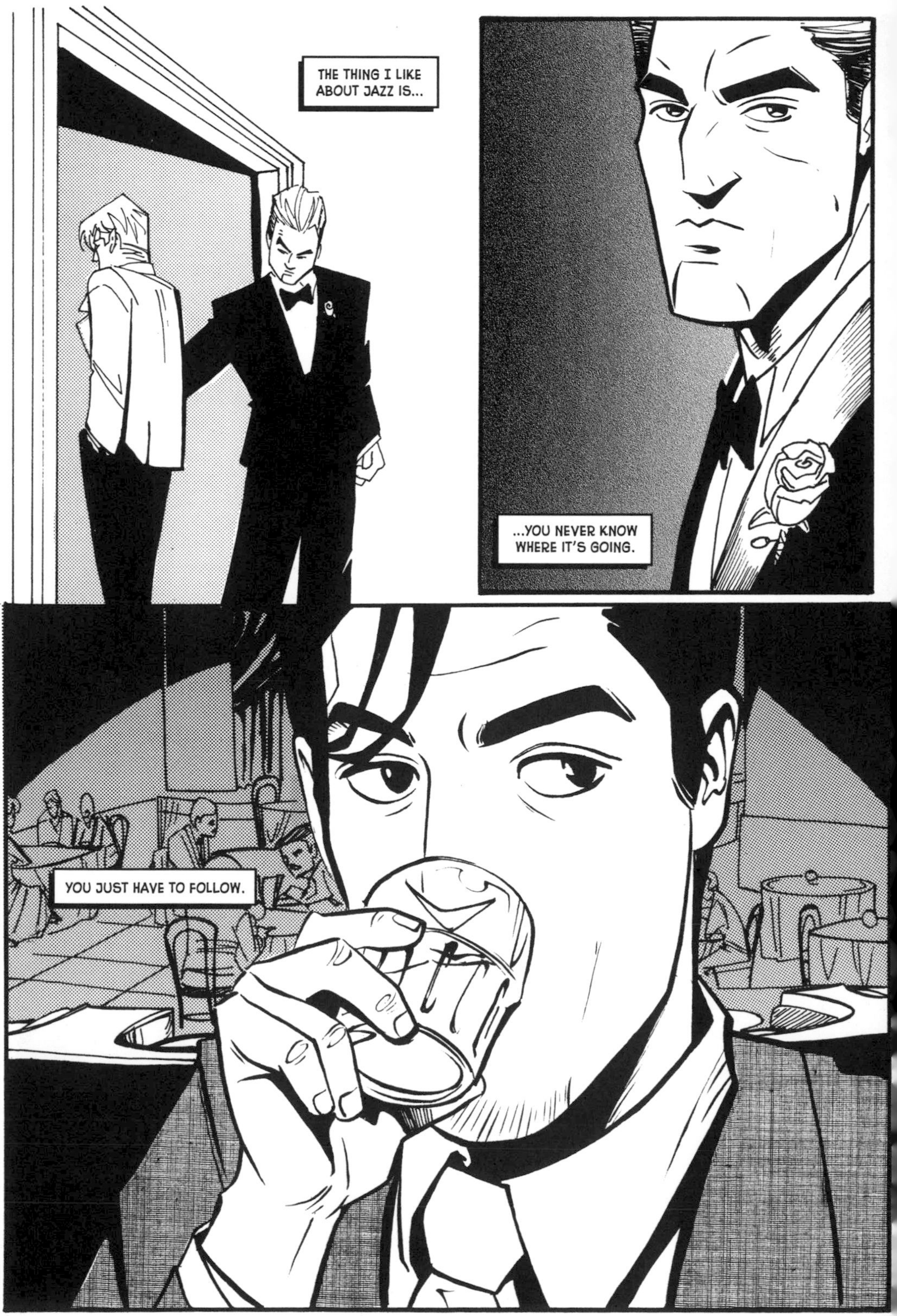
THE THING I LIKE ABOUT JAZZ IS...
...YOU NEVER KNOW WHERE IT'S GOING.
YOU JUST HAVE TO FOLLOW.

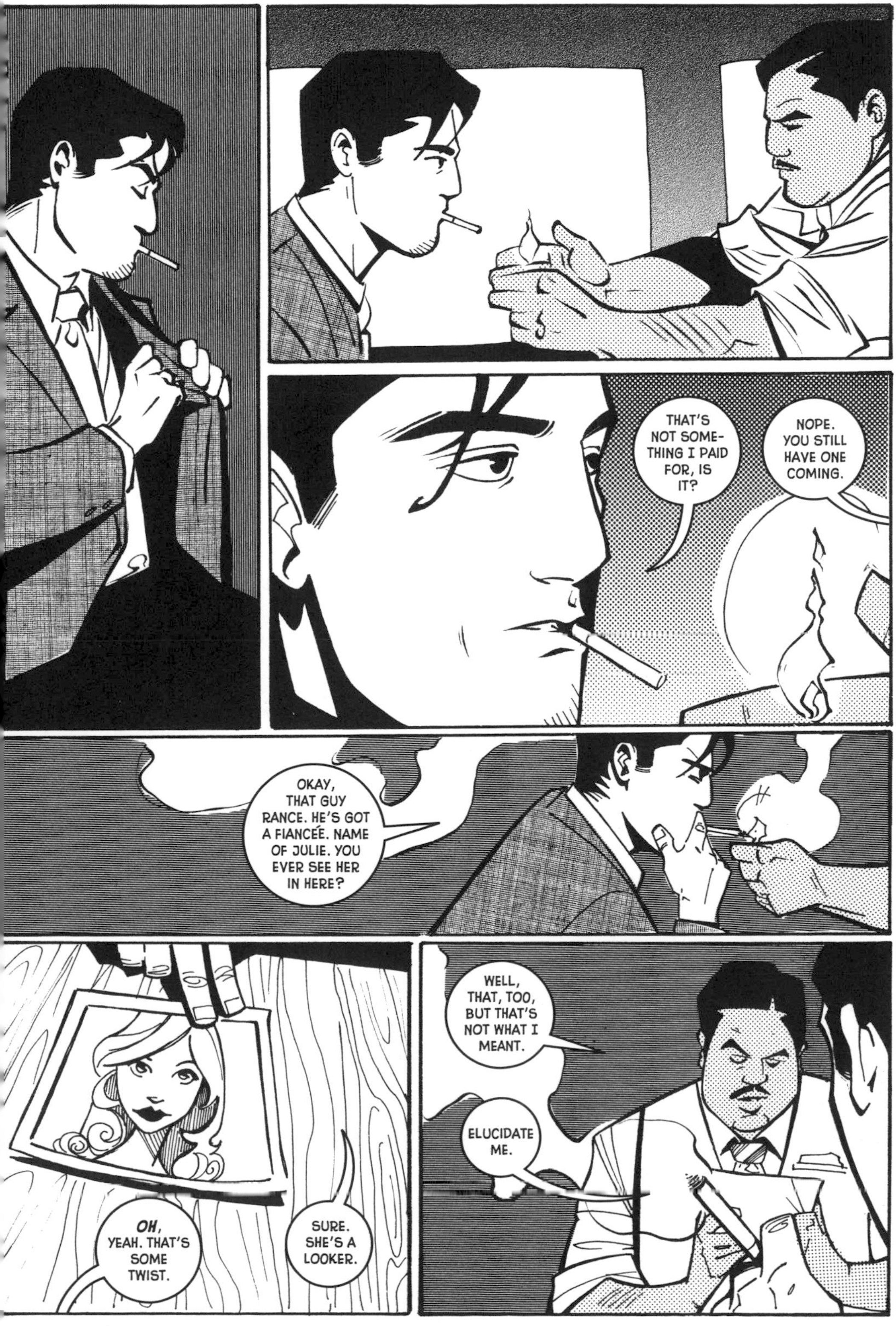
THAT'S NOT SOME-THING I PAID FOR, IS IT?
NOPE. YOU STILL HAVE ONE COMING.
OKAY, THAT GUY RANCE. HE'S GOT A FIANCÉE. NAME OF JULIE. YOU EVER SEE HER IN HERE?
OH, YEAH. THAT'S SOME TWIST.
SURE. SHE'S A LOOKER.
WELL, THAT, TOO, BUT THAT'S NOT WHAT I MEANT.
ELUCIDATE ME.

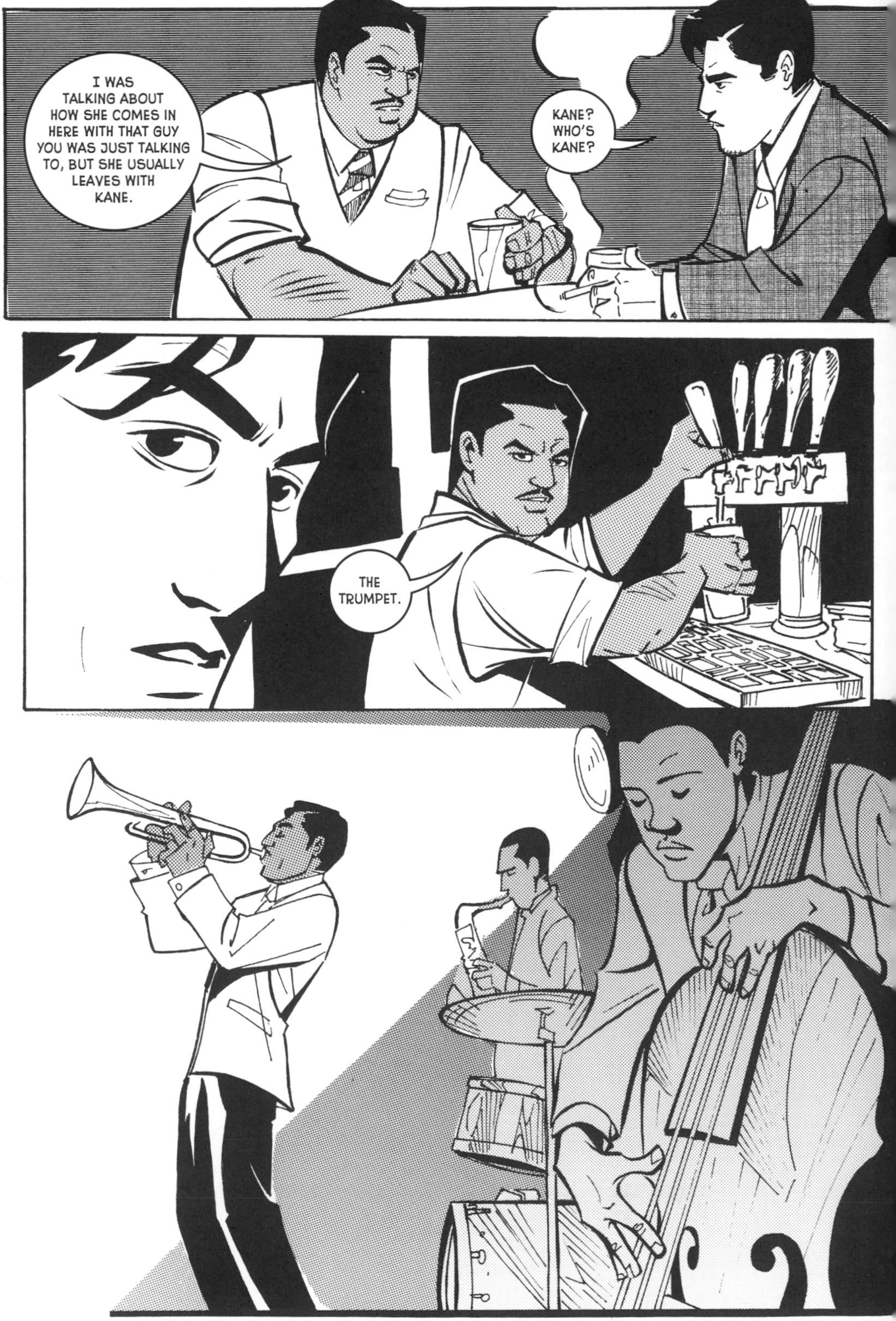
I WAS TALKING ABOUT HOW SHE COMES IN HERE WITH THAT GUY YOU WAS JUST TALKING TO, BUT SHE USUALLY LEAVES WITH KANE.
KANE? WHO'S KANE?
THE TRUMPET.

CHAPTER 3

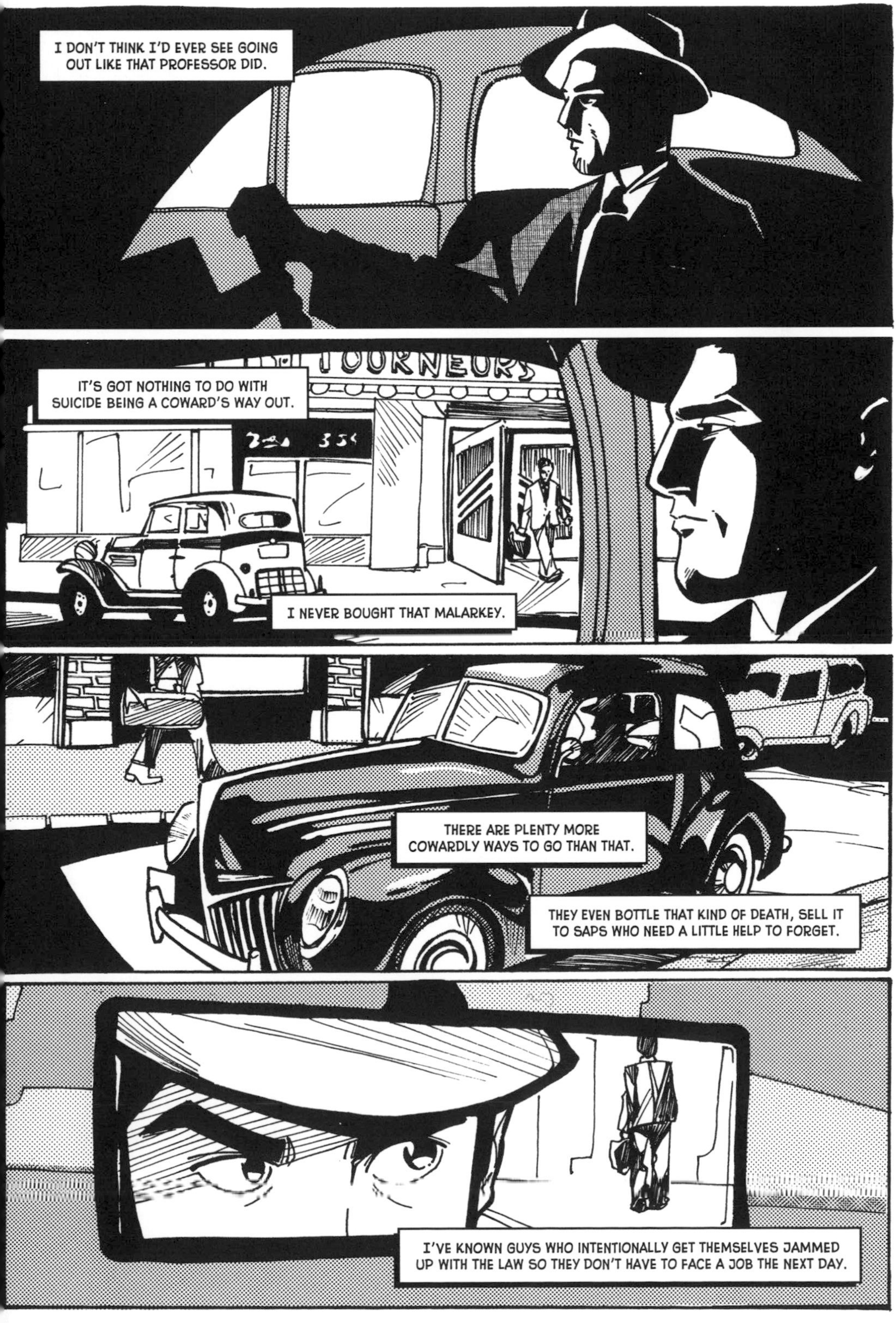
I DON'T THINK I'D EVER SEE GOING OUT LIKE THAT PROFESSOR DID.
IT'S GOT NOTHING TO DO WITH SUICIDE BEING A COWARD'S WAY OUT.
I NEVER BOUGHT THAT MALARKEY.
THERE ARE PLENTY MORE COWARDLY WAYS TO GO THAN THAT.
THEY EVEN BOTTLE THAT KIND OF DEATH, SELL IT TO SAPS WHO NEED A LITTLE HELP TO FORGET.
I'VE KNOWN GUYS WHO INTENTIONALLY GET THEMSELVES JAMMED UP WITH THE LAW SO THEY DON'T HAVE TO FACE A JOB THE NEXT DAY.

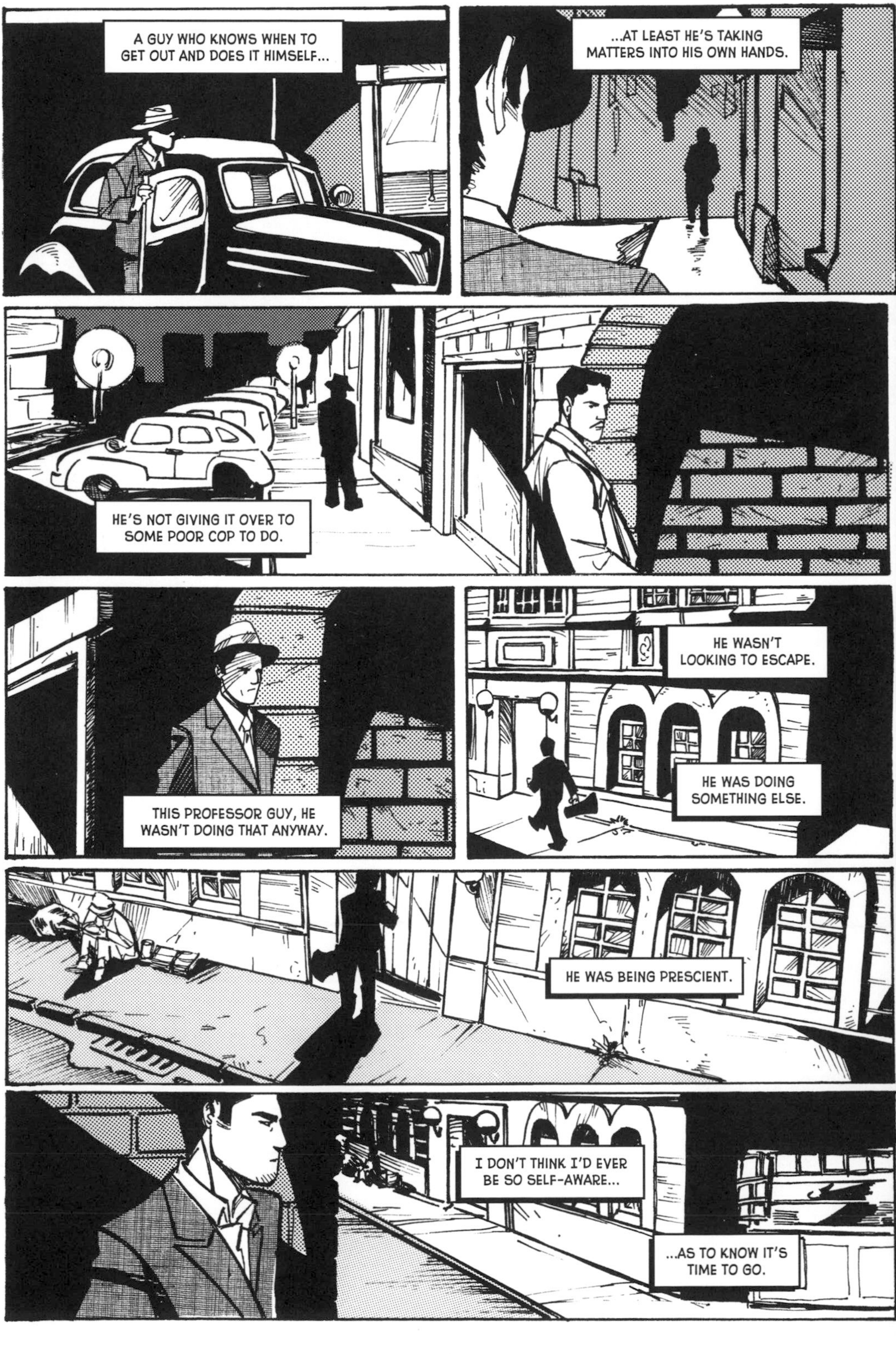
A GUY WHO KNOWS WHEN TO GET OUT AND DOES IT HIMSELF...
...AT LEAST HE'S TAKING MATTERS INTO HIS OWN HANDS.
HE'S NOT GIVING IT OVER TO SOME POOR COP TO DO.
THIS PROFESSOR GUY, HE WASN'T DOING THAT ANYWAY.
HE WASN'T LOOKING TO ESCAPE.
HE WAS DOING SOMETHING ELSE.
HE WAS BEING PRESCIENT.
I DON'T THINK I'D EVER BE SO SELF-AWARE...
...AS TO KNOW IT'S TIME TO GO.

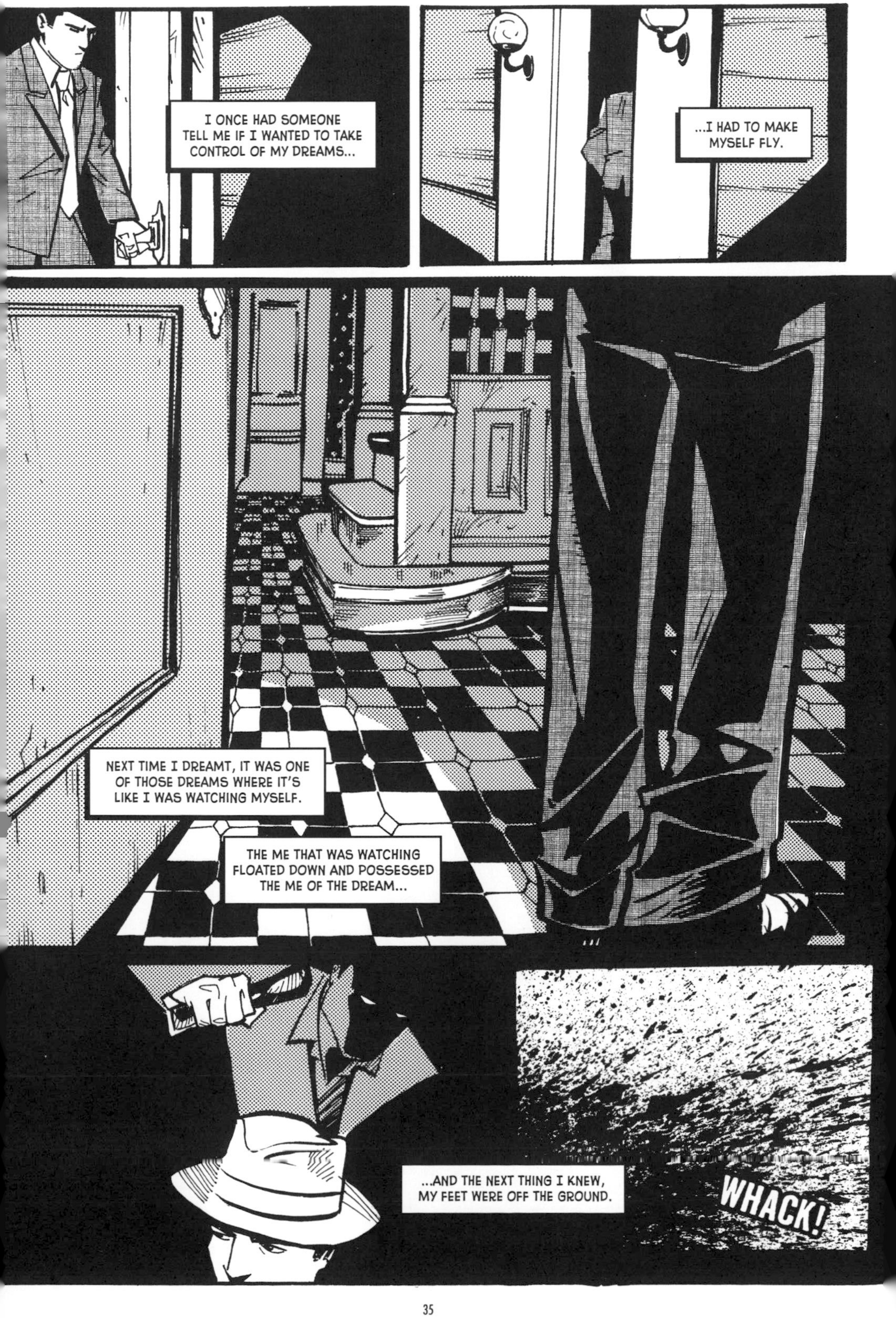
I ONCE HAD SOMEONE TELL ME IF I WANTED TO TAKE CONTROL OF MY DREAMS...
...I HAD TO MAKE MYSELF FLY.
NEXT TIME I DREAMT, IT WAS ONE OF THOSE DREAMS WHERE IT'S LIKE I WAS WATCHING MYSELF.
THE ME THAT WAS WATCHING FLOATED DOWN AND POSSESSED THE ME OF THE DREAM...
...AND THE NEXT THING I KNEW, MY FEET WERE OFF THE GROUND.
WHACK!

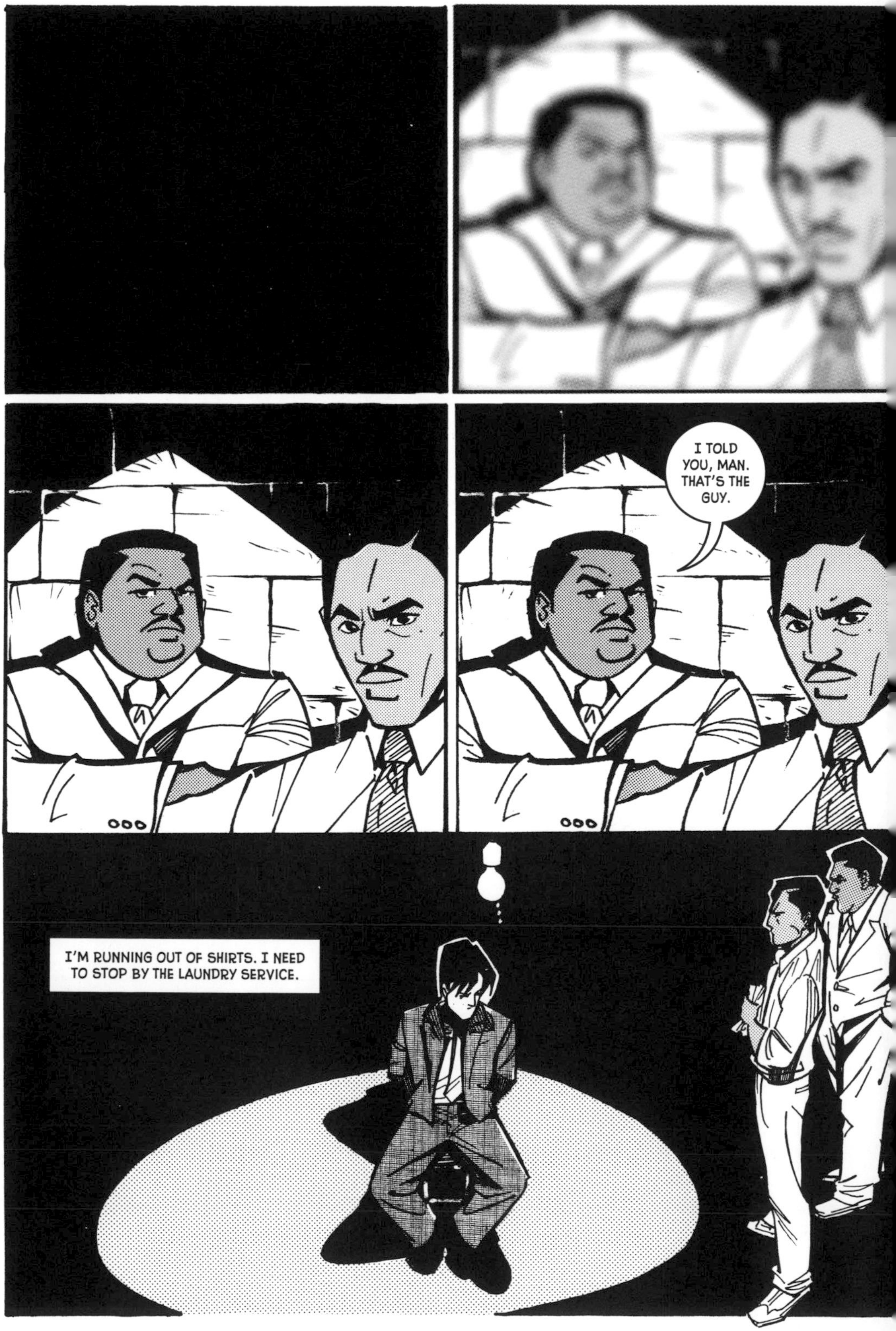
I TOLD YOU, MAN. THAT'S THE GUY.
I'M RUNNING OUT OF SHIRTS. I NEED TO STOP BY THE LAUNDRY SERVICE.

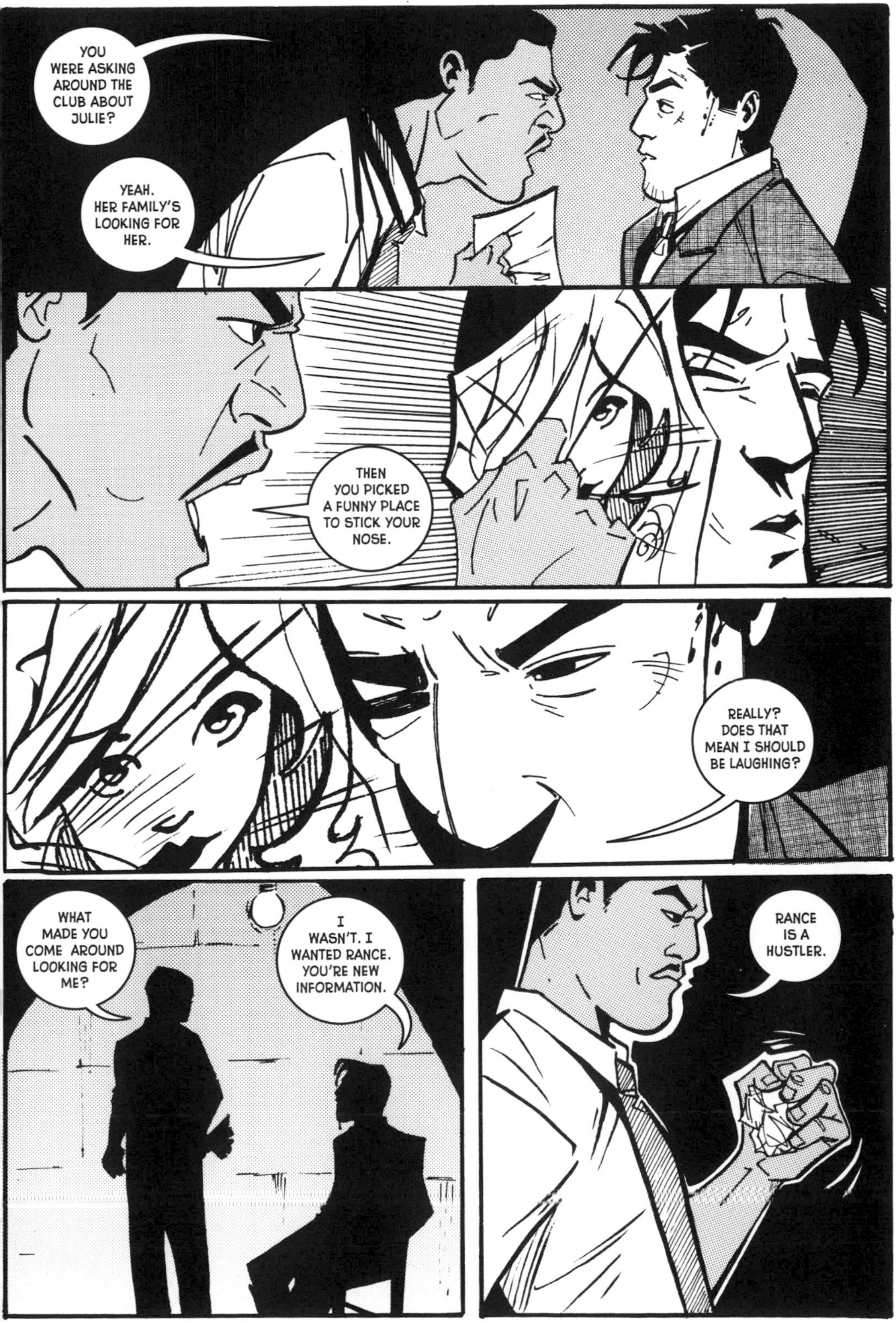
YOU WERE ASKING AROUND THE CLUB ABOUT JULIE?
YEAH. HER FAMILY'S LOOKING FOR HER.
THEN YOU PICKED A FUNNY PLACE TO STICK YOUR NOSE.
REALLY? DOES THAT MEAN I SHOULD BE LAUGHING?
WHAT MADE YOU COME AROUND LOOKING FOR ME?
I WASN'T. I WANTED RANCE. YOU'RE NEW INFORMATION.
RANCE IS A HUSTLER.

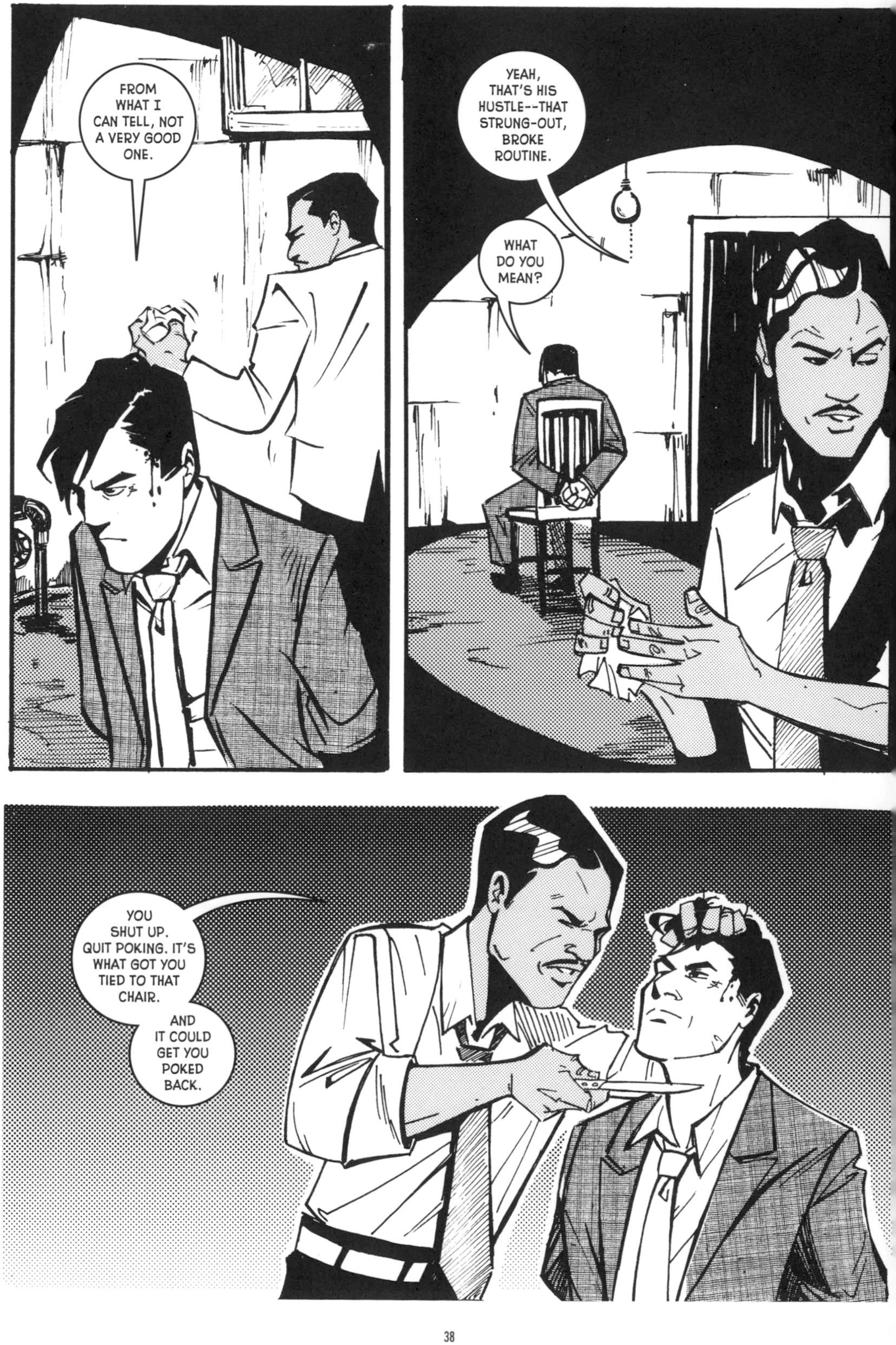
FROM WHAT I CAN TELL, NOT A VERY GOOD ONE.
YEAH, THAT'S HIS HUSTLE--THAT STRUNG-OUT, BROKE ROUTINE.
WHAT DO YOU MEAN?
YOU SHUT UP. QUIT POKING. IT'S WHAT GOT YOU TIED TO THAT CHAIR.
AND IT COULD GET YOU POKED BACK.

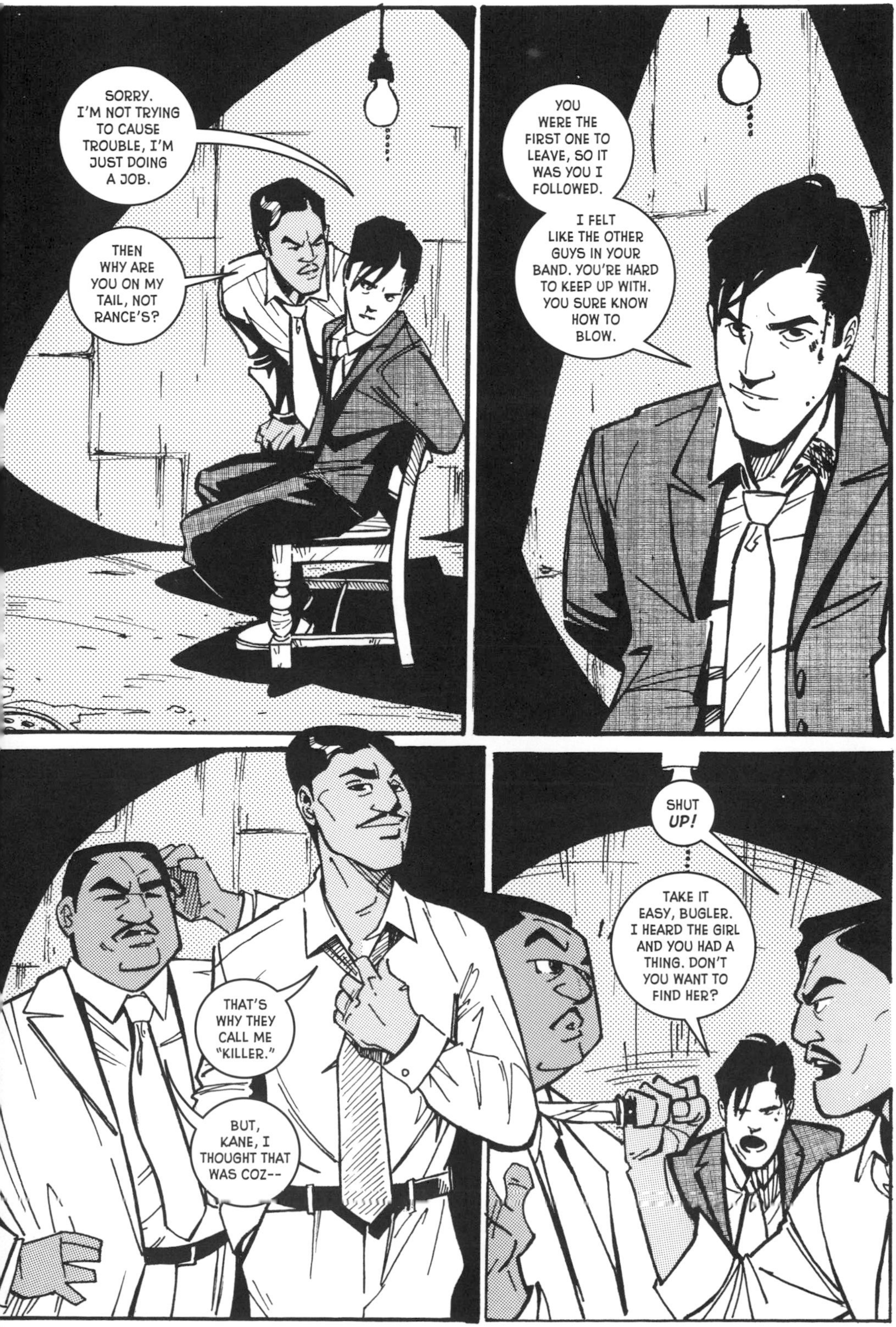
SORRY. I'M NOT TRYING TO CAUSE TROUBLE, I'M JUST DOING A JOB.
THEN WHY ARE YOU ON MY TAIL, NOT RANCE'S?
YOU WERE THE FIRST ONE TO LEAVE, SO IT WAS YOU I FOLLOWED.
I FELT LIKE THE OTHER GUYS IN YOUR BAND. YOU'RE HARD TO KEEP UP WITH. YOU SURE KNOW HOW TO BLOW.
THAT'S WHY THEY CALL ME "KILLER."
BUT, KANE, I THOUGHT THAT WAS COZ--
SHUT *UP!*
TAKE IT EASY, BUGLER. I HEARD THE GIRL AND YOU HAD A THING. DON'T YOU WANT TO FIND HER?

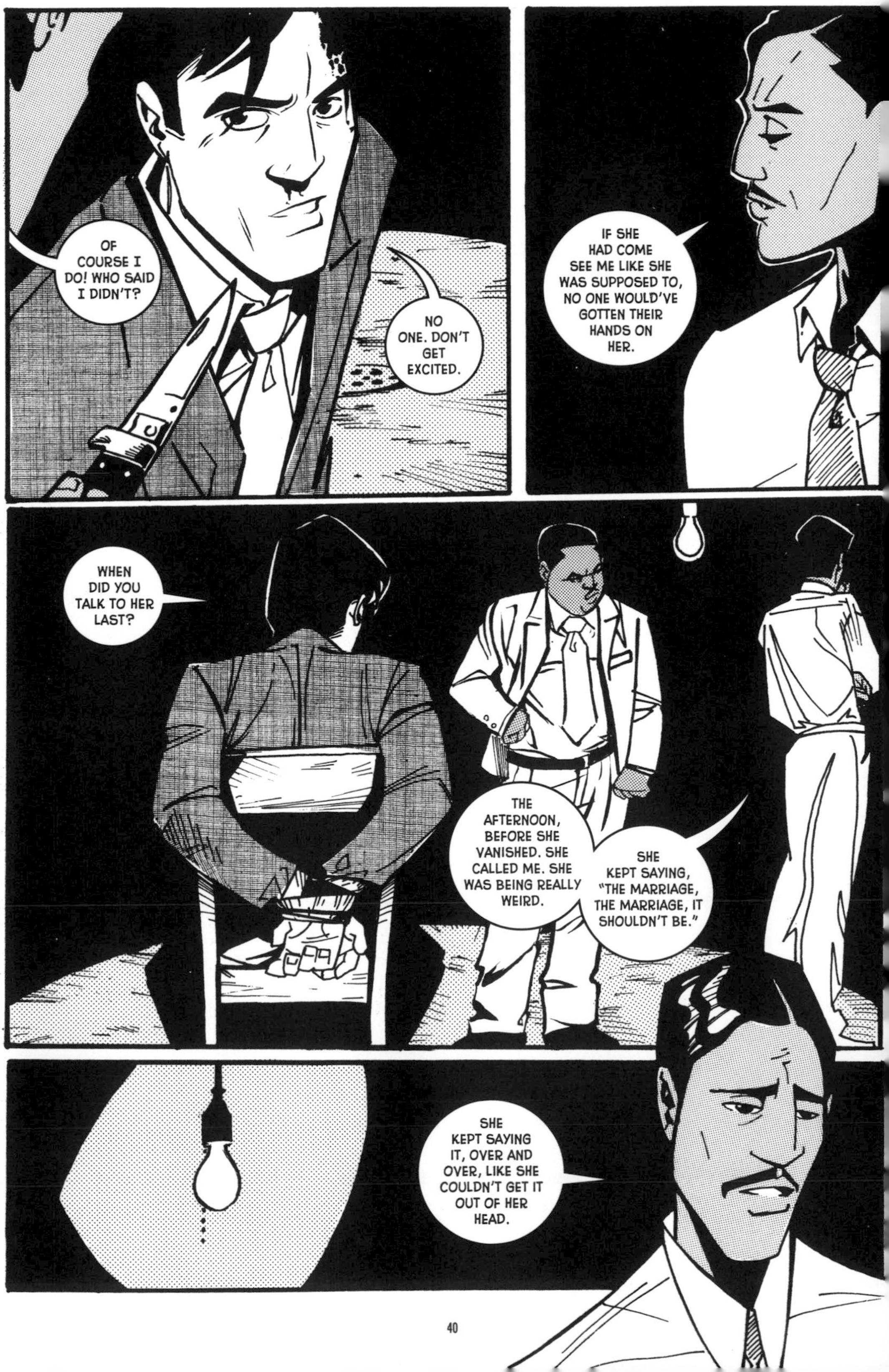
OF COURSE I DO! WHO SAID I DIDN'T?
NO ONE. DON'T GET EXCITED.
IF SHE HAD COME SEE ME LIKE SHE WAS SUPPOSED TO, NO ONE WOULD'VE GOTTEN THEIR HANDS ON HER.
WHEN DID YOU TALK TO HER LAST?
THE AFTERNOON, BEFORE SHE VANISHED. SHE CALLED ME. SHE WAS BEING REALLY WEIRD.
SHE KEPT SAYING, "THE MARRIAGE, THE MARRIAGE, IT SHOULDN'T BE."
SHE KEPT SAYING IT, OVER AND OVER, LIKE SHE COULDN'T GET IT OUT OF HER HEAD.

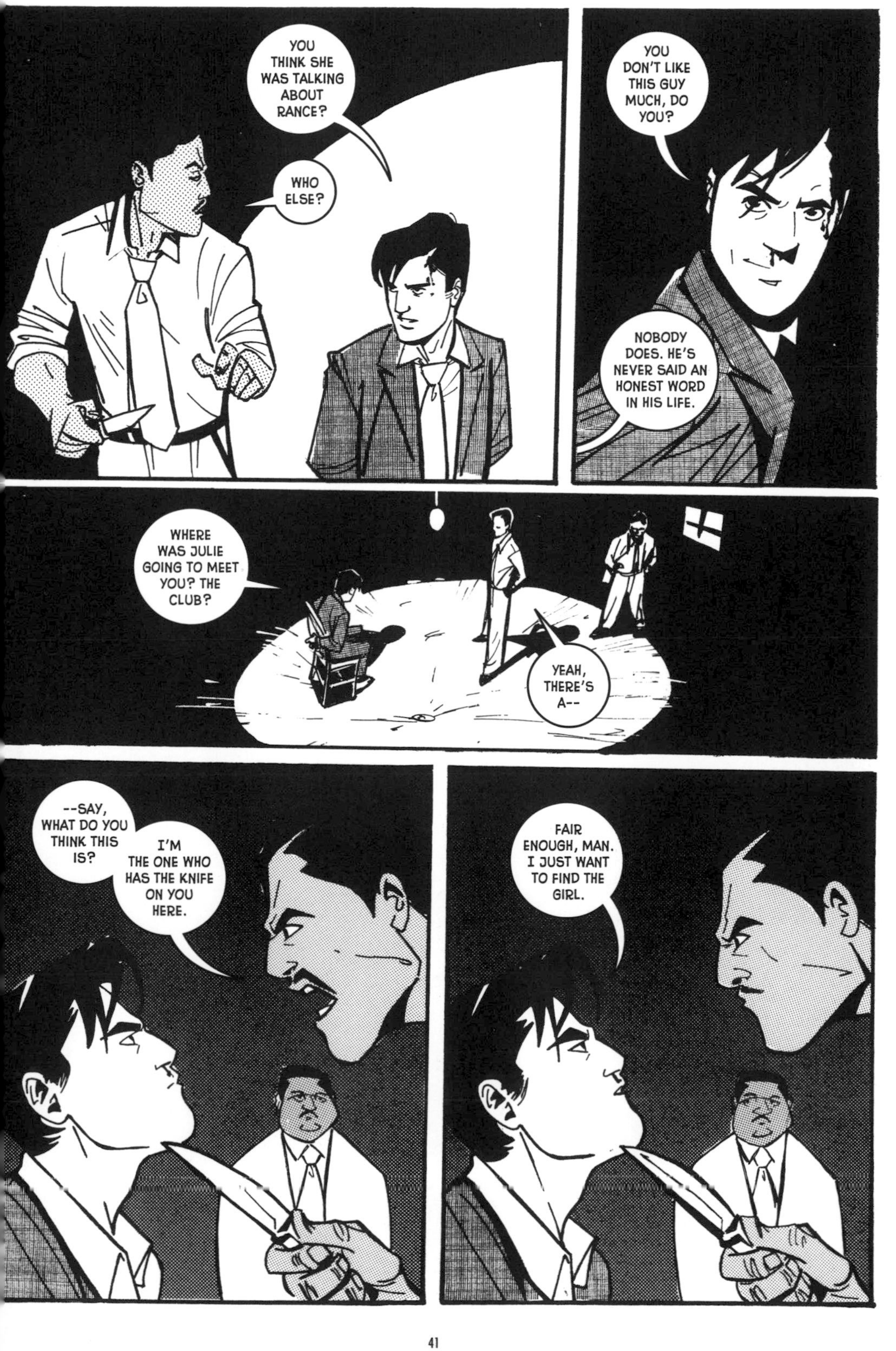
YOU THINK SHE WAS TALKING ABOUT RANCE?
WHO ELSE?
YOU DON'T LIKE THIS GUY MUCH, DO YOU?
NOBODY DOES. HE'S NEVER SAID AN HONEST WORD IN HIS LIFE.
WHERE WAS JULIE GOING TO MEET YOU? THE CLUB?
YEAH, THERE'S A--
--SAY, WHAT DO YOU THINK THIS IS?
I'M THE ONE WHO HAS THE KNIFE ON YOU HERE.
FAIR ENOUGH, MAN. I JUST WANT TO FIND THE GIRL.

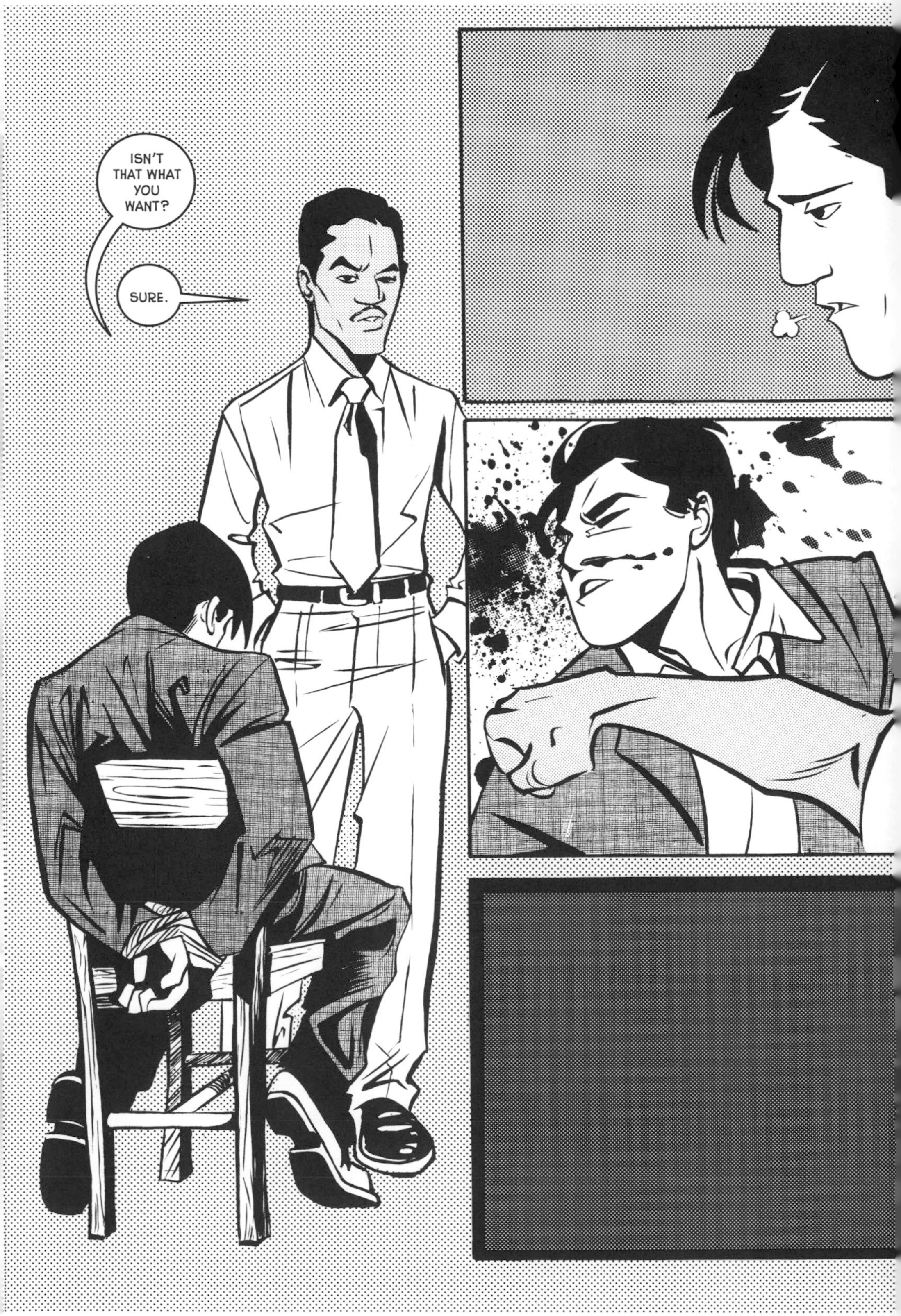
ISN'T THAT WHAT YOU WANT?
SURE.

CHAPTER 4

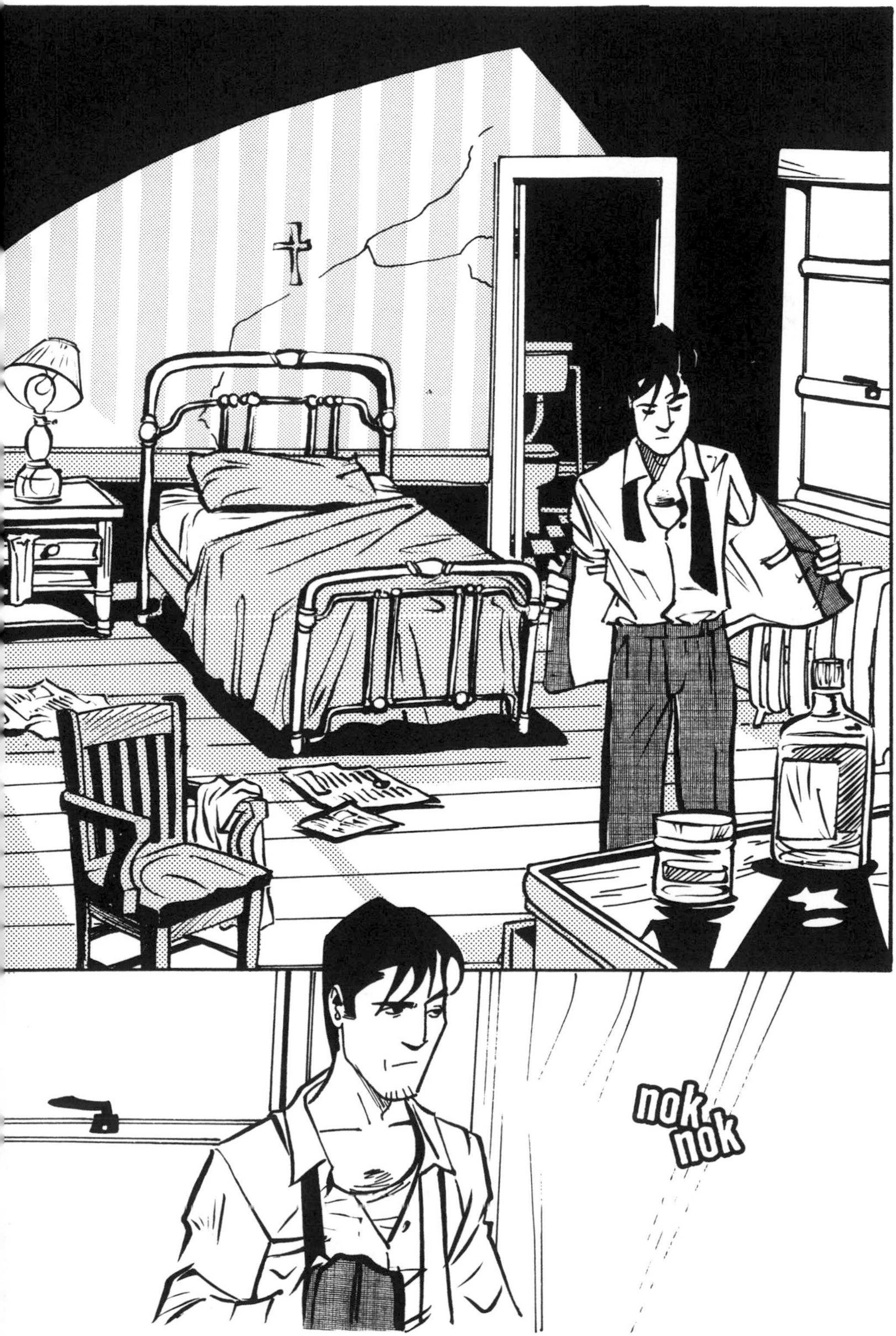
nok
nok

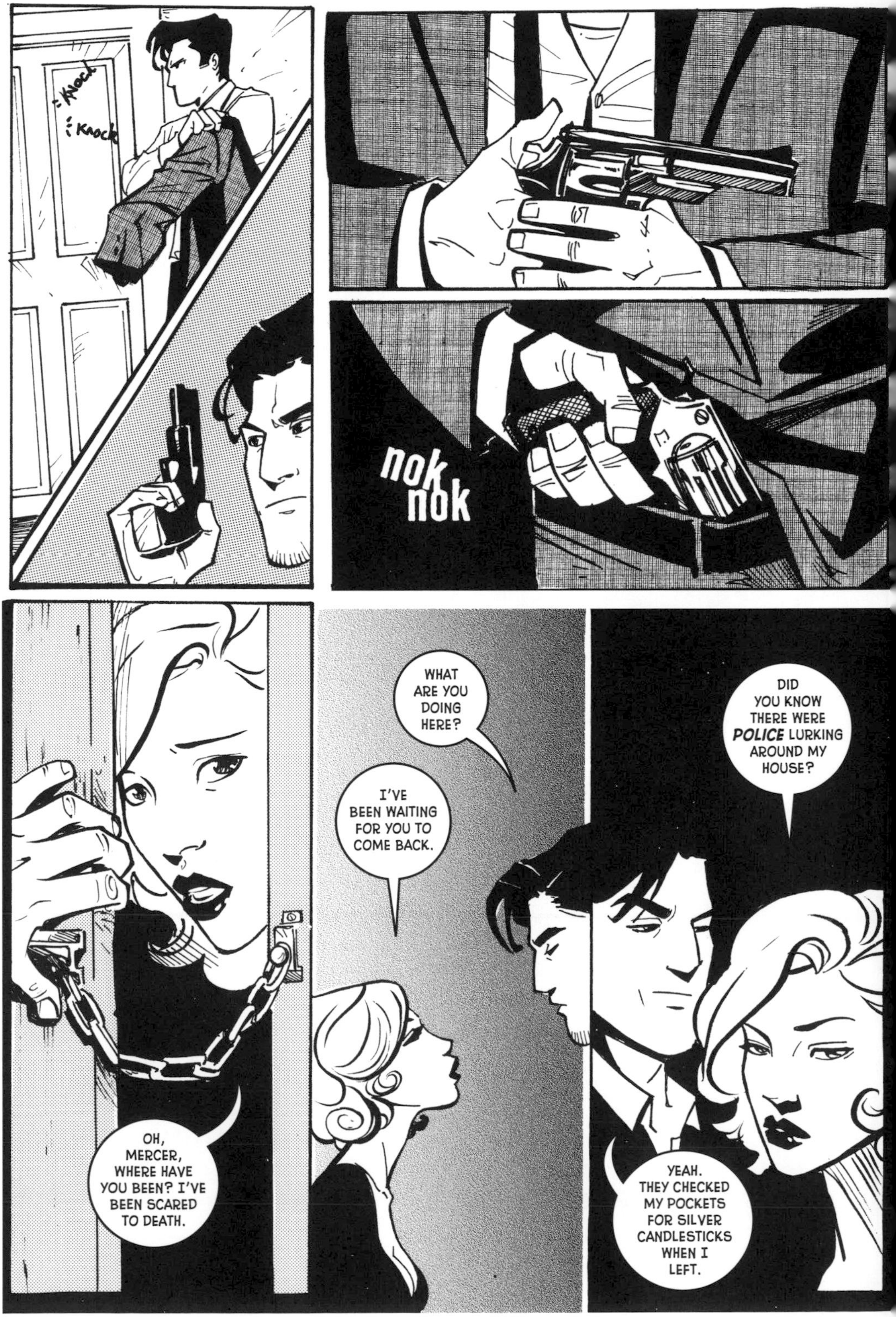
KNOCK
KNOCK
nok nok
OH, MERCER, WHERE HAVE YOU BEEN? I'VE BEEN SCARED TO DEATH.
WHAT ARE YOU DOING HERE?
I'VE BEEN WAITING FOR YOU TO COME BACK.
DID YOU KNOW THERE WERE POLICE LURKING AROUND MY HOUSE?
YEAH. THEY CHECKED MY POCKETS FOR SILVER CANDLESTICKS WHEN I LEFT.

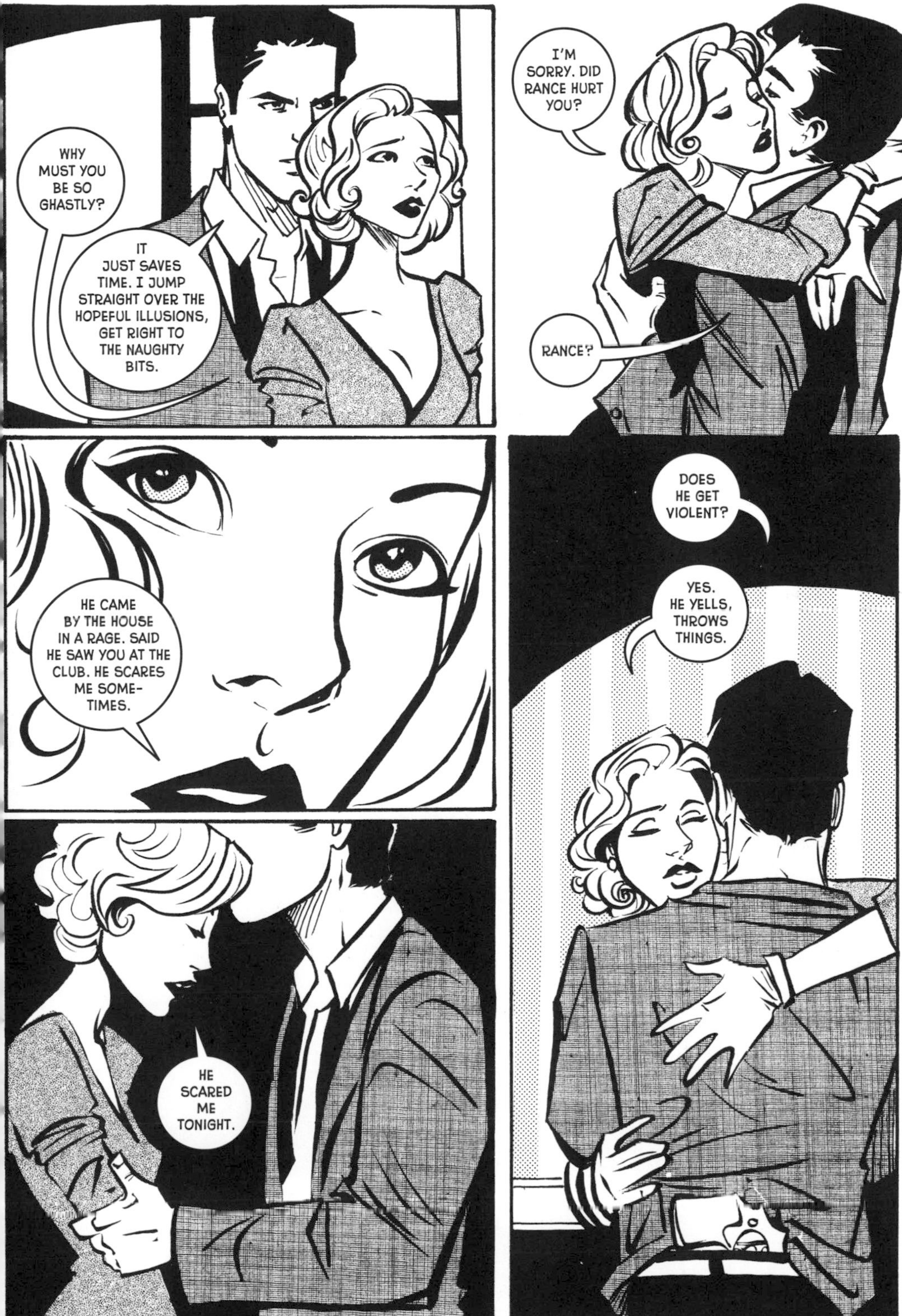
WHY MUST YOU BE SO GHASTLY?
IT JUST SAVES TIME. I JUMP STRAIGHT OVER THE HOPEFUL ILLUSIONS, GET RIGHT TO THE NAUGHTY BITS.
I'M SORRY. DID RANCE HURT YOU?
RANCE?
HE CAME BY THE HOUSE IN A RAGE. SAID HE SAW YOU AT THE CLUB. HE SCARES ME SOME-TIMES.
HE SCARED ME TONIGHT.
DOES HE GET VIOLENT?
YES. HE YELLS, THROWS THINGS.

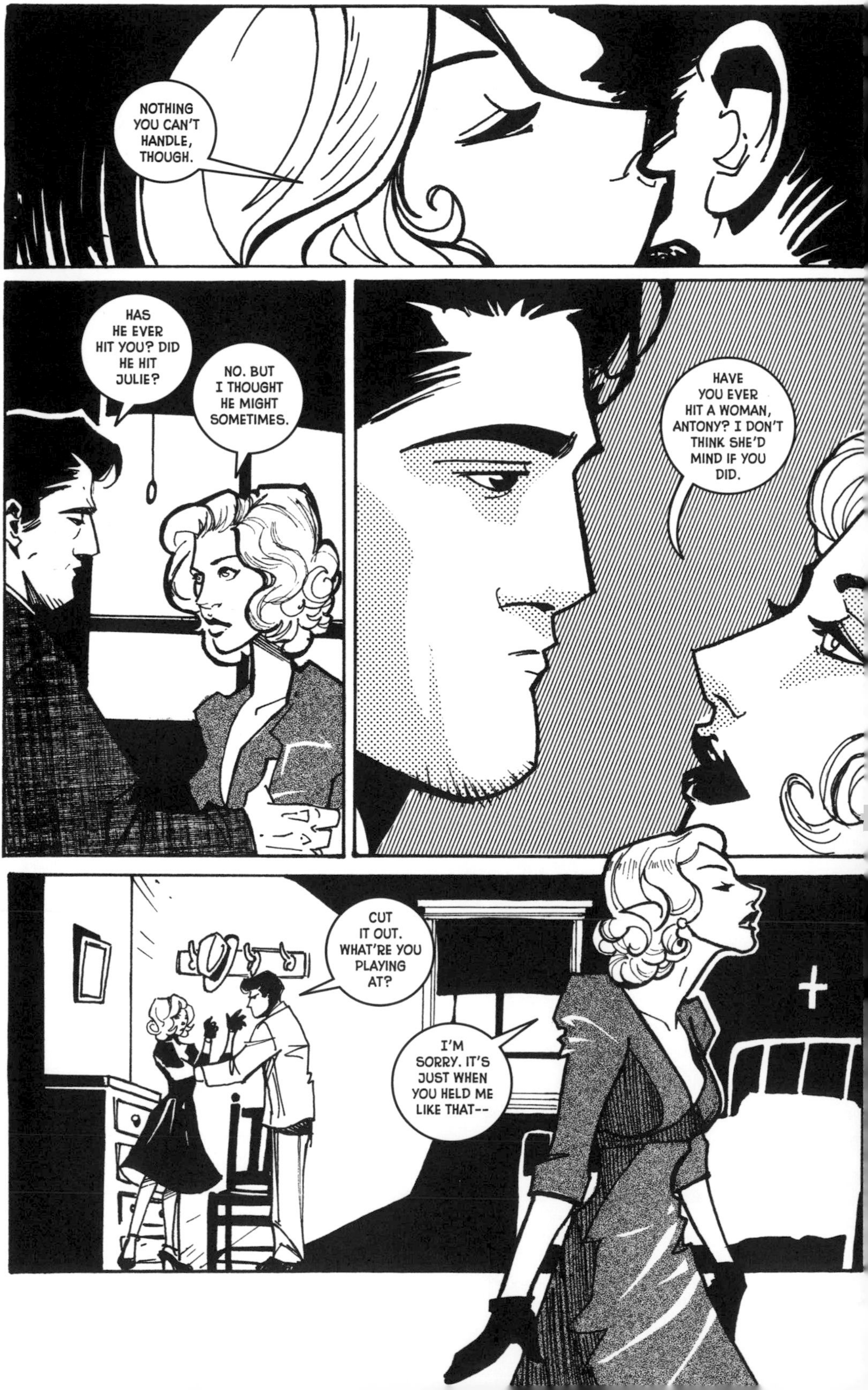
NOTHING YOU CAN'T HANDLE, THOUGH.
HAS HE EVER HIT YOU? DID HE HIT JULIE?
NO. BUT I THOUGHT HE MIGHT SOMETIMES.
HAVE YOU EVER HIT A WOMAN, ANTONY? I DON'T THINK SHE'D MIND IF YOU DID.
CUT IT OUT. WHAT'RE YOU PLAYING AT?
I'M SORRY. IT'S JUST WHEN YOU HELD ME LIKE THAT--

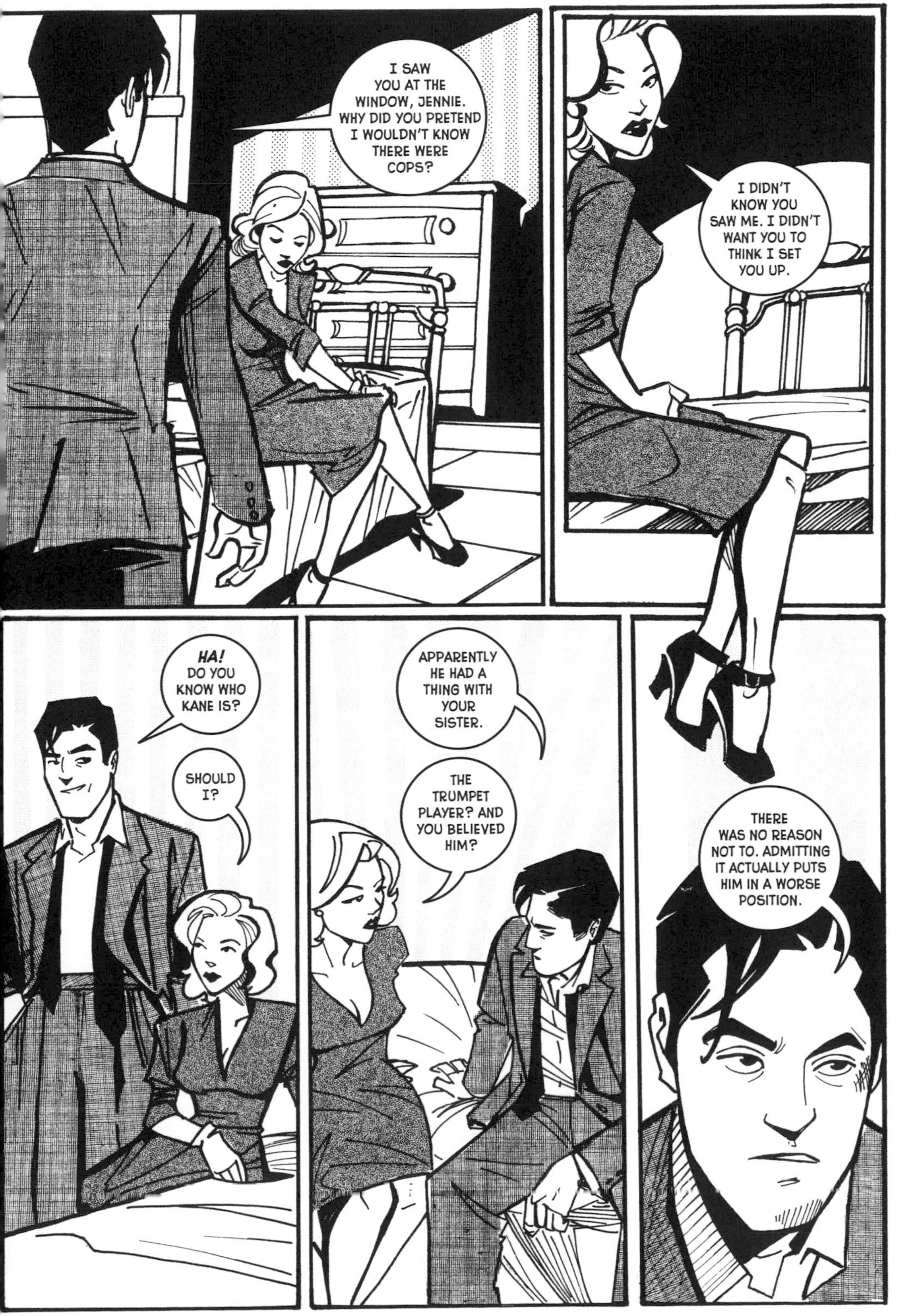

I SAW YOU AT THE WINDOW, JENNIE. WHY DID YOU PRETEND I WOULDN'T KNOW THERE WERE COPS?
I DIDN'T KNOW YOU SAW ME. I DIDN'T WANT YOU TO THINK I SET YOU UP.
HA! DO YOU KNOW WHO KANE IS?
SHOULD I?
APPARENTLY HE HAD A THING WITH YOUR SISTER.
THE TRUMPET PLAYER? AND YOU BELIEVED HIM?
THERE WAS NO REASON NOT TO. ADMITTING IT ACTUALLY PUTS HIM IN A WORSE POSITION.

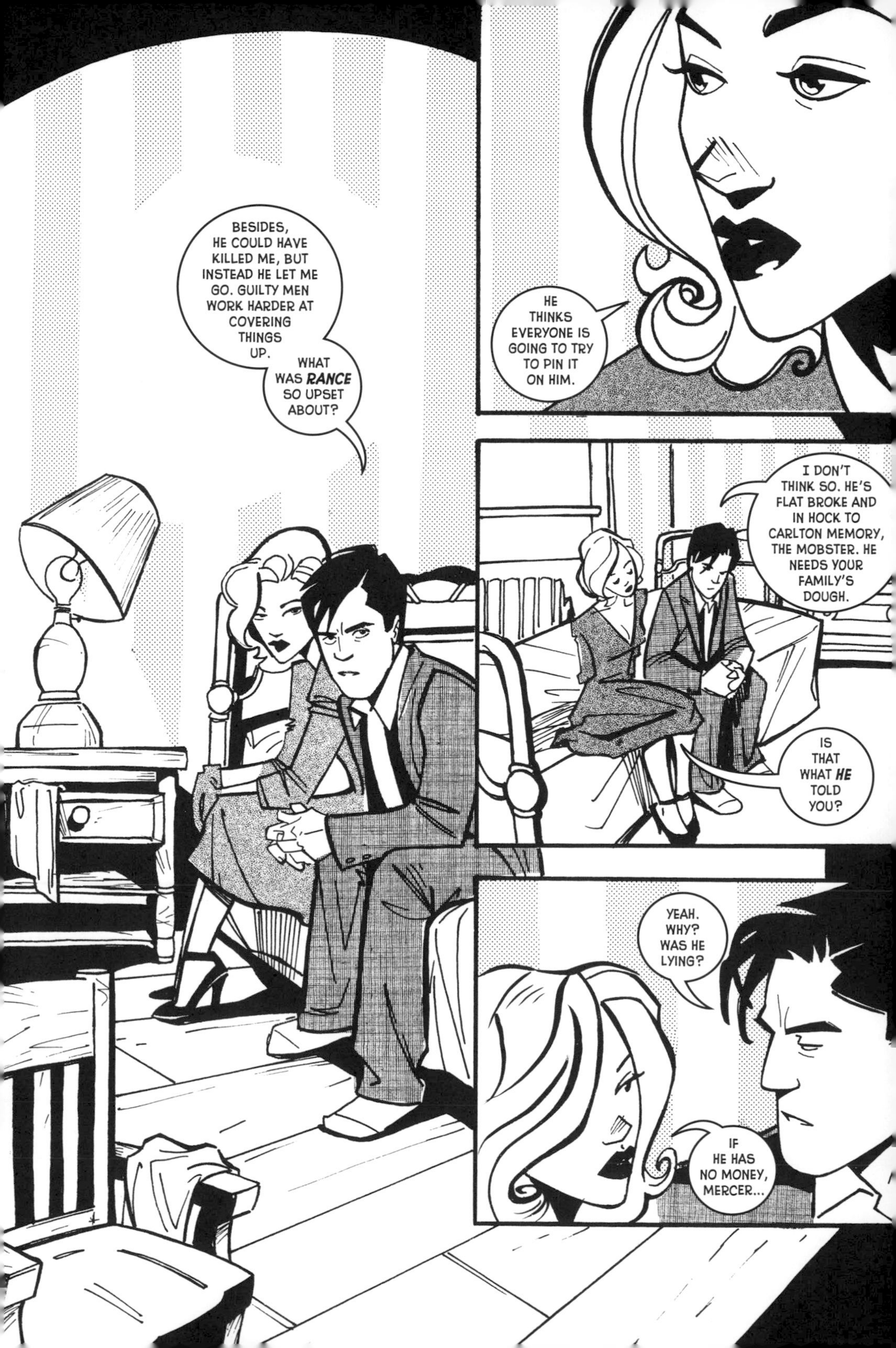
BESIDES, HE COULD HAVE KILLED ME, BUT INSTEAD HE LET ME GO. GUILTY MEN WORK HARDER AT COVERING THINGS UP.
WHAT WAS **RANCE** SO UPSET ABOUT?
HE THINKS EVERYONE IS GOING TO TRY TO PIN IT ON HIM.
I DON'T THINK SO. HE'S FLAT BROKE AND IN HOCK TO CARLTON MEMORY, THE MOBSTER. HE NEEDS YOUR FAMILY'S DOUGH.
IS THAT WHAT **HE** TOLD YOU?
YEAH. WHY? WAS HE LYING?
IF HE HAS NO MONEY, MERCER...

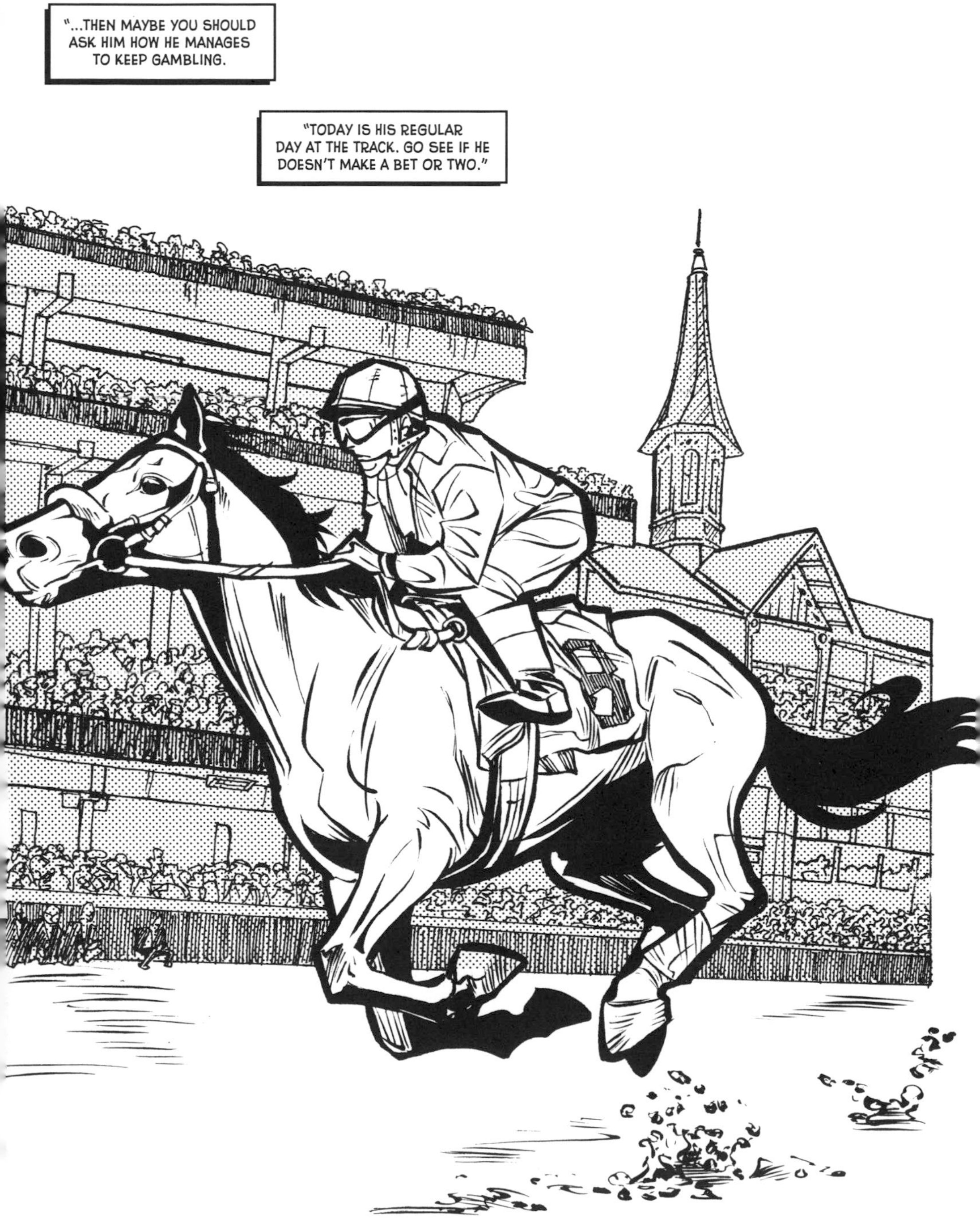
"...THEN MAYBE YOU SHOULD ASK HIM HOW HE MANAGES TO KEEP GAMBLING.
"TODAY IS HIS REGULAR DAY AT THE TRACK. GO SEE IF HE DOESN'T MAKE A BET OR TWO."

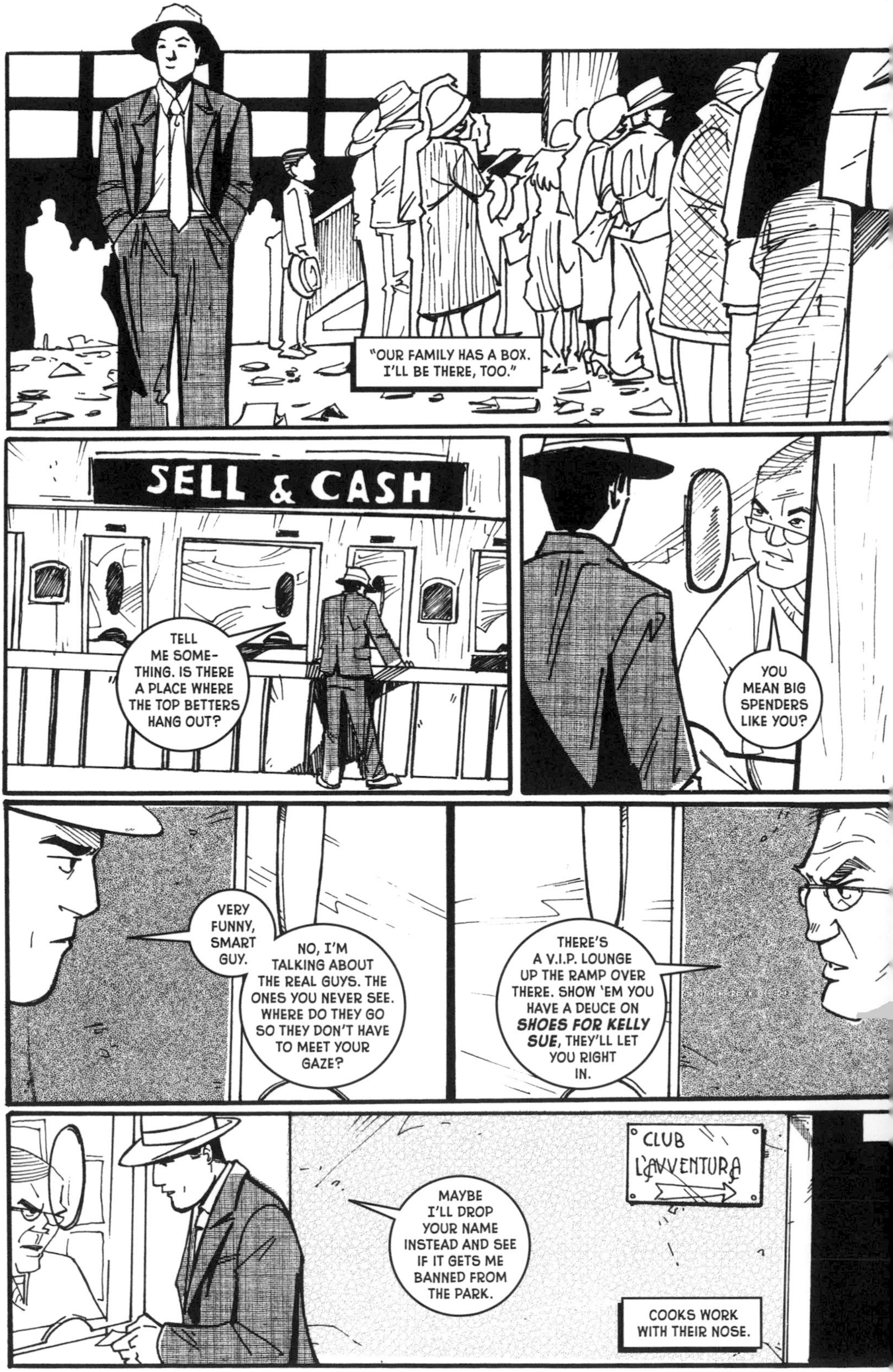
"OUR FAMILY HAS A BOX. I'LL BE THERE, TOO."
SELL & CASH
TELL ME SOME-THING. IS THERE A PLACE WHERE THE TOP BETTERS HANG OUT?
YOU MEAN BIG SPENDERS LIKE YOU?
VERY FUNNY, SMART GUY.
NO, I'M TALKING ABOUT THE REAL GUYS. THE ONES YOU NEVER SEE. WHERE DO THEY GO SO THEY DON'T HAVE TO MEET YOUR GAZE?
THERE'S A V.I.P. LOUNGE UP THE RAMP OVER THERE. SHOW 'EM YOU HAVE A DEUCE ON SHOES FOR KELLY SUE, THEY'LL LET YOU RIGHT IN.
CLUB L'AVVENTURA
MAYBE I'LL DROP YOUR NAME INSTEAD AND SEE IF IT GETS ME BANNED FROM THE PARK.
COOKS WORK WITH THEIR NOSE.

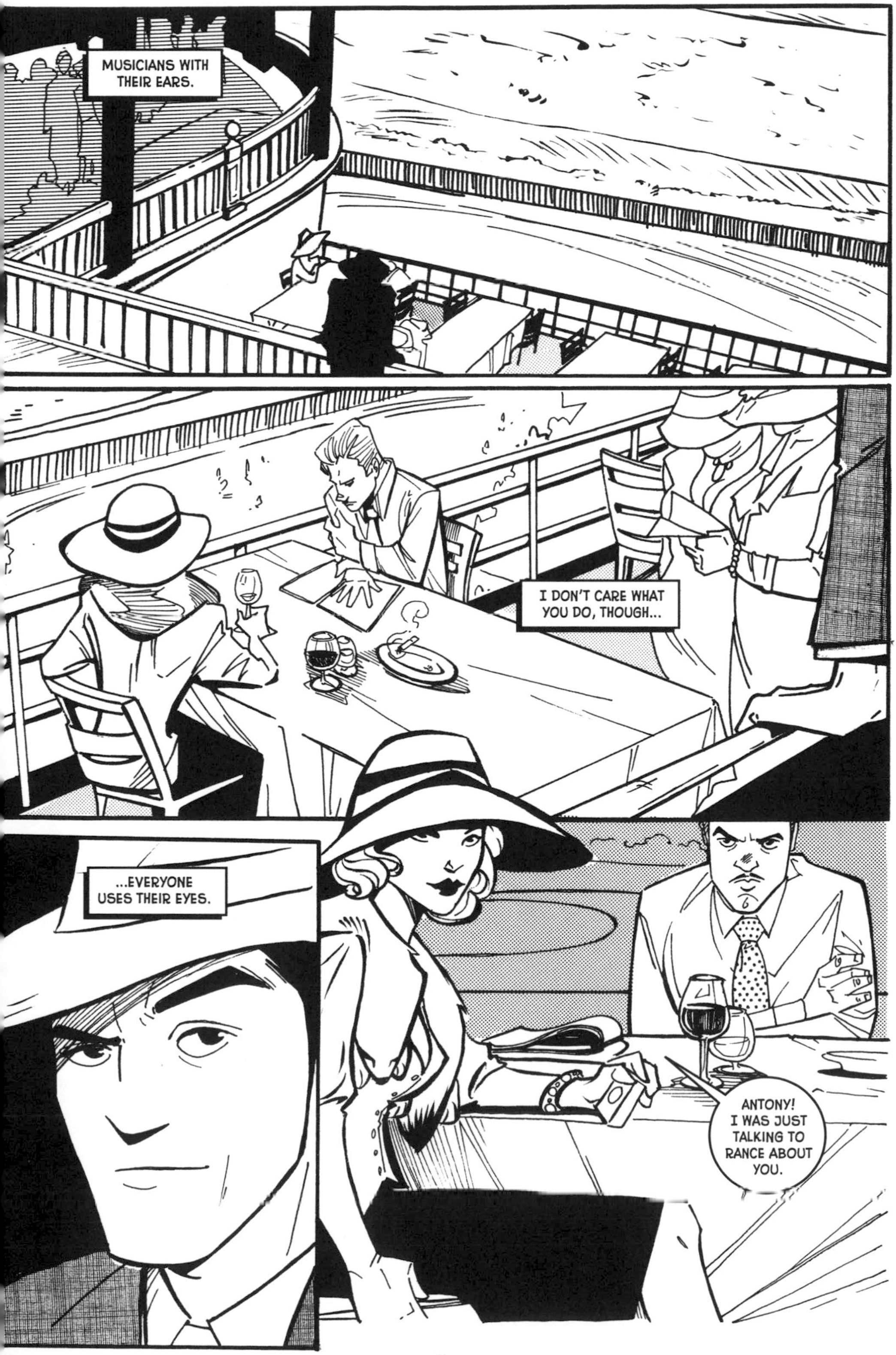
MUSICIANS WITH THEIR EARS.
I DON'T CARE WHAT YOU DO, THOUGH...
...EVERYONE USES THEIR EYES.
ANTONY! I WAS JUST TALKING TO RANCE ABOUT YOU.

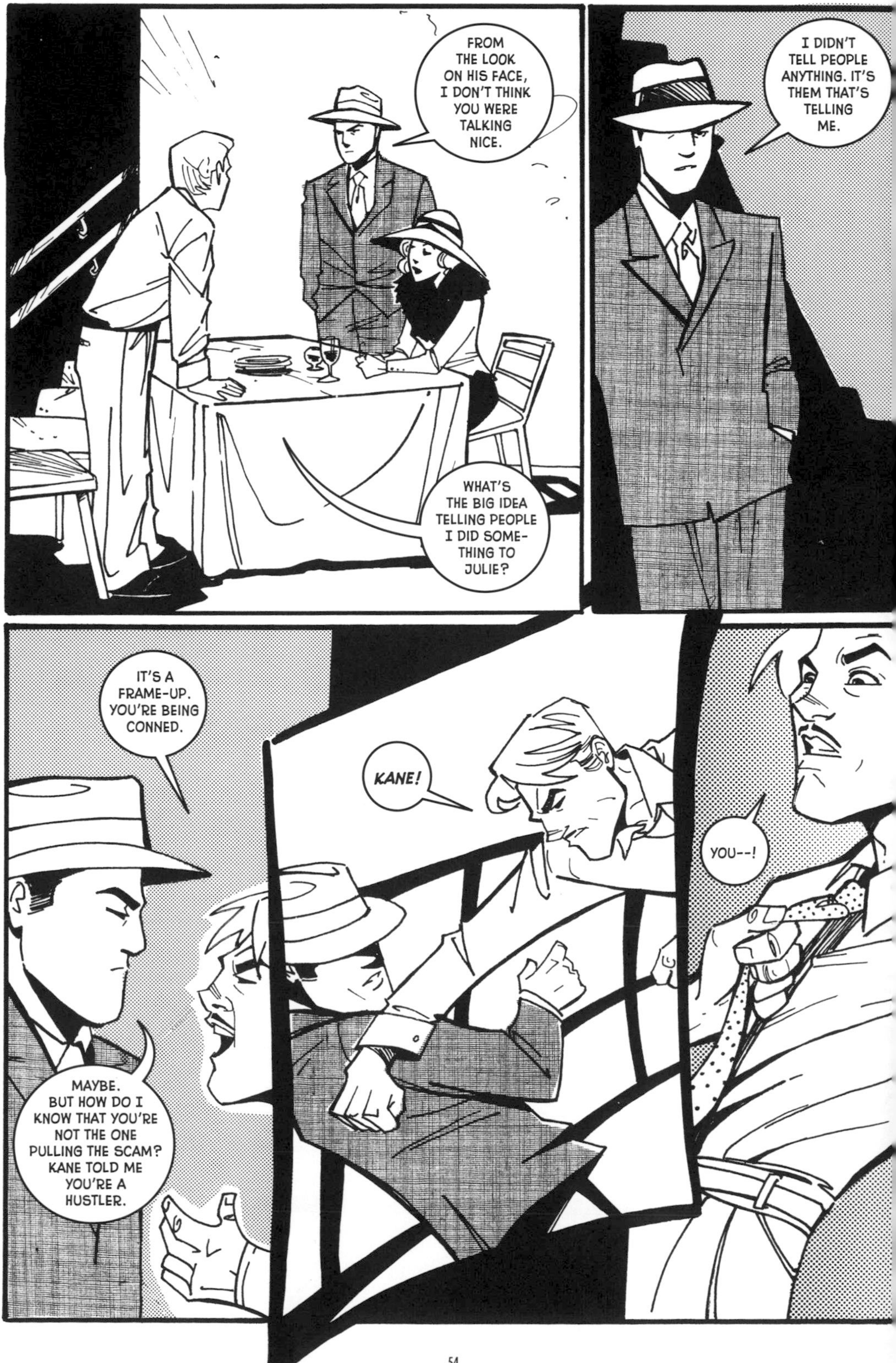
FROM THE LOOK ON HIS FACE, I DON'T THINK YOU WERE TALKING NICE.
WHAT'S THE BIG IDEA TELLING PEOPLE I DID SOME-THING TO JULIE?
I DIDN'T TELL PEOPLE ANYTHING. IT'S THEM THAT'S TELLING ME.
IT'S A FRAME-UP. YOU'RE BEING CONNED.
MAYBE. BUT HOW DO I KNOW THAT YOU'RE NOT THE ONE PULLING THE SCAM? KANE TOLD ME YOU'RE A HUSTLER.
KANE!
YOU--!

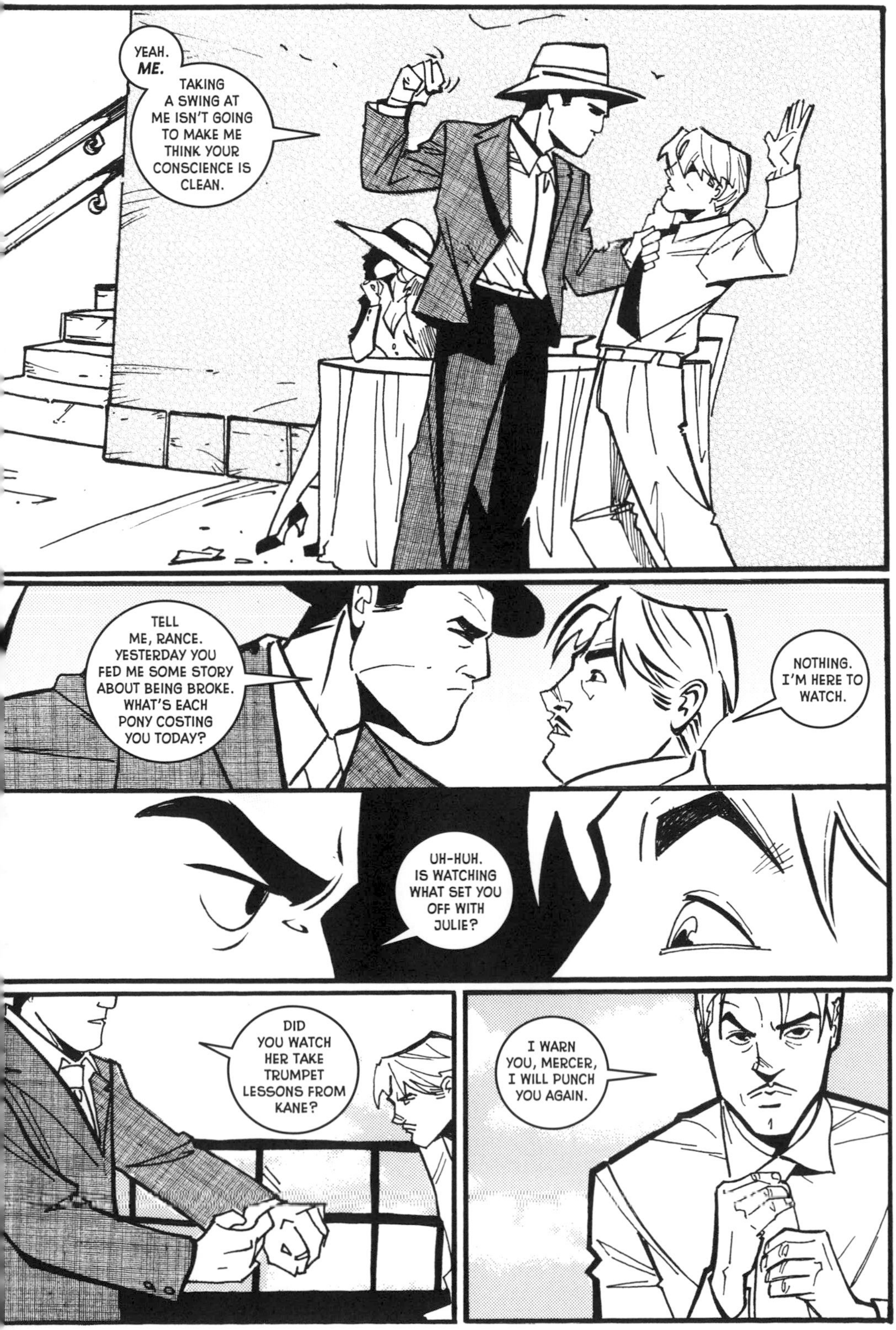
YEAH. *ME.*
TAKING A SWING AT ME ISN'T GOING TO MAKE ME THINK YOUR CONSCIENCE IS CLEAN.
TELL ME, RANCE. YESTERDAY YOU FED ME SOME STORY ABOUT BEING BROKE. WHAT'S EACH PONY COSTING YOU TODAY?
NOTHING. I'M HERE TO WATCH.
UH-HUH. IS WATCHING WHAT SET YOU OFF WITH JULIE?
DID YOU WATCH HER TAKE TRUMPET LESSONS FROM KANE?
I WARN YOU, MERCER, I WILL PUNCH YOU AGAIN.

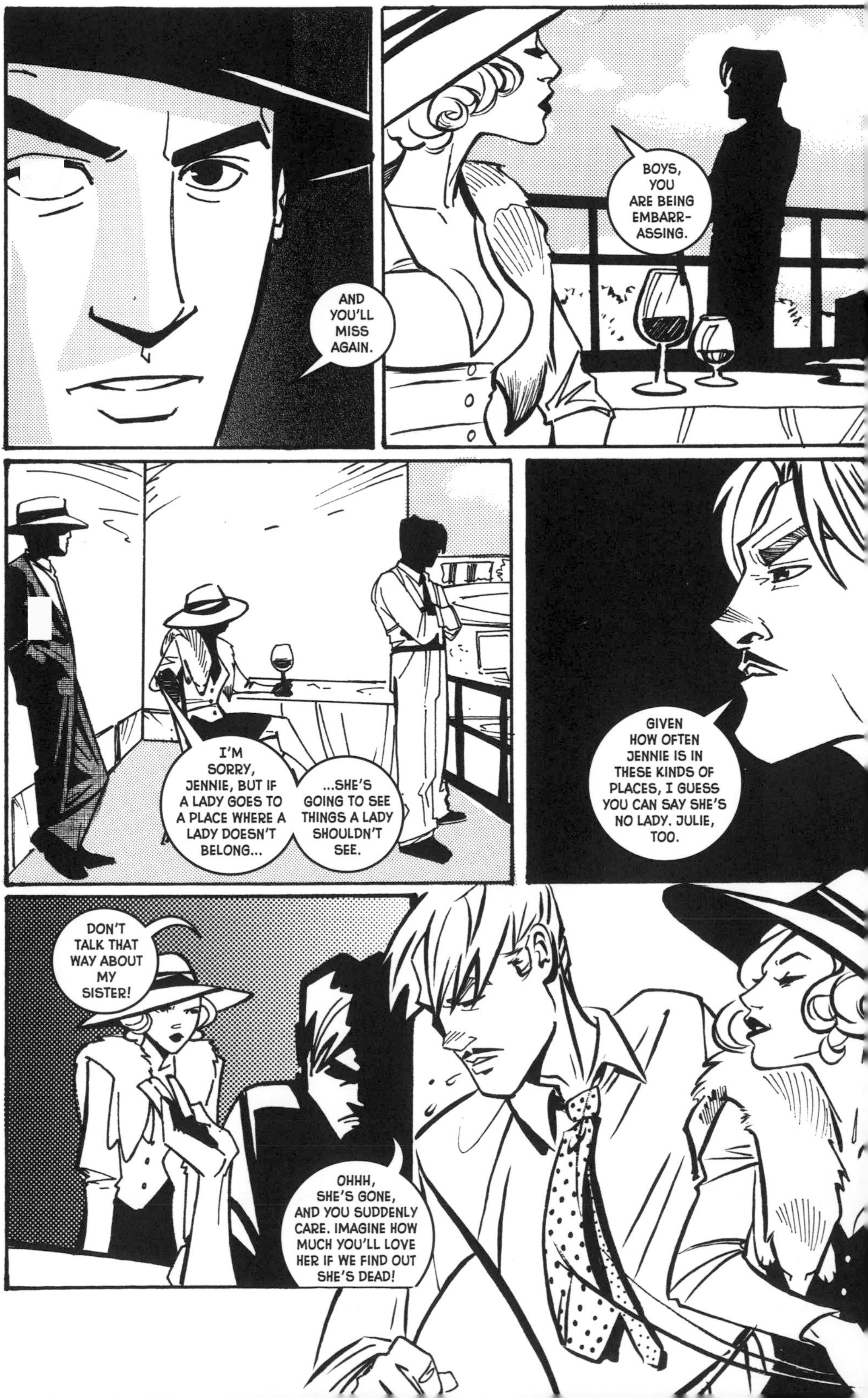
AND YOU'LL MISS AGAIN.
BOYS, YOU ARE BEING EMBARR-ASSING.
I'M SORRY, JENNIE, BUT IF A LADY GOES TO A PLACE WHERE A LADY DOESN'T BELONG...
...SHE'S GOING TO SEE THINGS A LADY SHOULDN'T SEE.
GIVEN HOW OFTEN JENNIE IS IN THESE KINDS OF PLACES, I GUESS YOU CAN SAY SHE'S NO LADY. JULIE, TOO.
DON'T TALK THAT WAY ABOUT MY SISTER!
OHHH, SHE'S GONE, AND YOU SUDDENLY CARE. IMAGINE HOW MUCH YOU'LL LOVE HER IF WE FIND OUT SHE'S DEAD!

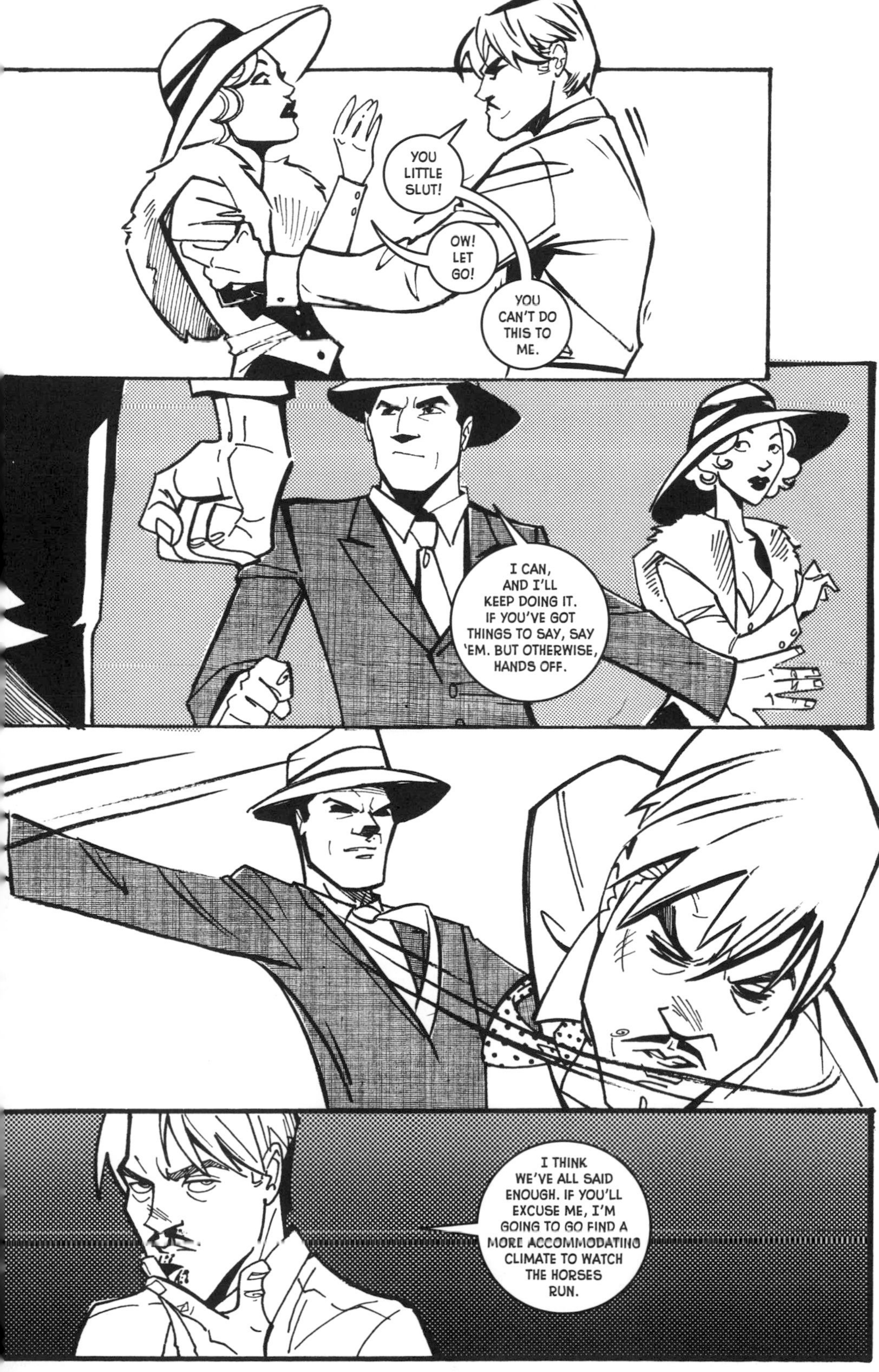
YOU LITTLE SLUT!
OW! LET GO!
YOU CAN'T DO THIS TO ME.
I CAN, AND I'LL KEEP DOING IT. IF YOU'VE GOT THINGS TO SAY, SAY 'EM. BUT OTHERWISE, HANDS OFF.
I THINK WE'VE ALL SAID ENOUGH. IF YOU'LL EXCUSE ME, I'M GOING TO GO FIND A MORE ACCOMMODATING CLIMATE TO WATCH THE HORSES RUN.

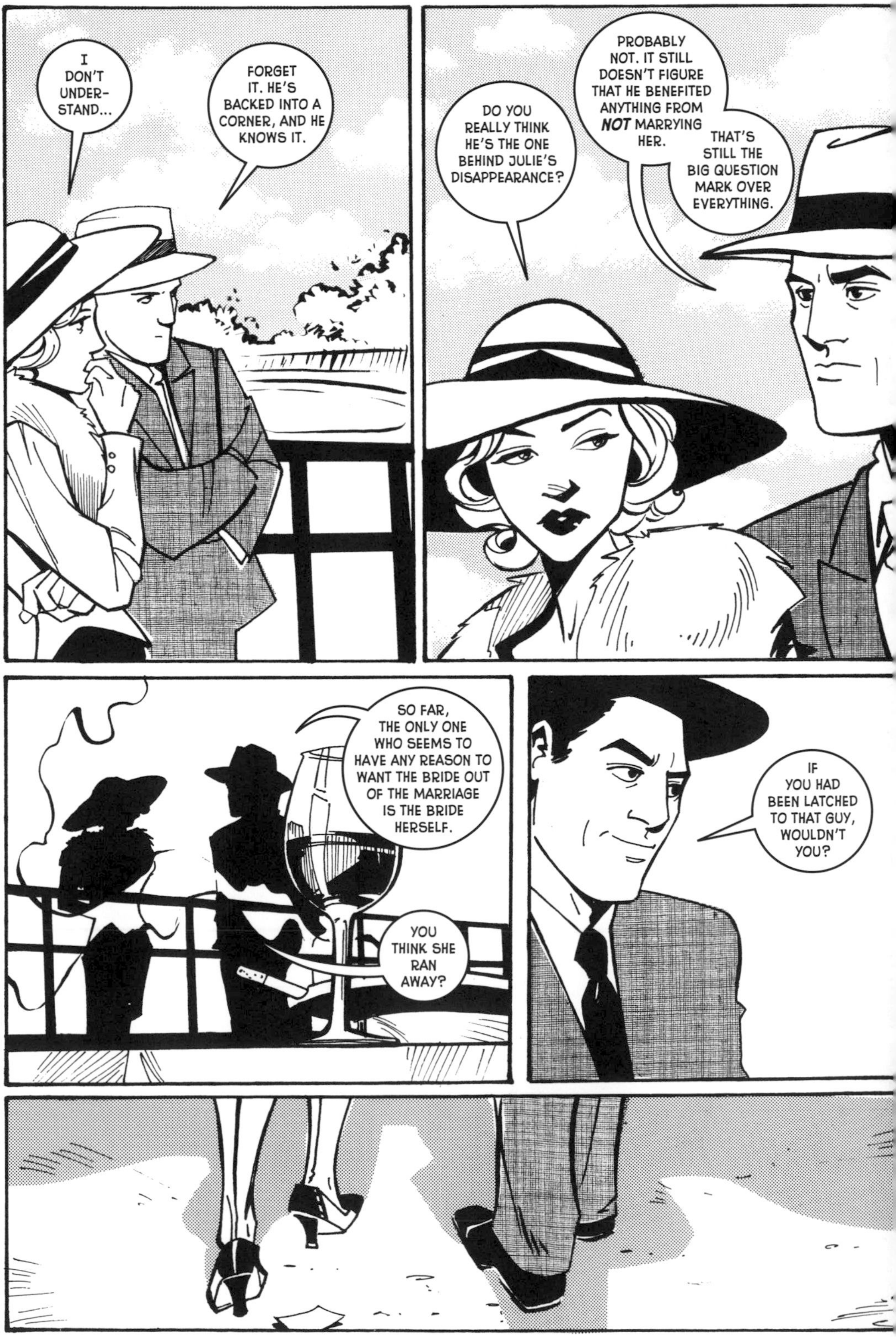
I DON'T UNDER-STAND...
FORGET IT. HE'S BACKED INTO A CORNER, AND HE KNOWS IT.
DO YOU REALLY THINK HE'S THE ONE BEHIND JULIE'S DISAPPEARANCE?
PROBABLY NOT. IT STILL DOESN'T FIGURE THAT HE BENEFITED ANYTHING FROM NOT MARRYING HER.
THAT'S STILL THE BIG QUESTION MARK OVER EVERYTHING.
SO FAR, THE ONLY ONE WHO SEEMS TO HAVE ANY REASON TO WANT THE BRIDE OUT OF THE MARRIAGE IS THE BRIDE HERSELF.
YOU THINK SHE RAN AWAY?
IF YOU HAD BEEN LATCHED TO THAT GUY, WOULDN'T YOU?

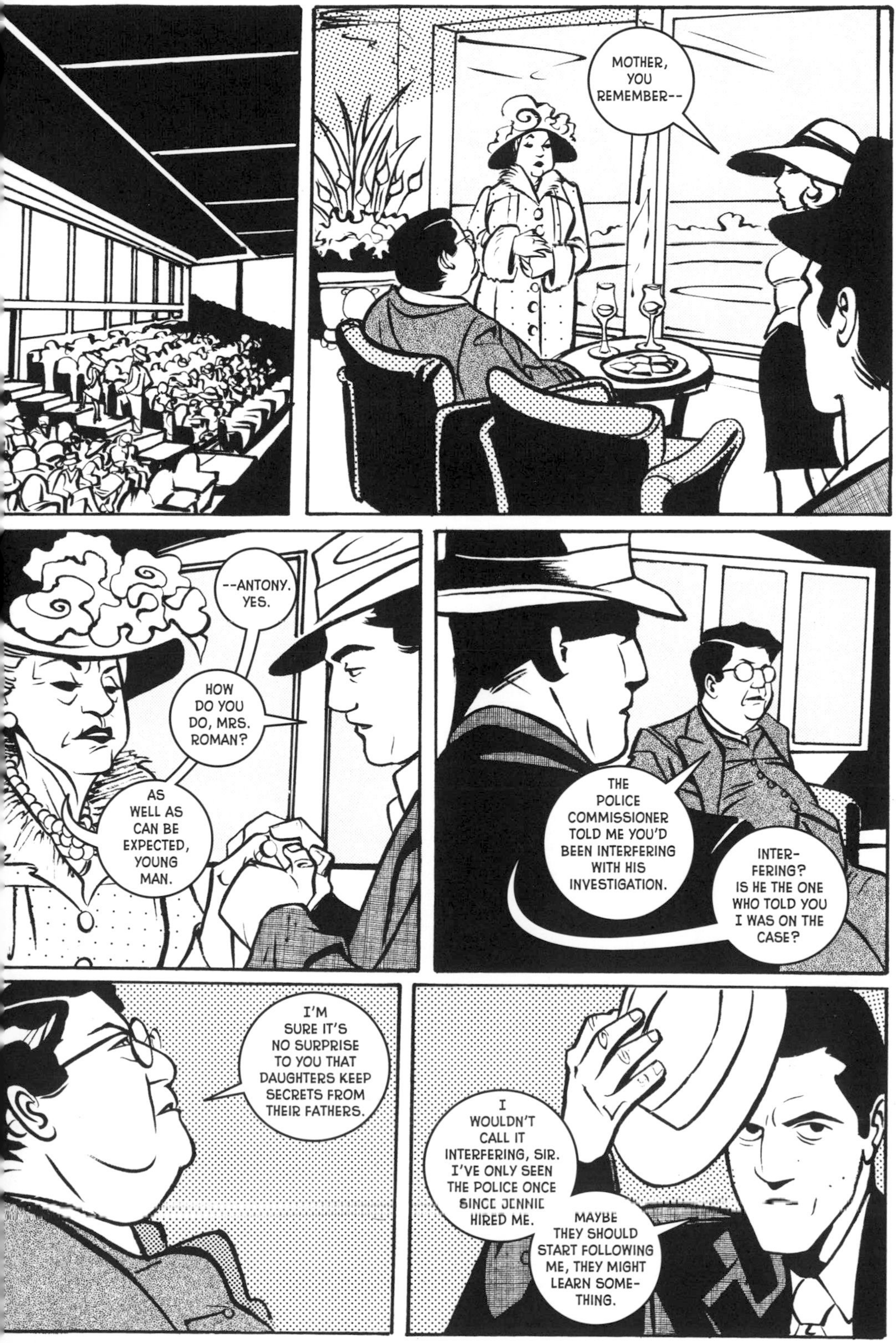
MOTHER, YOU REMEMBER--
--ANTONY. YES.
HOW DO YOU DO, MRS. ROMAN?
AS WELL AS CAN BE EXPECTED, YOUNG MAN.
THE POLICE COMMISSIONER TOLD ME YOU'D BEEN INTERFERING WITH HIS INVESTIGATION.
INTER-FERING? IS HE THE ONE WHO TOLD YOU I WAS ON THE CASE?
I'M SURE IT'S NO SURPRISE TO YOU THAT DAUGHTERS KEEP SECRETS FROM THEIR FATHERS.
I WOULDN'T CALL IT INTERFERING, SIR. I'VE ONLY SEEN THE POLICE ONCE SINCE JENNIE HIRED ME.
MAYBE THEY SHOULD START FOLLOWING ME, THEY MIGHT LEARN SOME-THING.

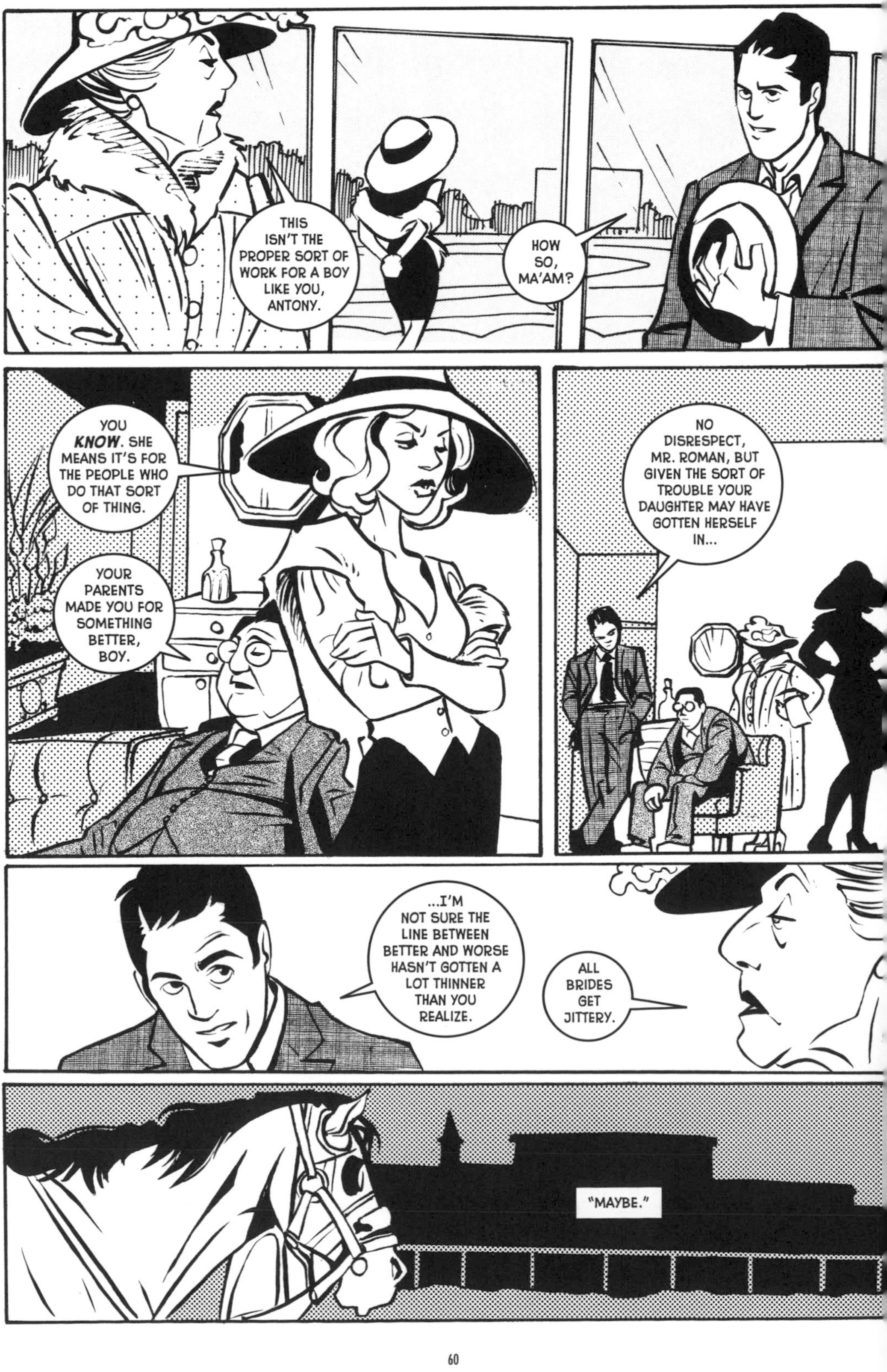
THIS ISN'T THE PROPER SORT OF WORK FOR A BOY LIKE YOU, ANTONY.
HOW SO, MA'AM?
YOU **KNOW**. SHE MEANS IT'S FOR THE PEOPLE WHO DO THAT SORT OF THING.
YOUR PARENTS MADE YOU FOR SOMETHING BETTER, BOY.
NO DISRESPECT, MR. ROMAN, BUT GIVEN THE SORT OF TROUBLE YOUR DAUGHTER MAY HAVE GOTTEN HERSELF IN...
...I'M NOT SURE THE LINE BETWEEN BETTER AND WORSE HASN'T GOTTEN A LOT THINNER THAN YOU REALIZE.
ALL BRIDES GET JITTERY.
"MAYBE."

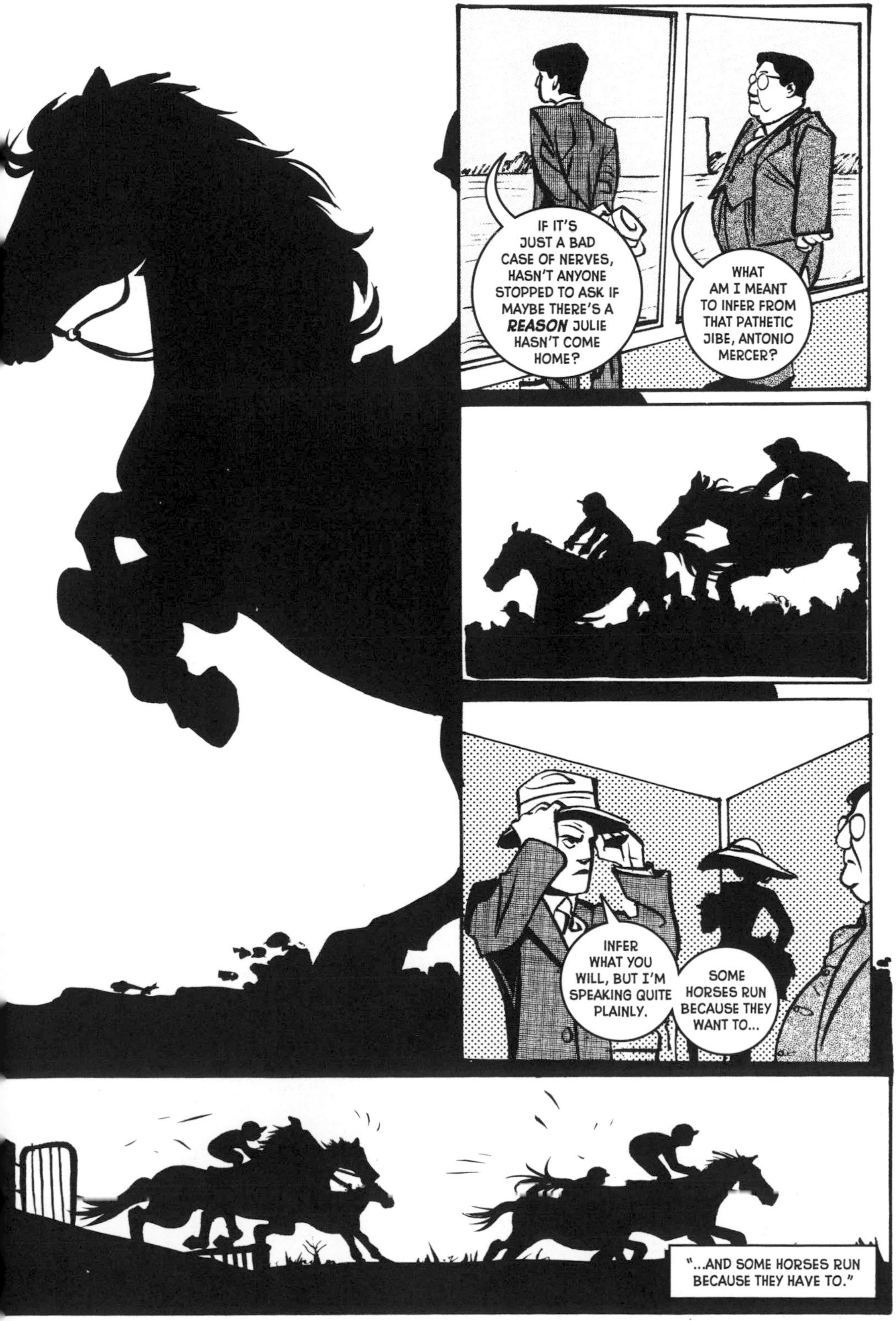
IF IT'S JUST A BAD CASE OF NERVES, HASN'T ANYONE STOPPED TO ASK IF MAYBE THERE'S A REASON JULIE HASN'T COME HOME?
WHAT AM I MEANT TO INFER FROM THAT PATHETIC JIBE, ANTONIO MERCER?
INFER WHAT YOU WILL, BUT I'M SPEAKING QUITE PLAINLY.
SOME HORSES RUN BECAUSE THEY WANT TO...
"...AND SOME HORSES RUN BECAUSE THEY HAVE TO."

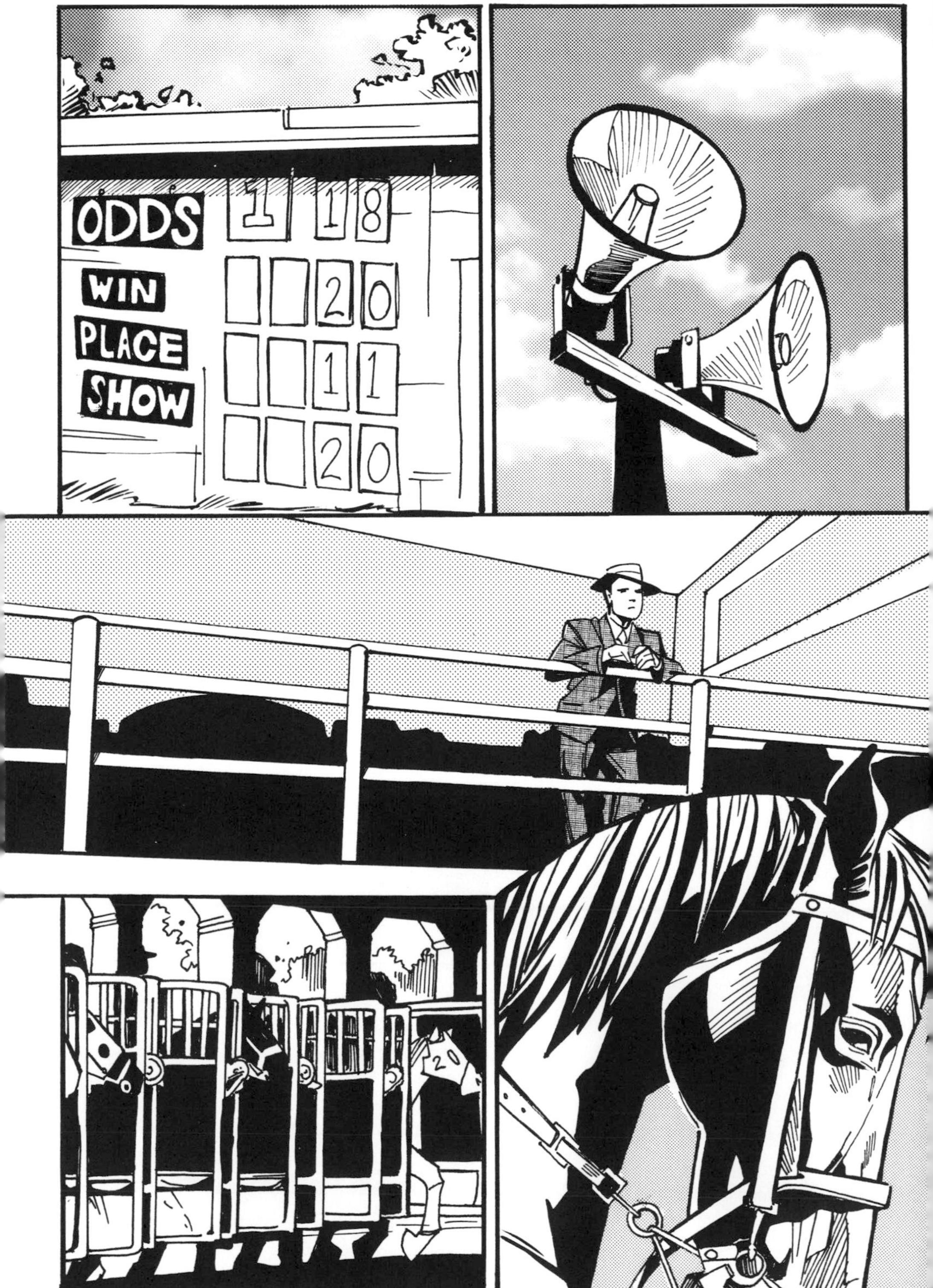
ODDS
1 18
WIN 20
PLACE 11
SHOW 20
20

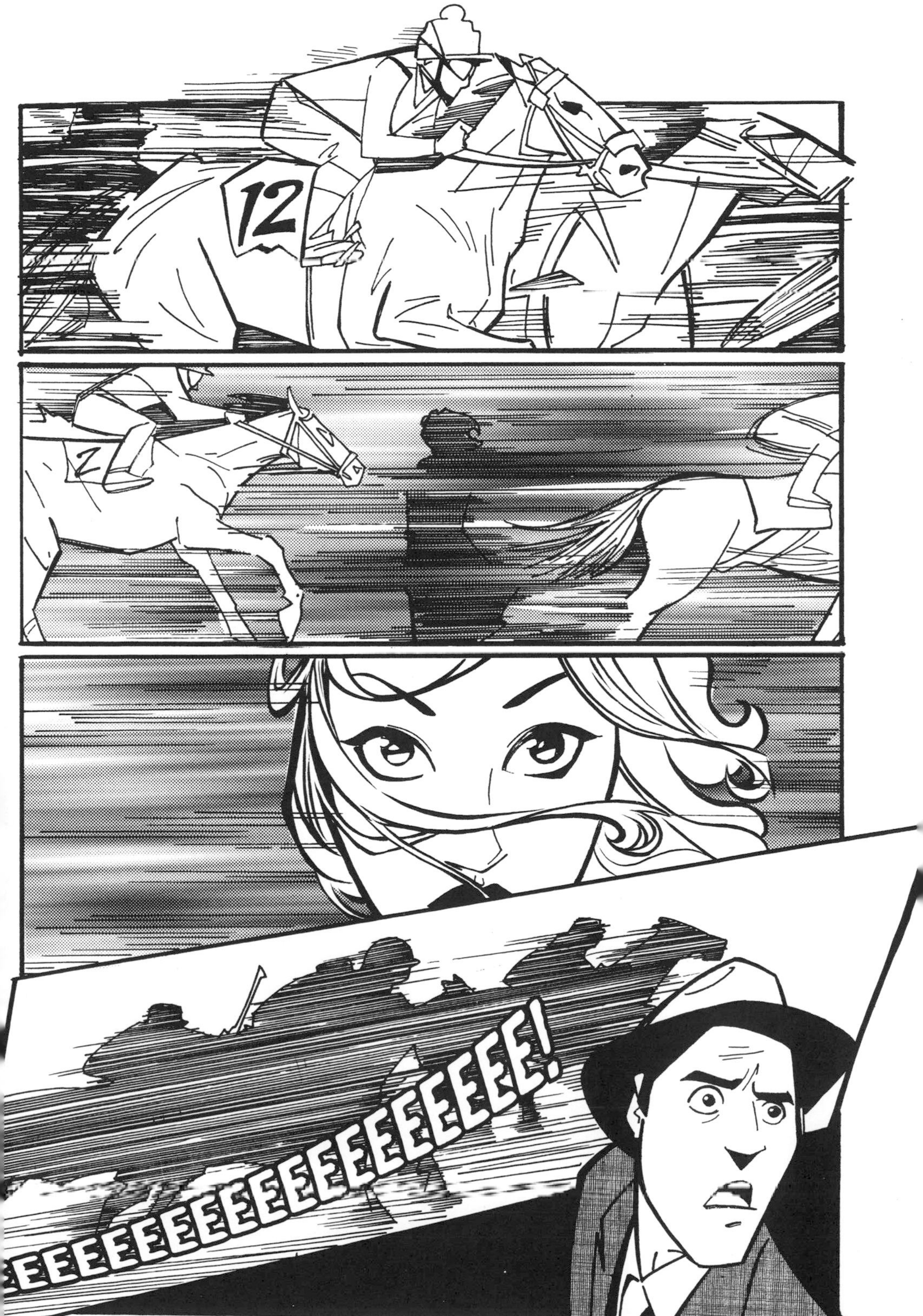
EEEEEEEEEEEEEEEEEEEEEEEE!

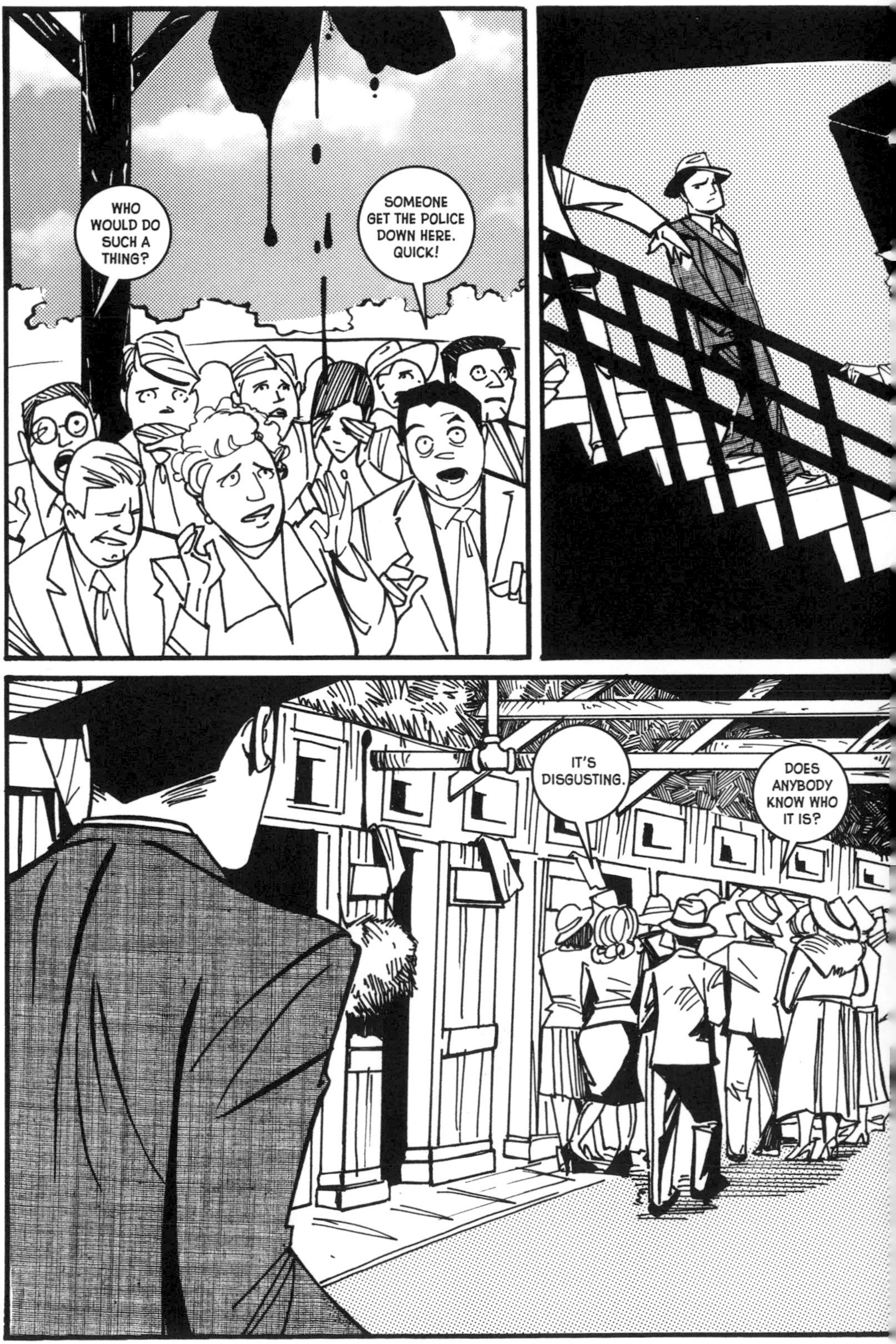
WHO WOULD DO SUCH A THING?
SOMEONE GET THE POLICE DOWN HERE. QUICK!
IT'S DISGUSTING.
DOES ANYBODY KNOW WHO IT IS?

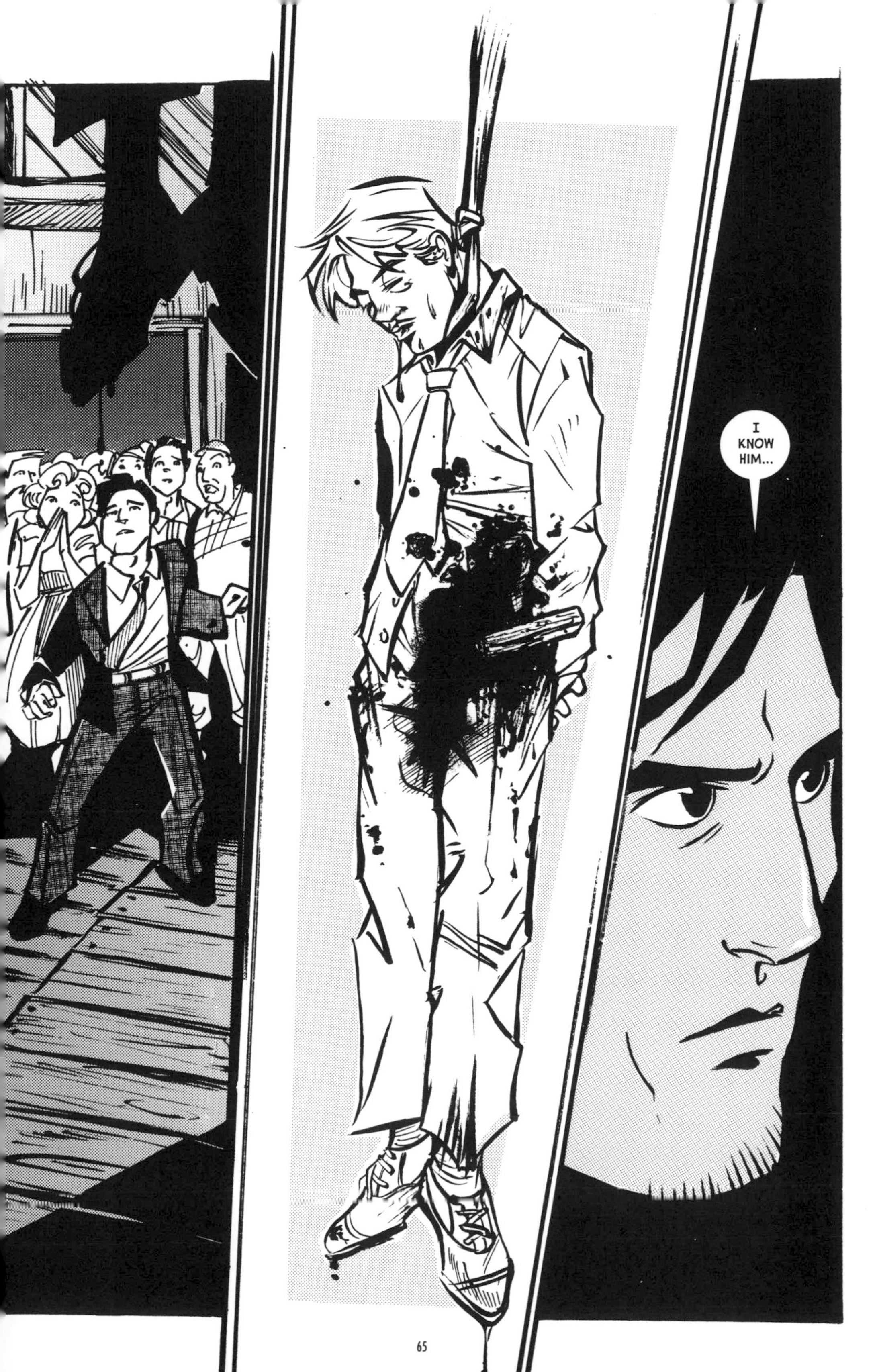
I KNOW HIM...

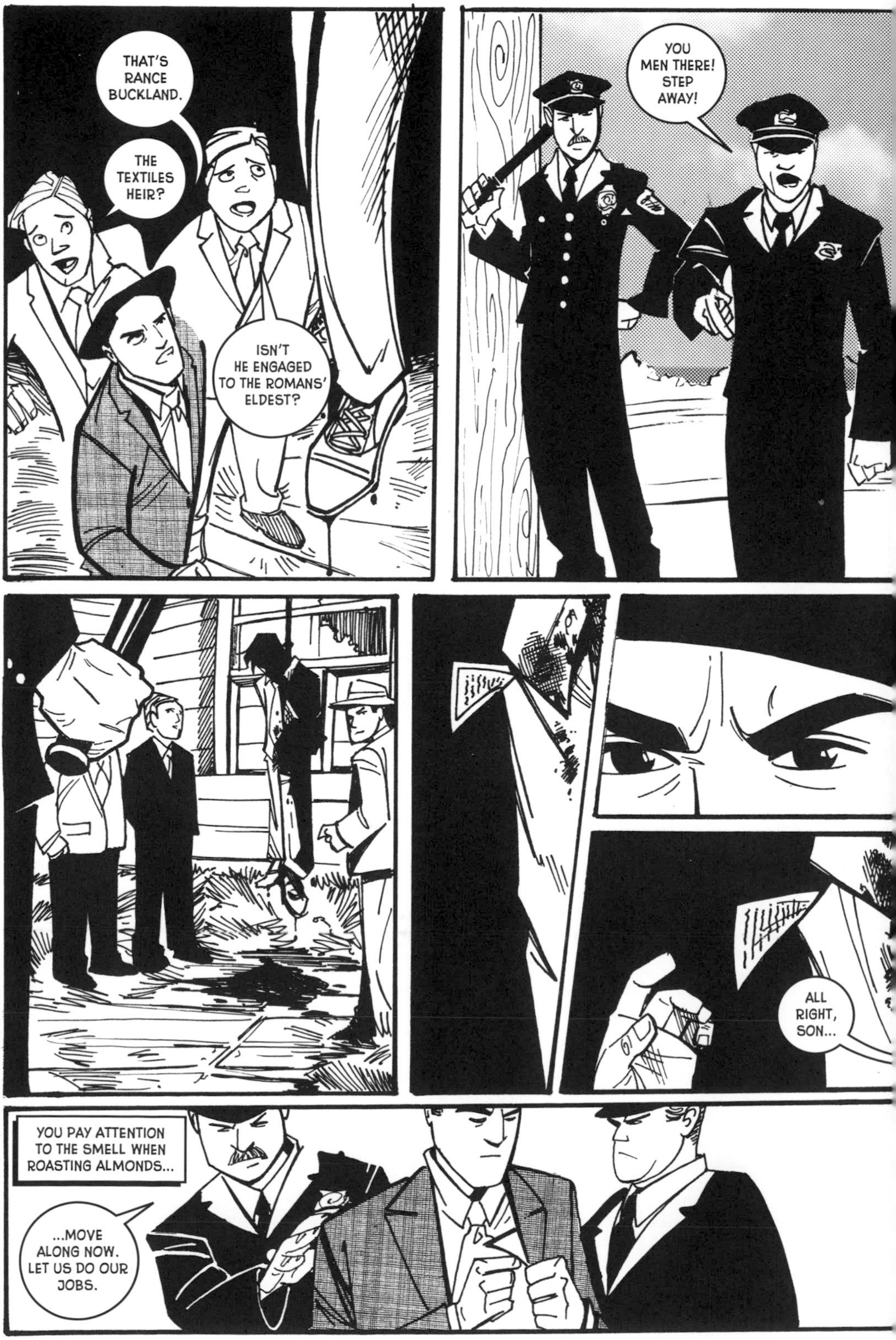
THAT'S RANCE BUCKLAND.
THE TEXTILES HEIR?
ISN'T HE ENGAGED TO THE ROMANS' ELDEST?
YOU MEN THERE! STEP AWAY!
ALL RIGHT, SON...
YOU PAY ATTENTION TO THE SMELL WHEN ROASTING ALMONDS...
...MOVE ALONG NOW. LET US DO OUR JOBS.

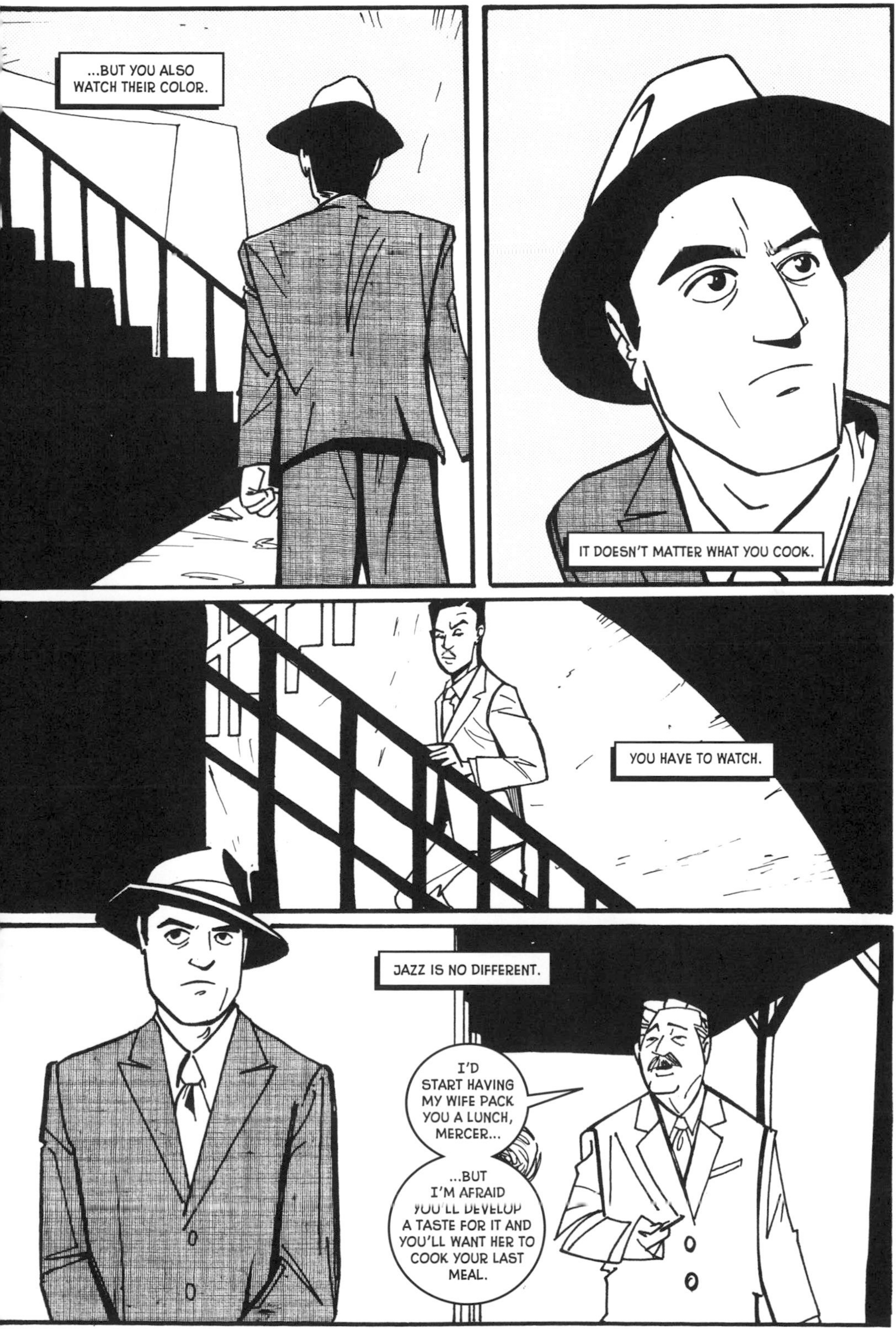

...BUT YOU ALSO WATCH THEIR COLOR.
IT DOESN'T MATTER WHAT YOU COOK.
YOU HAVE TO WATCH.
JAZZ IS NO DIFFERENT.
I'D START HAVING MY WIFE PACK YOU A LUNCH, MERCER...
...BUT I'M AFRAID YOU'LL DEVELOP A TASTE FOR IT AND YOU'LL WANT HER TO COOK YOUR LAST MEAL.

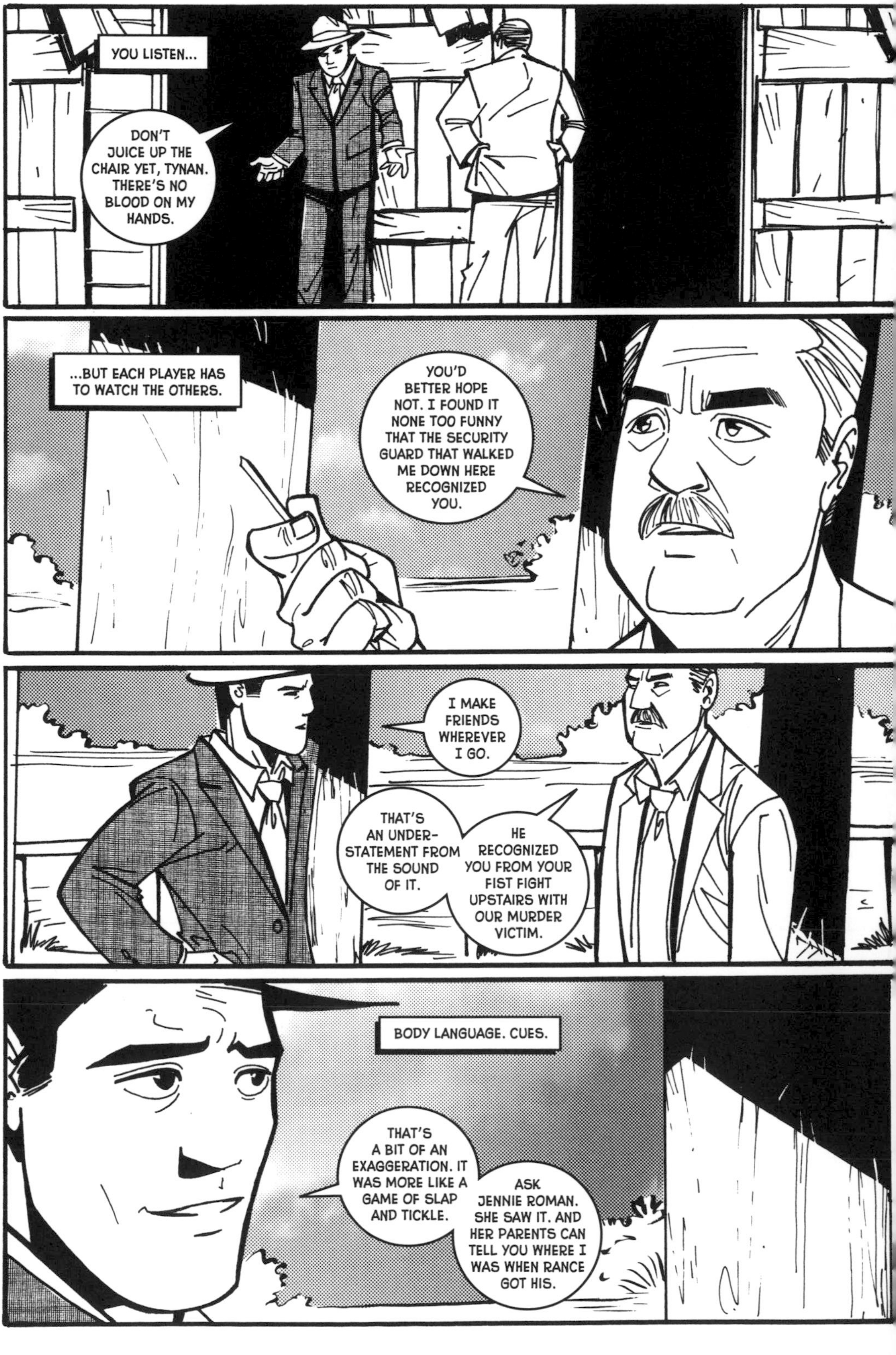
YOU LISTEN...
DON'T JUICE UP THE CHAIR YET, TYNAN. THERE'S NO BLOOD ON MY HANDS.
...BUT EACH PLAYER HAS TO WATCH THE OTHERS.
YOU'D BETTER HOPE NOT. I FOUND IT NONE TOO FUNNY THAT THE SECURITY GUARD THAT WALKED ME DOWN HERE RECOGNIZED YOU.
I MAKE FRIENDS WHEREVER I GO.
HE RECOGNIZED YOU FROM YOUR FIST FIGHT UPSTAIRS WITH OUR MURDER VICTIM.
THAT'S AN UNDER-STATEMENT FROM THE SOUND OF IT.
BODY LANGUAGE. CUES.
THAT'S A BIT OF AN EXAGGERATION. IT WAS MORE LIKE A GAME OF SLAP AND TICKLE.
ASK JENNIE ROMAN. SHE SAW IT. AND HER PARENTS CAN TELL YOU WHERE I WAS WHEN RANCE GOT HIS.

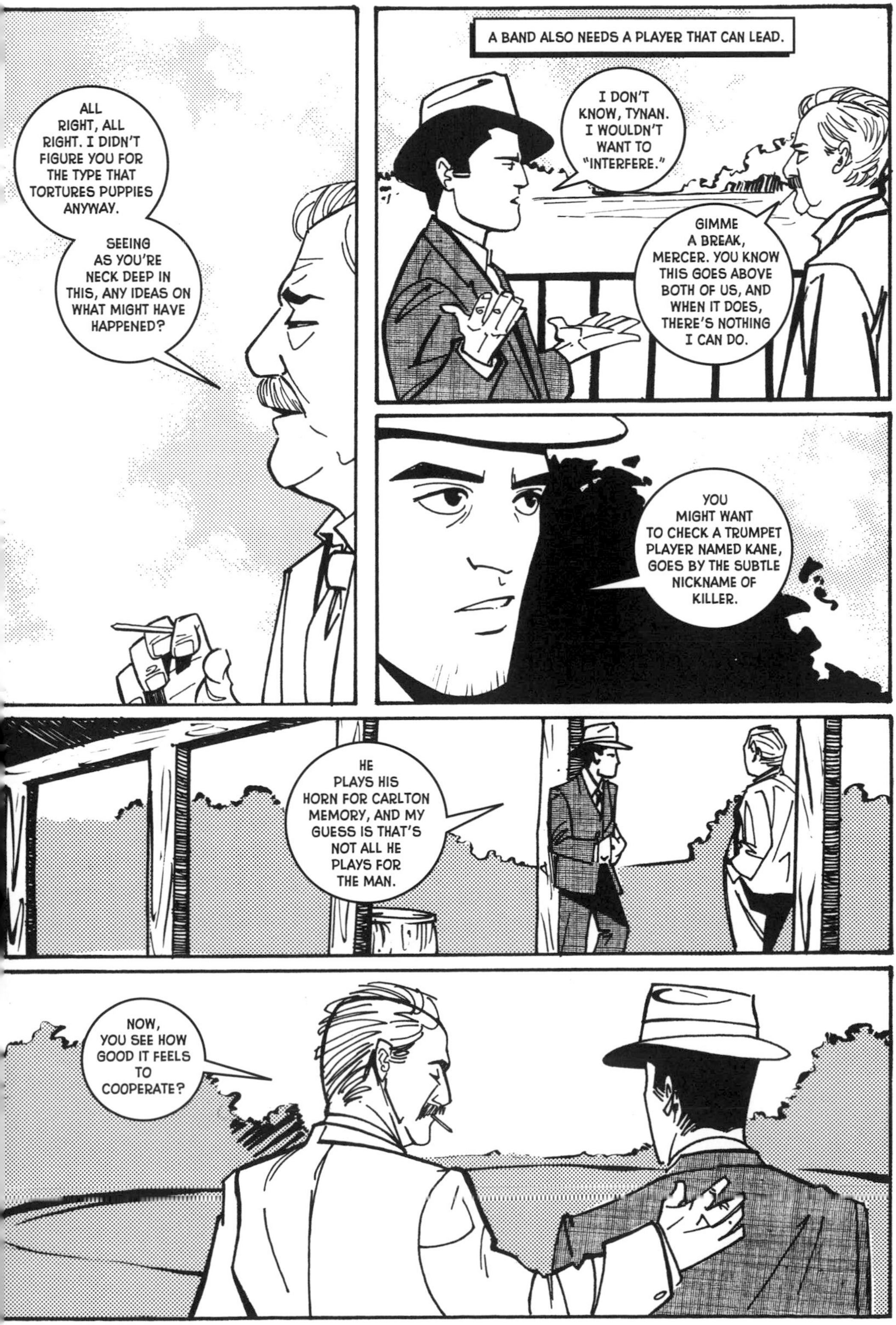
ALL RIGHT, ALL RIGHT. I DIDN'T FIGURE YOU FOR THE TYPE THAT TORTURES PUPPIES ANYWAY.
SEEING AS YOU'RE NECK DEEP IN THIS, ANY IDEAS ON WHAT MIGHT HAVE HAPPENED?
A BAND ALSO NEEDS A PLAYER THAT CAN LEAD.
I DON'T KNOW, TYNAN. I WOULDN'T WANT TO "INTERFERE."
GIMME A BREAK, MERCER. YOU KNOW THIS GOES ABOVE BOTH OF US, AND WHEN IT DOES, THERE'S NOTHING I CAN DO.
YOU MIGHT WANT TO CHECK A TRUMPET PLAYER NAMED KANE, GOES BY THE SUBTLE NICKNAME OF KILLER.
HE PLAYS HIS HORN FOR CARLTON MEMORY, AND MY GUESS IS THAT'S NOT ALL HE PLAYS FOR THE MAN.
NOW, YOU SEE HOW GOOD IT FEELS TO COOPERATE?

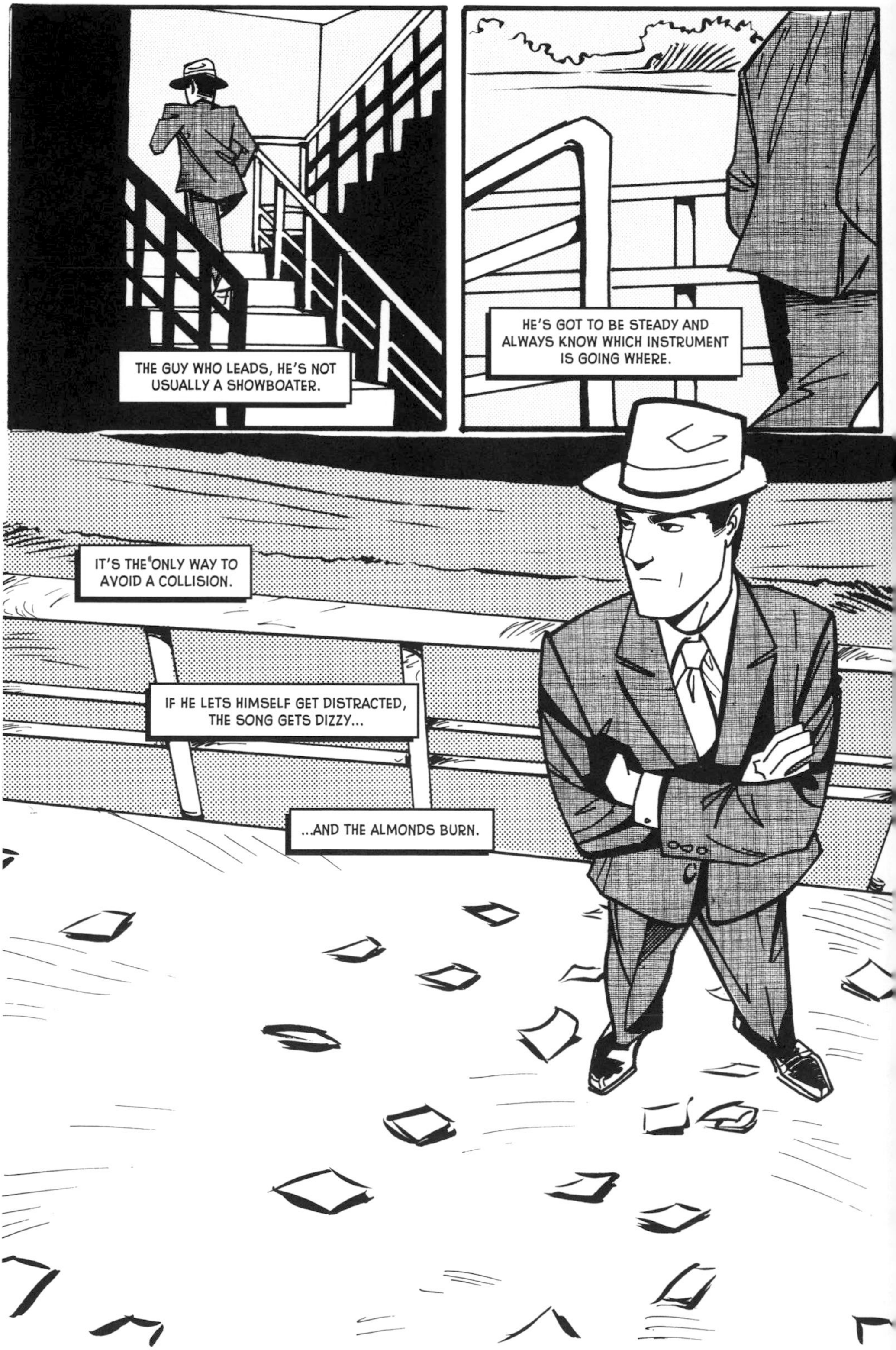
THE GUY WHO LEADS, HE'S NOT USUALLY A SHOWBOATER.
HE'S GOT TO BE STEADY AND ALWAYS KNOW WHICH INSTRUMENT IS GOING WHERE.
IT'S THE ONLY WAY TO AVOID A COLLISION.
IF HE LETS HIMSELF GET DISTRACTED, THE SONG GETS DIZZY...
...AND THE ALMONDS BURN.

CHAPTER 5

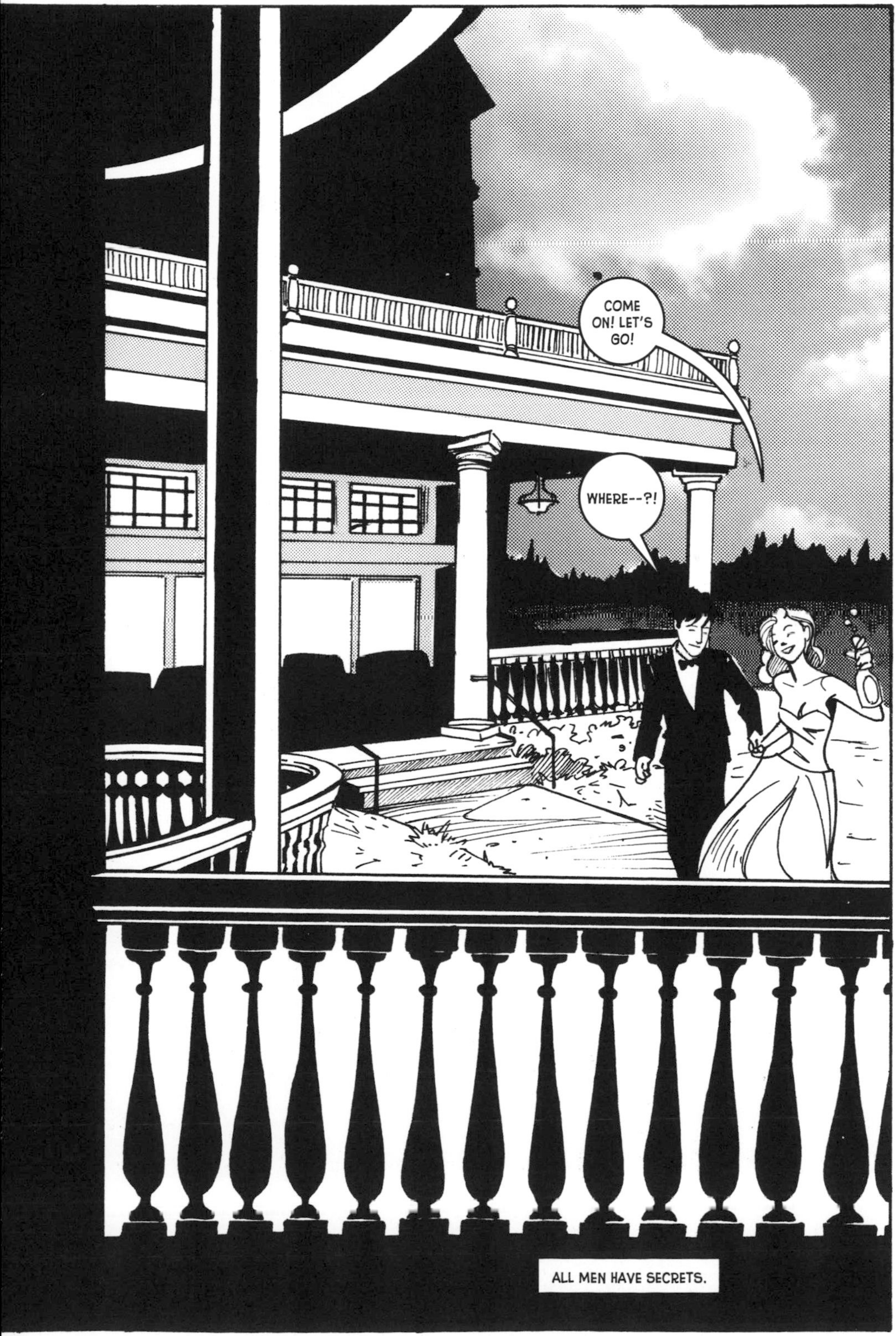
COME ON! LET'S GO!
WHERE--?!
ALL MEN HAVE SECRETS.

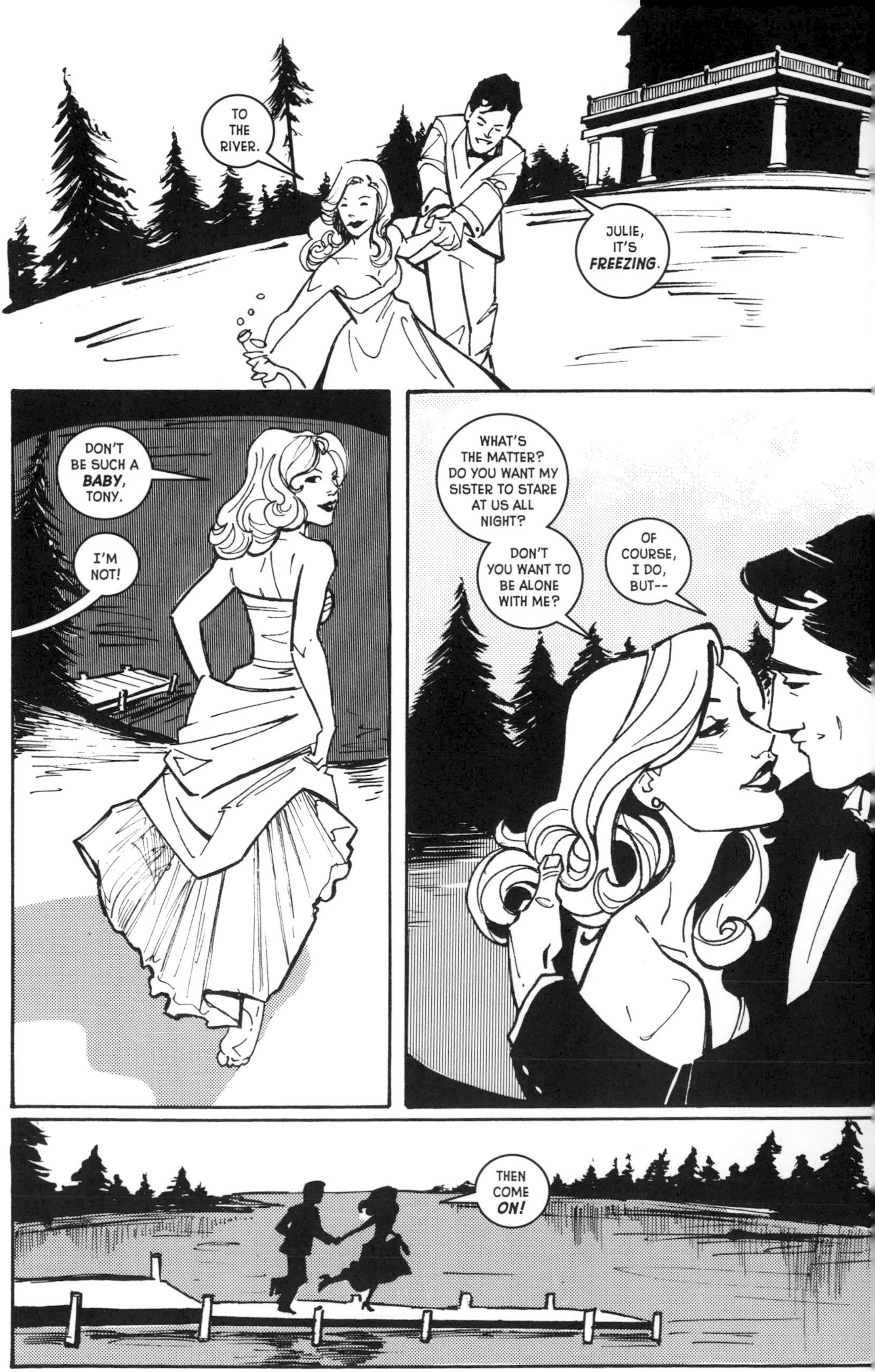
TO THE RIVER.
JULIE, IT'S FREEZING.
DON'T BE SUCH A BABY, TONY.
I'M NOT!
WHAT'S THE MATTER? DO YOU WANT MY SISTER TO STARE AT US ALL NIGHT?
DON'T YOU WANT TO BE ALONE WITH ME?
OF COURSE, I DO, BUT--
THEN COME ON!

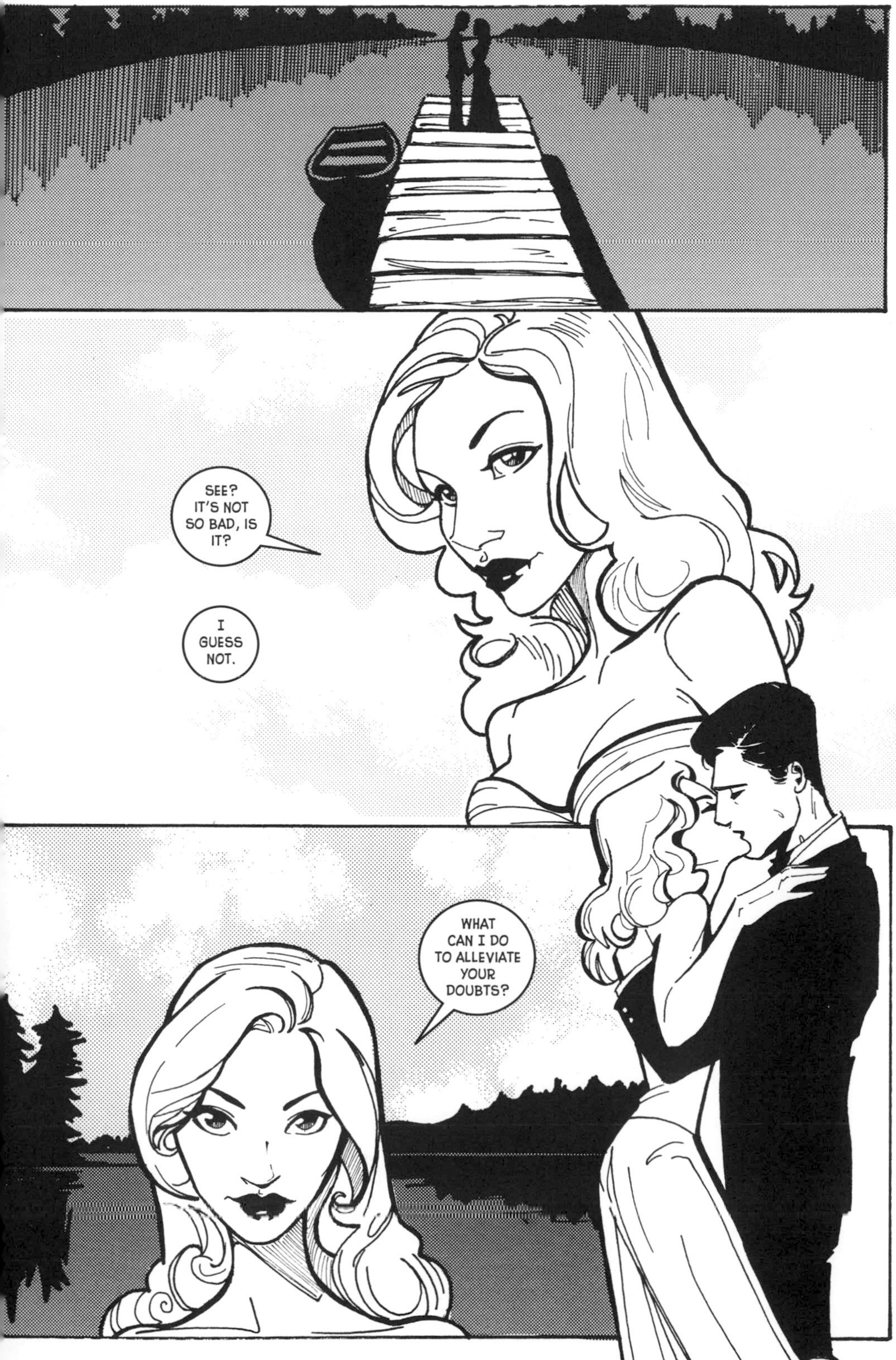
SEE? IT'S NOT SO BAD, IS IT?
I GUESS NOT.
WHAT CAN I DO TO ALLEVIATE YOUR DOUBTS?

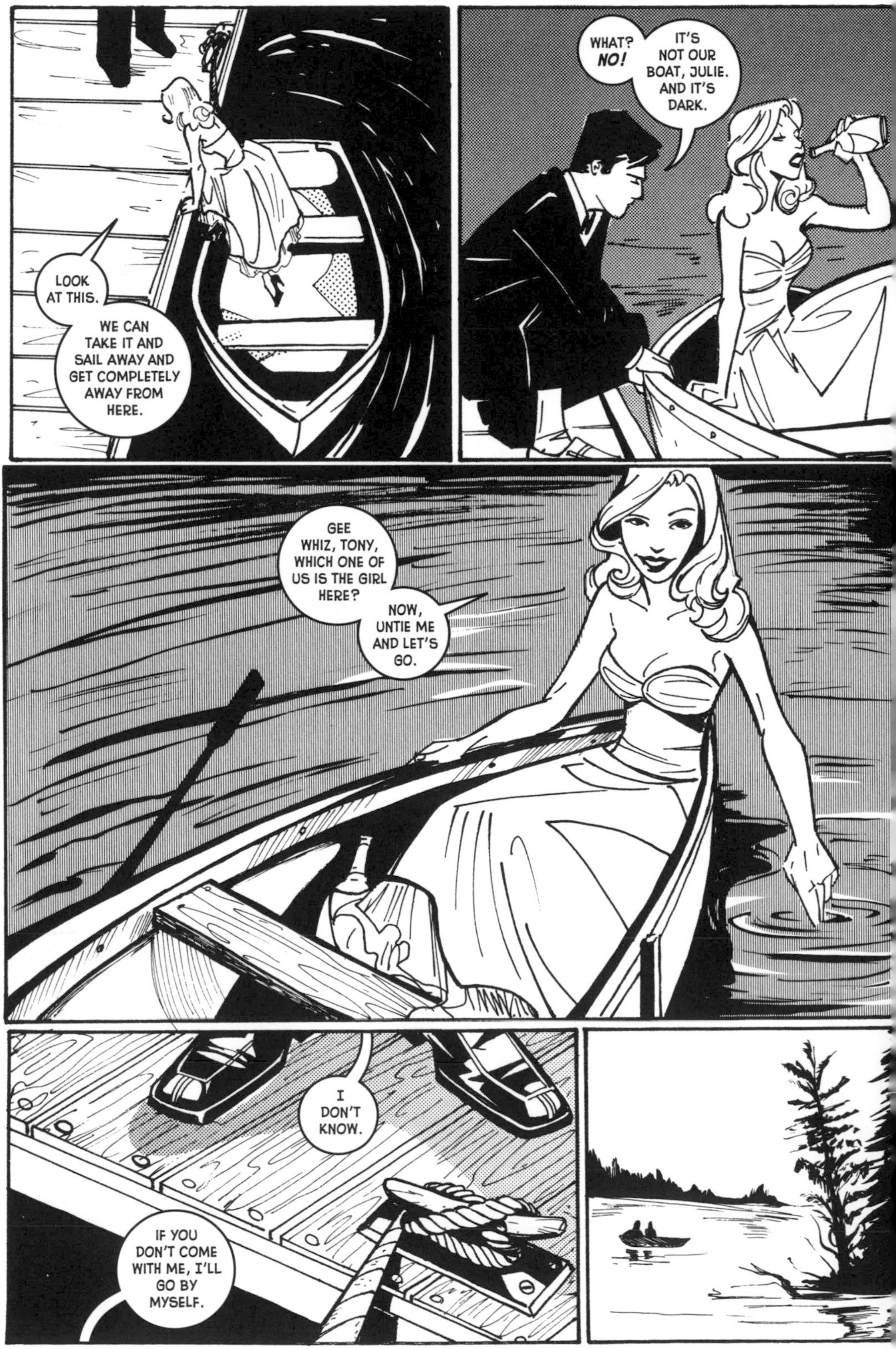
LOOK AT THIS.
WE CAN TAKE IT AND SAIL AWAY AND GET COMPLETELY AWAY FROM HERE.
WHAT? NO!
IT'S NOT OUR BOAT, JULIE. AND IT'S DARK.
GEE WHIZ, TONY, WHICH ONE OF US IS THE GIRL HERE?
NOW, UNTIE ME AND LET'S GO.
I DON'T KNOW.
IF YOU DON'T COME WITH ME, I'LL GO BY MYSELF.

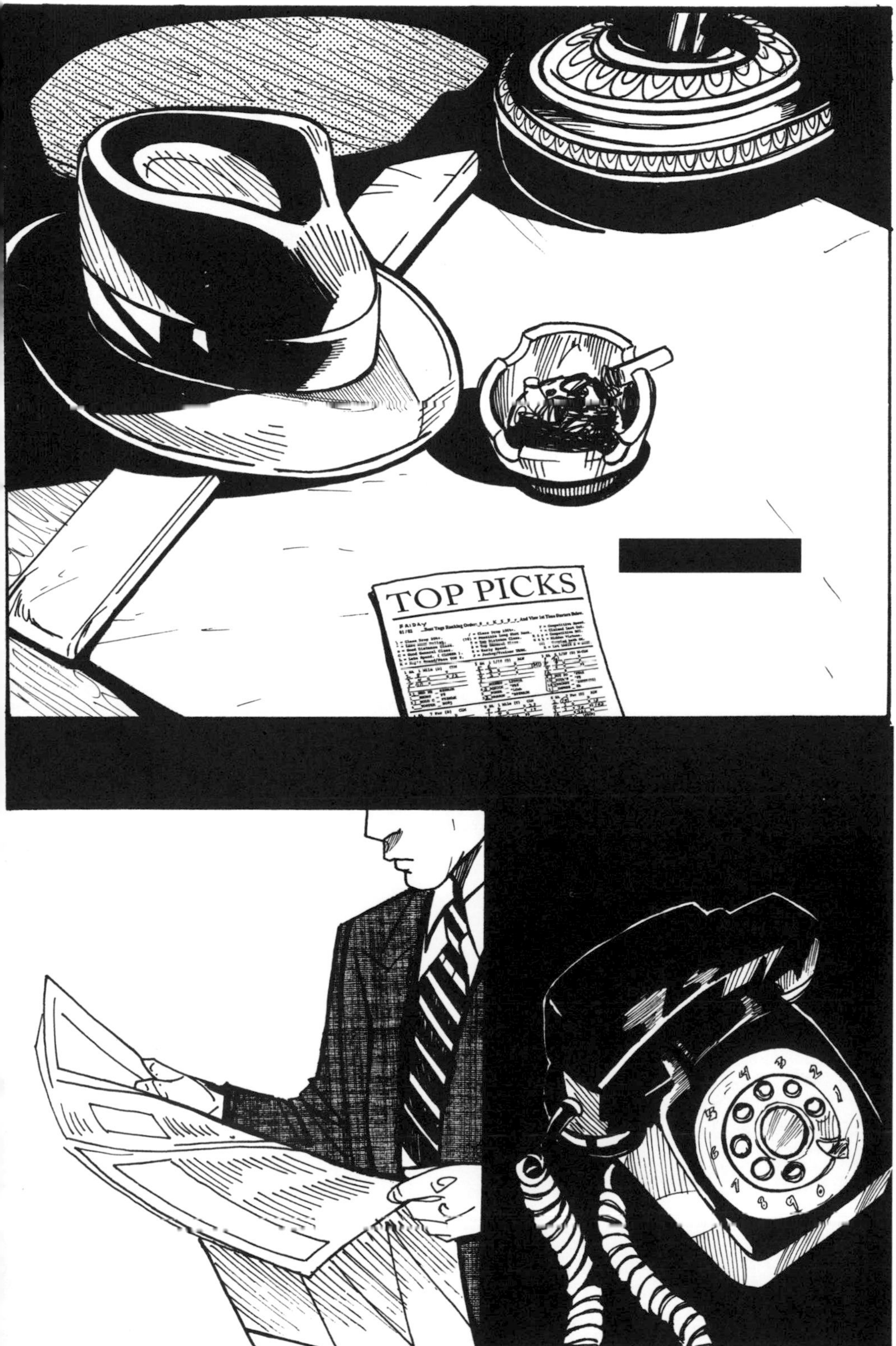
TOP PICKS

BRRING BRRII--
HELLO?

JENNIE IS THAT YOU?

YES. MERCER?

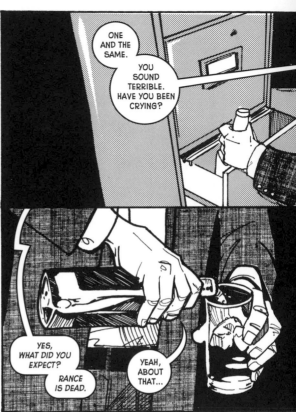

ONE AND THE SAME.

YOU SOUND TERRIBLE. HAVE YOU BEEN CRYING?

YES, WHAT DID YOU EXPECT?

RANCE IS DEAD.

YEAH, ABOUT THAT...

...ARE YOU SURE THAT HE WAS SUCH A BIG LOSER?

WHAT DO YOU MEAN?

I'VE SEEN HIS BETTING SHEET. I'M LOOKING AT YESTERDAY, AND HE WAS WINNING ALL OVER THE PLACE.

FROM THE LOOK OF THINGS TODAY, THE STREAK WASN'T GOING TO END.

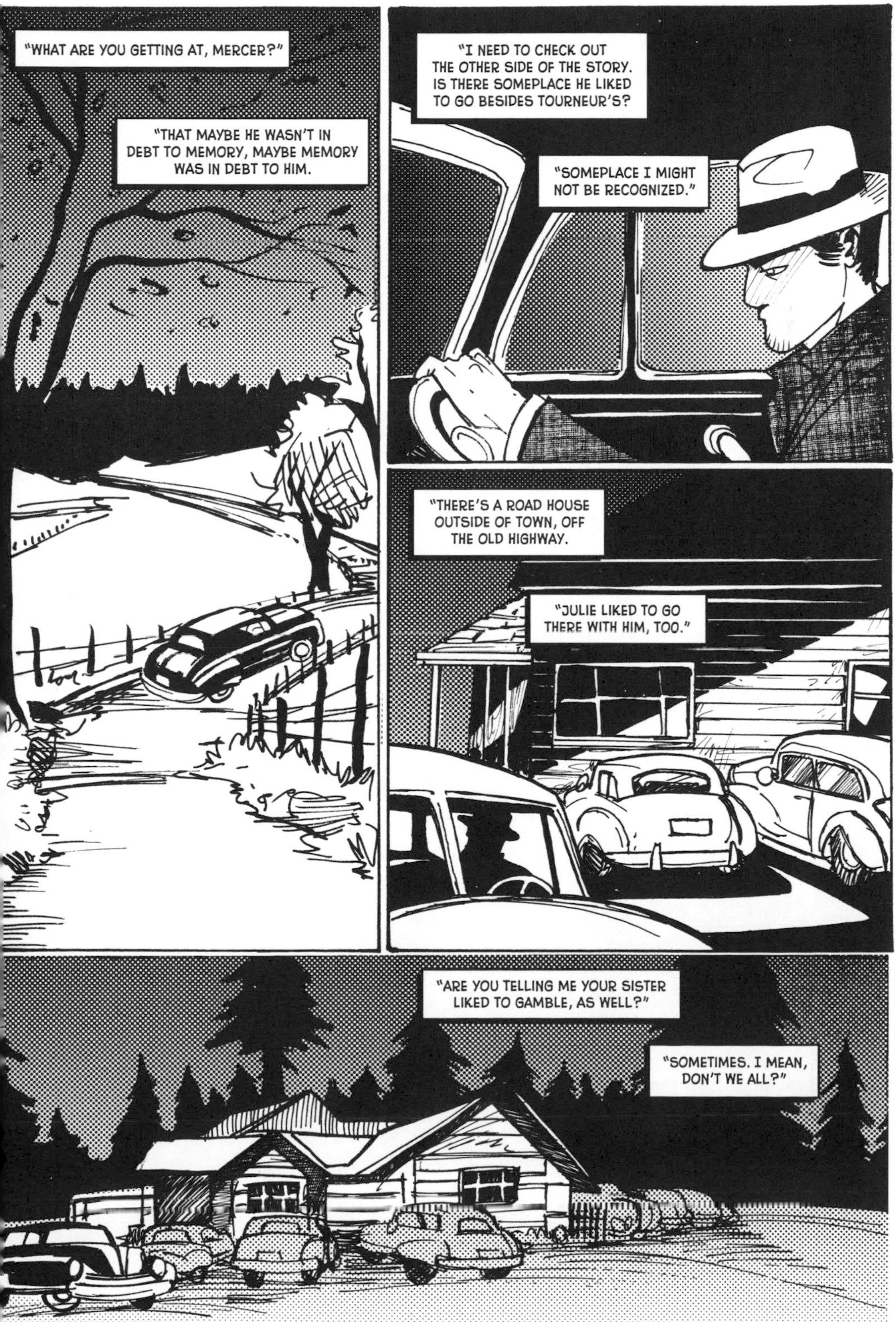
"WHAT ARE YOU GETTING AT, MERCER?"
"THAT MAYBE HE WASN'T IN DEBT TO MEMORY, MAYBE MEMORY WAS IN DEBT TO HIM.
"I NEED TO CHECK OUT THE OTHER SIDE OF THE STORY. IS THERE SOMEPLACE HE LIKED TO GO BESIDES TOURNEUR'S?
"SOMEPLACE I MIGHT NOT BE RECOGNIZED."
"THERE'S A ROAD HOUSE OUTSIDE OF TOWN, OFF THE OLD HIGHWAY.
"JULIE LIKED TO GO THERE WITH HIM, TOO."
"ARE YOU TELLING ME YOUR SISTER LIKED TO GAMBLE, AS WELL?"
"SOMETIMES. I MEAN, DON'T WE ALL?"

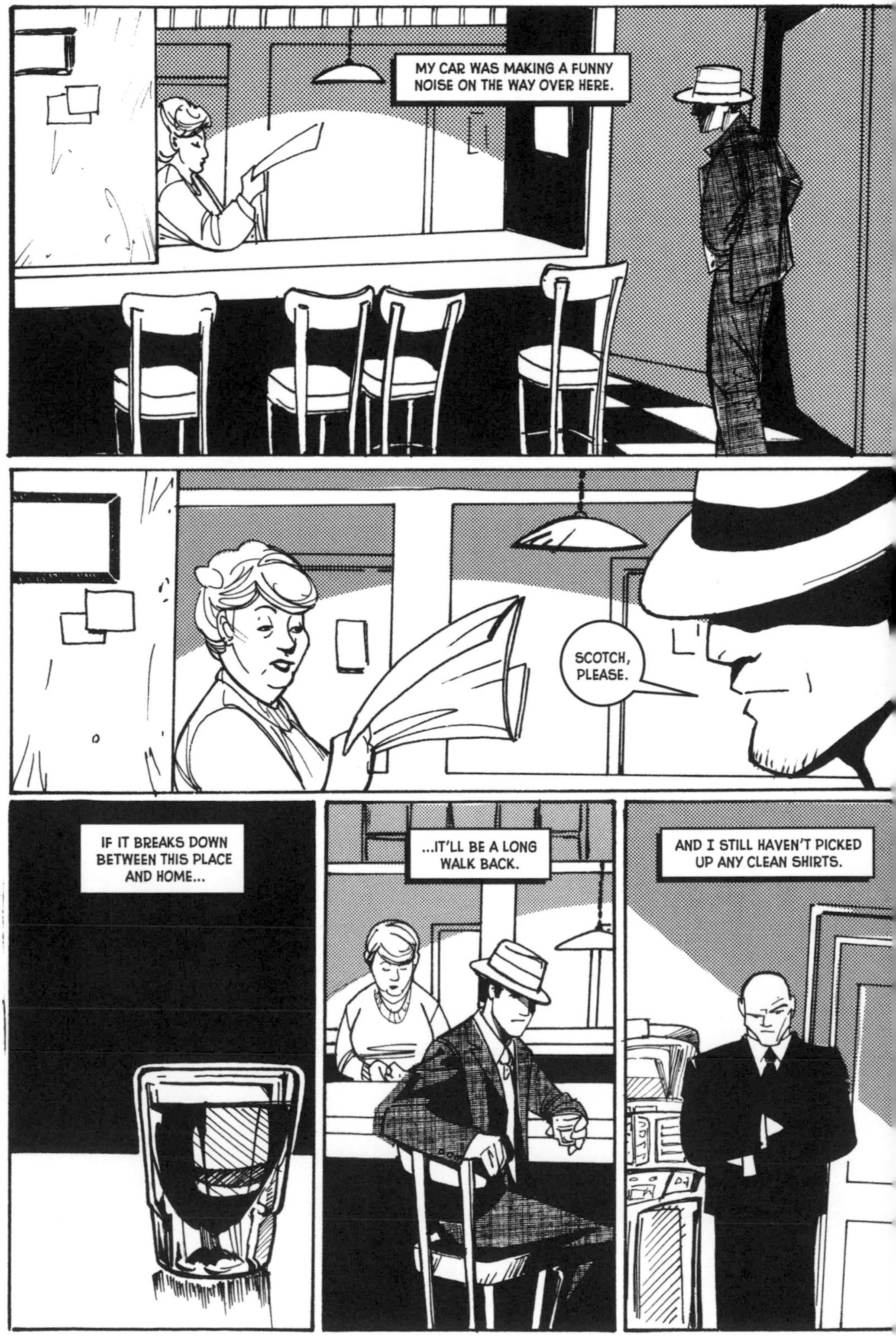
MY CAR WAS MAKING A FUNNY NOISE ON THE WAY OVER HERE.
SCOTCH, PLEASE.
IF IT BREAKS DOWN BETWEEN THIS PLACE AND HOME...
...IT'LL BE A LONG WALK BACK.
AND I STILL HAVEN'T PICKED UP ANY CLEAN SHIRTS.

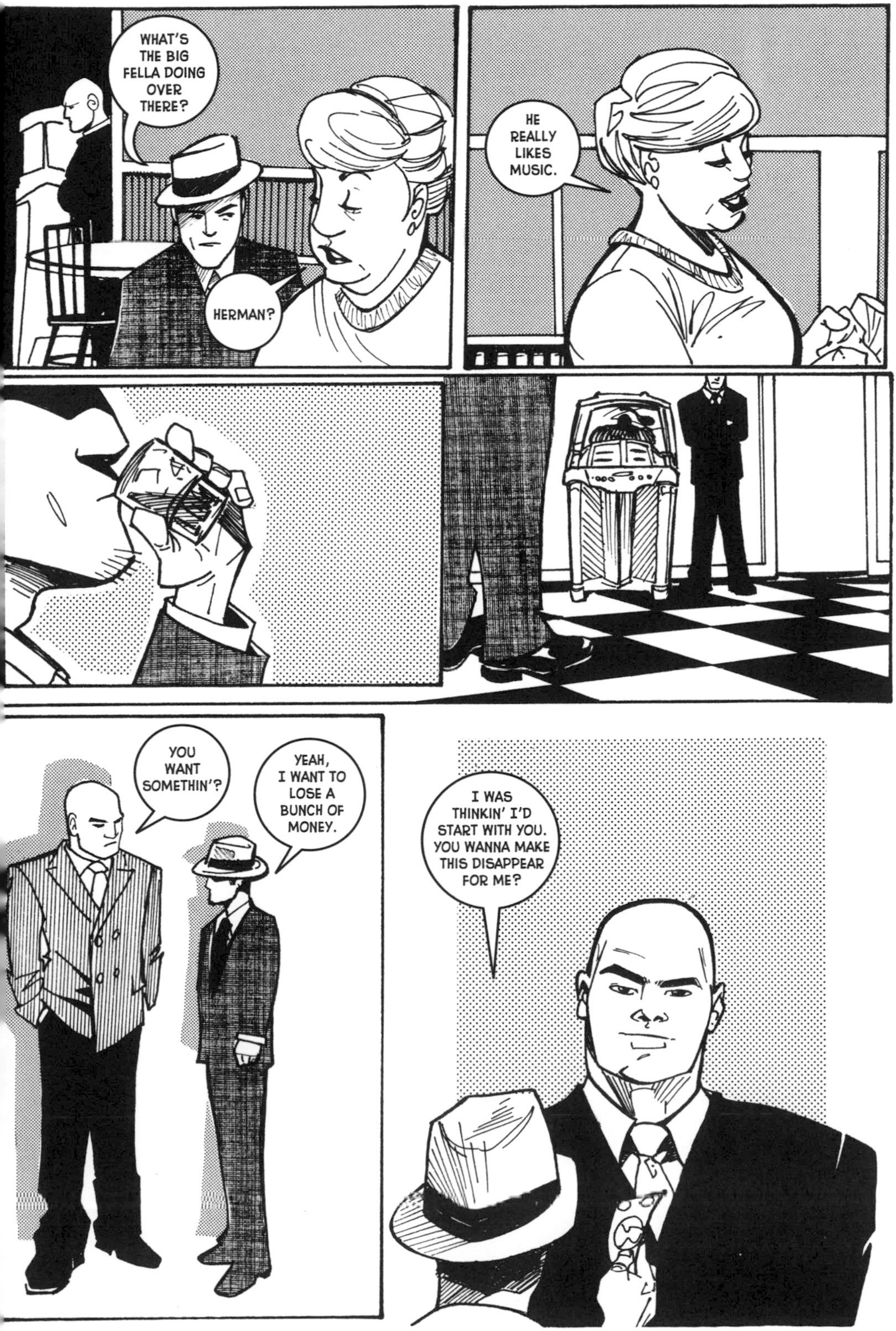
WHAT'S THE BIG FELLA DOING OVER THERE?
HERMAN?
HE REALLY LIKES MUSIC.
YOU WANT SOMETHIN'?
YEAH, I WANT TO LOSE A BUNCH OF MONEY.
I WAS THINKIN' I'D START WITH YOU. YOU WANNA MAKE THIS DISAPPEAR FOR ME?

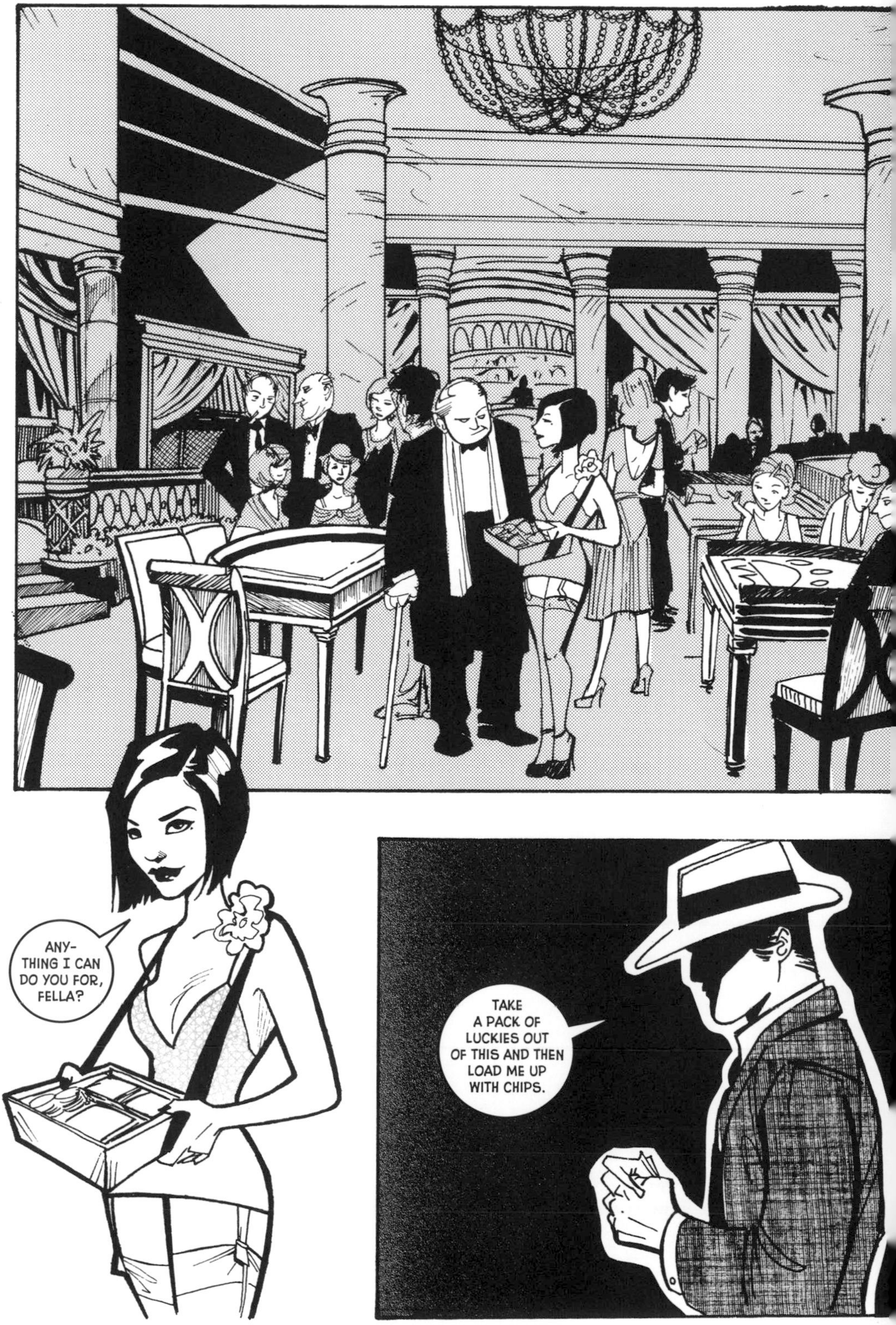
ANY-THING I CAN DO YOU FOR, FELLA?
TAKE A PACK OF LUCKIES OUT OF THIS AND THEN LOAD ME UP WITH CHIPS.

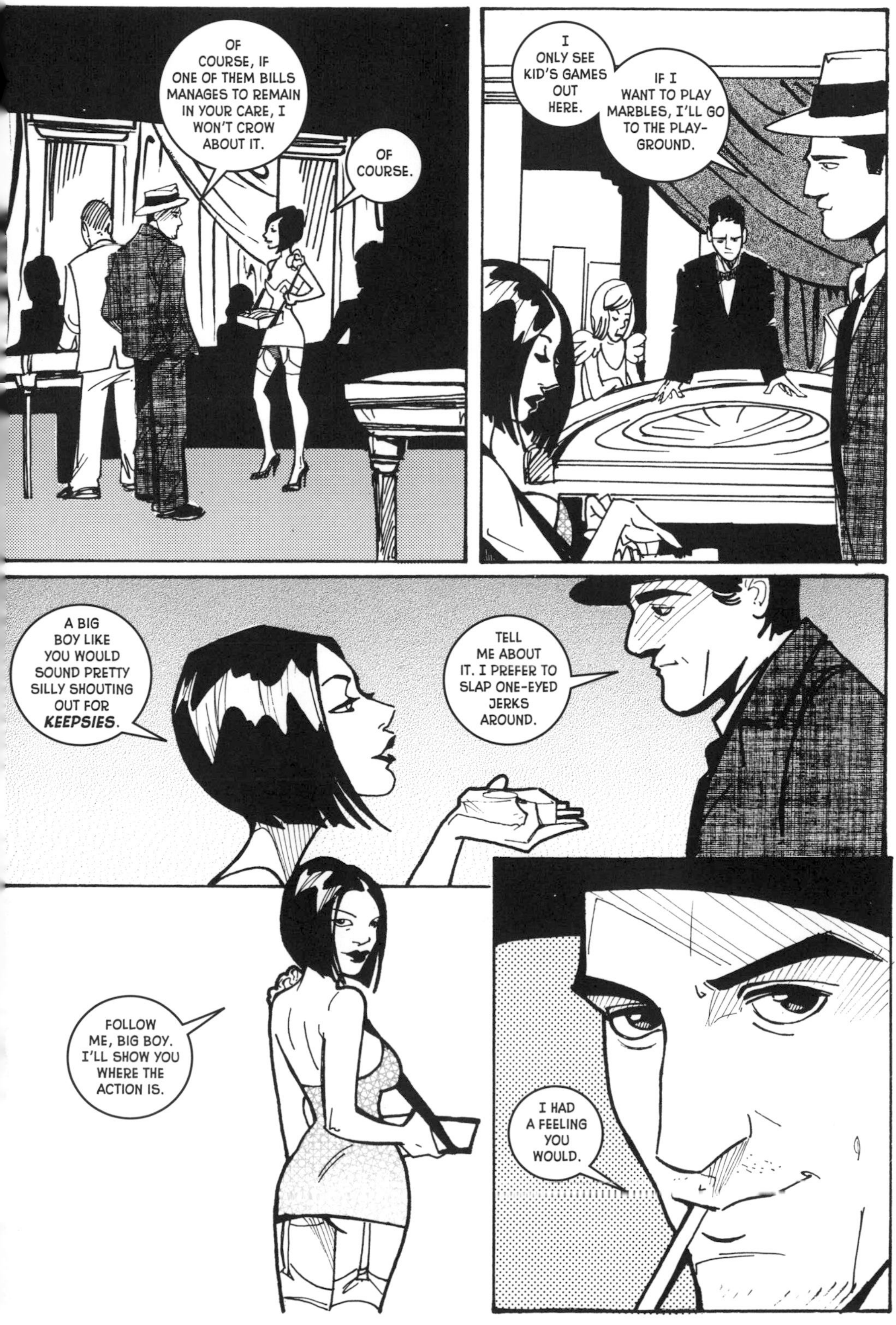
OF COURSE, IF ONE OF THEM BILLS MANAGES TO REMAIN IN YOUR CARE, I WON'T CROW ABOUT IT.
OF COURSE.
I ONLY SEE KID'S GAMES OUT HERE.
IF I WANT TO PLAY MARBLES, I'LL GO TO THE PLAY-GROUND.
A BIG BOY LIKE YOU WOULD SOUND PRETTY SILLY SHOUTING OUT FOR ***KEEPSIES***.
TELL ME ABOUT IT. I PREFER TO SLAP ONE-EYED JERKS AROUND.
FOLLOW ME, BIG BOY. I'LL SHOW YOU WHERE THE ACTION IS.
I HAD A FEELING YOU WOULD.

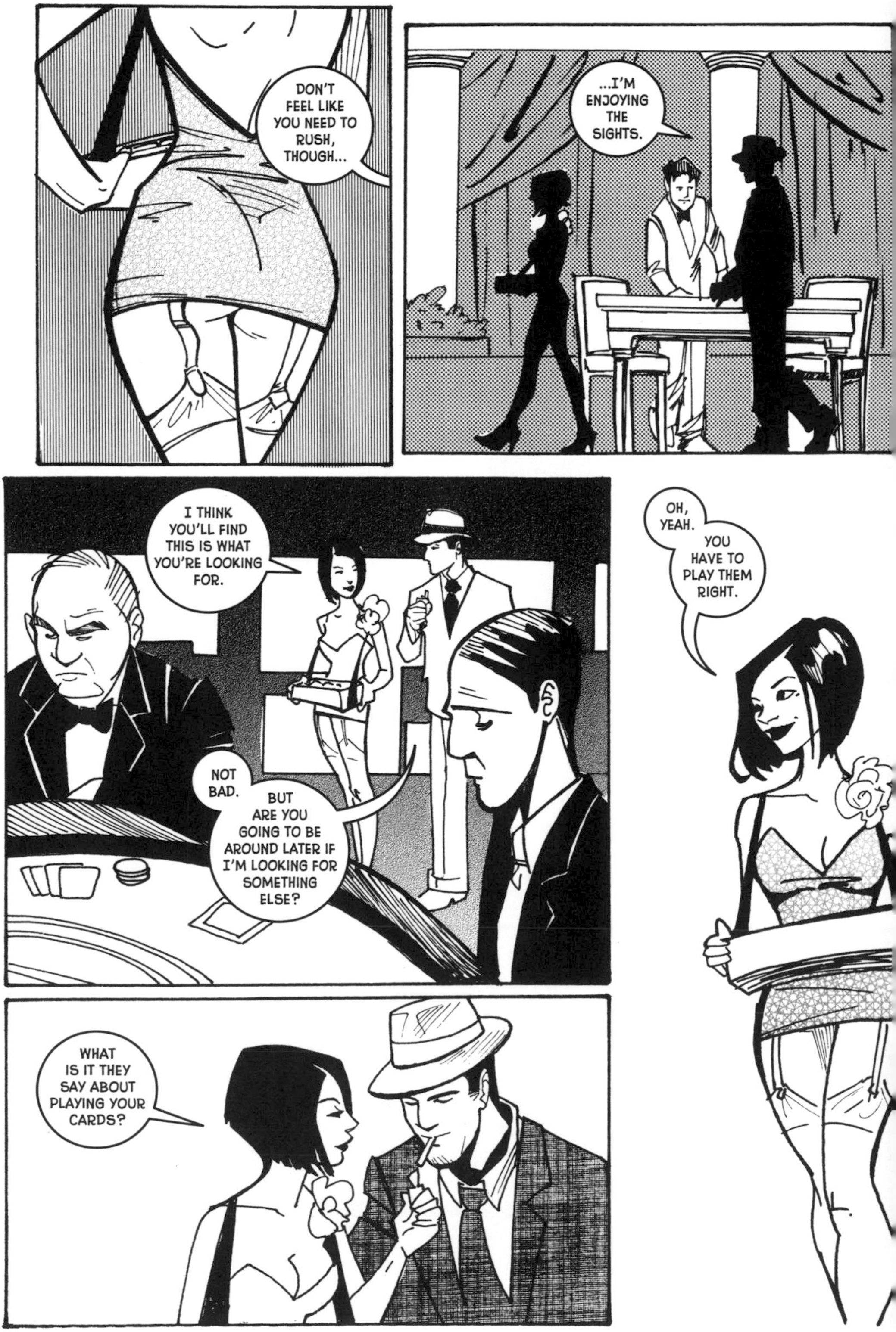
DON'T FEEL LIKE YOU NEED TO RUSH, THOUGH...
...I'M ENJOYING THE SIGHTS.
I THINK YOU'LL FIND THIS IS WHAT YOU'RE LOOKING FOR.
NOT BAD.
BUT ARE YOU GOING TO BE AROUND LATER IF I'M LOOKING FOR SOMETHING ELSE?
OH, YEAH.
YOU HAVE TO PLAY THEM RIGHT.
WHAT IS IT THEY SAY ABOUT PLAYING YOUR CARDS?

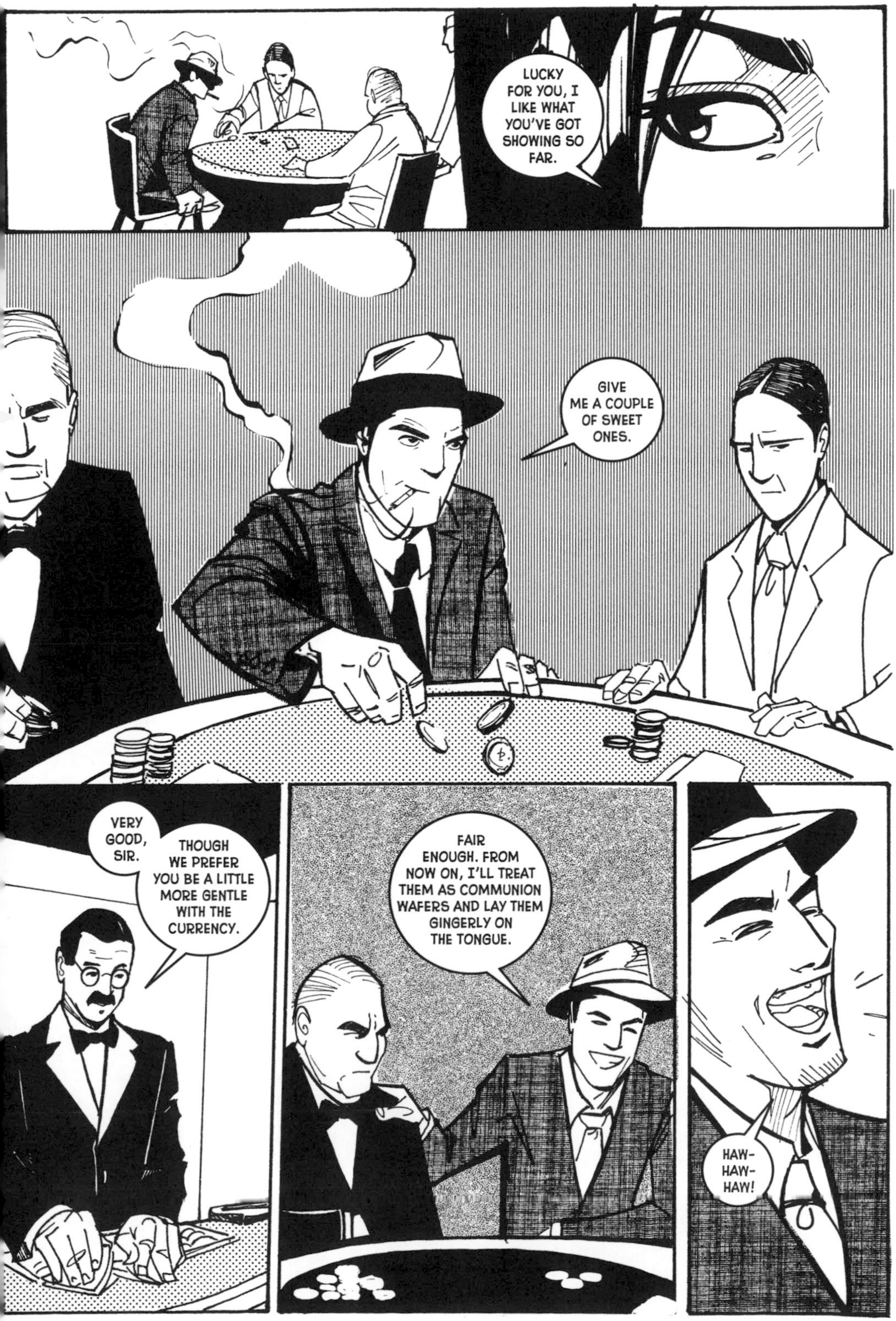
LUCKY FOR YOU, I LIKE WHAT YOU'VE GOT SHOWING SO FAR.
GIVE ME A COUPLE OF SWEET ONES.
VERY GOOD, SIR.
THOUGH WE PREFER YOU BE A LITTLE MORE GENTLE WITH THE CURRENCY.
FAIR ENOUGH. FROM NOW ON, I'LL TREAT THEM AS COMMUNION WAFERS AND LAY THEM GINGERLY ON THE TONGUE.
HAW-HAW-HAW!

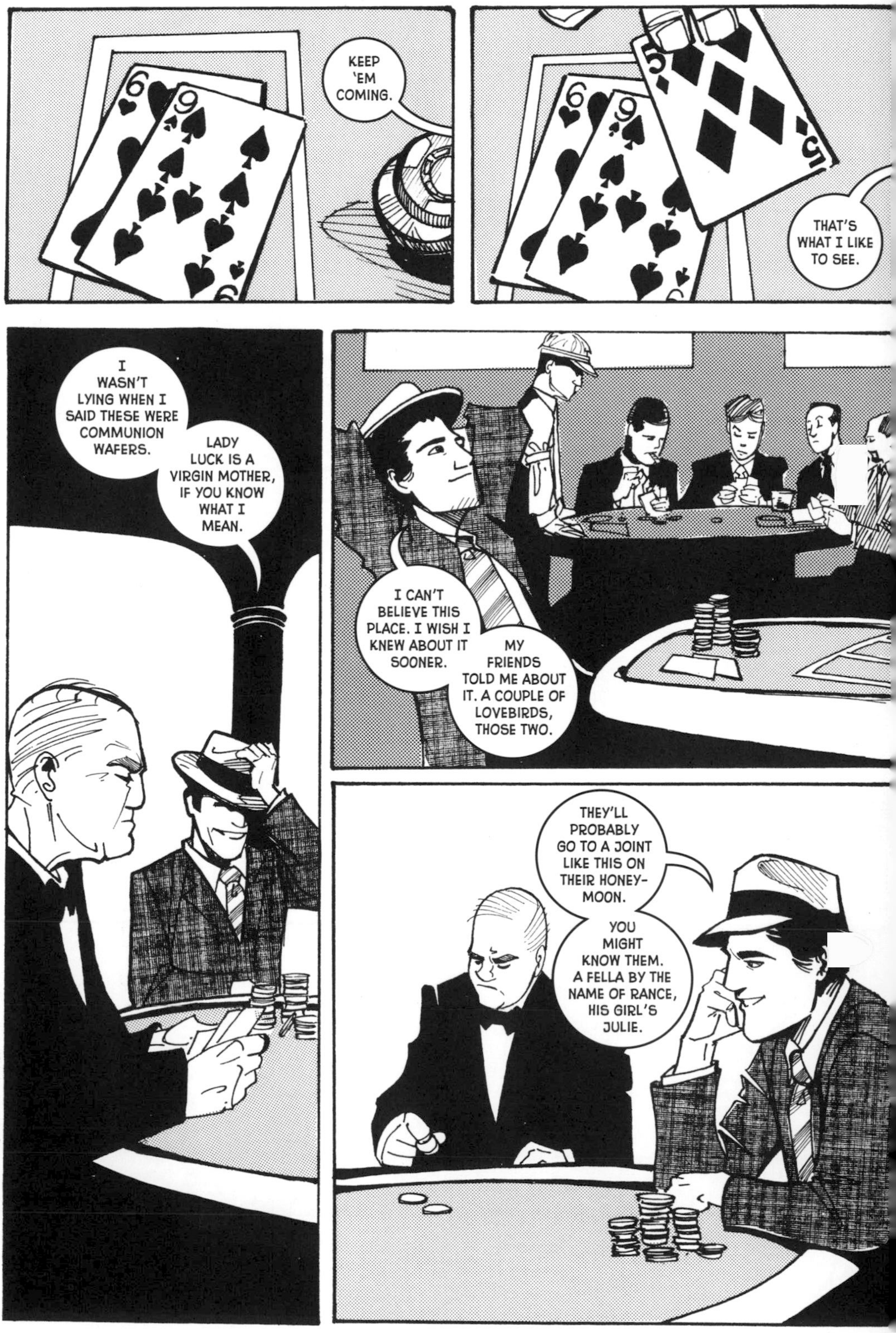
KEEP 'EM COMING.
THAT'S WHAT I LIKE TO SEE.
I WASN'T LYING WHEN I SAID THESE WERE COMMUNION WAFERS.
LADY LUCK IS A VIRGIN MOTHER, IF YOU KNOW WHAT I MEAN.
I CAN'T BELIEVE THIS PLACE. I WISH I KNEW ABOUT IT SOONER.
MY FRIENDS TOLD ME ABOUT IT. A COUPLE OF LOVEBIRDS, THOSE TWO.
THEY'LL PROBABLY GO TO A JOINT LIKE THIS ON THEIR HONEY-MOON.
YOU MIGHT KNOW THEM. A FELLA BY THE NAME OF RANCE, HIS GIRL'S JULIE.

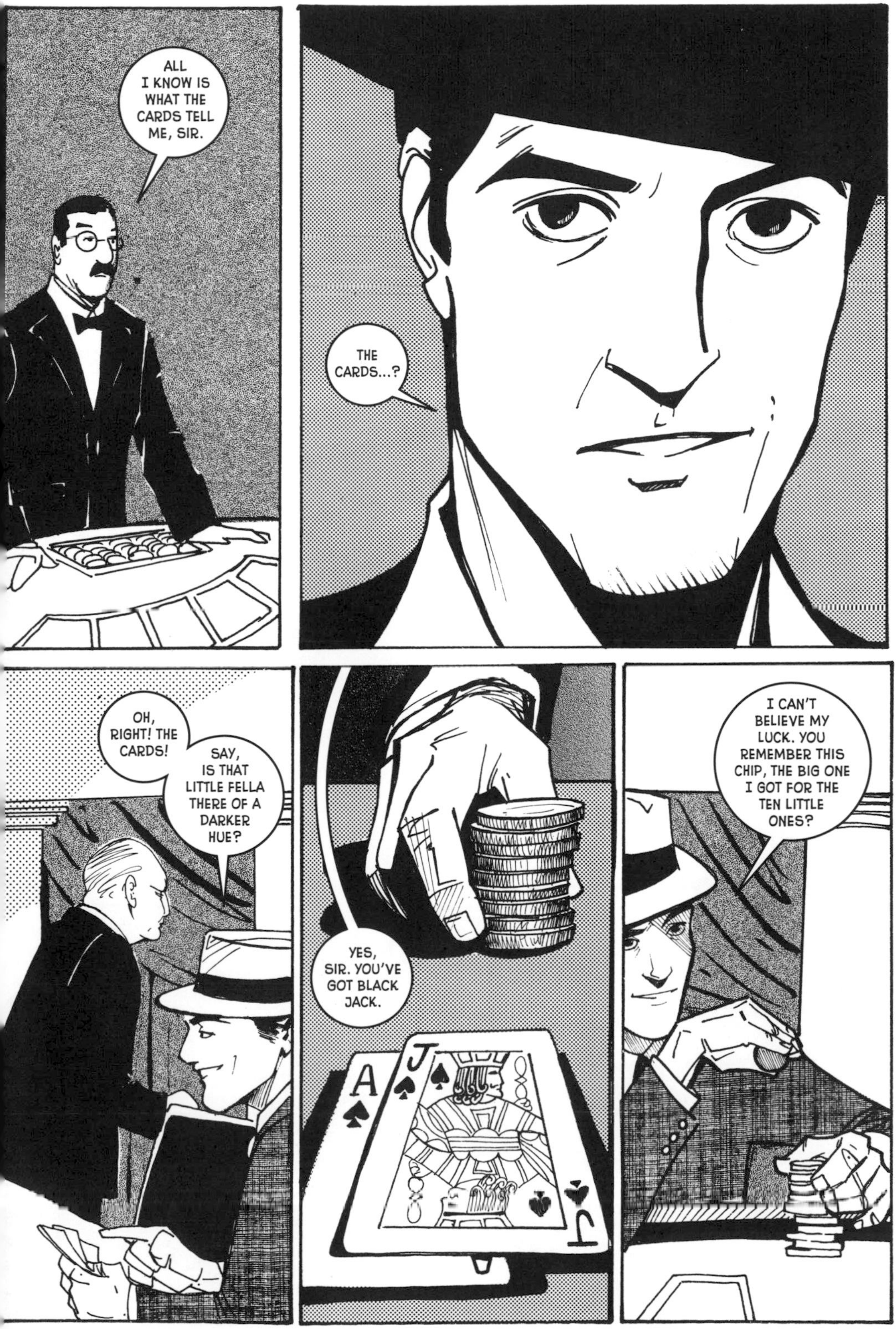
ALL I KNOW IS WHAT THE CARDS TELL ME, SIR.
THE CARDS...?
OH, RIGHT! THE CARDS!
SAY, IS THAT LITTLE FELLA THERE OF A DARKER HUE?
YES, SIR. YOU'VE GOT BLACK JACK.
I CAN'T BELIEVE MY LUCK. YOU REMEMBER THIS CHIP, THE BIG ONE I GOT FOR THE TEN LITTLE ONES?

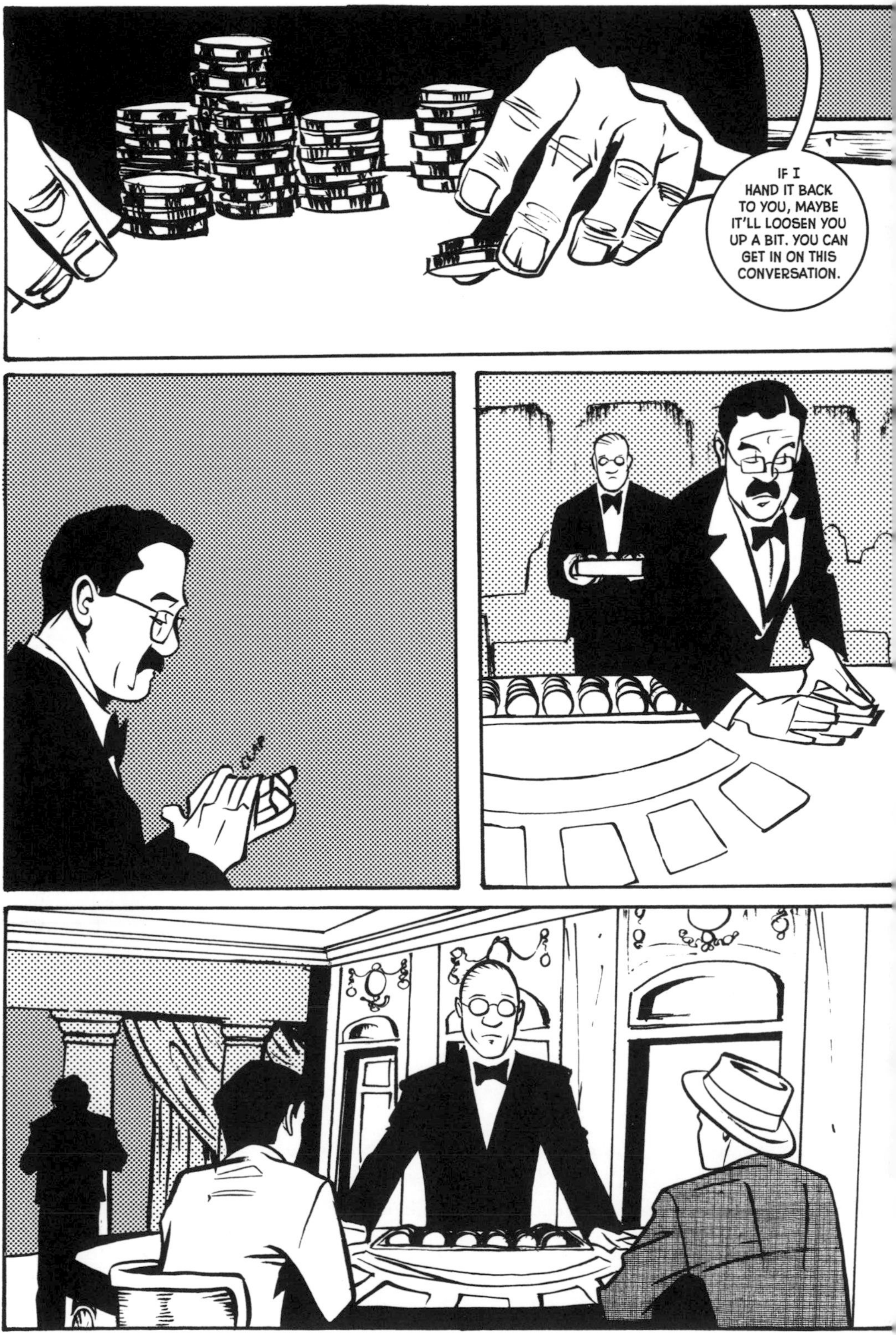
IF I HAND IT BACK TO YOU, MAYBE IT'LL LOOSEN YOU UP A BIT. YOU CAN GET IN ON THIS CONVERSATION.

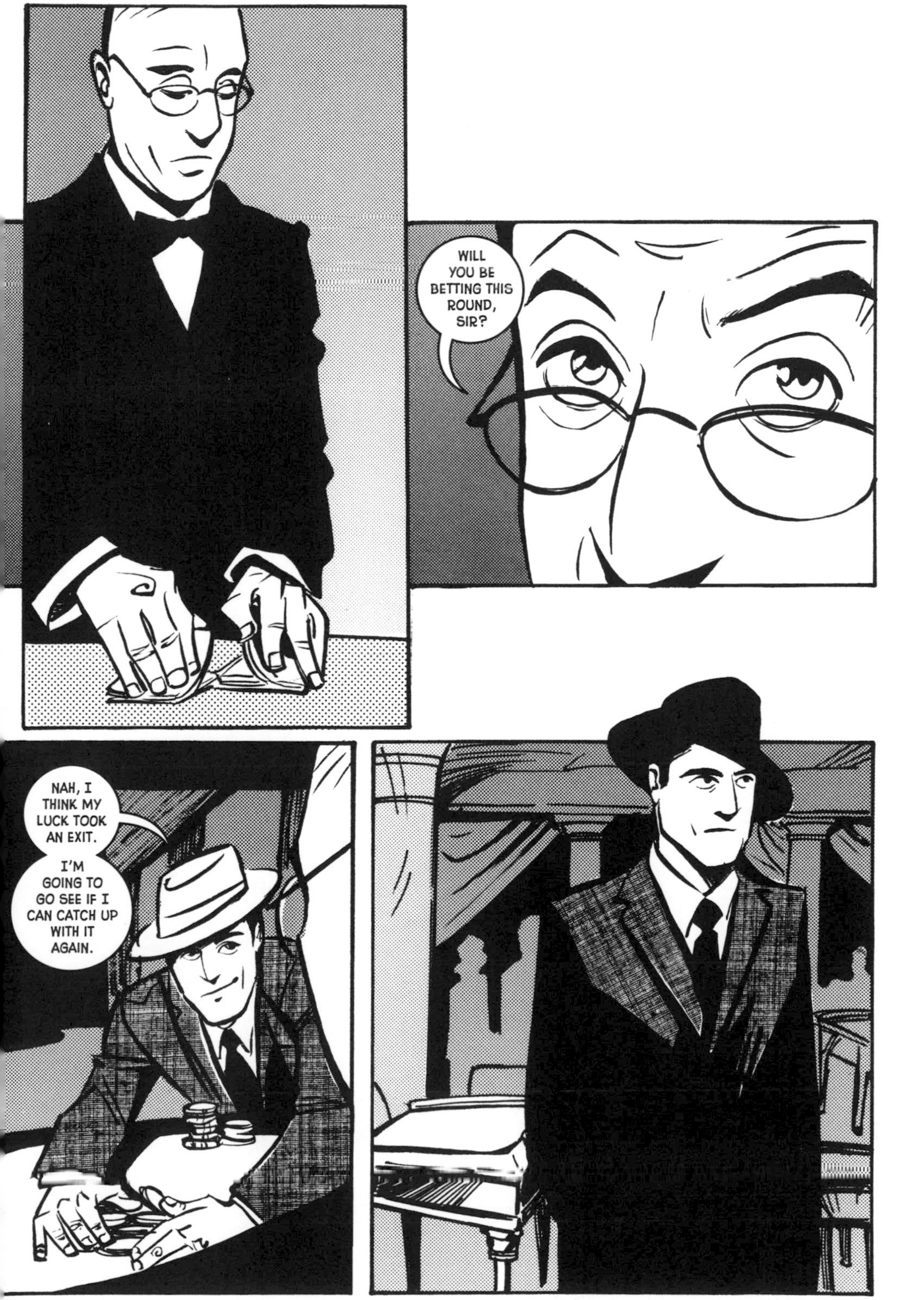
WILL YOU BE BETTING THIS ROUND, SIR?
NAH, I THINK MY LUCK TOOK AN EXIT.
I'M GOING TO GO SEE IF I CAN CATCH UP WITH IT AGAIN.

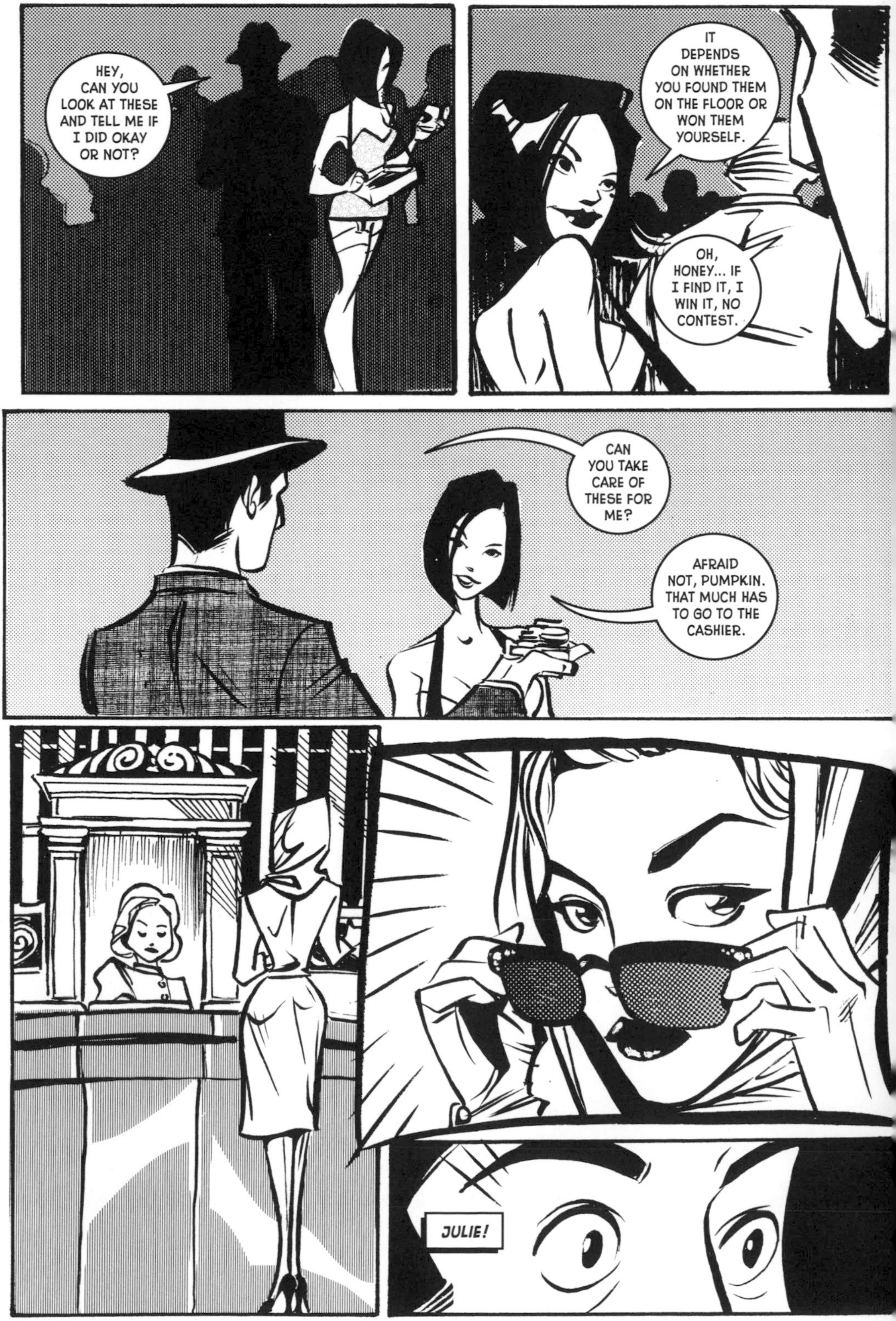
HEY, CAN YOU LOOK AT THESE AND TELL ME IF I DID OKAY OR NOT?
IT DEPENDS ON WHETHER YOU FOUND THEM ON THE FLOOR OR WON THEM YOURSELF.
OH, HONEY... IF I FIND IT, I WIN IT, NO CONTEST.
CAN YOU TAKE CARE OF THESE FOR ME?
AFRAID NOT, PUMPKIN. THAT MUCH HAS TO GO TO THE CASHIER.
JULIE!

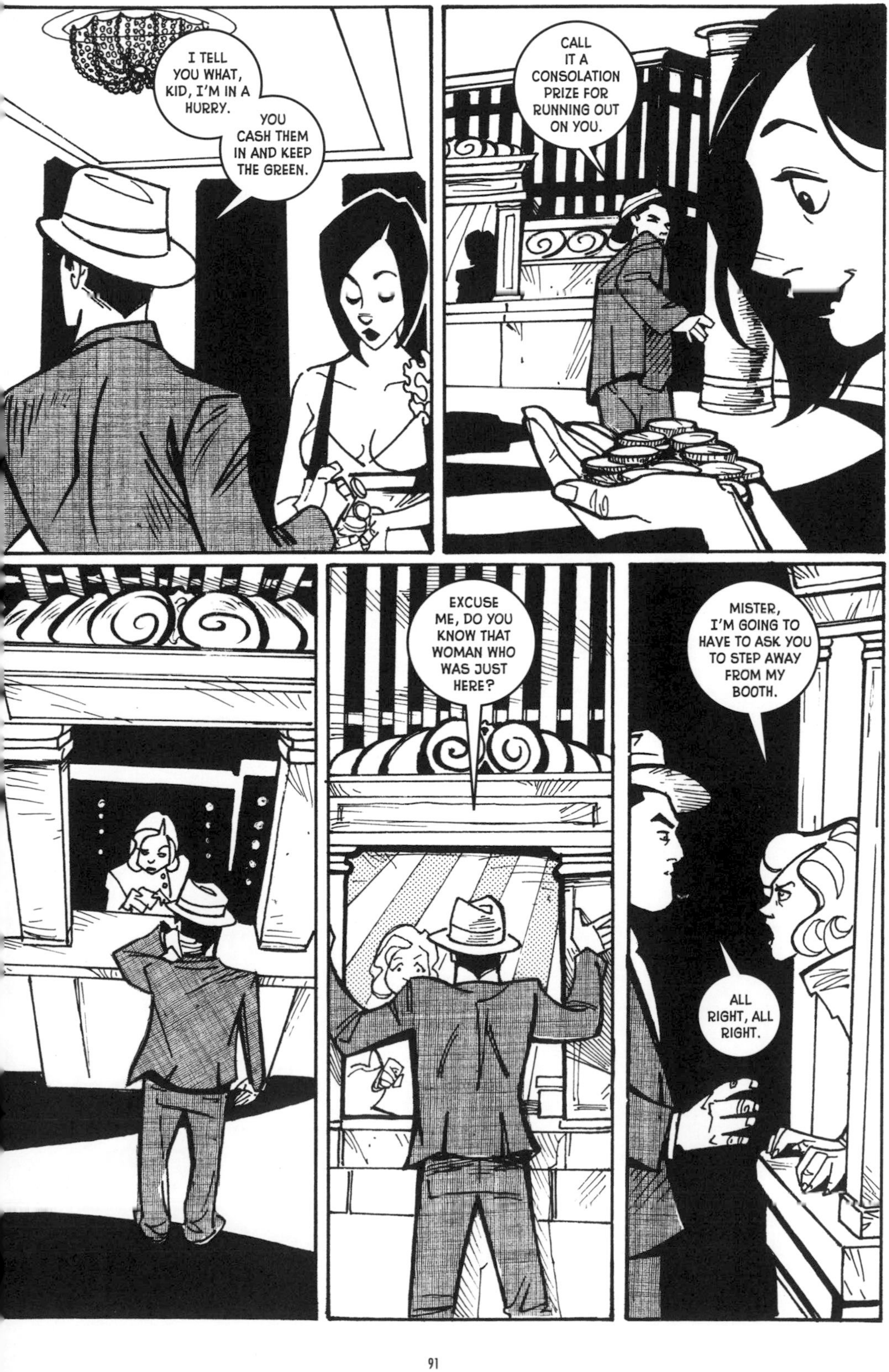
I TELL YOU WHAT, KID, I'M IN A HURRY.
YOU CASH THEM IN AND KEEP THE GREEN.
CALL IT A CONSOLATION PRIZE FOR RUNNING OUT ON YOU.
EXCUSE ME, DO YOU KNOW THAT WOMAN WHO WAS JUST HERE?
MISTER, I'M GOING TO HAVE TO ASK YOU TO STEP AWAY FROM MY BOOTH.
ALL RIGHT, ALL RIGHT.

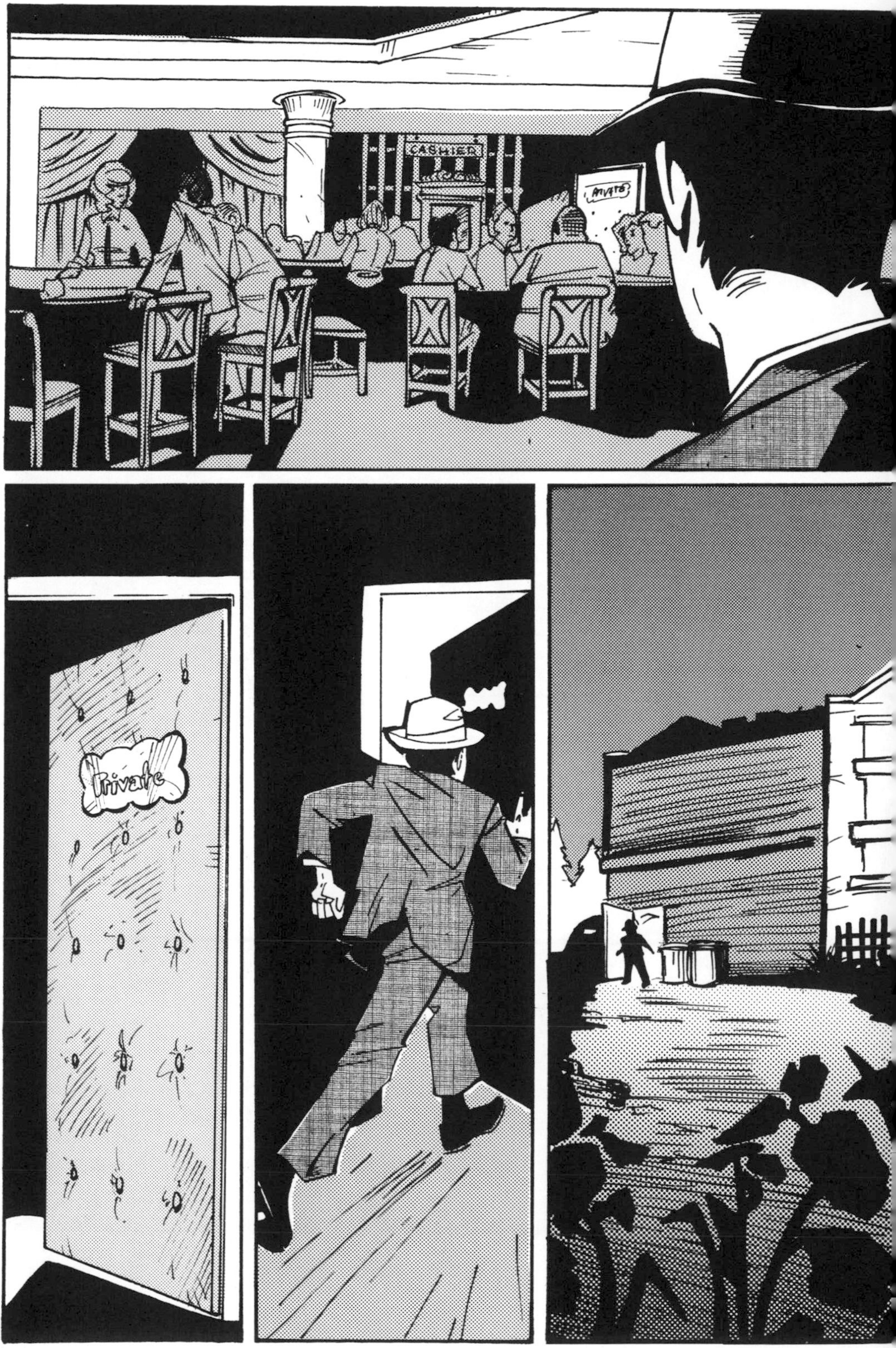
CASHIER
PRIVATE
Private

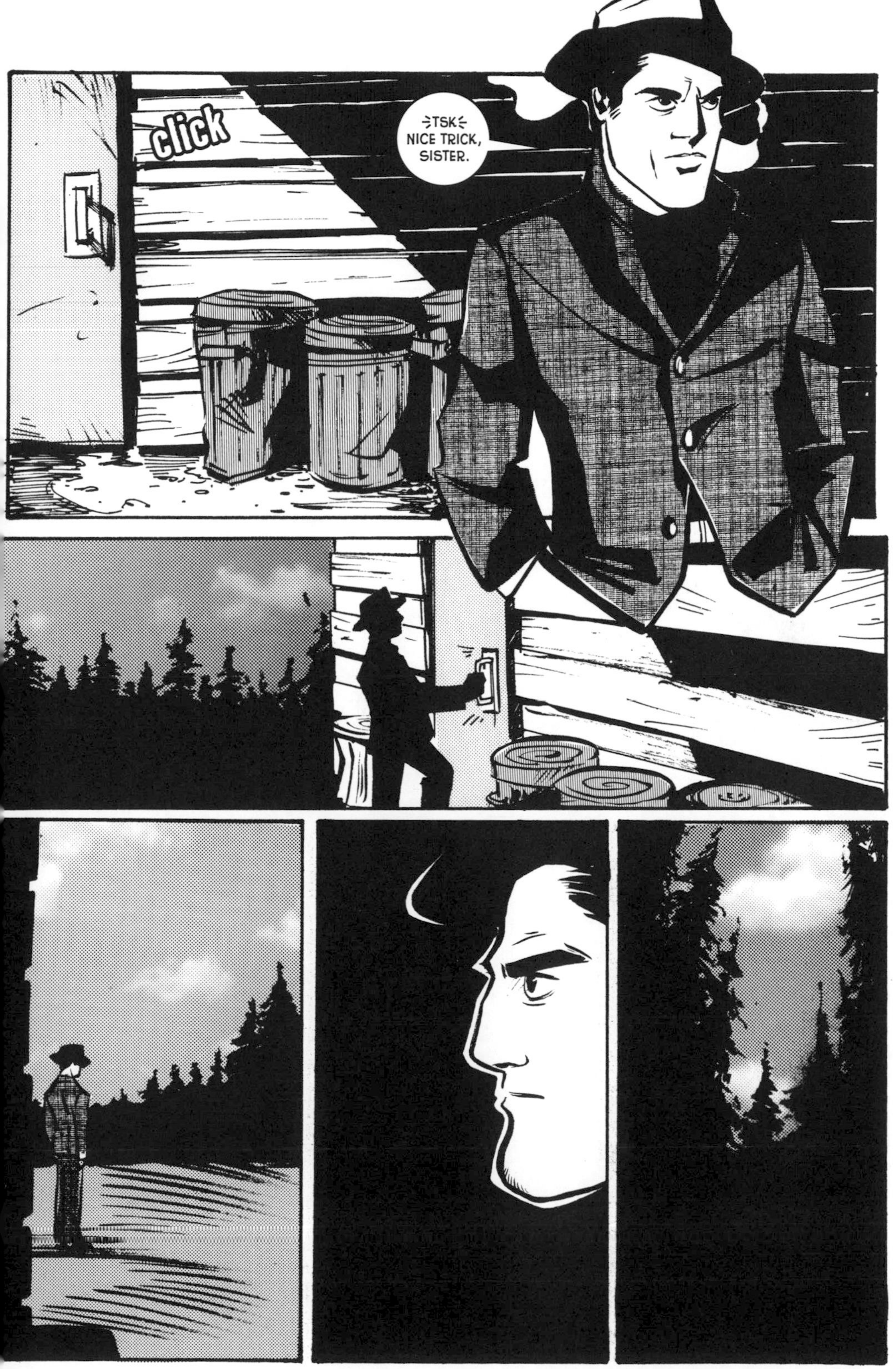
click
TSK
NICE TRICK, SISTER.

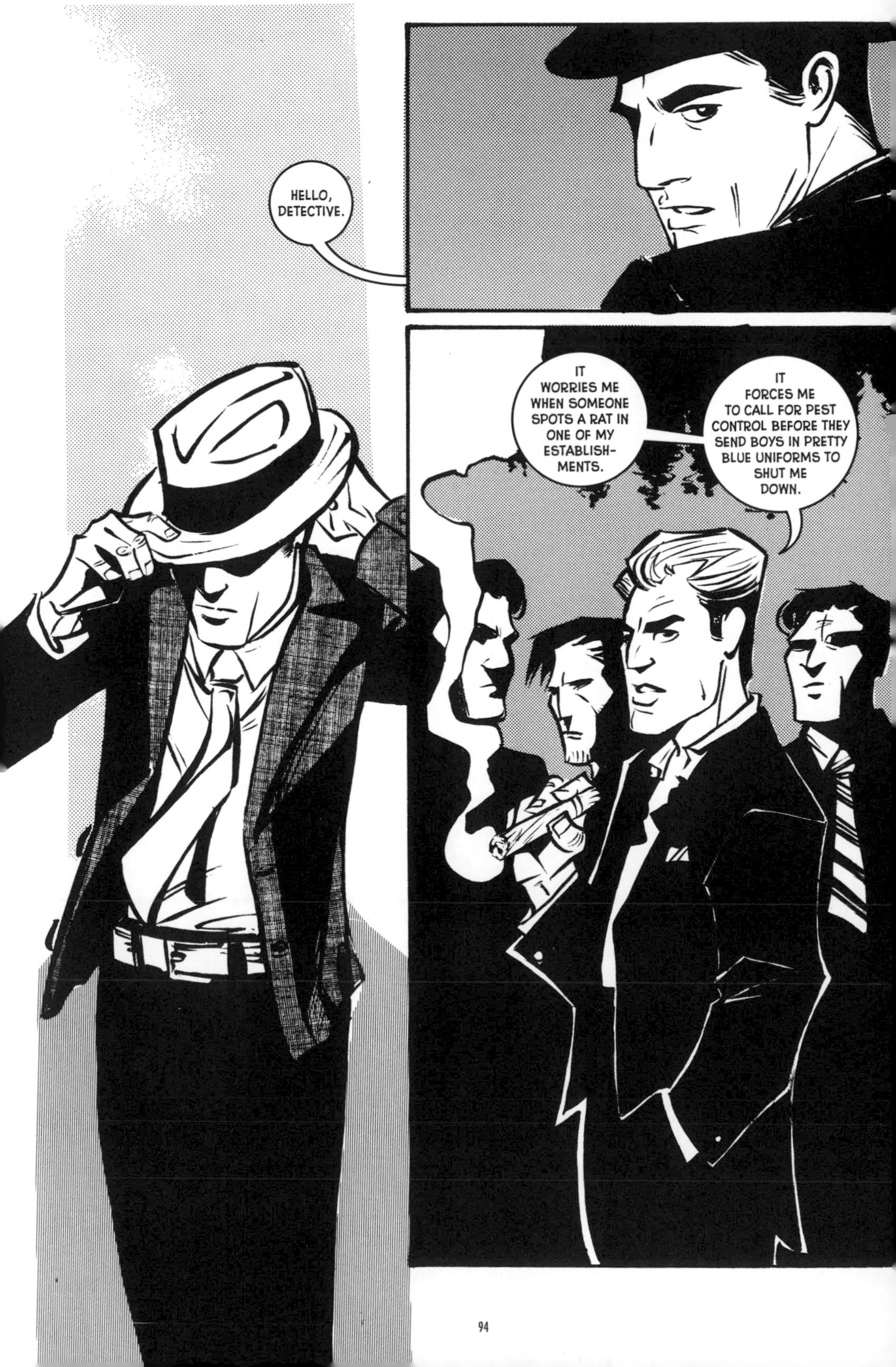
HELLO, DETECTIVE.
IT WORRIES ME WHEN SOMEONE SPOTS A RAT IN ONE OF MY ESTABLISH- MENTS.
IT FORCES ME TO CALL FOR PEST CONTROL BEFORE THEY SEND BOYS IN PRETTY BLUE UNIFORMS TO SHUT ME DOWN.

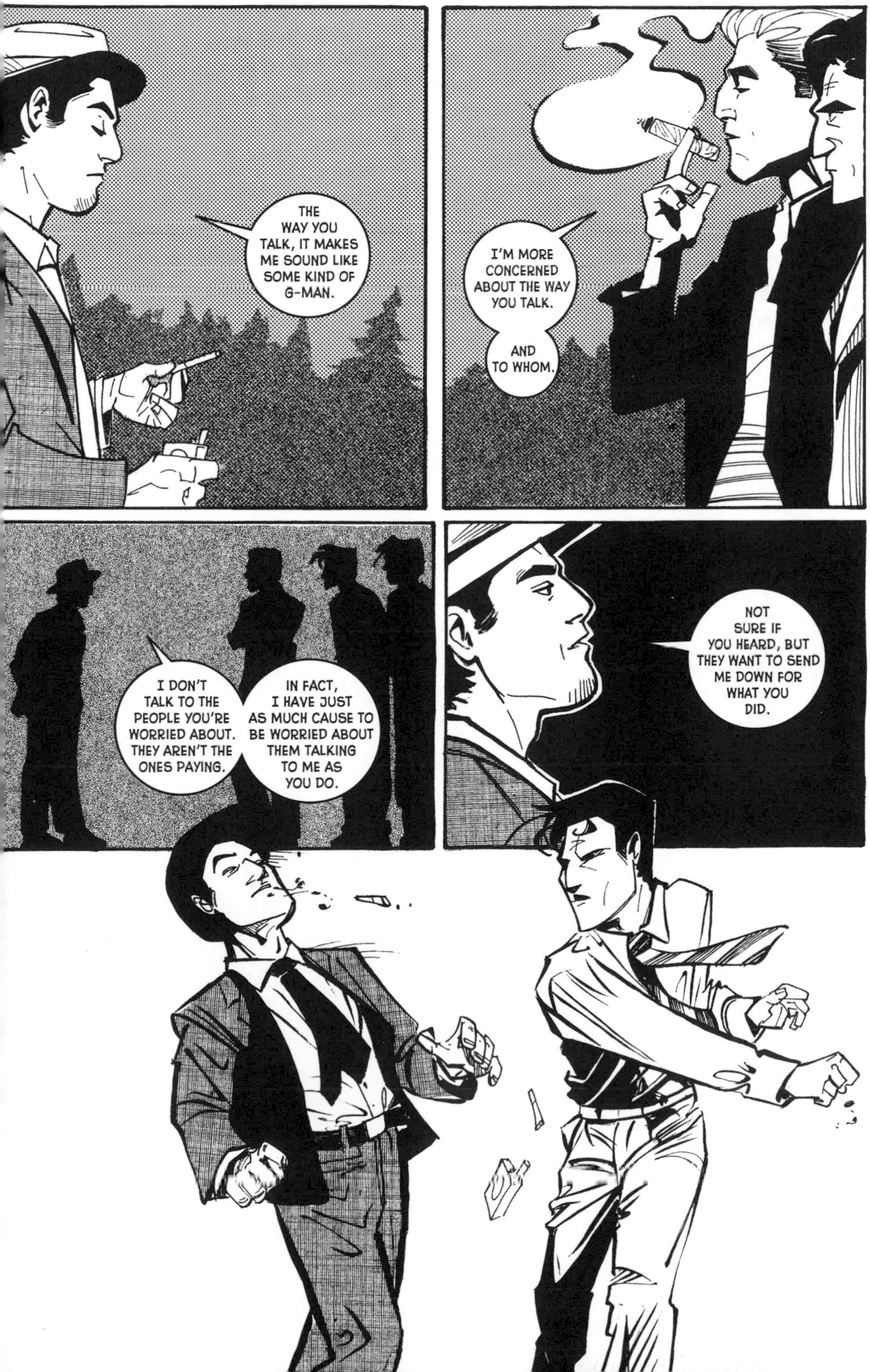
THE WAY YOU TALK, IT MAKES ME SOUND LIKE SOME KIND OF G-MAN.
I'M MORE CONCERNED ABOUT THE WAY YOU TALK.
AND TO WHOM.
I DON'T TALK TO THE PEOPLE YOU'RE WORRIED ABOUT. THEY AREN'T THE ONES PAYING.
IN FACT, I HAVE JUST AS MUCH CAUSE TO BE WORRIED ABOUT THEM TALKING TO ME AS YOU DO.
NOT SURE IF YOU HEARD, BUT THEY WANT TO SEND ME DOWN FOR WHAT YOU DID.

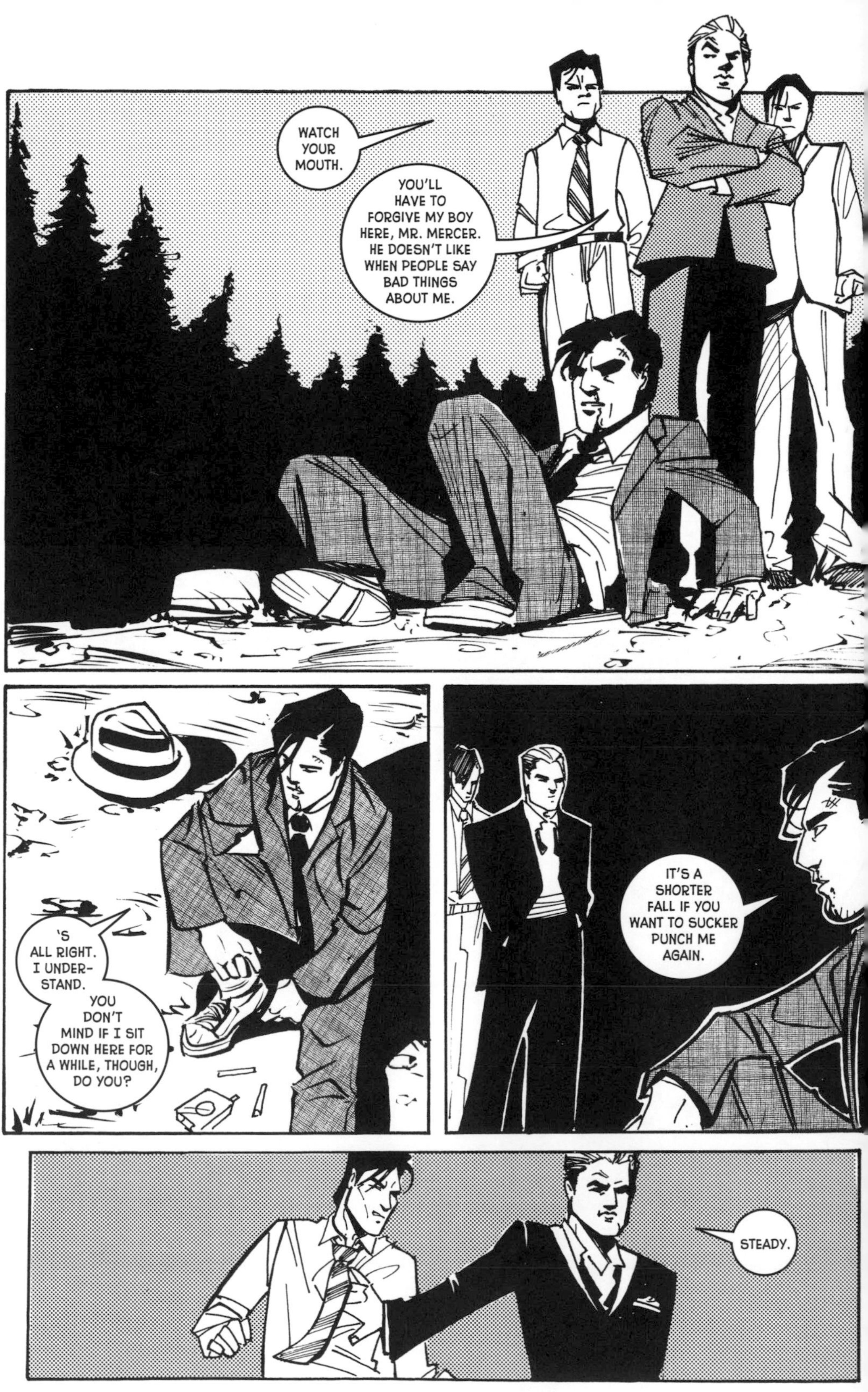
WATCH YOUR MOUTH.
YOU'LL HAVE TO FORGIVE MY BOY HERE, MR. MERCER. HE DOESN'T LIKE WHEN PEOPLE SAY BAD THINGS ABOUT ME.
'S ALL RIGHT. I UNDER-STAND.
YOU DON'T MIND IF I SIT DOWN HERE FOR A WHILE, THOUGH, DO YOU?
IT'S A SHORTER FALL IF YOU WANT TO SUCKER PUNCH ME AGAIN.
STEADY.

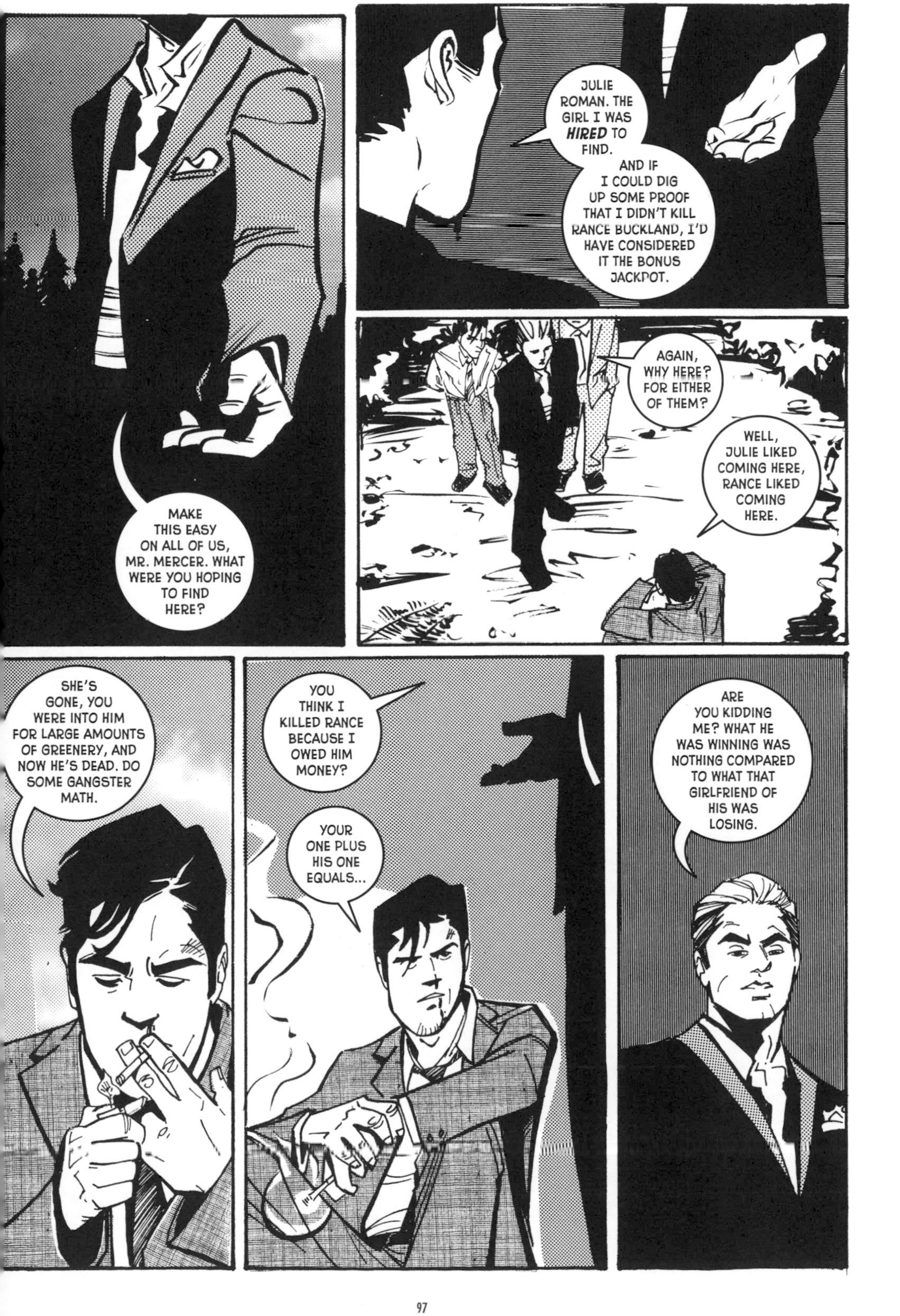
JULIE ROMAN. THE GIRL I WAS *HIRED* TO FIND.
AND IF I COULD DIG UP SOME PROOF THAT I DIDN'T KILL RANCE BUCKLAND, I'D HAVE CONSIDERED IT THE BONUS JACKPOT.
MAKE THIS EASY ON ALL OF US, MR. MERCER. WHAT WERE YOU HOPING TO FIND HERE?
AGAIN, WHY HERE? FOR EITHER OF THEM?
WELL, JULIE LIKED COMING HERE, RANCE LIKED COMING HERE.
SHE'S GONE, YOU WERE INTO HIM FOR LARGE AMOUNTS OF GREENERY, AND NOW HE'S DEAD. DO SOME GANGSTER MATH.
YOU THINK I KILLED RANCE BECAUSE I OWED HIM MONEY?
YOUR ONE PLUS HIS ONE EQUALS...
ARE YOU KIDDING ME? WHAT HE WAS WINNING WAS NOTHING COMPARED TO WHAT THAT GIRLFRIEND OF HIS WAS LOSING.

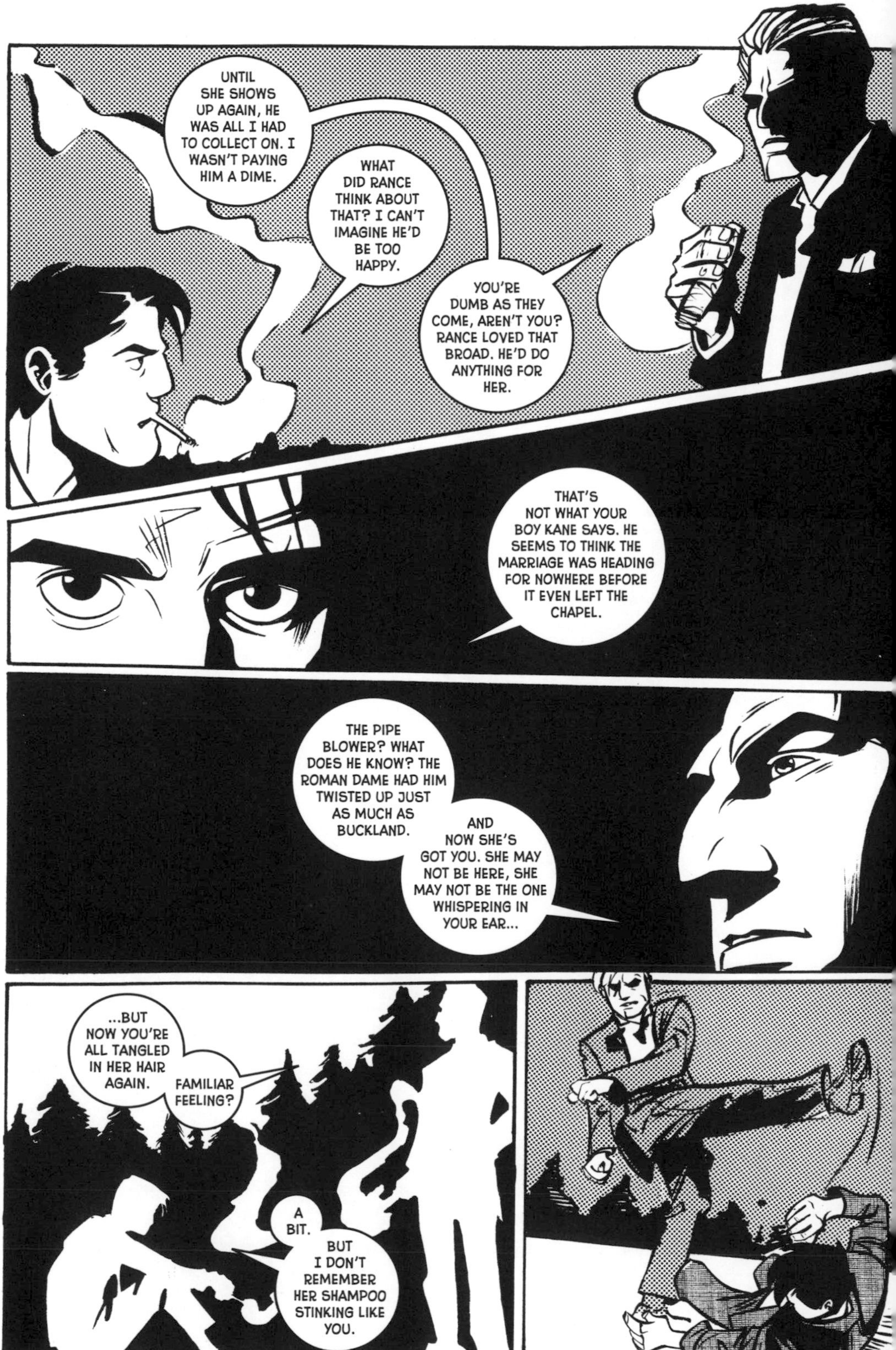
UNTIL SHE SHOWS UP AGAIN, HE WAS ALL I HAD TO COLLECT ON. I WASN'T PAYING HIM A DIME.
WHAT DID RANCE THINK ABOUT THAT? I CAN'T IMAGINE HE'D BE TOO HAPPY.
YOU'RE DUMB AS THEY COME, AREN'T YOU? RANCE LOVED THAT BROAD. HE'D DO ANYTHING FOR HER.
THAT'S NOT WHAT YOUR BOY KANE SAYS. HE SEEMS TO THINK THE MARRIAGE WAS HEADING FOR NOWHERE BEFORE IT EVEN LEFT THE CHAPEL.
THE PIPE BLOWER? WHAT DOES HE KNOW? THE ROMAN DAME HAD HIM TWISTED UP JUST AS MUCH AS BUCKLAND.
AND NOW SHE'S GOT YOU. SHE MAY NOT BE HERE, SHE MAY NOT BE THE ONE WHISPERING IN YOUR EAR...
...BUT NOW YOU'RE ALL TANGLED IN HER HAIR AGAIN.
FAMILIAR FEELING?
A BIT.
BUT I DON'T REMEMBER HER SHAMPOO STINKING LIKE YOU.

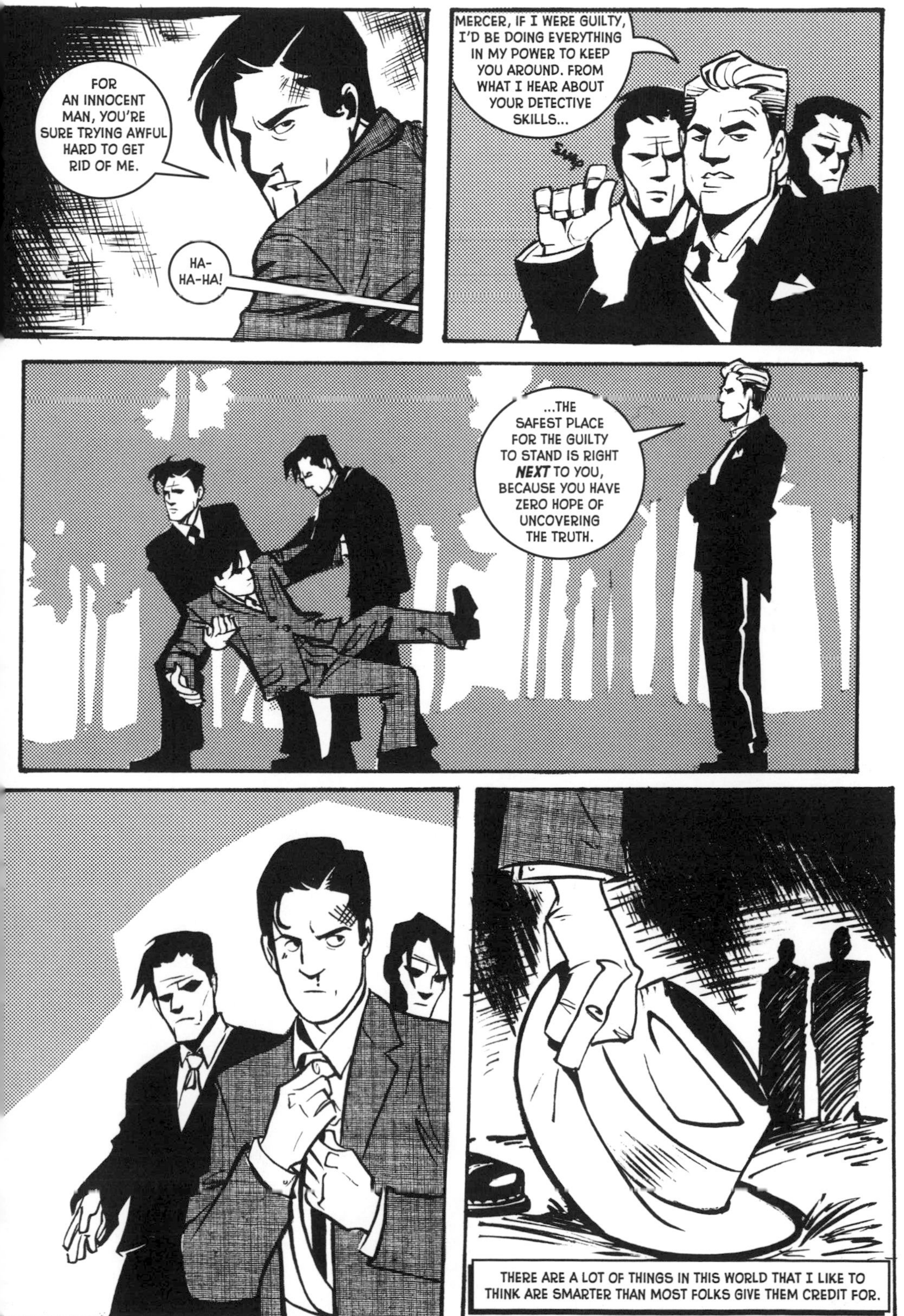
FOR AN INNOCENT MAN, YOU'RE SURE TRYING AWFUL HARD TO GET RID OF ME.
HA-HA-HA!
MERCER, IF I WERE GUILTY, I'D BE DOING EVERYTHING IN MY POWER TO KEEP YOU AROUND. FROM WHAT I HEAR ABOUT YOUR DETECTIVE SKILLS...
...THE SAFEST PLACE FOR THE GUILTY TO STAND IS RIGHT NEXT TO YOU, BECAUSE YOU HAVE ZERO HOPE OF UNCOVERING THE TRUTH.
THERE ARE A LOT OF THINGS IN THIS WORLD THAT I LIKE TO THINK ARE SMARTER THAN MOST FOLKS GIVE THEM CREDIT FOR.

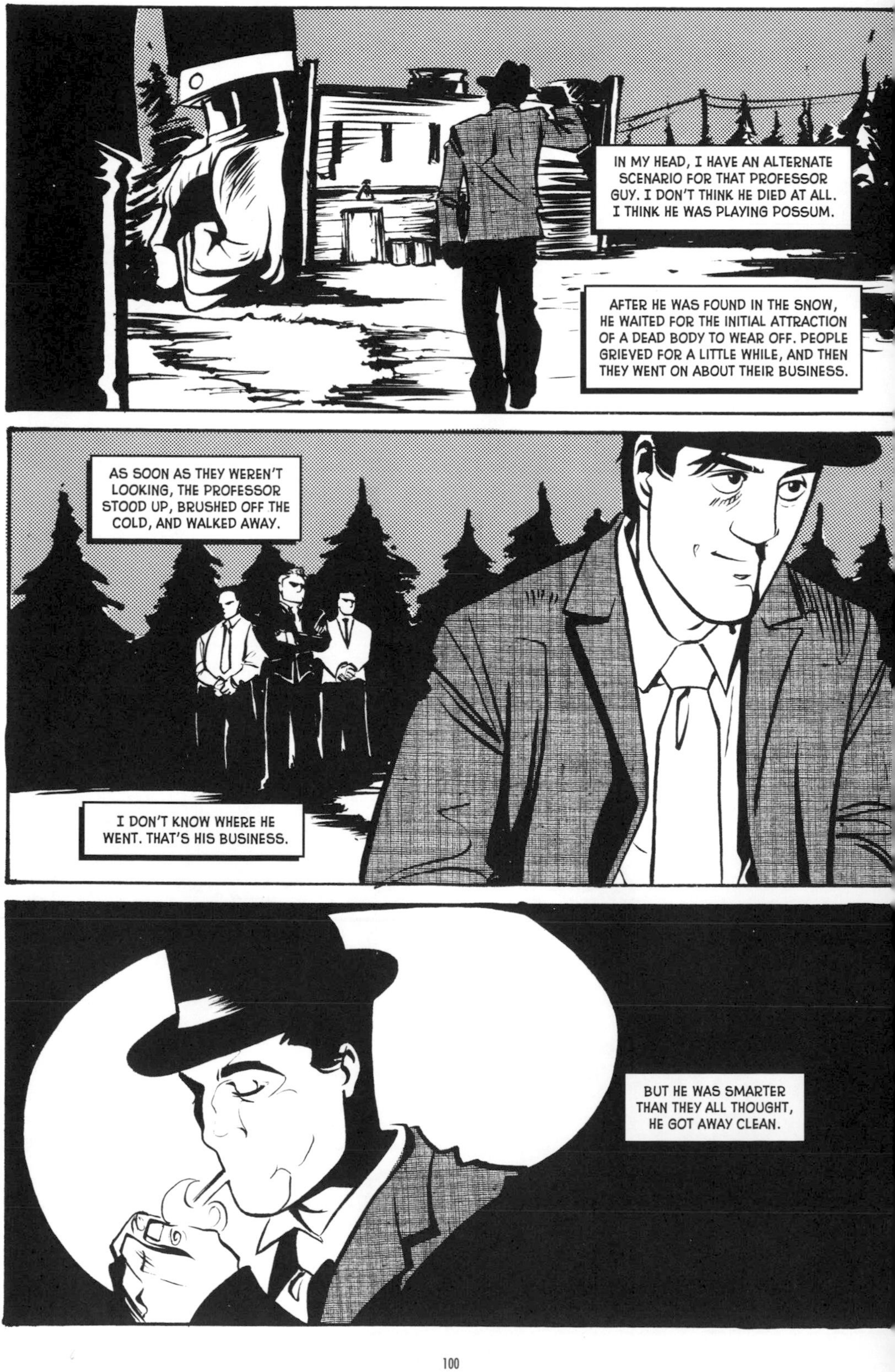
IN MY HEAD, I HAVE AN ALTERNATE SCENARIO FOR THAT PROFESSOR GUY. I DON'T THINK HE DIED AT ALL. I THINK HE WAS PLAYING POSSUM.
AFTER HE WAS FOUND IN THE SNOW, HE WAITED FOR THE INITIAL ATTRACTION OF A DEAD BODY TO WEAR OFF. PEOPLE GRIEVED FOR A LITTLE WHILE, AND THEN THEY WENT ON ABOUT THEIR BUSINESS.
AS SOON AS THEY WEREN'T LOOKING, THE PROFESSOR STOOD UP, BRUSHED OFF THE COLD, AND WALKED AWAY.
I DON'T KNOW WHERE HE WENT. THAT'S HIS BUSINESS.
BUT HE WAS SMARTER THAN THEY ALL THOUGHT, HE GOT AWAY CLEAN.

CHAPTER 6

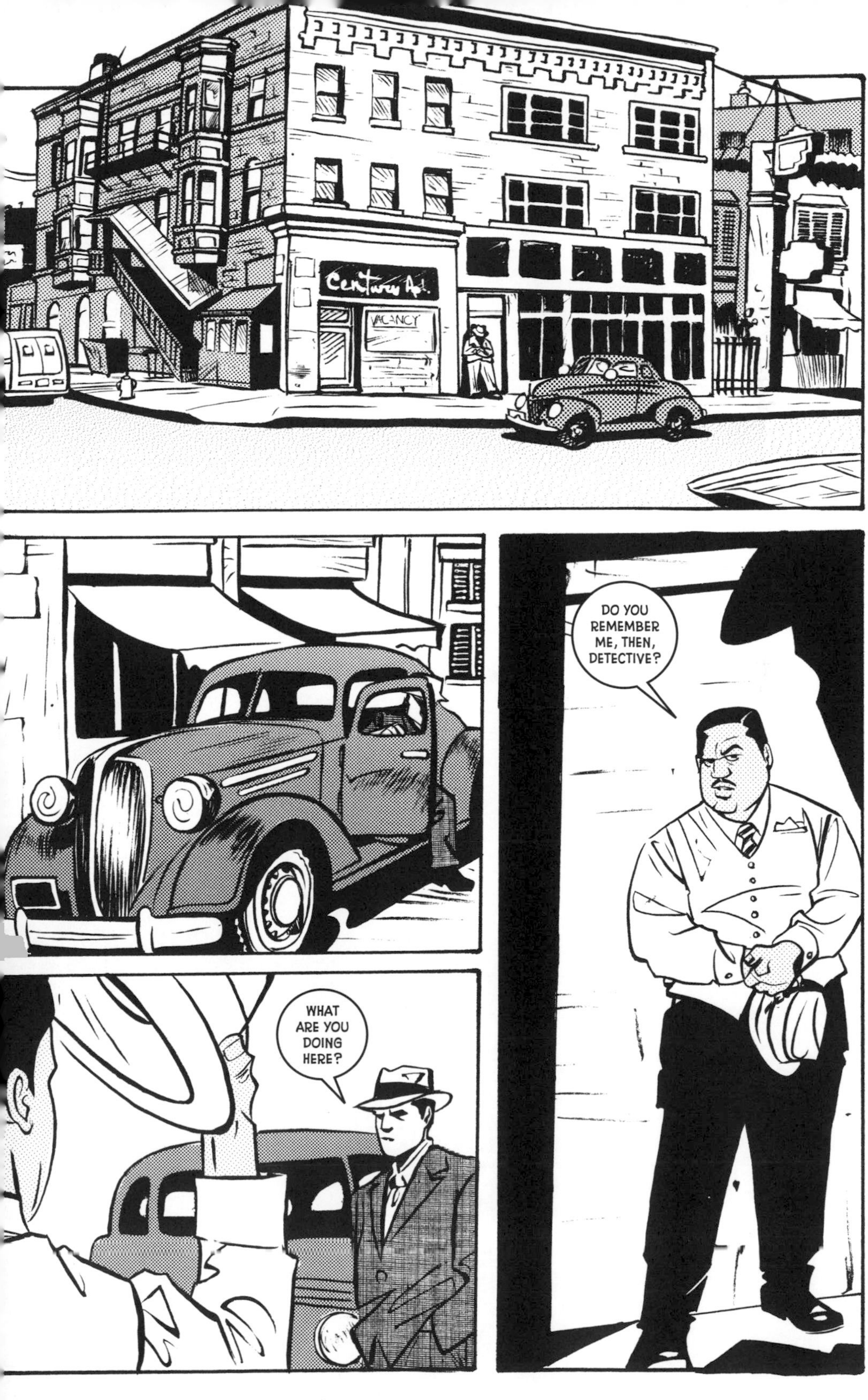
Century Apt.
VACANCY
WHAT ARE YOU DOING HERE?
DO YOU REMEMBER ME, THEN, DETECTIVE?

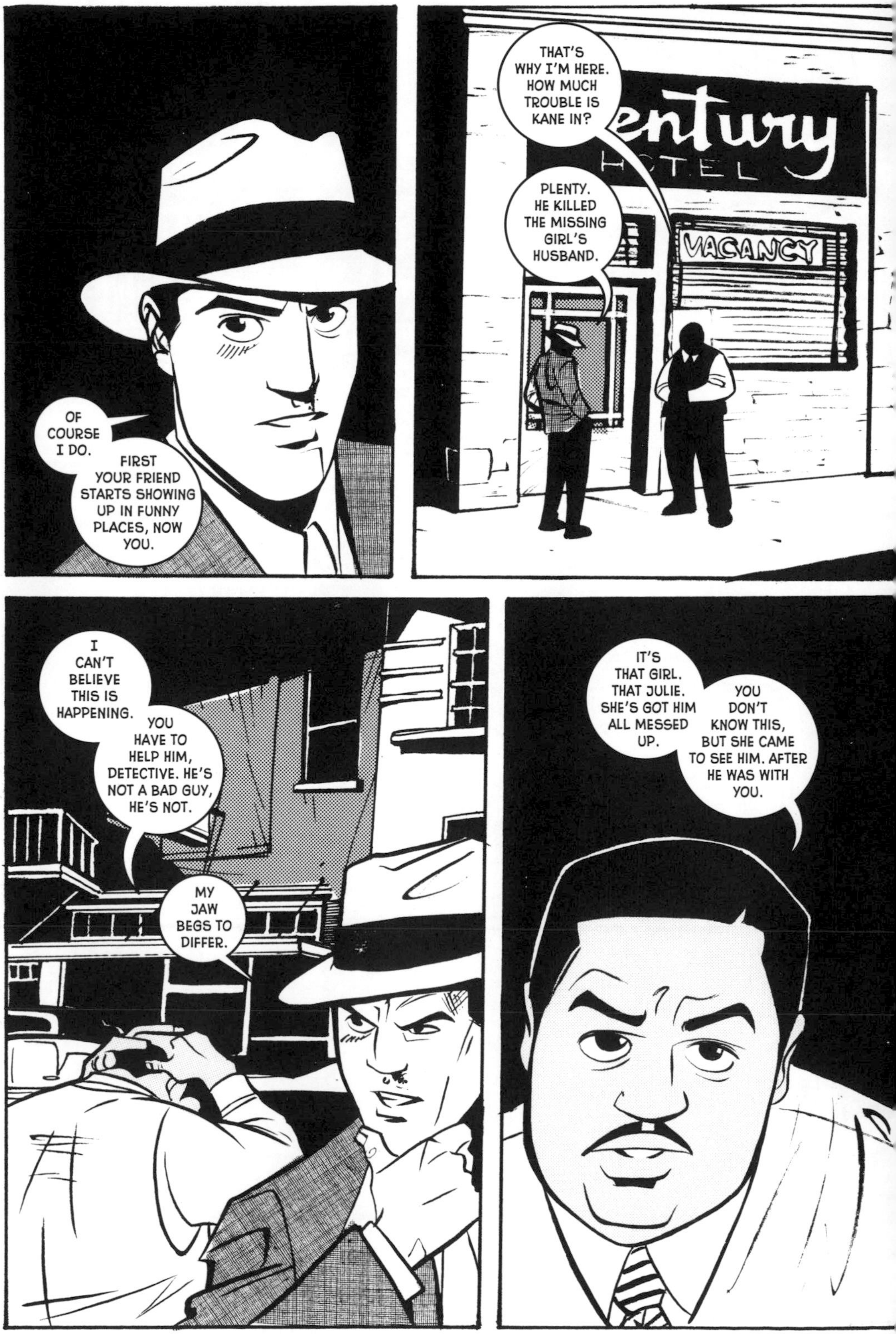
OF COURSE I DO.
FIRST YOUR FRIEND STARTS SHOWING UP IN FUNNY PLACES, NOW YOU.
THAT'S WHY I'M HERE. HOW MUCH TROUBLE IS KANE IN?
PLENTY. HE KILLED THE MISSING GIRL'S HUSBAND.
Century HOTEL
VACANCY
I CAN'T BELIEVE THIS IS HAPPENING.
YOU HAVE TO HELP HIM, DETECTIVE. HE'S NOT A BAD GUY, HE'S NOT.
MY JAW BEGS TO DIFFER.
IT'S THAT GIRL. THAT JULIE. SHE'S GOT HIM ALL MESSED UP.
YOU DON'T KNOW THIS, BUT SHE CAME TO SEE HIM. AFTER HE WAS WITH YOU.

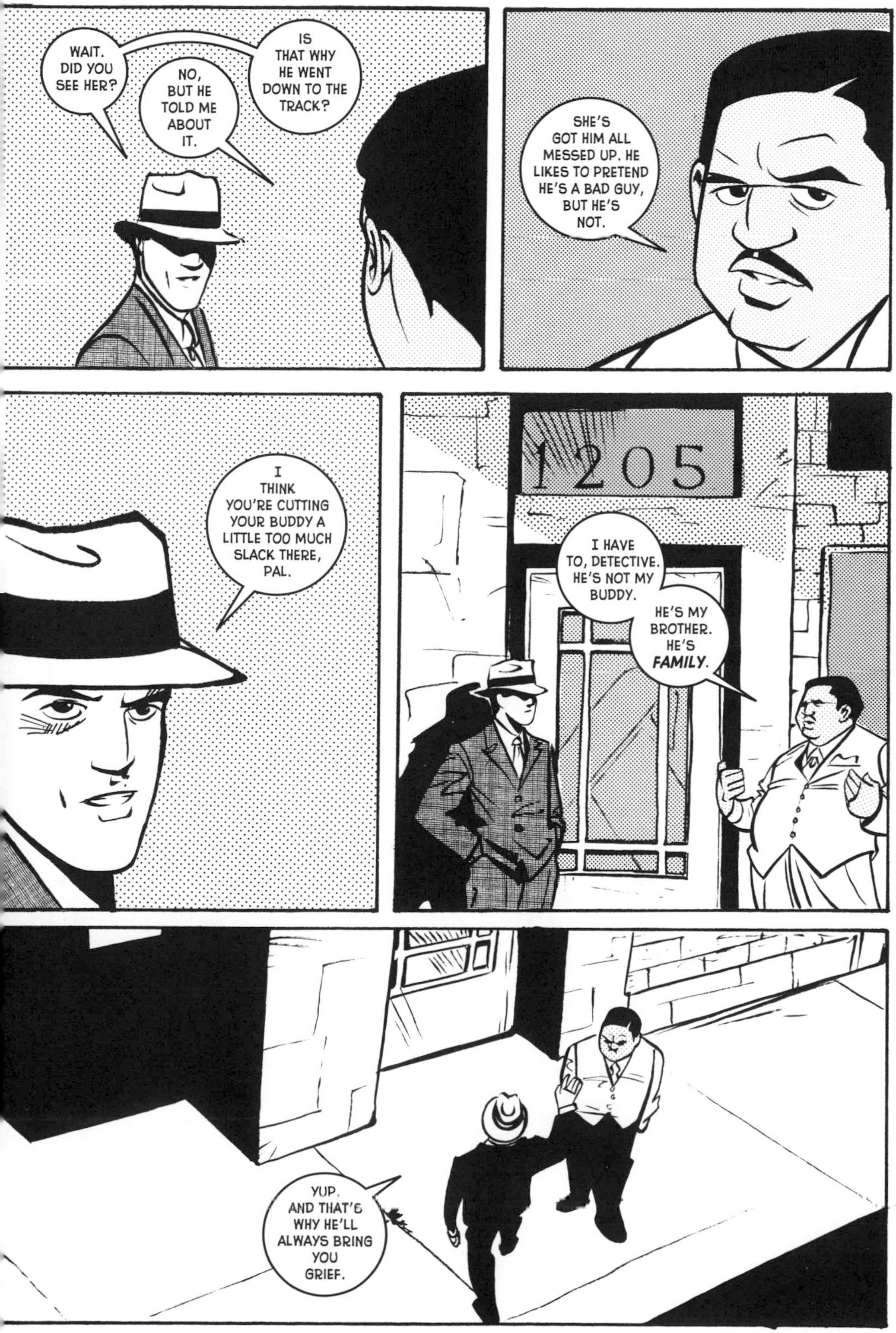
WAIT. DID YOU SEE HER?
NO, BUT HE TOLD ME ABOUT IT.
IS THAT WHY HE WENT DOWN TO THE TRACK?
SHE'S GOT HIM ALL MESSED UP. HE LIKES TO PRETEND HE'S A BAD GUY, BUT HE'S NOT.
I THINK YOU'RE CUTTING YOUR BUDDY A LITTLE TOO MUCH SLACK THERE, PAL.
1205
I HAVE TO, DETECTIVE. HE'S NOT MY BUDDY.
HE'S MY BROTHER. HE'S FAMILY.
YUP. AND THAT'S WHY HE'LL ALWAYS BRING YOU GRIEF.

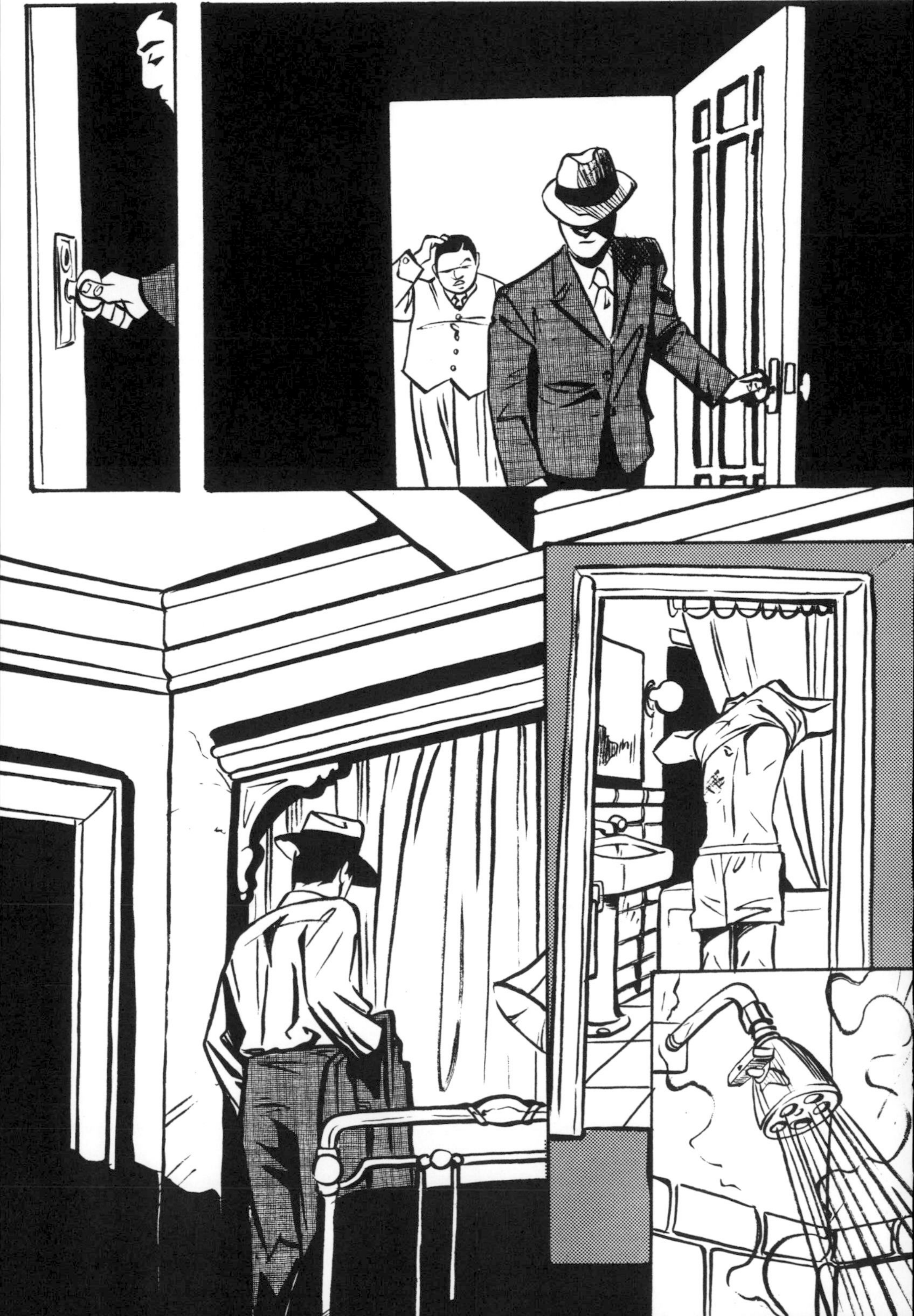

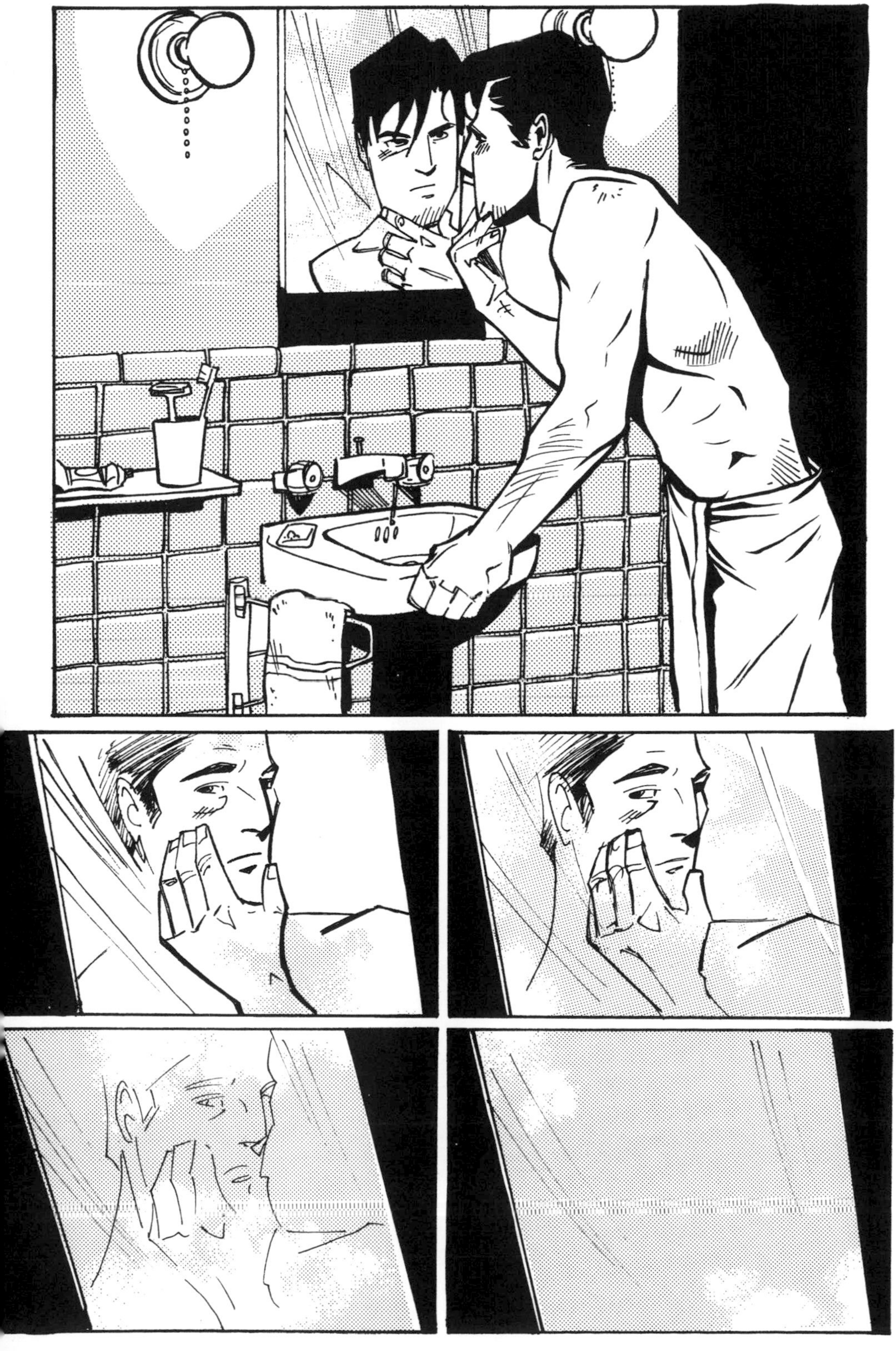

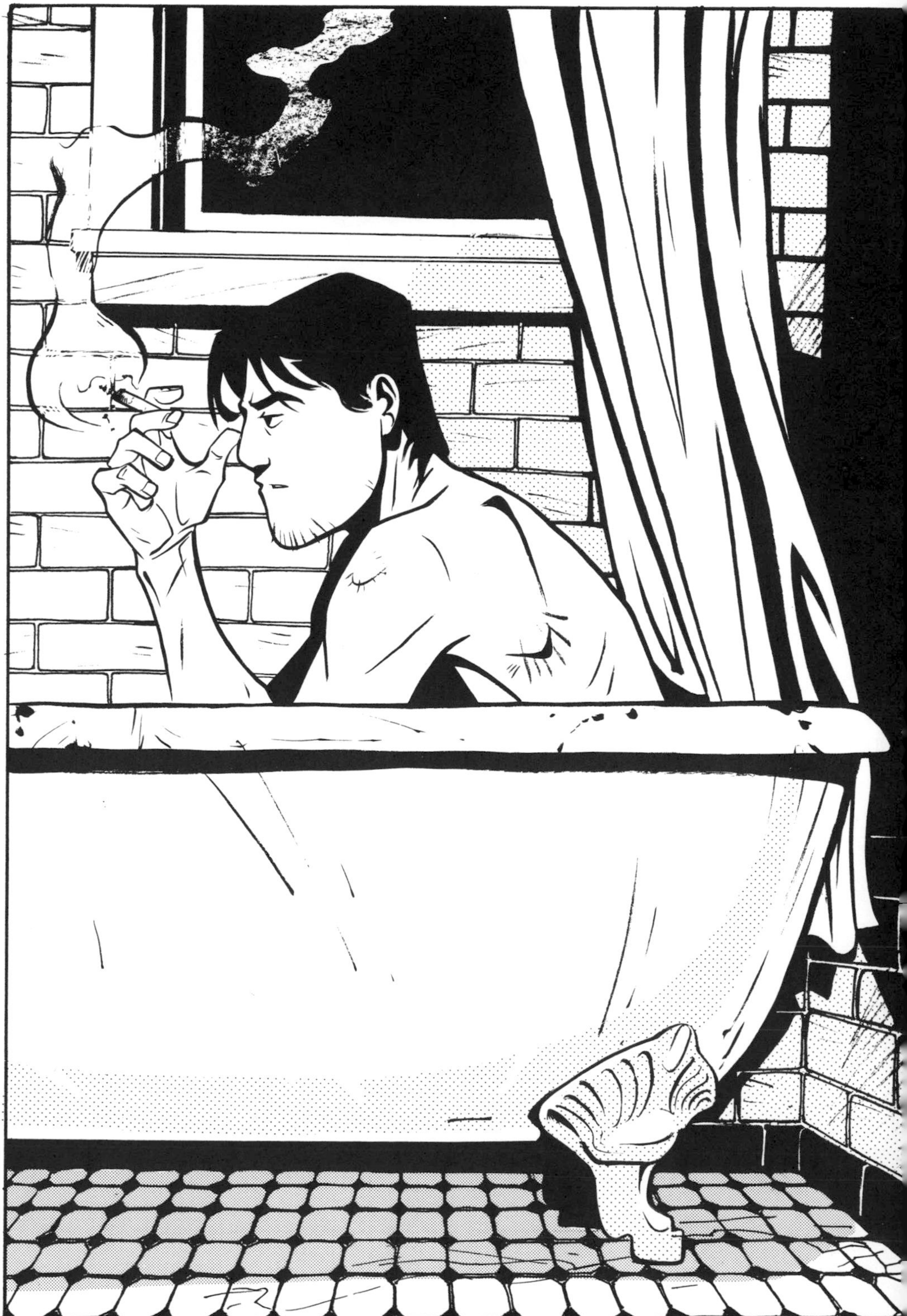

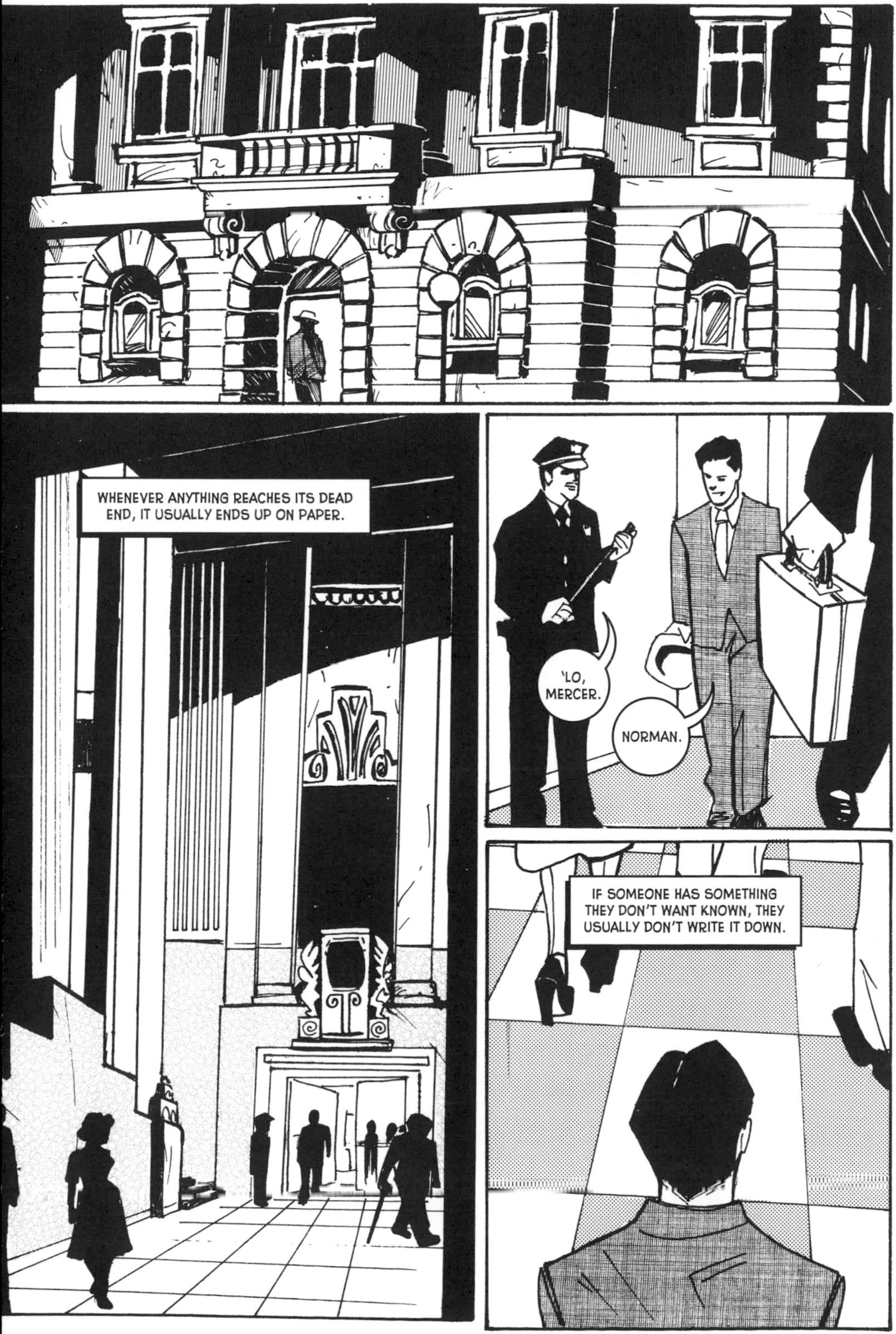
WHENEVER ANYTHING REACHES ITS DEAD END, IT USUALLY ENDS UP ON PAPER.
'LO, MERCER.
NORMAN.
IF SOMEONE HAS SOMETHING THEY DON'T WANT KNOWN, THEY USUALLY DON'T WRITE IT DOWN.

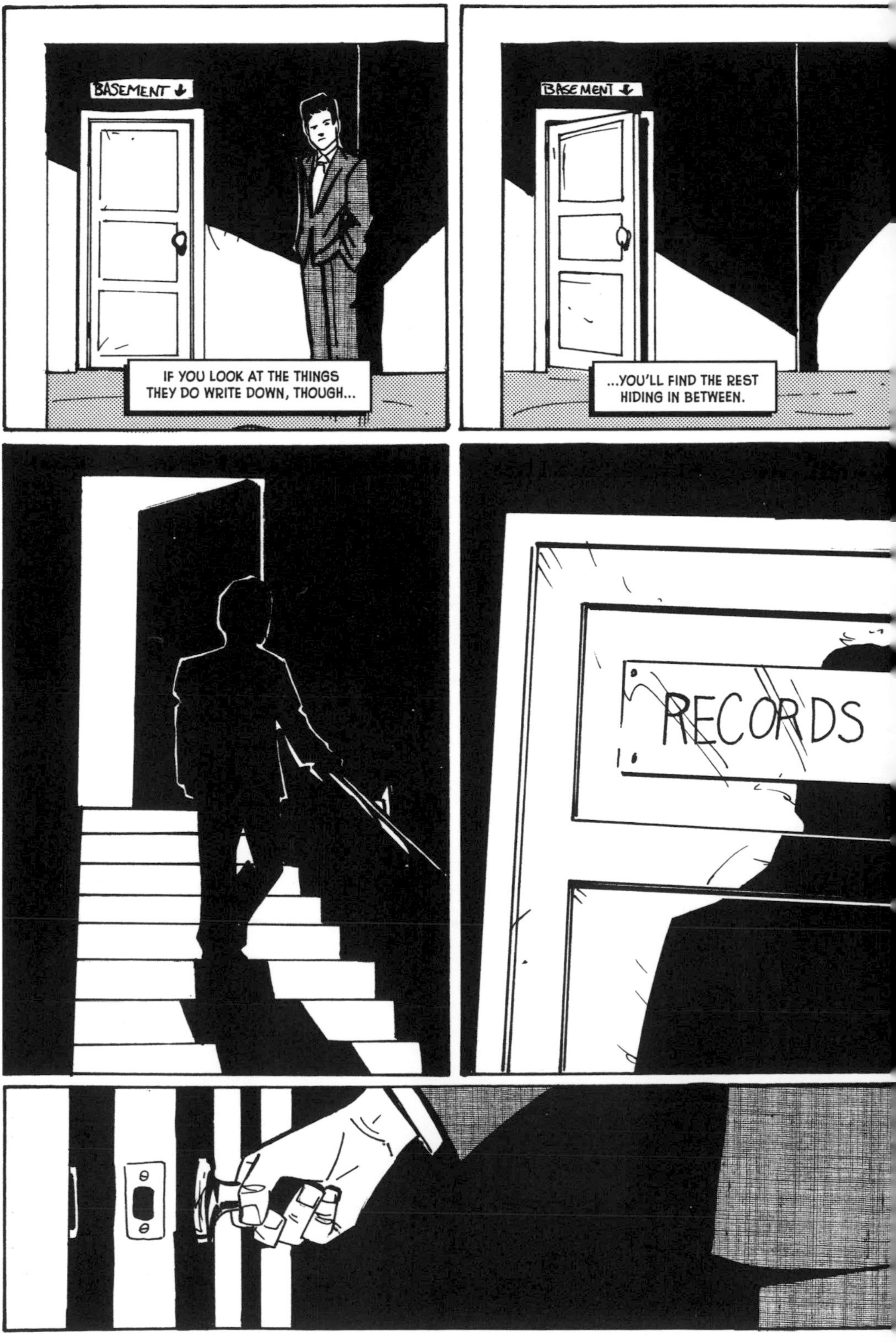
BASEMENT
IF YOU LOOK AT THE THINGS THEY DO WRITE DOWN, THOUGH...
BASEMENT
...YOU'LL FIND THE REST HIDING IN BETWEEN.
RECORDS

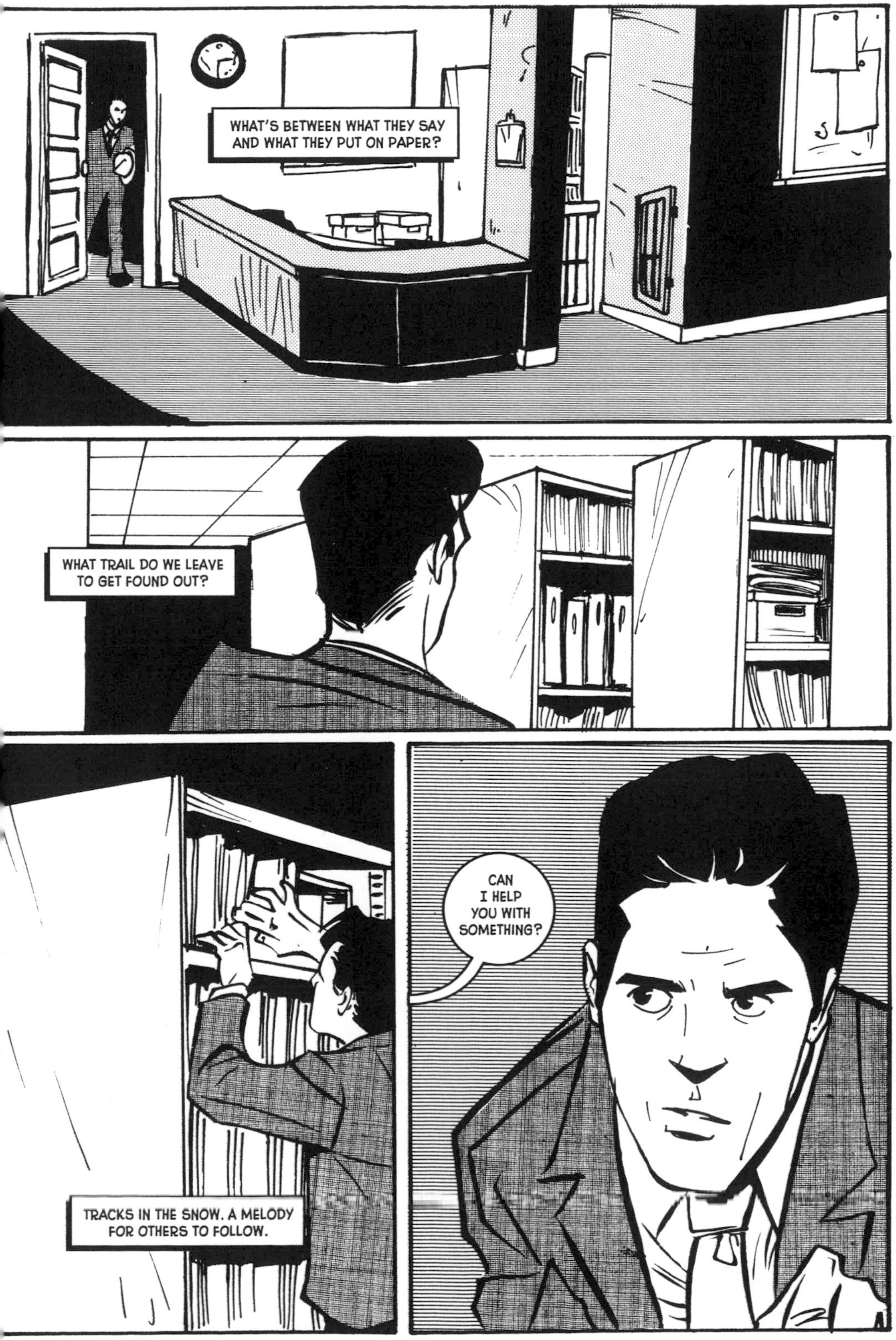
WHAT'S BETWEEN WHAT THEY SAY AND WHAT THEY PUT ON PAPER?
WHAT TRAIL DO WE LEAVE TO GET FOUND OUT?
TRACKS IN THE SNOW. A MELODY FOR OTHERS TO FOLLOW.
CAN I HELP YOU WITH SOMETHING?

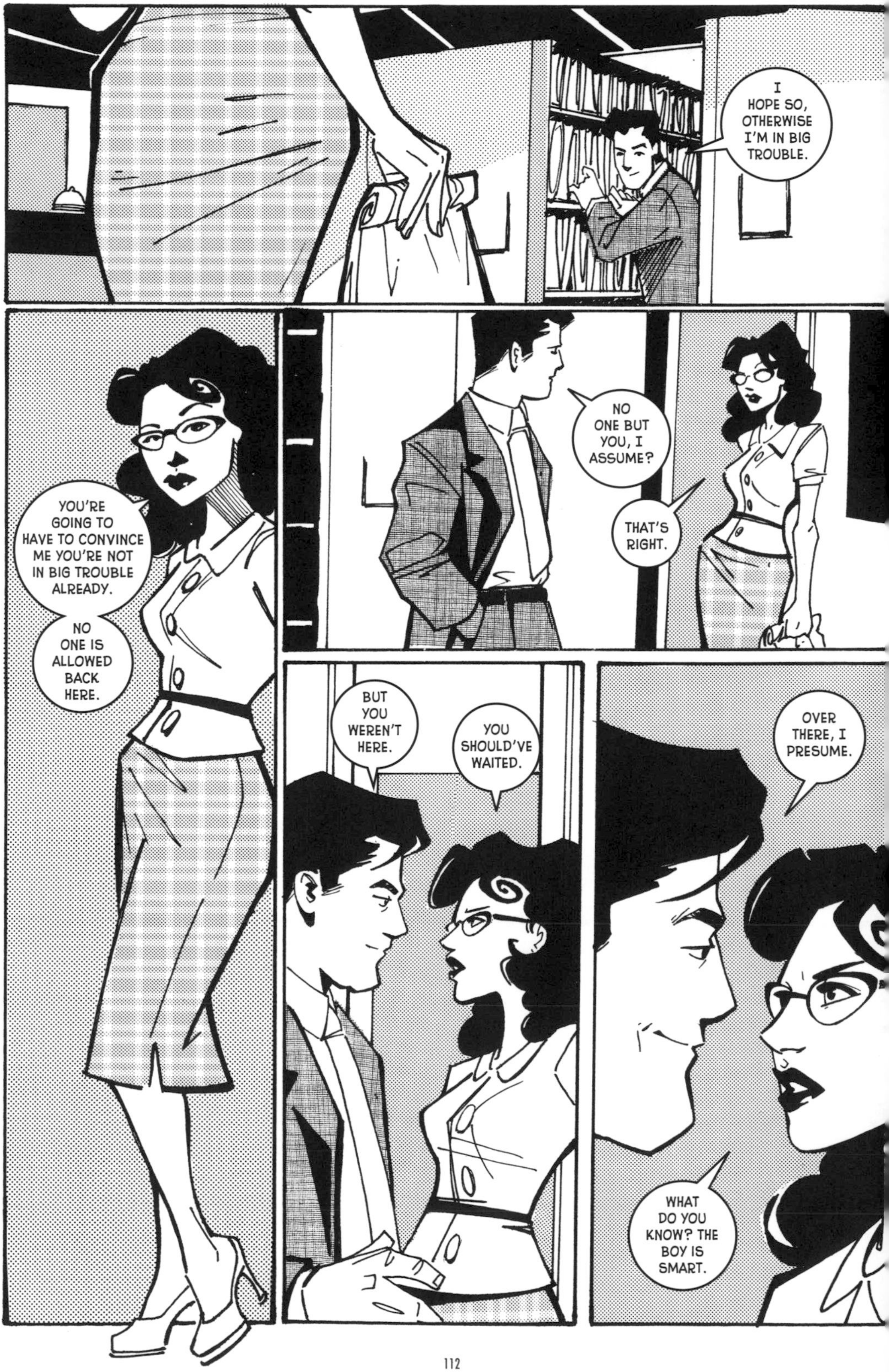
I HOPE SO, OTHERWISE I'M IN BIG TROUBLE.
YOU'RE GOING TO HAVE TO CONVINCE ME YOU'RE NOT IN BIG TROUBLE ALREADY.
NO ONE IS ALLOWED BACK HERE.
NO ONE BUT YOU, I ASSUME?
THAT'S RIGHT.
BUT YOU WEREN'T HERE.
YOU SHOULD'VE WAITED.
OVER THERE, I PRESUME.
WHAT DO YOU KNOW? THE BOY IS SMART.

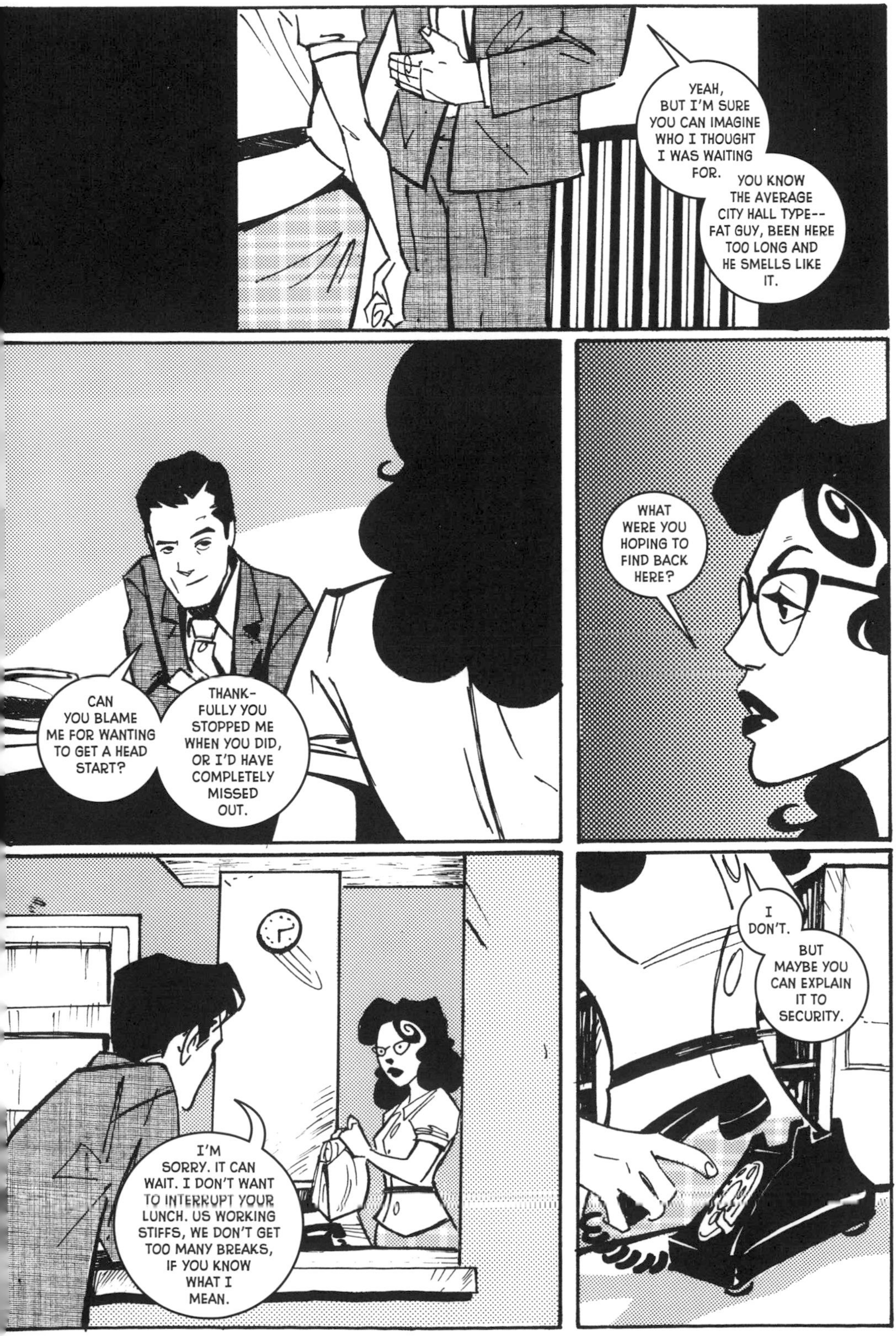
YEAH, BUT I'M SURE YOU CAN IMAGINE WHO I THOUGHT I WAS WAITING FOR.
YOU KNOW THE AVERAGE CITY HALL TYPE-- FAT GUY, BEEN HERE TOO LONG AND HE SMELLS LIKE IT.
CAN YOU BLAME ME FOR WANTING TO GET A HEAD START?
THANK-FULLY YOU STOPPED ME WHEN YOU DID, OR I'D HAVE COMPLETELY MISSED OUT.
WHAT WERE YOU HOPING TO FIND BACK HERE?
I'M SORRY. IT CAN WAIT. I DON'T WANT TO INTERRUPT YOUR LUNCH. US WORKING STIFFS, WE DON'T GET TOO MANY BREAKS, IF YOU KNOW WHAT I MEAN.
I DON'T.
BUT MAYBE YOU CAN EXPLAIN IT TO SECURITY.

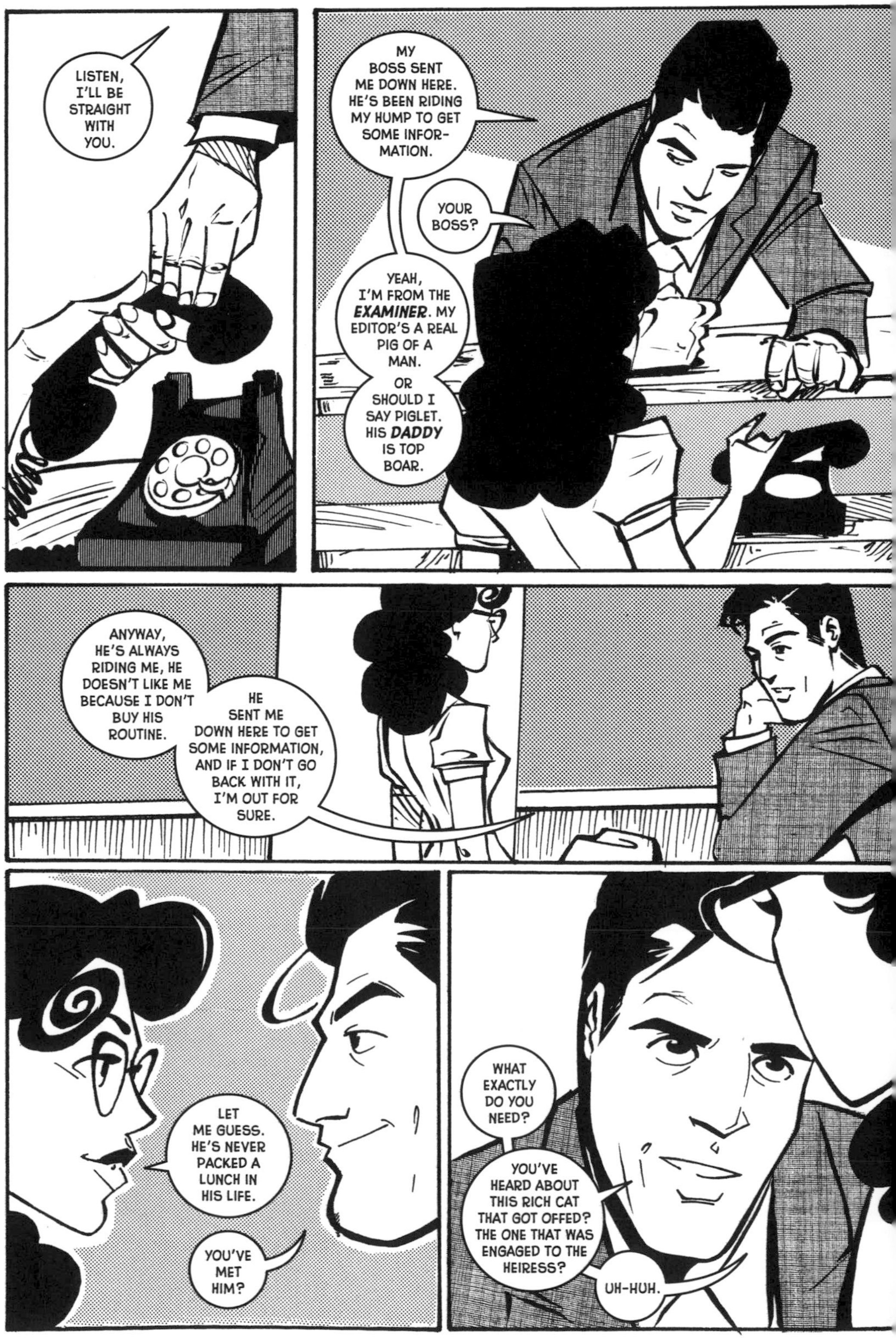
LISTEN, I'LL BE STRAIGHT WITH YOU.
MY BOSS SENT ME DOWN HERE. HE'S BEEN RIDING MY HUMP TO GET SOME INFOR-MATION.
YOUR BOSS?
YEAH, I'M FROM THE **EXAMINER**. MY EDITOR'S A REAL PIG OF A MAN.
OR SHOULD I SAY PIGLET. HIS **DADDY** IS TOP BOAR.
ANYWAY, HE'S ALWAYS RIDING ME, HE DOESN'T LIKE ME BECAUSE I DON'T BUY HIS ROUTINE.
HE SENT ME DOWN HERE TO GET SOME INFORMATION, AND IF I DON'T GO BACK WITH IT, I'M OUT FOR SURE.
LET ME GUESS. HE'S NEVER PACKED A LUNCH IN HIS LIFE.
YOU'VE MET HIM?
WHAT EXACTLY DO YOU NEED?
YOU'VE HEARD ABOUT THIS RICH CAT THAT GOT OFFED? THE ONE THAT WAS ENGAGED TO THE HEIRESS?
UH-HUH.

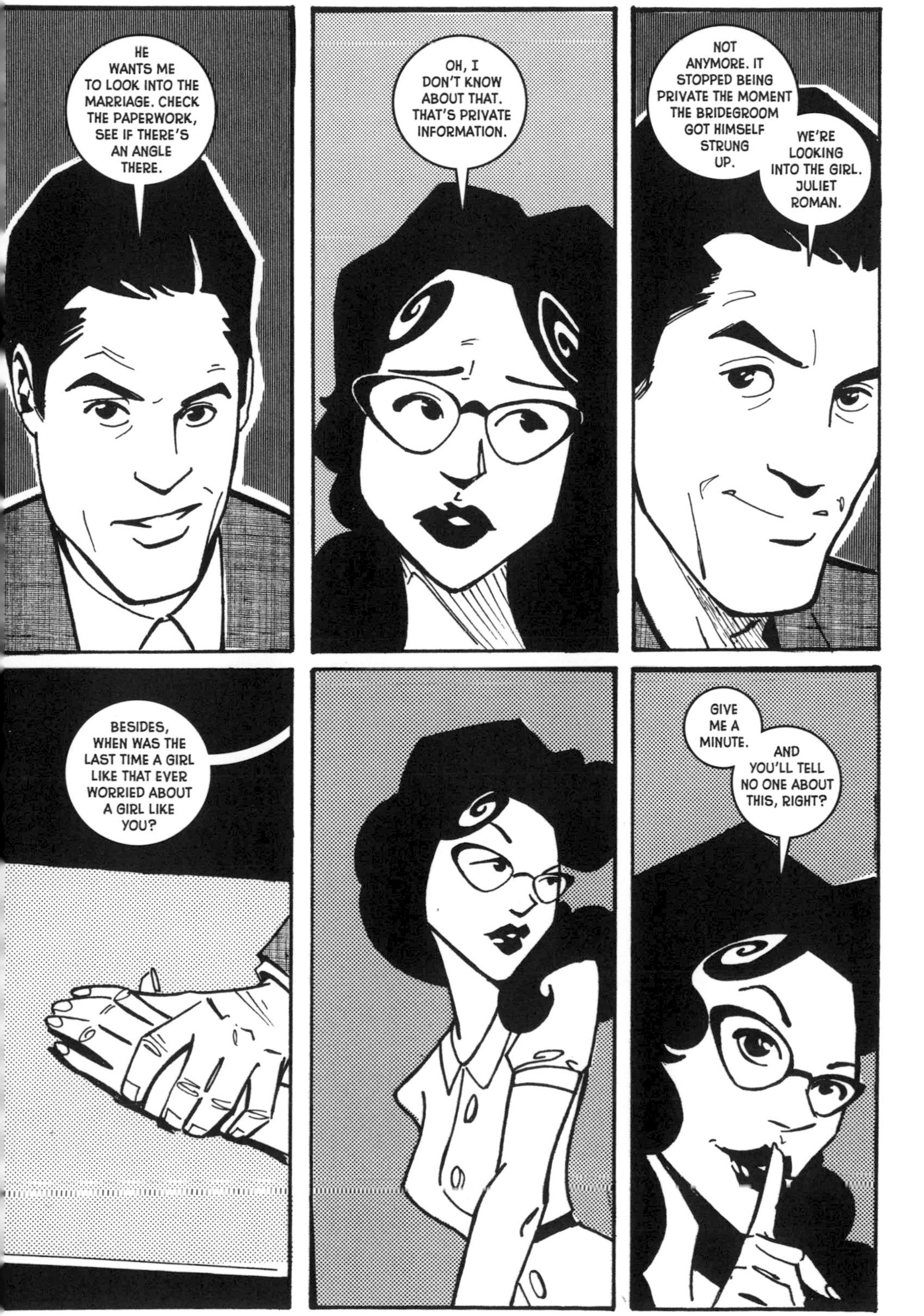
HE WANTS ME TO LOOK INTO THE MARRIAGE. CHECK THE PAPERWORK, SEE IF THERE'S AN ANGLE THERE.
OH, I DON'T KNOW ABOUT THAT. THAT'S PRIVATE INFORMATION.
NOT ANYMORE. IT STOPPED BEING PRIVATE THE MOMENT THE BRIDEGROOM GOT HIMSELF STRUNG UP.
WE'RE LOOKING INTO THE GIRL. JULIET ROMAN.
BESIDES, WHEN WAS THE LAST TIME A GIRL LIKE THAT EVER WORRIED ABOUT A GIRL LIKE YOU?
GIVE ME A MINUTE.
AND YOU'LL TELL NO ONE ABOUT THIS, RIGHT?

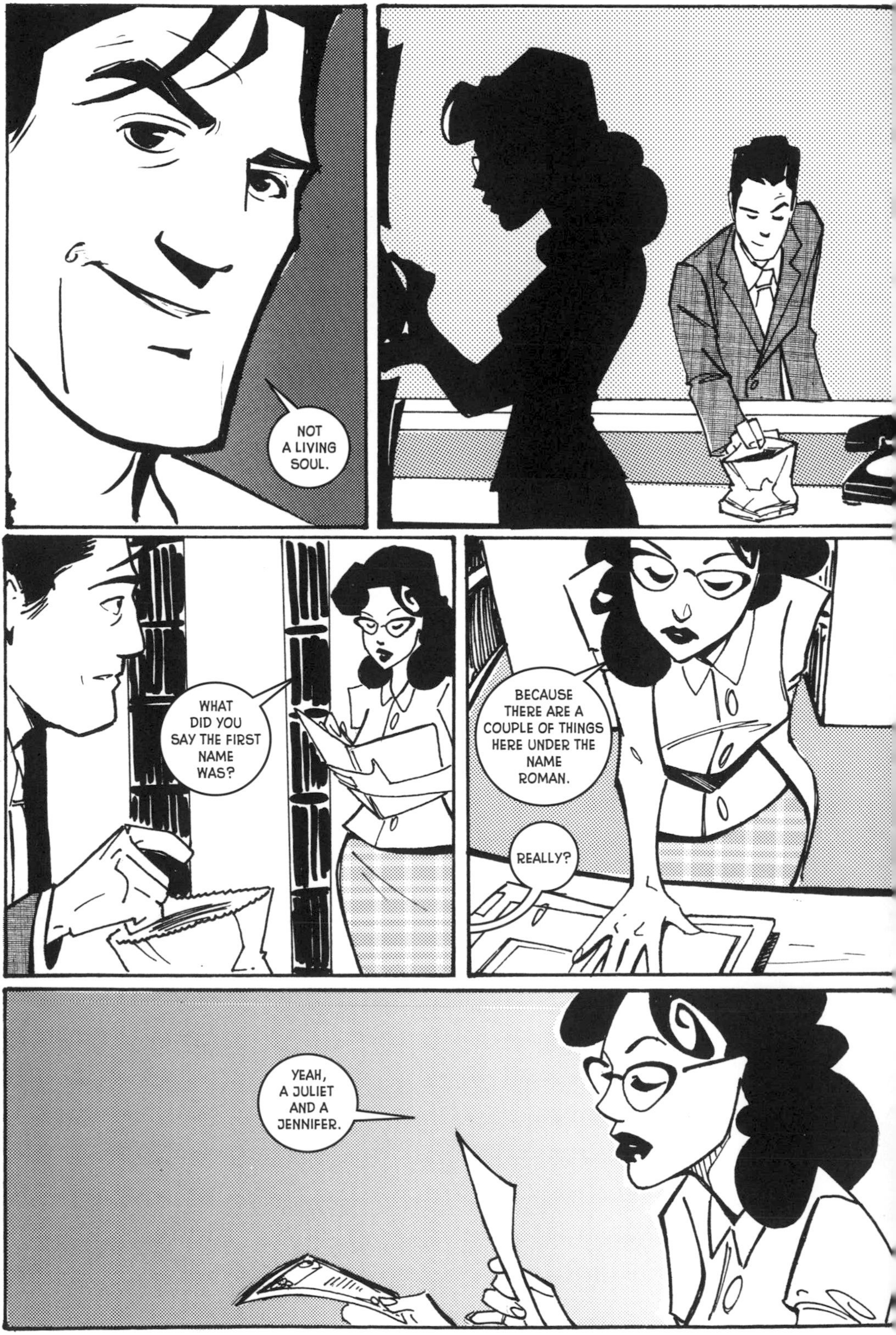
NOT A LIVING SOUL.
WHAT DID YOU SAY THE FIRST NAME WAS?
BECAUSE THERE ARE A COUPLE OF THINGS HERE UNDER THE NAME ROMAN.
REALLY?
YEAH, A JULIET AND A JENNIFER.

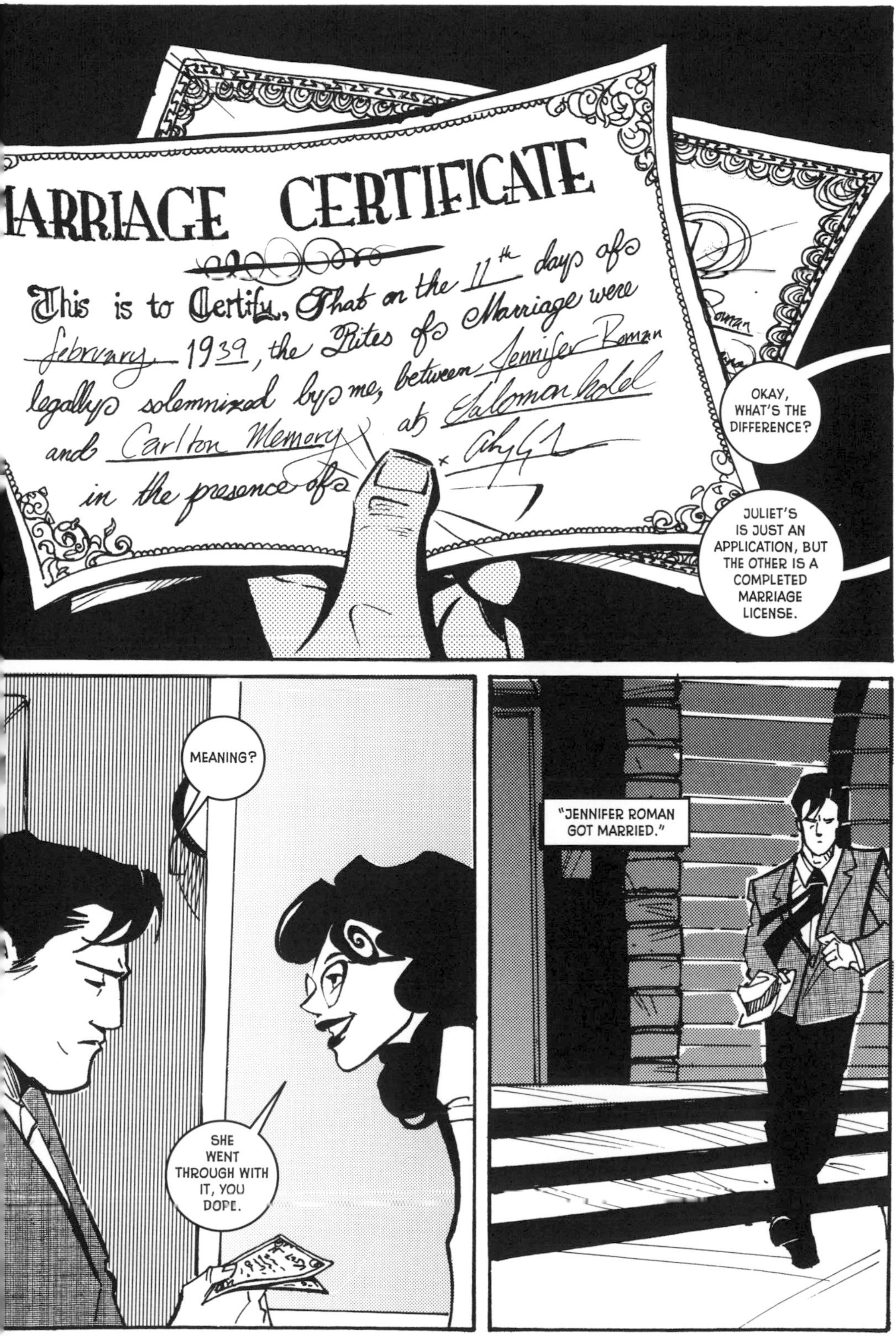
ARRIAGE CERTIFICATE
This is to Certify, That on the 11th days of February 1939, the Rites of Marriage were legally solemnized by me, between Jennifer Roman and Carlton Memory at Salomon Hotel
in the presence of
OKAY, WHAT'S THE DIFFERENCE?
JULIET'S IS JUST AN APPLICATION, BUT THE OTHER IS A COMPLETED MARRIAGE LICENSE.
MEANING?
SHE WENT THROUGH WITH IT, YOU DOPE.
"JENNIFER ROMAN GOT MARRIED."

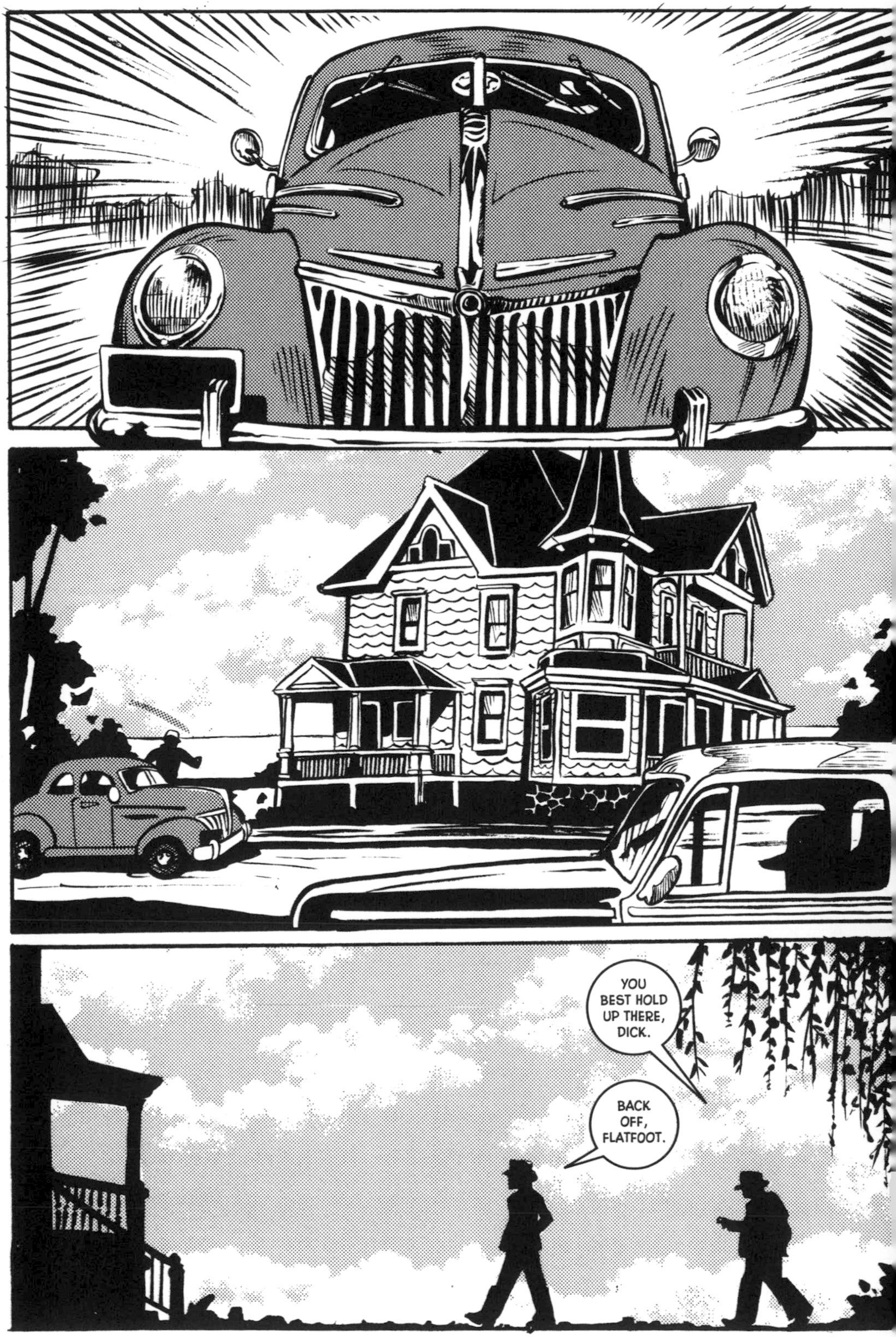
YOU BEST HOLD UP THERE, DICK.
BACK OFF, FLATFOOT.

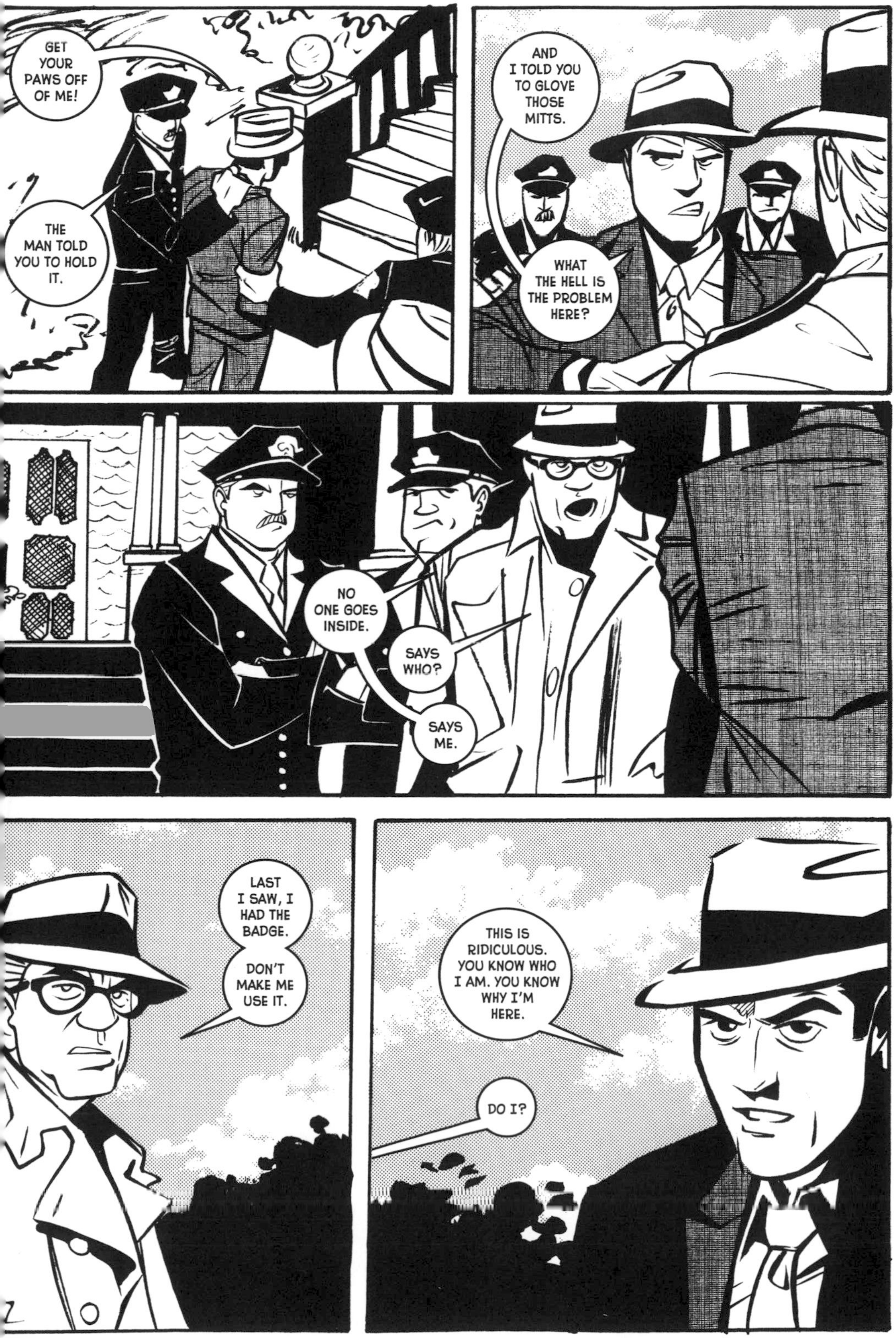
GET YOUR PAWS OFF OF ME!
THE MAN TOLD YOU TO HOLD IT.
AND I TOLD YOU TO GLOVE THOSE MITTS.
WHAT THE HELL IS THE PROBLEM HERE?
NO ONE GOES INSIDE.
SAYS WHO?
SAYS ME.
LAST I SAW, I HAD THE BADGE.
DON'T MAKE ME USE IT.
THIS IS RIDICULOUS. YOU KNOW WHO I AM. YOU KNOW WHY I'M HERE.
DO I?

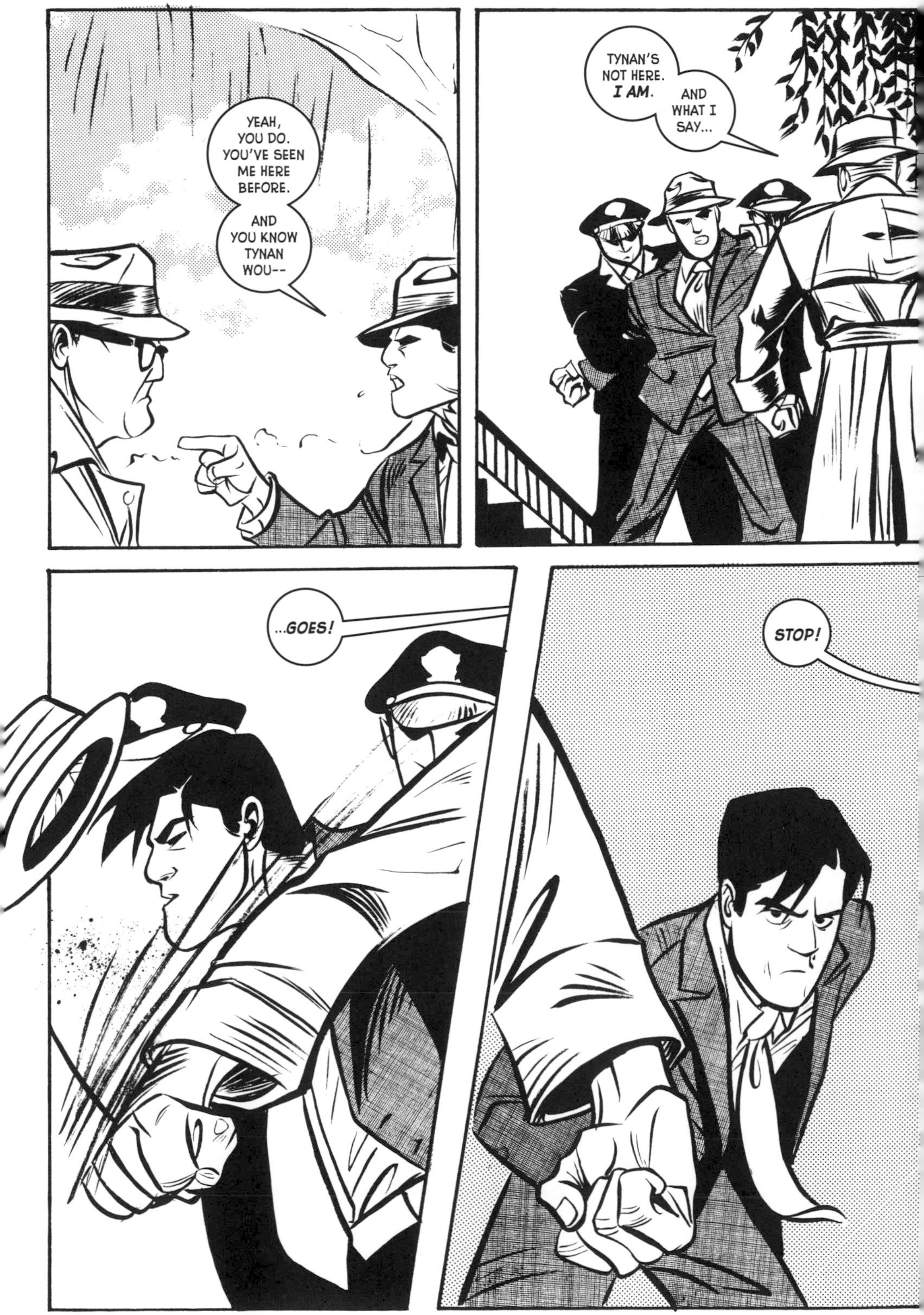
YEAH, YOU DO. YOU'VE SEEN ME HERE BEFORE.
AND YOU KNOW TYNAN WOU--
TYNAN'S NOT HERE. I AM.
AND WHAT I SAY...
...GOES!
STOP!

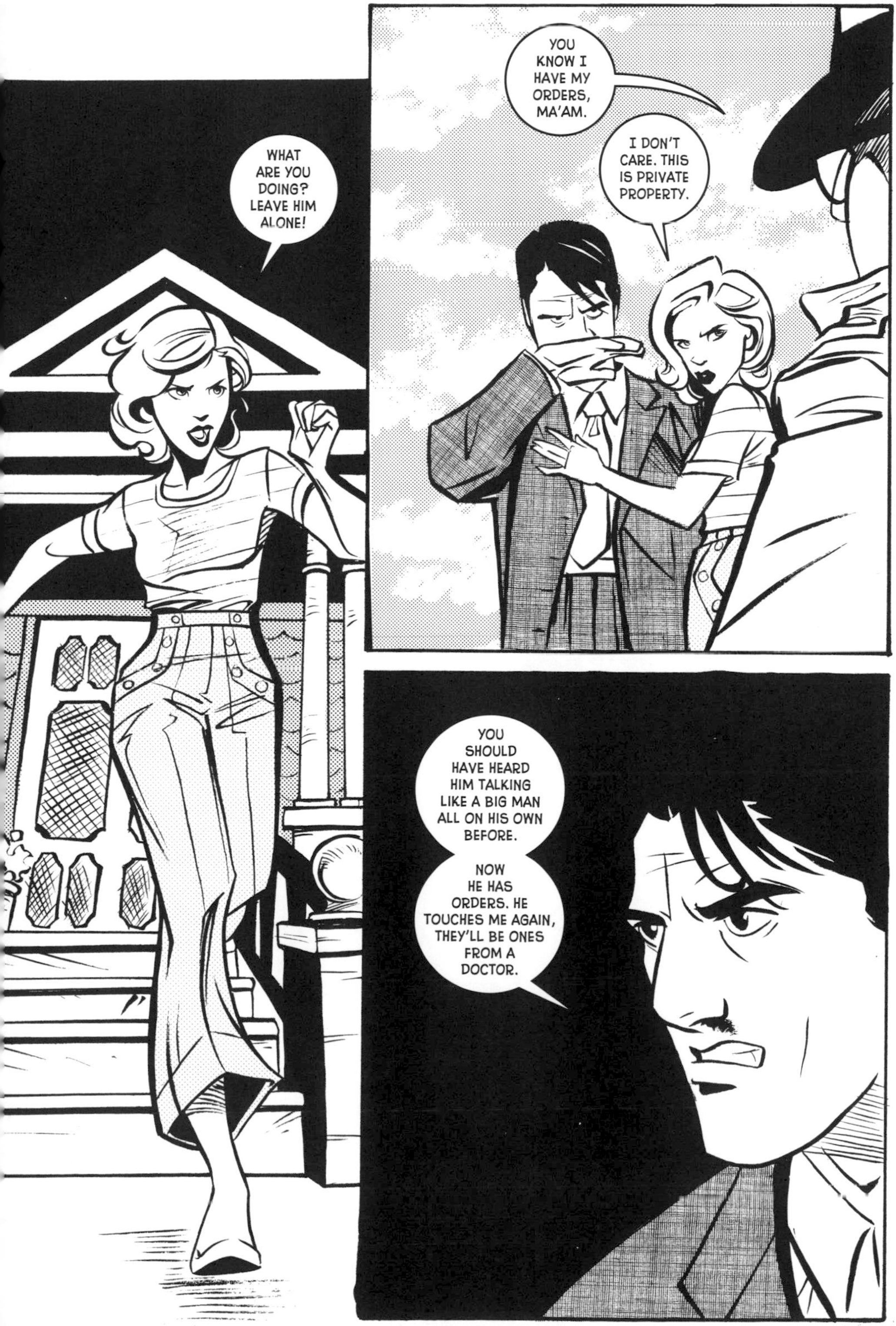
WHAT ARE YOU DOING? LEAVE HIM ALONE!
YOU KNOW I HAVE MY ORDERS, MA'AM.
I DON'T CARE. THIS IS PRIVATE PROPERTY.
YOU SHOULD HAVE HEARD HIM TALKING LIKE A BIG MAN ALL ON HIS OWN BEFORE.
NOW HE HAS ORDERS. HE TOUCHES ME AGAIN, THEY'LL BE ONES FROM A DOCTOR.

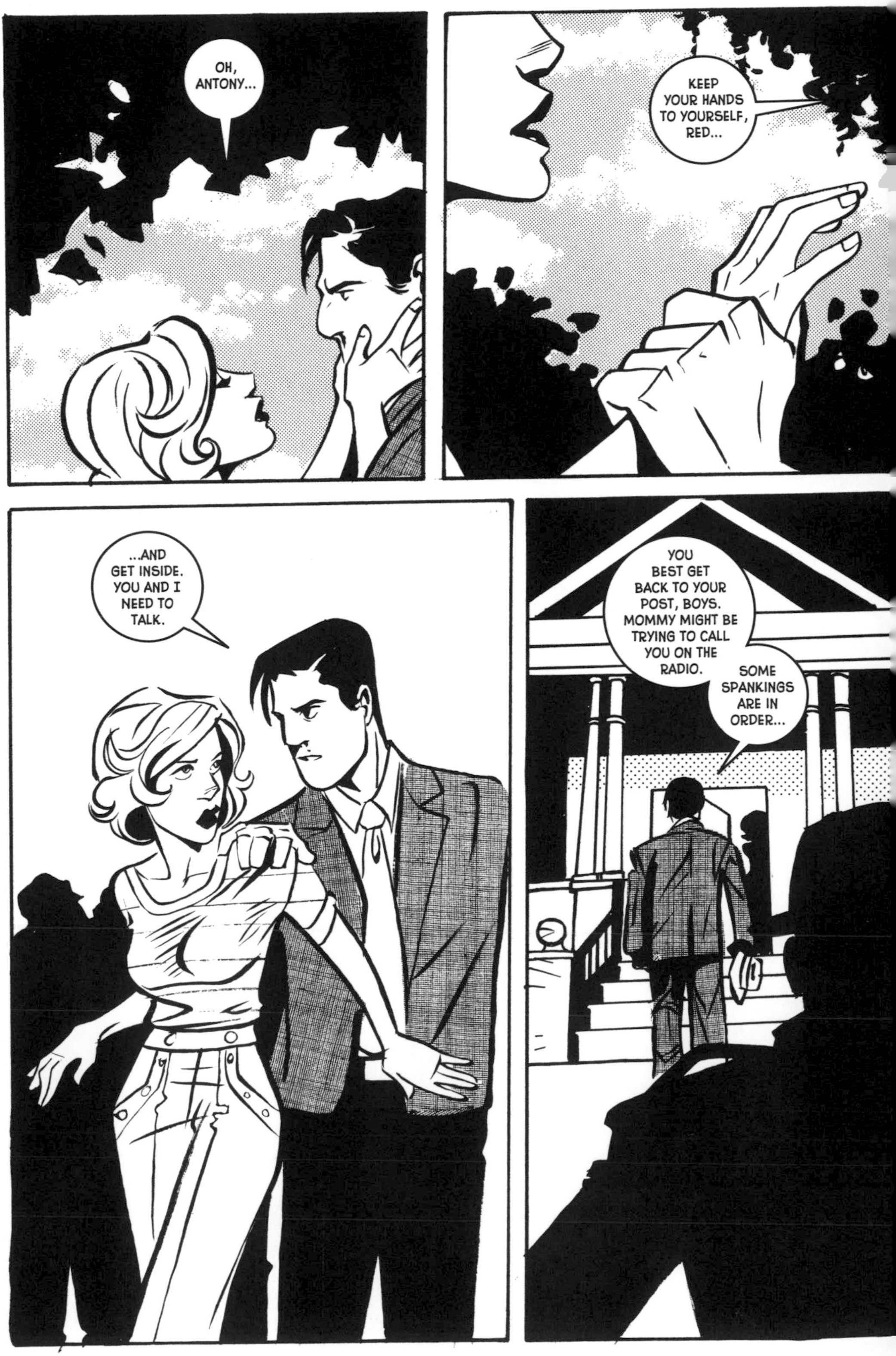
OH, ANTONY...
KEEP YOUR HANDS TO YOURSELF, RED...
...AND GET INSIDE. YOU AND I NEED TO TALK.
YOU BEST GET BACK TO YOUR POST, BOYS. MOMMY MIGHT BE TRYING TO CALL YOU ON THE RADIO.
SOME SPANKINGS ARE IN ORDER...

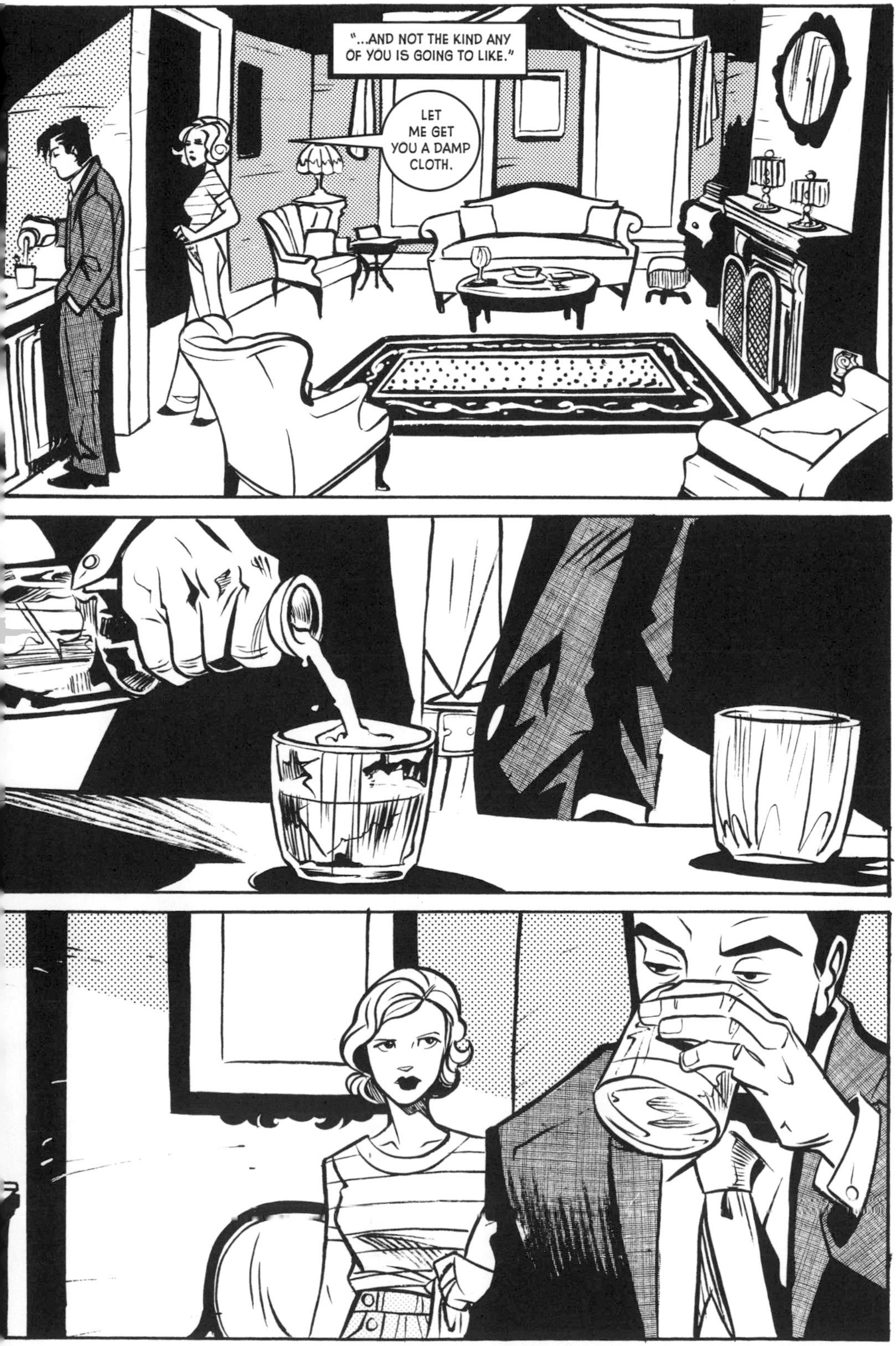
"...AND NOT THE KIND ANY OF YOU IS GOING TO LIKE."
LET ME GET YOU A DAMP CLOTH.

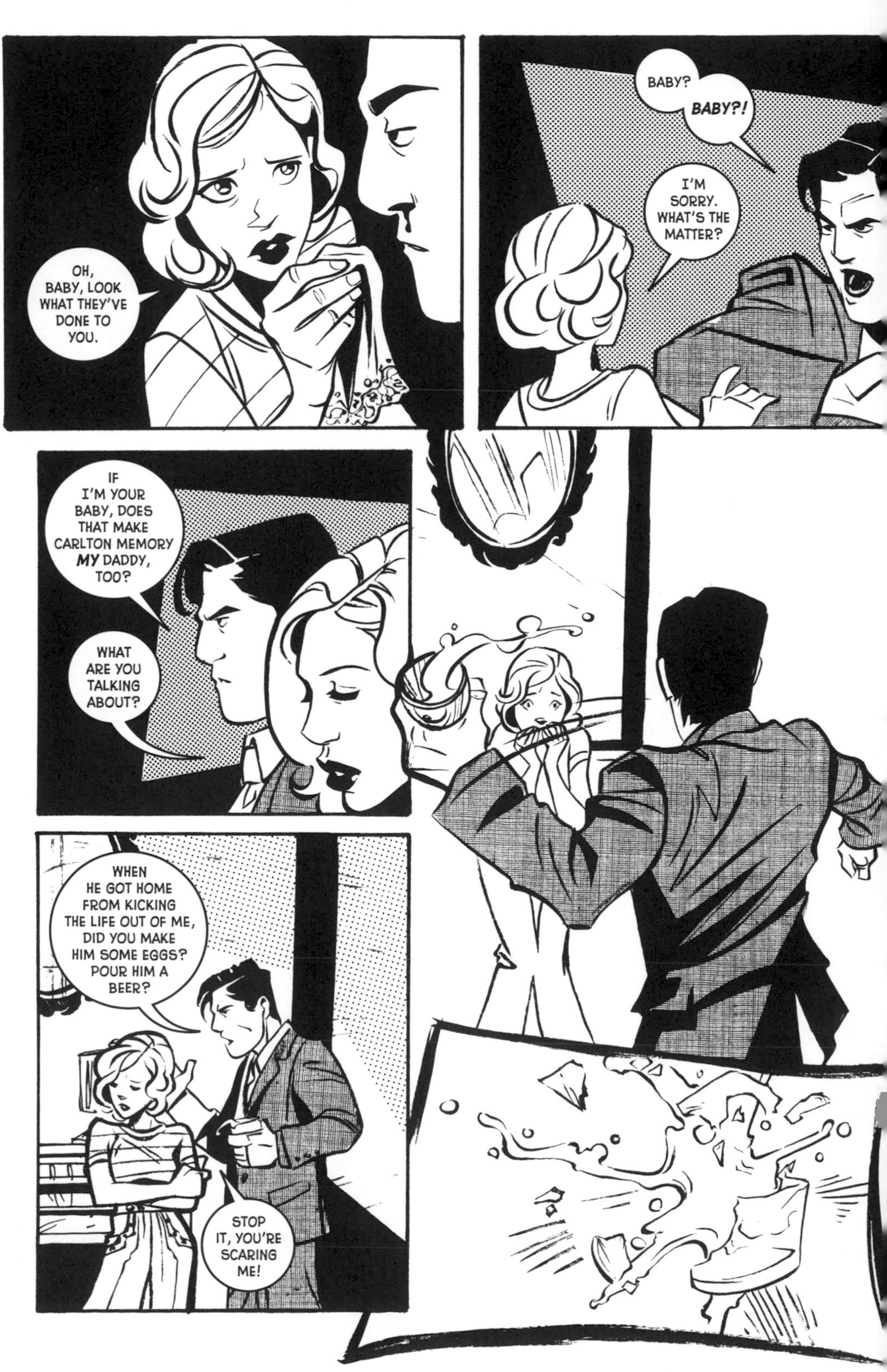
OH, BABY, LOOK WHAT THEY'VE DONE TO YOU.
BABY? BABY?!
I'M SORRY. WHAT'S THE MATTER?
IF I'M YOUR BABY, DOES THAT MAKE CARLTON MEMORY MY DADDY, TOO?
WHAT ARE YOU TALKING ABOUT?
WHEN HE GOT HOME FROM KICKING THE LIFE OUT OF ME, DID YOU MAKE HIM SOME EGGS? POUR HIM A BEER?
STOP IT, YOU'RE SCARING ME!

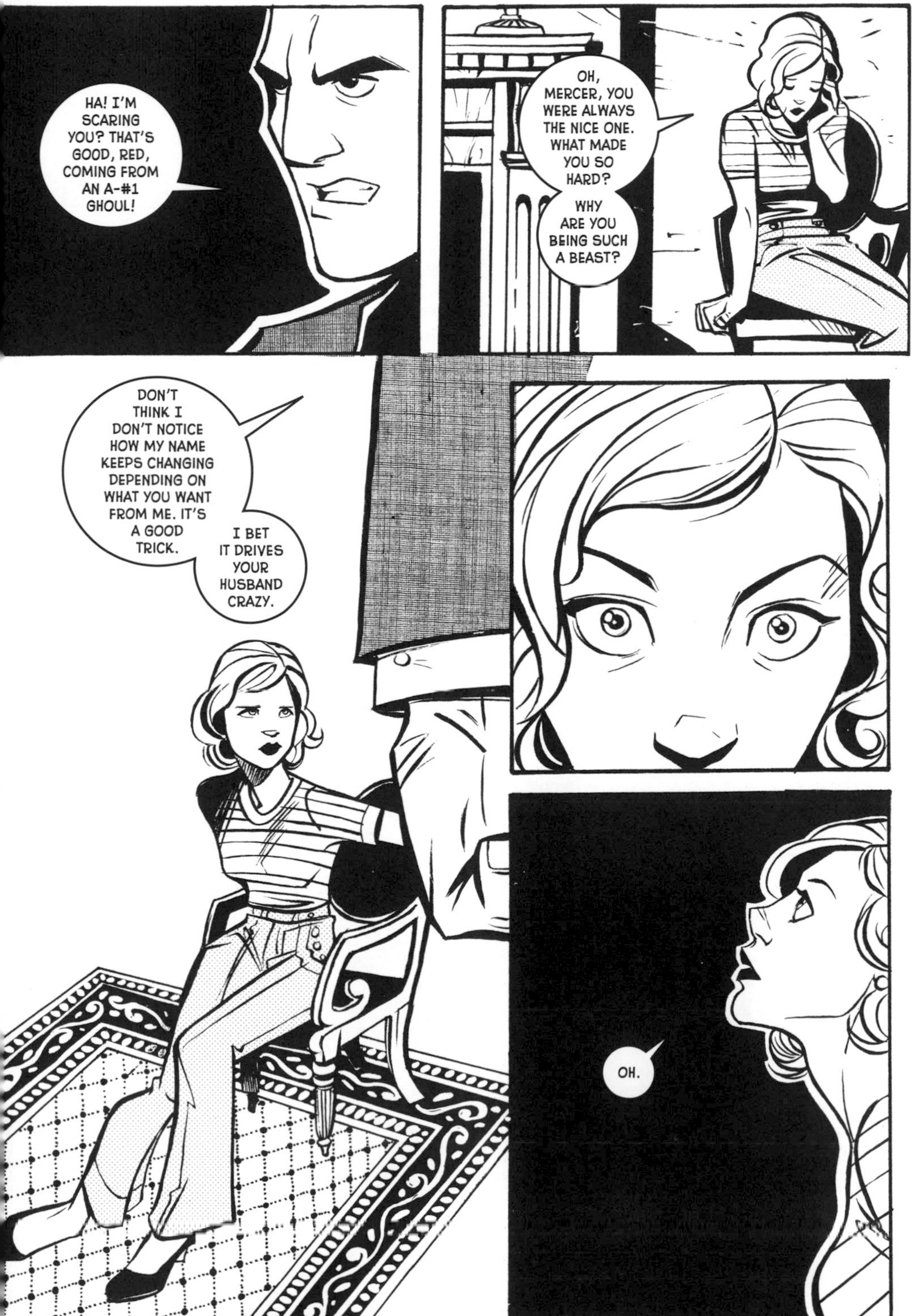
HA! I'M SCARING YOU? THAT'S GOOD, RED, COMING FROM AN A-#1 GHOUL!
OH, MERCER, YOU WERE ALWAYS THE NICE ONE. WHAT MADE YOU SO HARD?
WHY ARE YOU BEING SUCH A BEAST?
DON'T THINK I DON'T NOTICE HOW MY NAME KEEPS CHANGING DEPENDING ON WHAT YOU WANT FROM ME. IT'S A GOOD TRICK.
I BET IT DRIVES YOUR HUSBAND CRAZY.
OH.

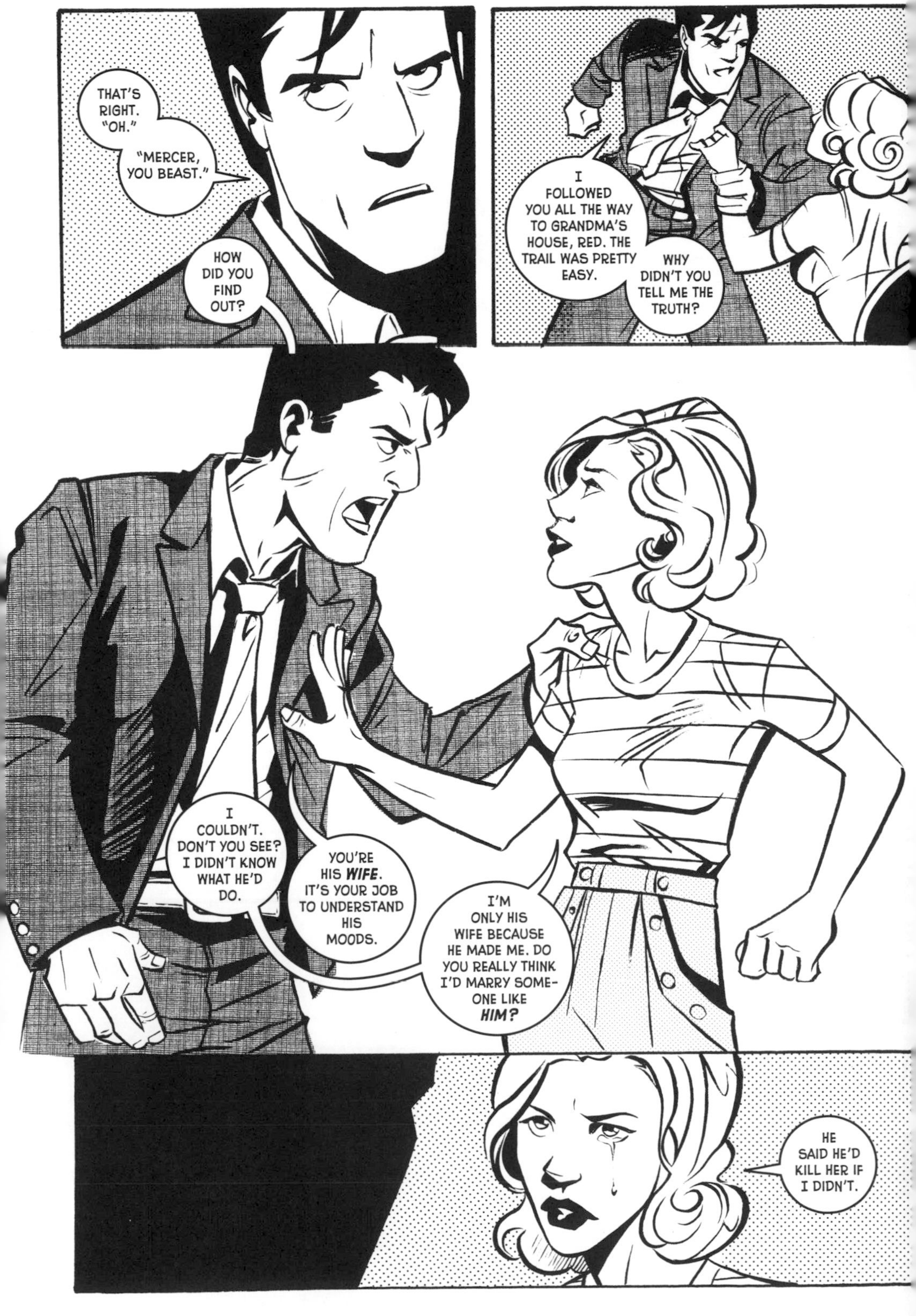
THAT'S RIGHT. "OH."
"MERCER, YOU BEAST."
HOW DID YOU FIND OUT?
I FOLLOWED YOU ALL THE WAY TO GRANDMA'S HOUSE, RED. THE TRAIL WAS PRETTY EASY.
WHY DIDN'T YOU TELL ME THE TRUTH?
I COULDN'T. DON'T YOU SEE? I DIDN'T KNOW WHAT HE'D DO.
YOU'RE HIS ***WIFE***. IT'S YOUR JOB TO UNDERSTAND HIS MOODS.
I'M ONLY HIS WIFE BECAUSE HE MADE ME. DO YOU REALLY THINK I'D MARRY SOME-ONE LIKE ***HIM?***
HE SAID HE'D KILL HER IF I DIDN'T.

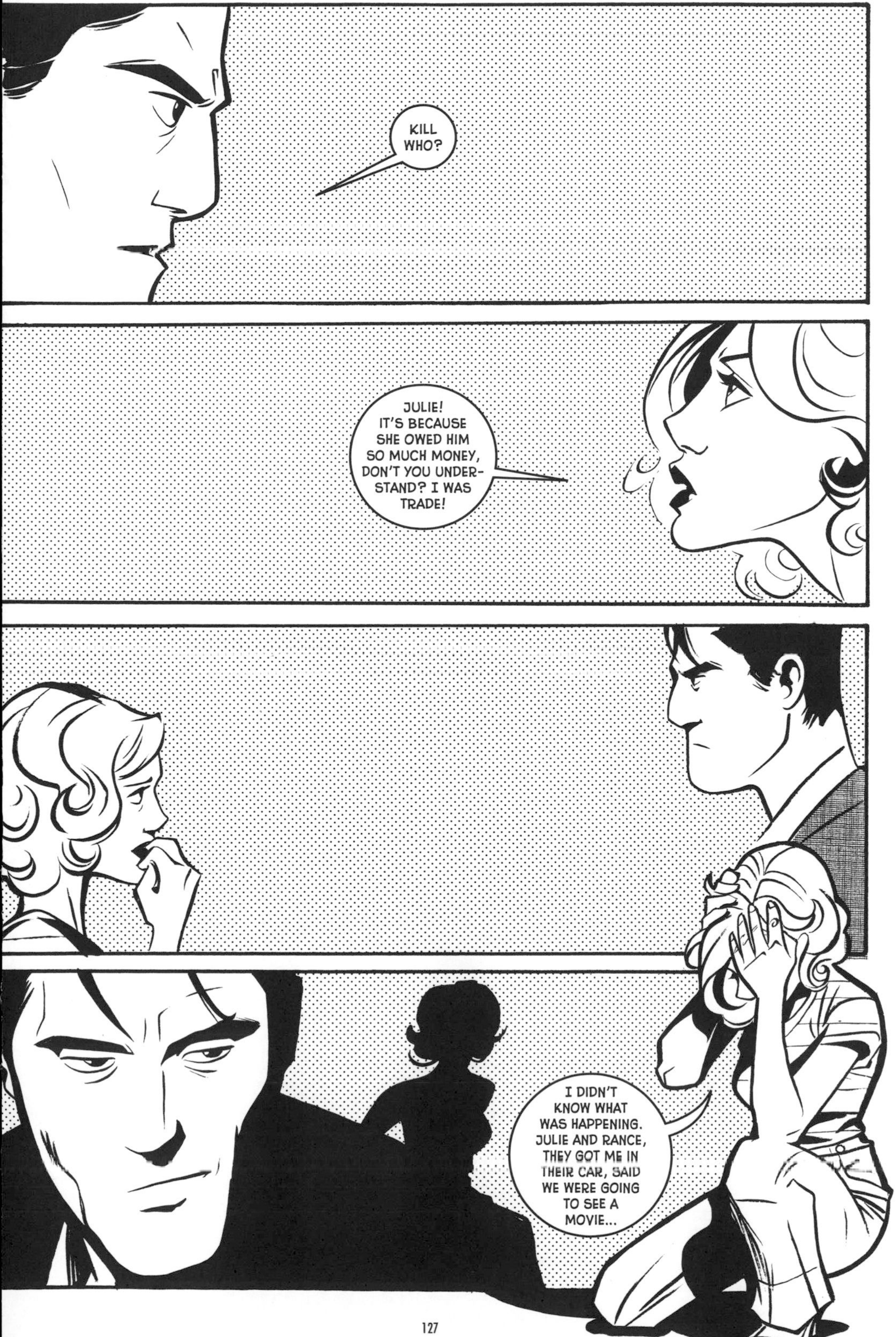
KILL WHO?
JULIE! IT'S BECAUSE SHE OWED HIM SO MUCH MONEY, DON'T YOU UNDERSTAND? I WAS TRADE!
I DIDN'T KNOW WHAT WAS HAPPENING. JULIE AND RANCE, THEY GOT ME IN THEIR CAR, SAID WE WERE GOING TO SEE A MOVIE...

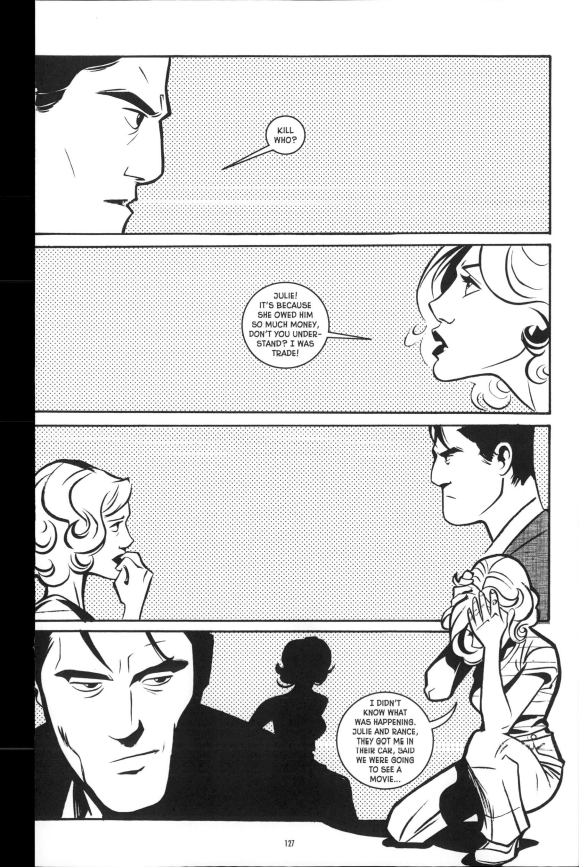

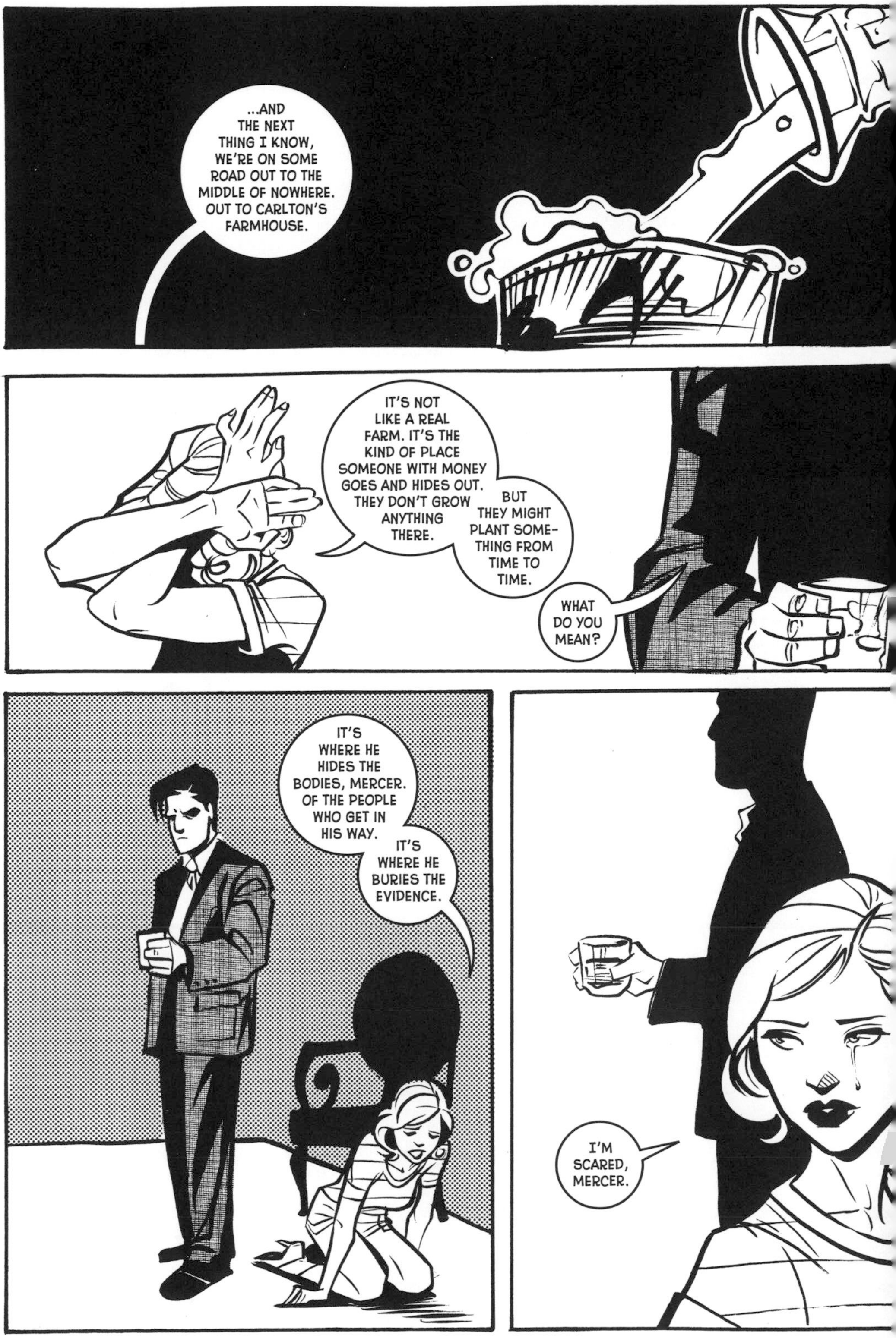
...AND THE NEXT THING I KNOW, WE'RE ON SOME ROAD OUT TO THE MIDDLE OF NOWHERE. OUT TO CARLTON'S FARMHOUSE.
IT'S NOT LIKE A REAL FARM. IT'S THE KIND OF PLACE SOMEONE WITH MONEY GOES AND HIDES OUT. THEY DON'T GROW ANYTHING THERE.
BUT THEY MIGHT PLANT SOME-THING FROM TIME TO TIME.
WHAT DO YOU MEAN?
IT'S WHERE HE HIDES THE BODIES, MERCER. OF THE PEOPLE WHO GET IN HIS WAY.
IT'S WHERE HE BURIES THE EVIDENCE.
I'M SCARED, MERCER.

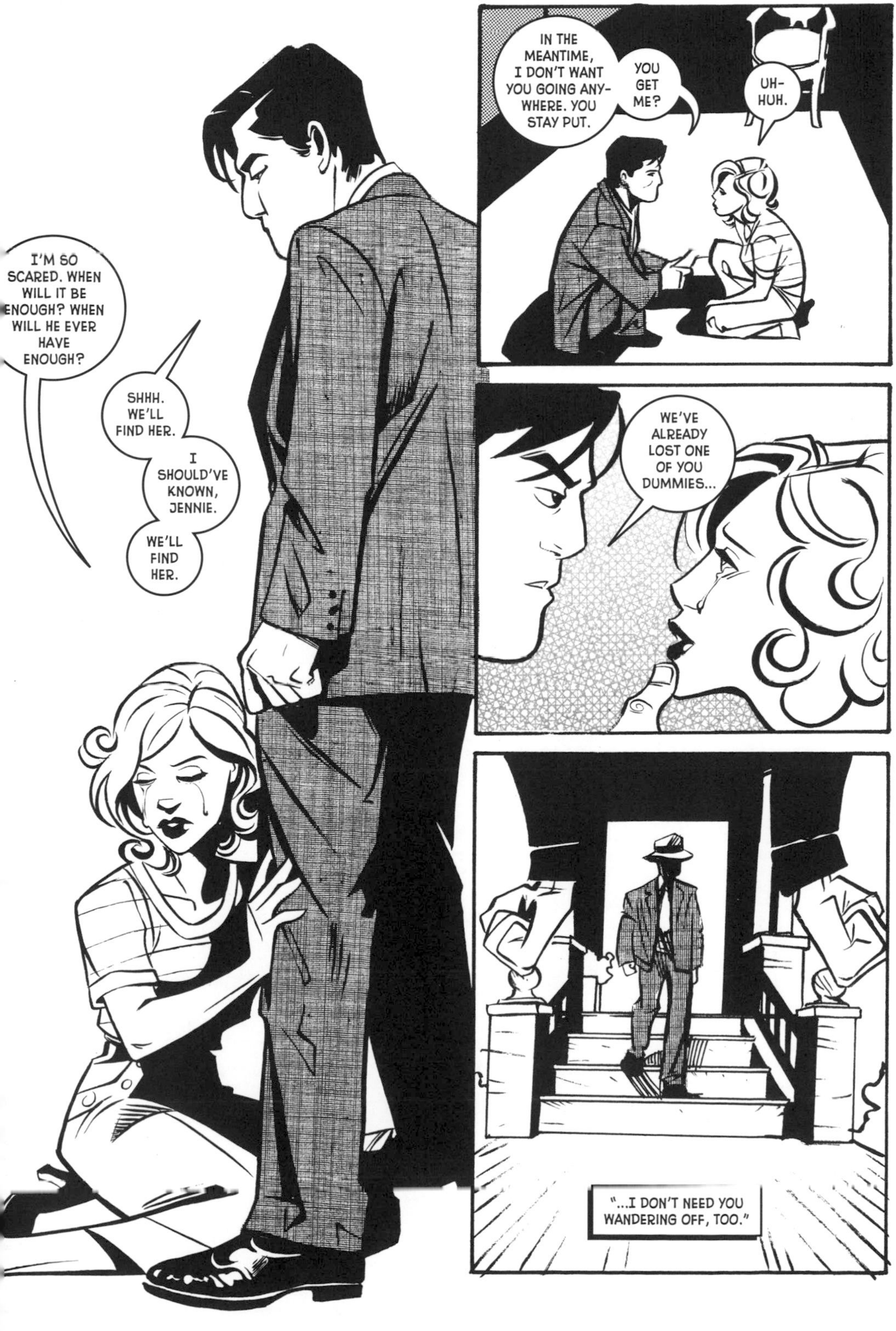
I'M SO SCARED. WHEN WILL IT BE ENOUGH? WHEN WILL HE EVER HAVE ENOUGH?
SHHH. WE'LL FIND HER.
I SHOULD'VE KNOWN, JENNIE.
WE'LL FIND HER.
IN THE MEANTIME, I DON'T WANT YOU GOING ANY-WHERE. YOU STAY PUT.
YOU GET ME?
UH-HUH.
WE'VE ALREADY LOST ONE OF YOU DUMMIES...
"...I DON'T NEED YOU WANDERING OFF, TOO."

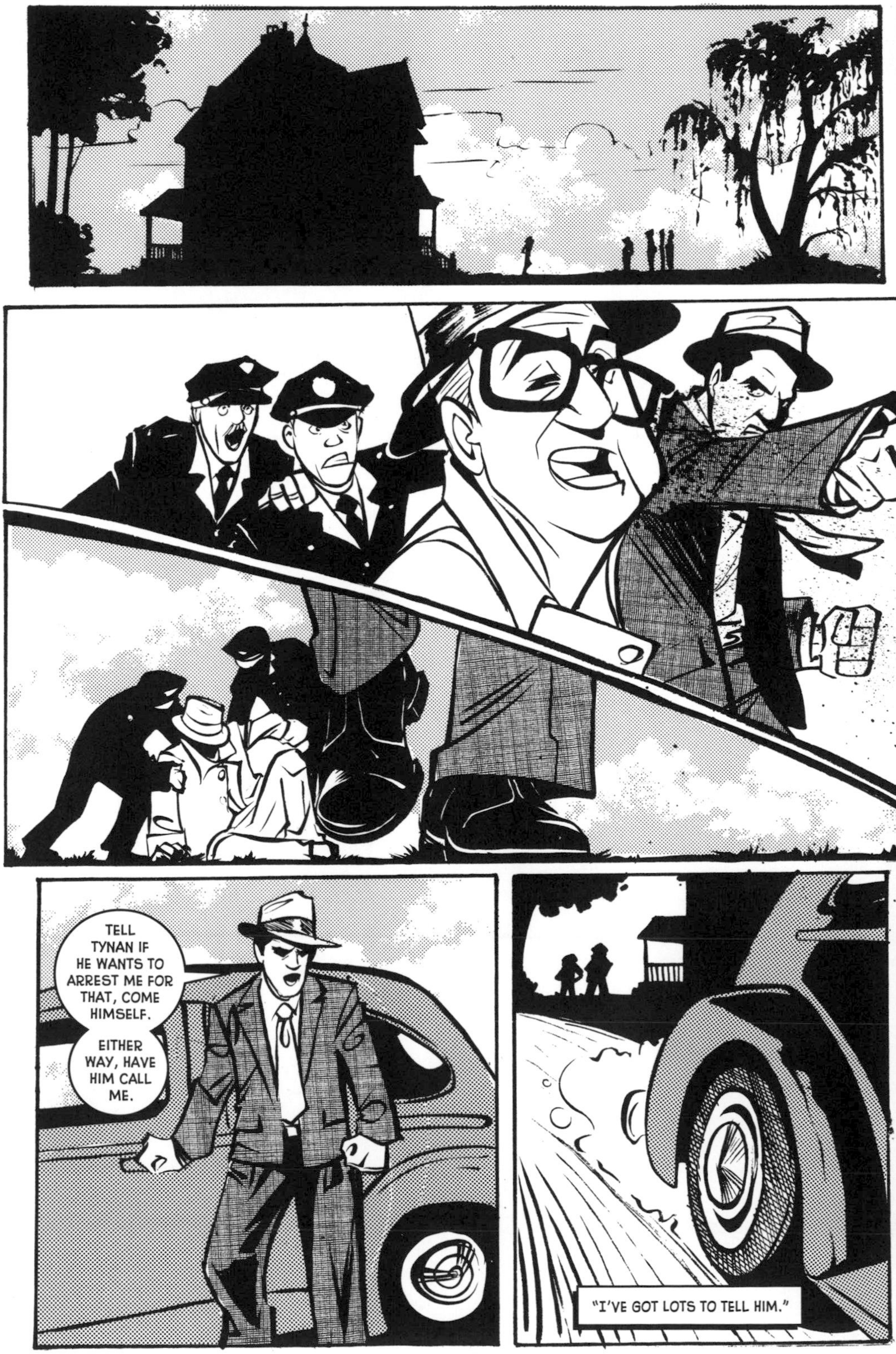
TELL TYNAN IF HE WANTS TO ARREST ME FOR THAT, COME HIMSELF.
EITHER WAY, HAVE HIM CALL ME.
"I'VE GOT LOTS TO TELL HIM."

CHAPTER 7

I DON'T MIND THE CUTS AND BRUISES.

ANYTHING YOU CAN PUT A BANDAGE OVER WILL EVENTUALLY CLOSE UP...

EVEN IF IT LEAVES A MARK, YOU'VE GOT A NEW ANECDOTE.

"SEE THIS HERE ON MY CHIN? THAT'S WHEN I WALKED INTO SOME GUY'S ELBOW."

...WILL EVENTUALLY FADE AWAY.

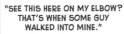

"SEE THIS HERE ON MY ELBOW? THAT'S WHEN SOME GUY WALKED INTO MINE."

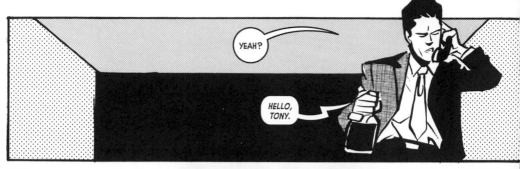

YEAH?

HELLO, TONY.

HELLO YOURSELF. WHO IS THIS?

MY, HOW QUICKLY THEY FORGET.

JULIE?

I HEAR YOU'VE BEEN MAKING ALL SORTS OF NOISE AROUND TOWN, BANGING ON POTS AND PANS AND SCREAMING YOUR HEAD OFF.

I NEED YOU TO CUT IT OUT, TONY. YOU'RE GOING TO GET ME IN TROUBLE.

I HATE TO BREAK IT TO YOU, BUT YOU'RE ALREADY IN TROUBLE.

LET ME SEE YOU, JULIE. ALL I NEED TO KNOW IS YOU'RE OKAY. JUST SO I CAN TELL YOUR FOLKS. THEN I'LL CALL IT OFF. I SWEAR.

...

FINE. MEET ME...

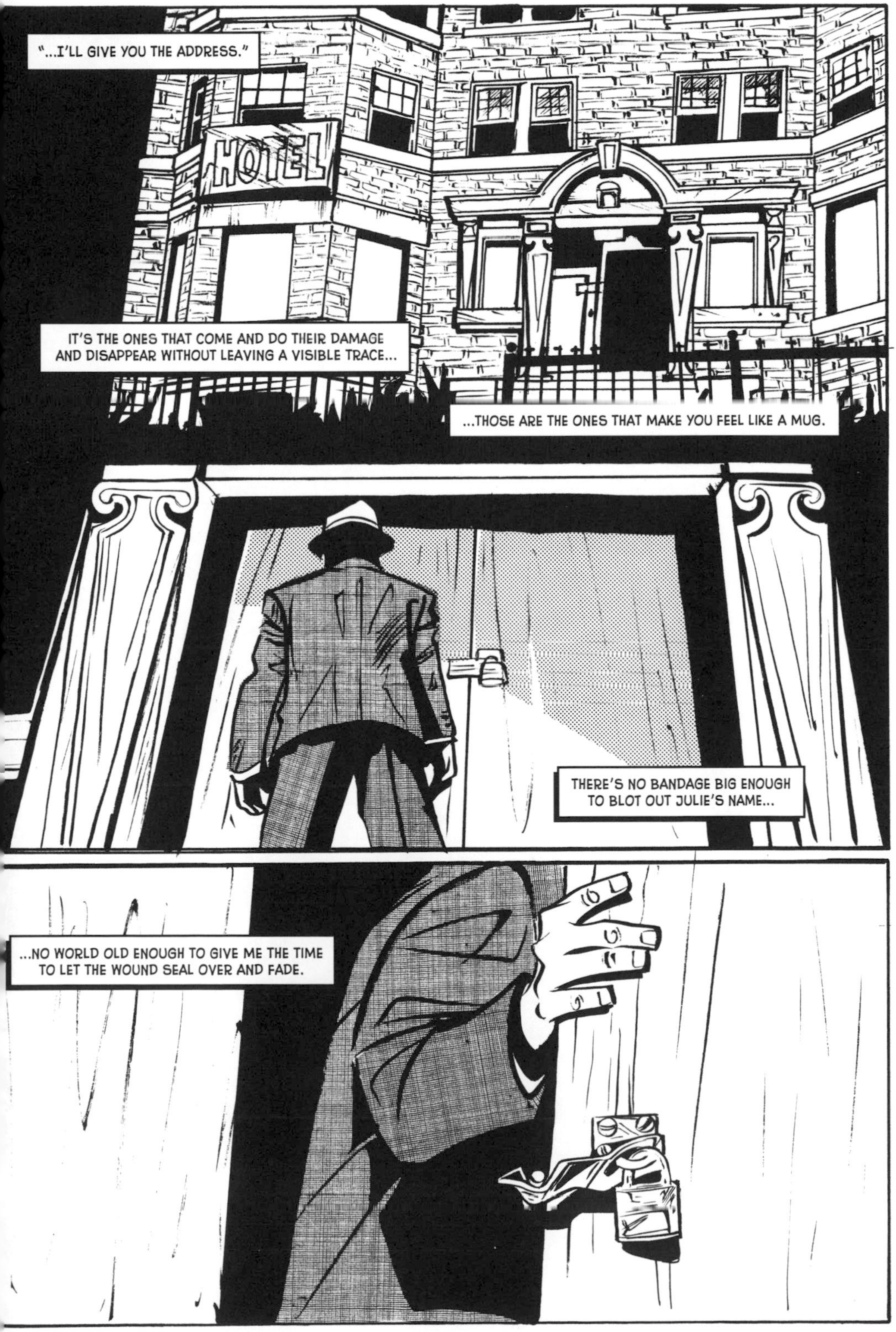
"...I'LL GIVE YOU THE ADDRESS."
IT'S THE ONES THAT COME AND DO THEIR DAMAGE AND DISAPPEAR WITHOUT LEAVING A VISIBLE TRACE...
HOTEL
...THOSE ARE THE ONES THAT MAKE YOU FEEL LIKE A MUG.
THERE'S NO BANDAGE BIG ENOUGH TO BLOT OUT JULIE'S NAME...
...NO WORLD OLD ENOUGH TO GIVE ME THE TIME TO LET THE WOUND SEAL OVER AND FADE.

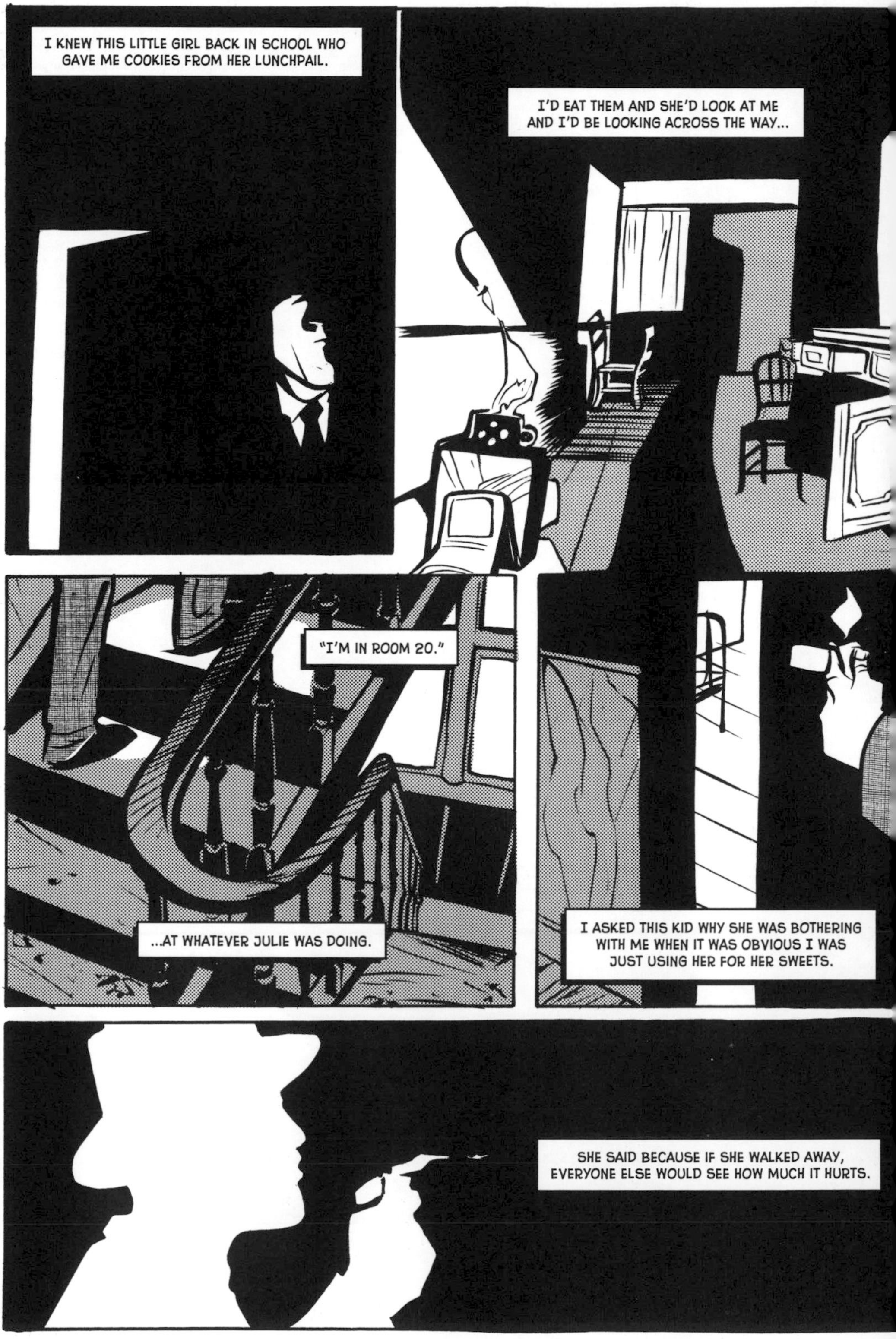
I KNEW THIS LITTLE GIRL BACK IN SCHOOL WHO GAVE ME COOKIES FROM HER LUNCHPAIL.
I'D EAT THEM AND SHE'D LOOK AT ME AND I'D BE LOOKING ACROSS THE WAY...
"I'M IN ROOM 20."
...AT WHATEVER JULIE WAS DOING.
I ASKED THIS KID WHY SHE WAS BOTHERING WITH ME WHEN IT WAS OBVIOUS I WAS JUST USING HER FOR HER SWEETS.
SHE SAID BECAUSE IF SHE WALKED AWAY, EVERYONE ELSE WOULD SEE HOW MUCH IT HURTS.

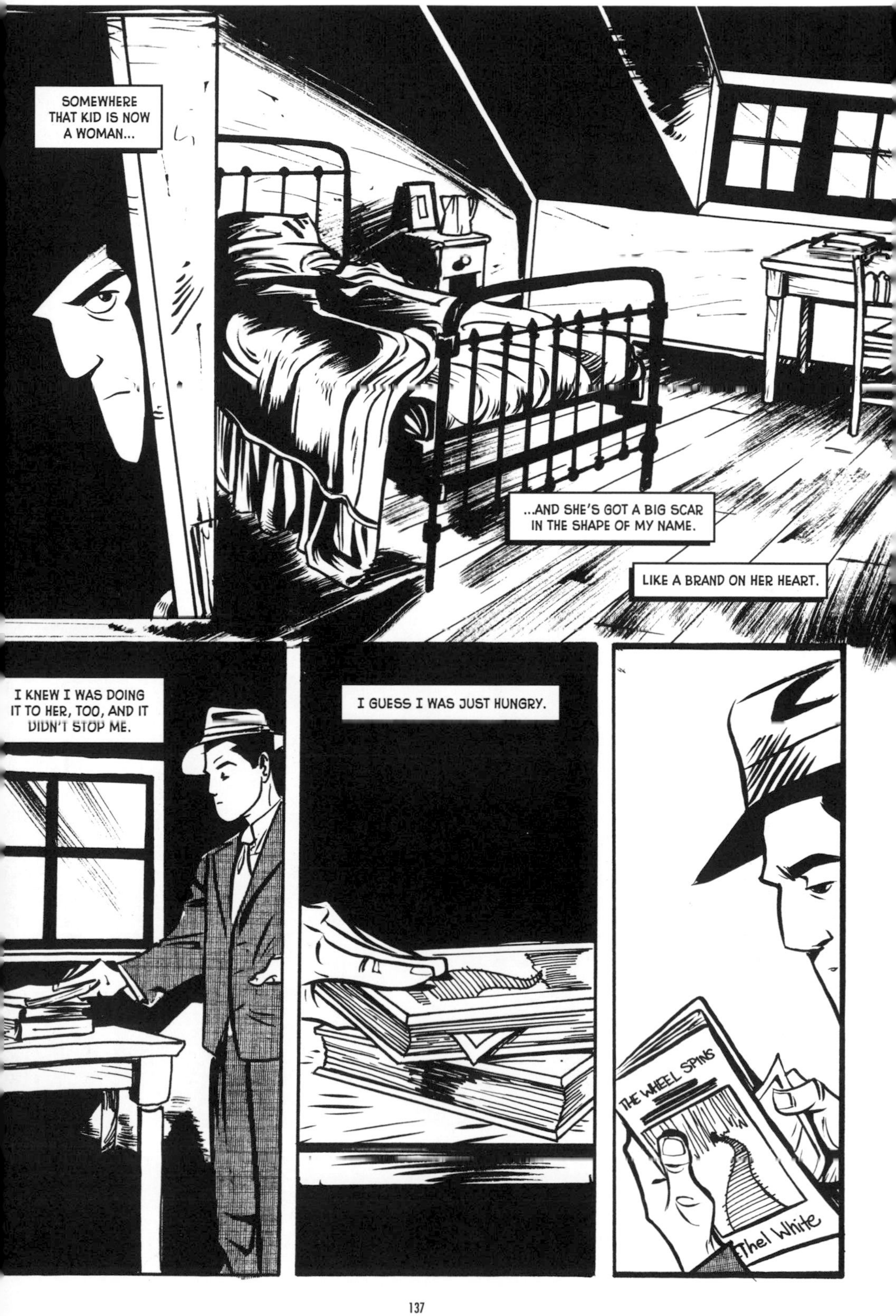
SOMEWHERE THAT KID IS NOW A WOMAN...
...AND SHE'S GOT A BIG SCAR IN THE SHAPE OF MY NAME.
LIKE A BRAND ON HER HEART.
I KNEW I WAS DOING IT TO HER, TOO, AND IT DIDN'T STOP ME.
I GUESS I WAS JUST HUNGRY.
THE WHEEL SPINS
Ethel White

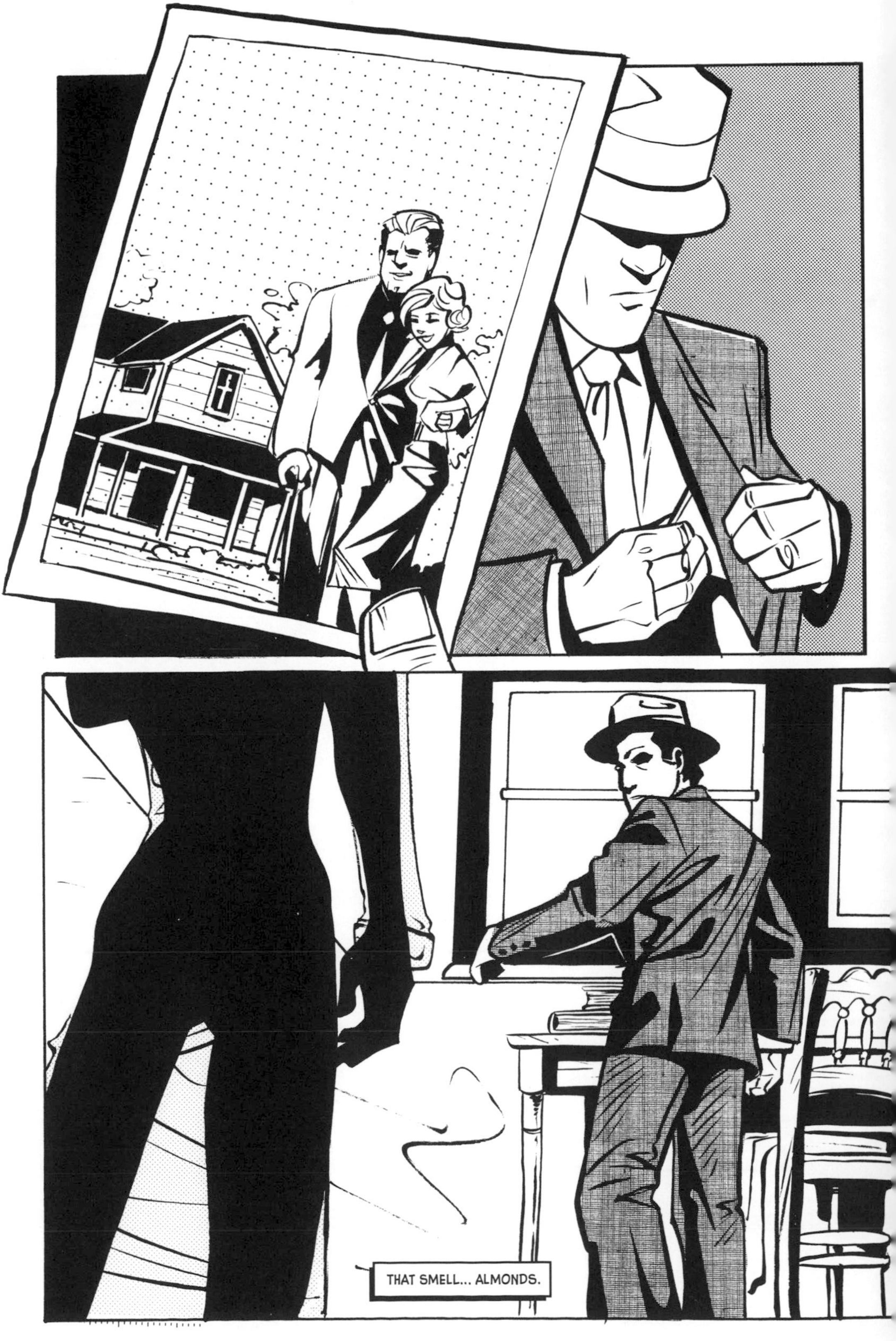
THAT SMELL... ALMONDS.

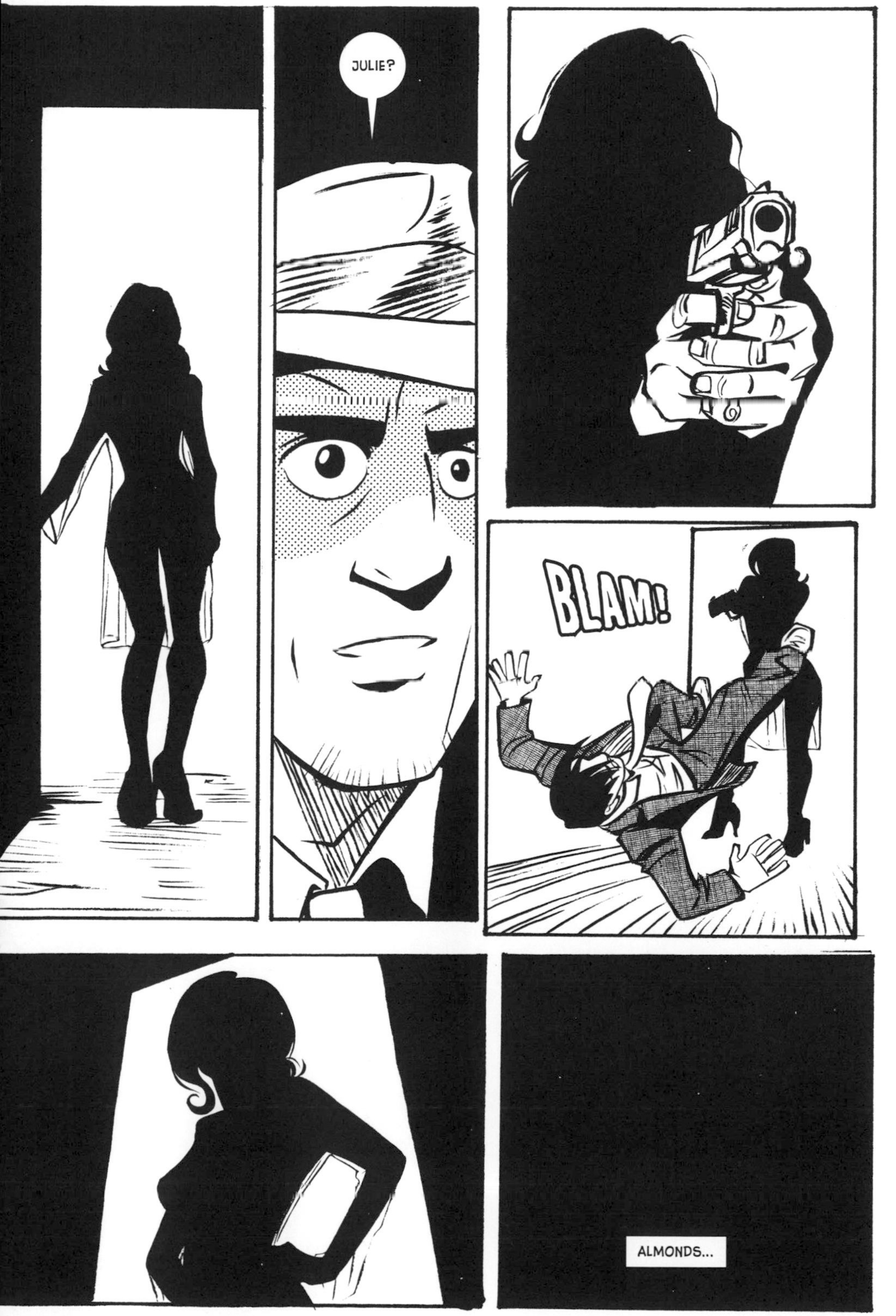
JULIE?
BLAM!
ALMONDS...

CHAPTER 8

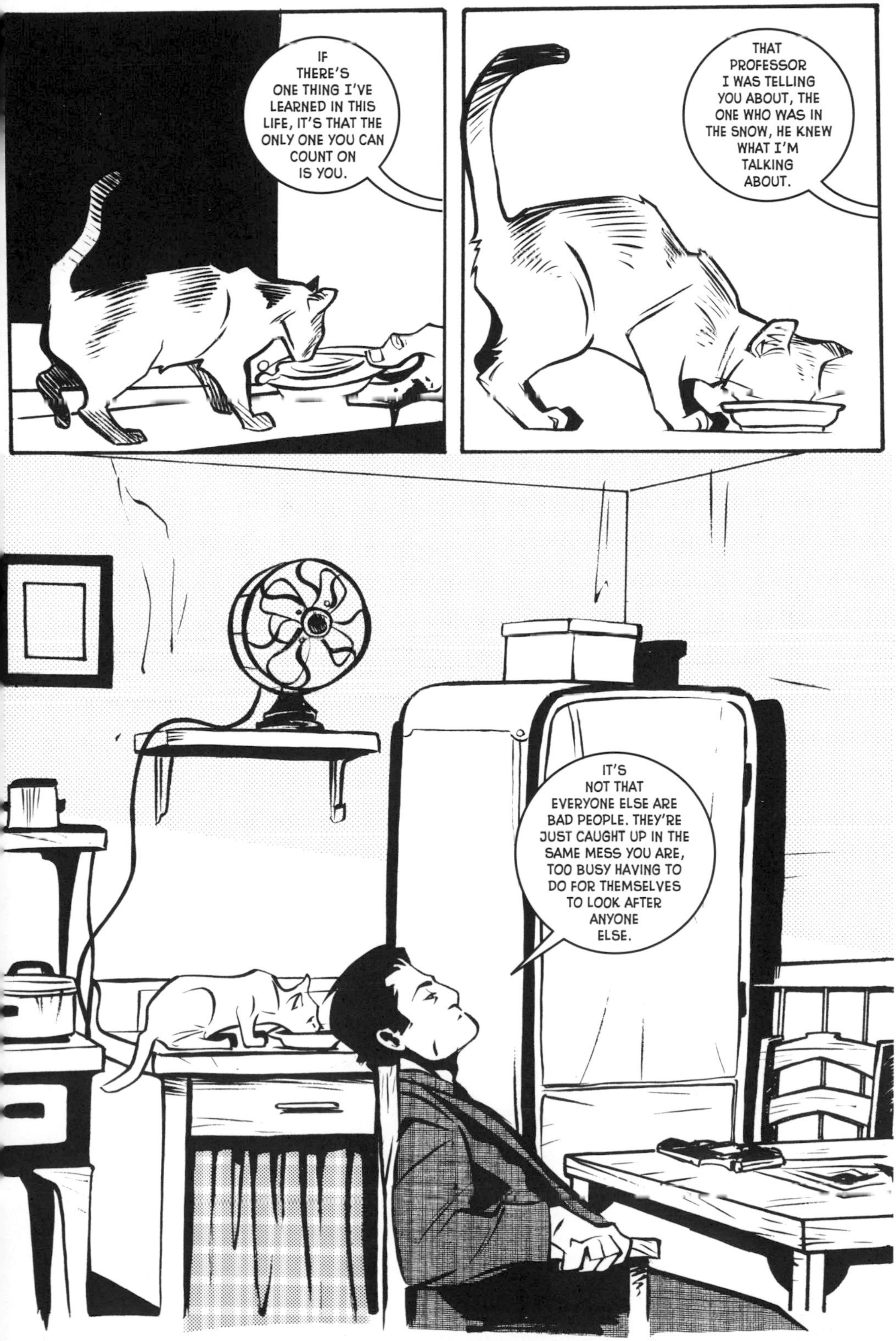
IF THERE'S ONE THING I'VE LEARNED IN THIS LIFE, IT'S THAT THE ONLY ONE YOU CAN COUNT ON IS YOU.
THAT PROFESSOR I WAS TELLING YOU ABOUT, THE ONE WHO WAS IN THE SNOW, HE KNEW WHAT I'M TALKING ABOUT.
IT'S NOT THAT EVERYONE ELSE ARE BAD PEOPLE. THEY'RE JUST CAUGHT UP IN THE SAME MESS YOU ARE, TOO BUSY HAVING TO DO FOR THEMSELVES TO LOOK AFTER ANYONE ELSE.

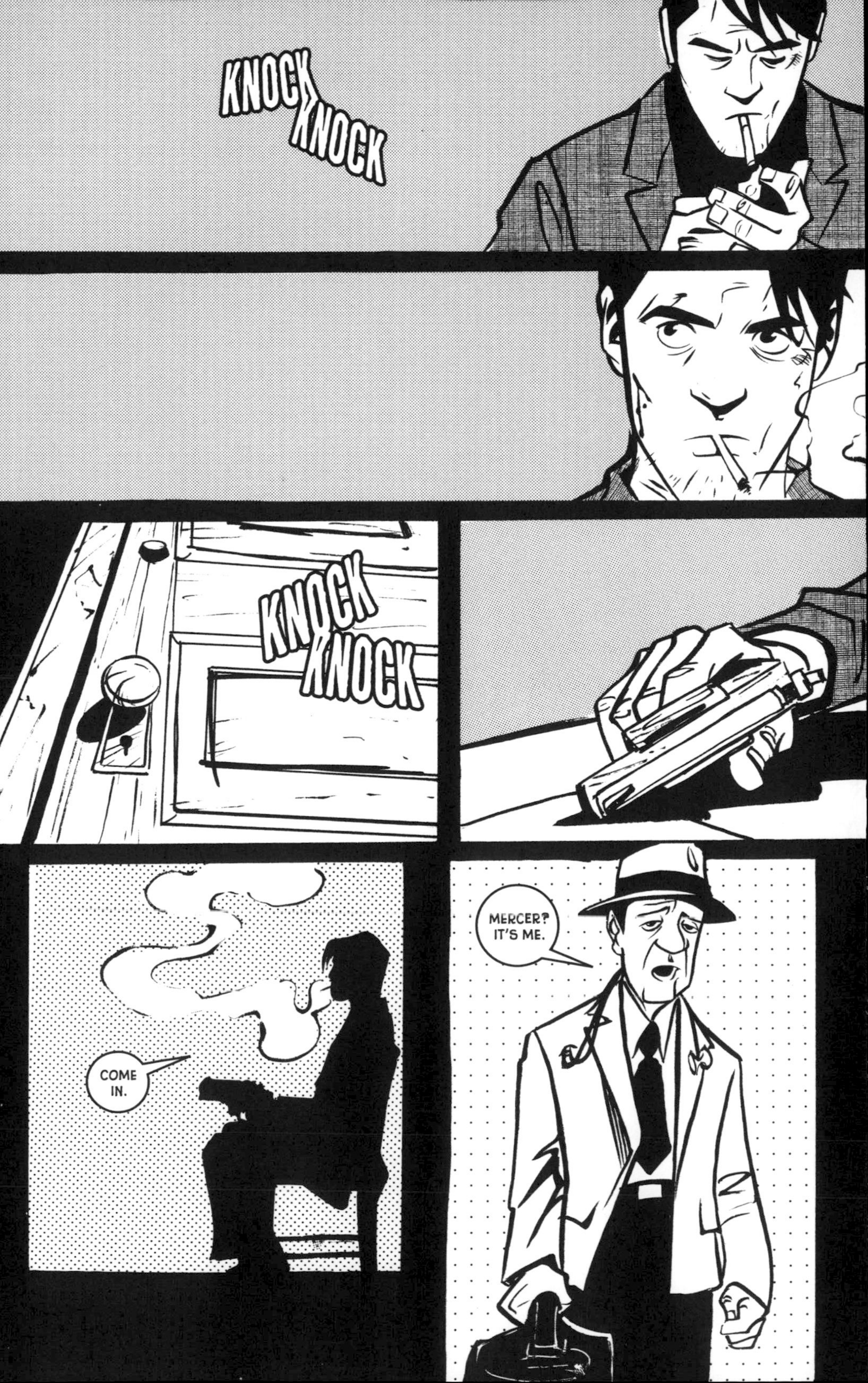
KNOCK KNOCK
KNOCK KNOCK
COME IN.
MERCER? IT'S ME.

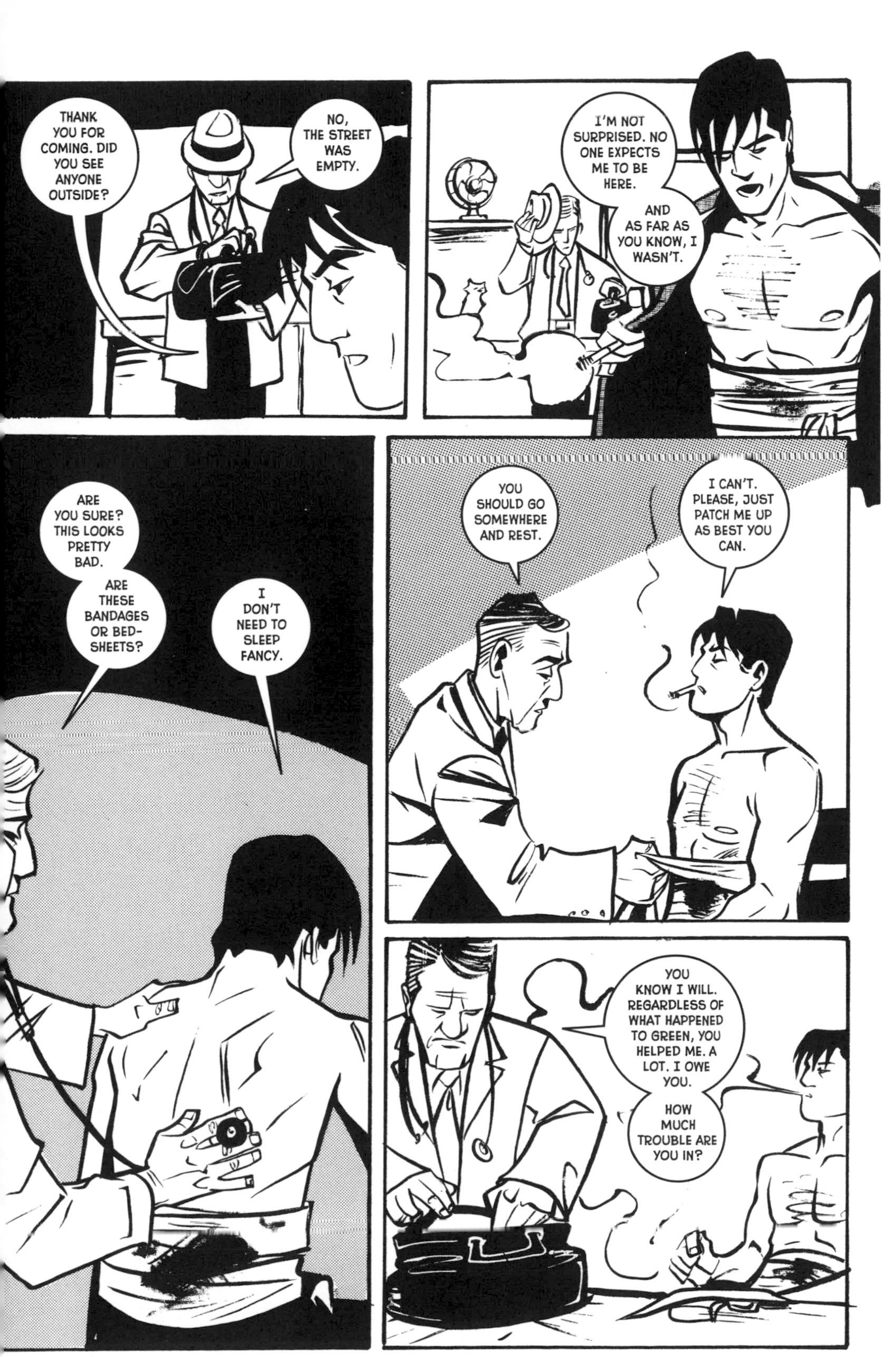
THANK YOU FOR COMING. DID YOU SEE ANYONE OUTSIDE?
NO, THE STREET WAS EMPTY.
I'M NOT SURPRISED. NO ONE EXPECTS ME TO BE HERE.
AND AS FAR AS YOU KNOW, I WASN'T.
ARE YOU SURE? THIS LOOKS PRETTY BAD.
ARE THESE BANDAGES OR BED-SHEETS?
I DON'T NEED TO SLEEP FANCY.
YOU SHOULD GO SOMEWHERE AND REST.
I CAN'T. PLEASE, JUST PATCH ME UP AS BEST YOU CAN.
YOU KNOW I WILL. REGARDLESS OF WHAT HAPPENED TO GREEN, YOU HELPED ME. A LOT. I OWE YOU.
HOW MUCH TROUBLE ARE YOU IN?

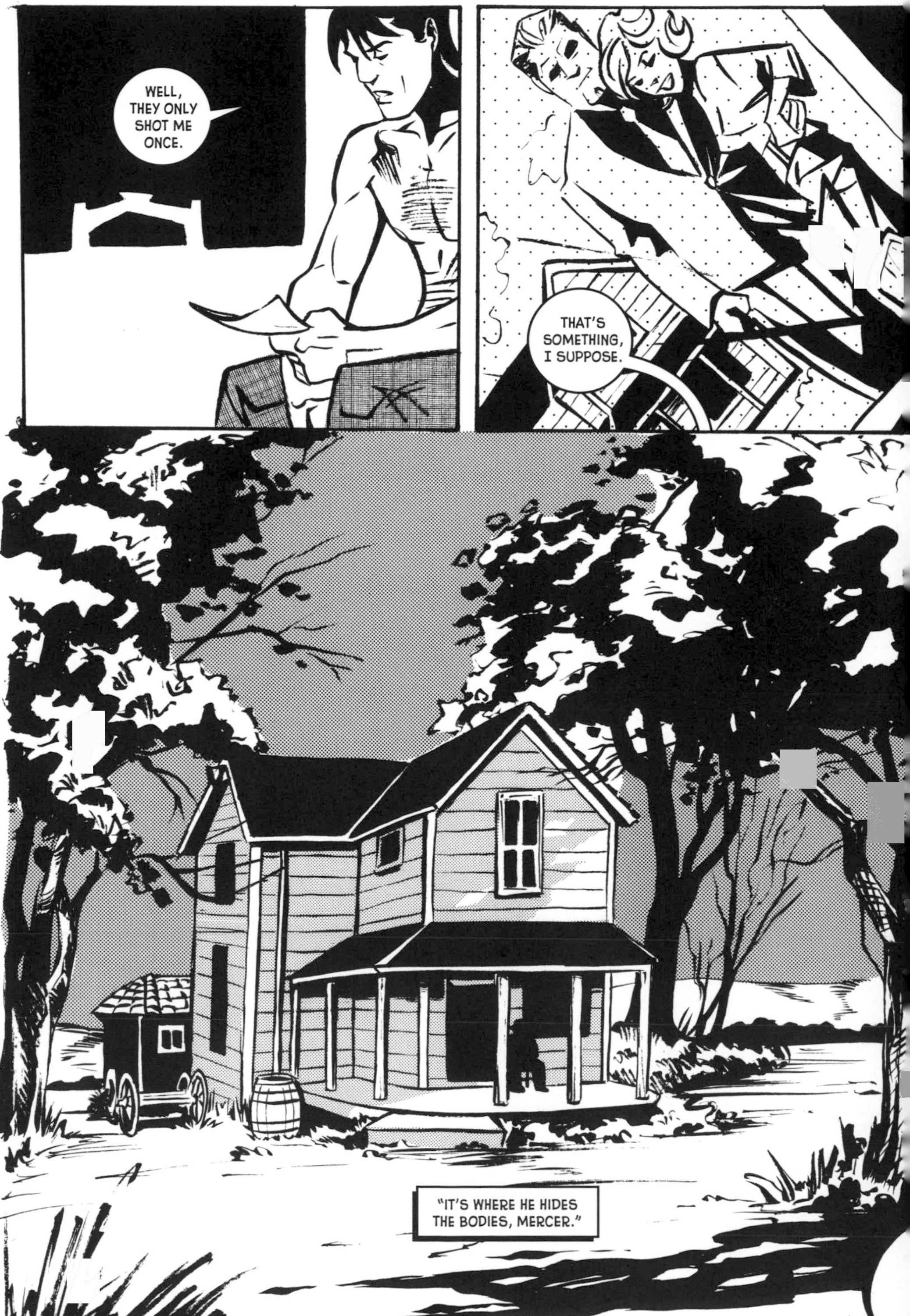
WELL, THEY ONLY SHOT ME ONCE.
THAT'S SOMETHING, I SUPPOSE.
"IT'S WHERE HE HIDES THE BODIES, MERCER."

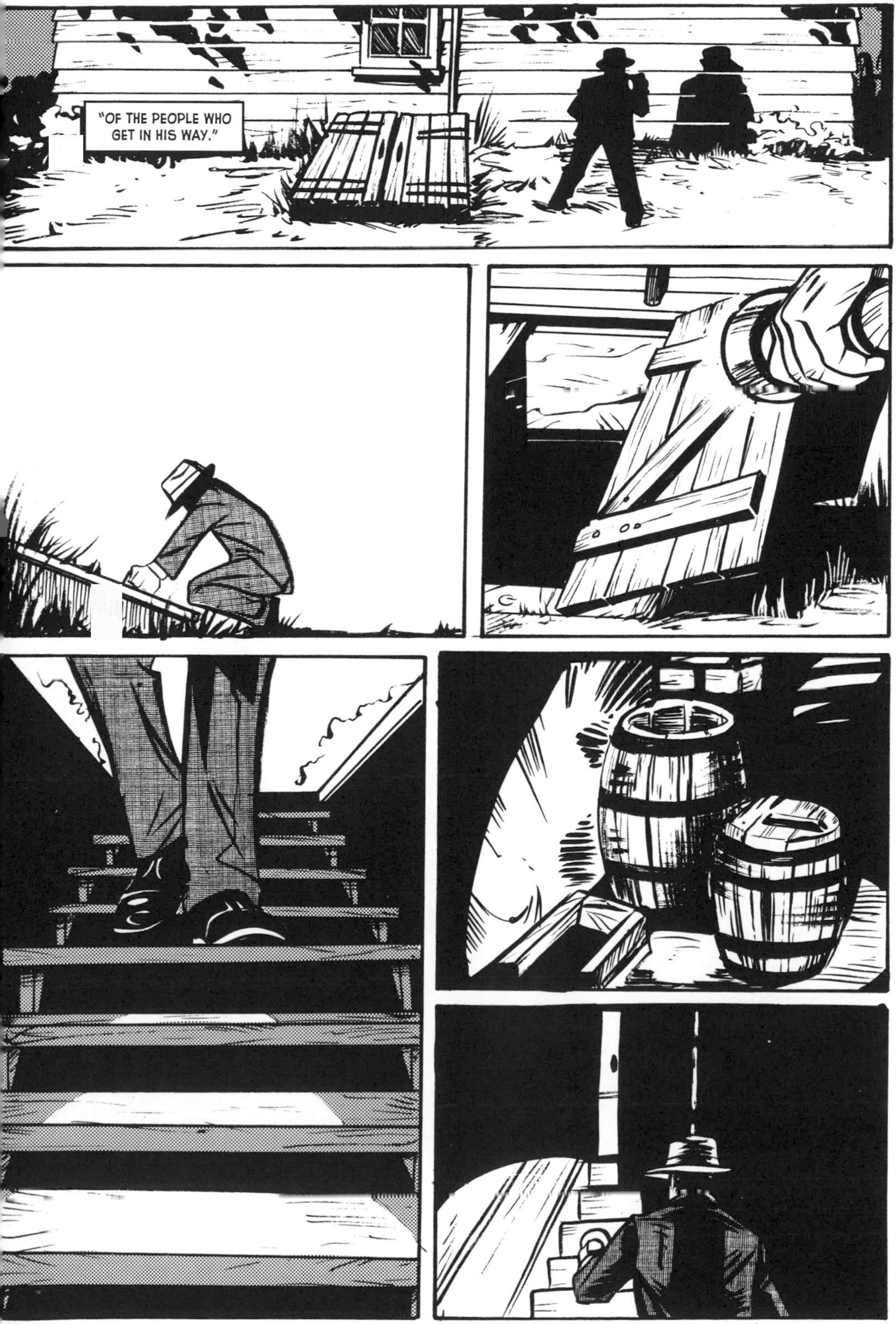
"OF THE PEOPLE WHO GET IN HIS WAY."

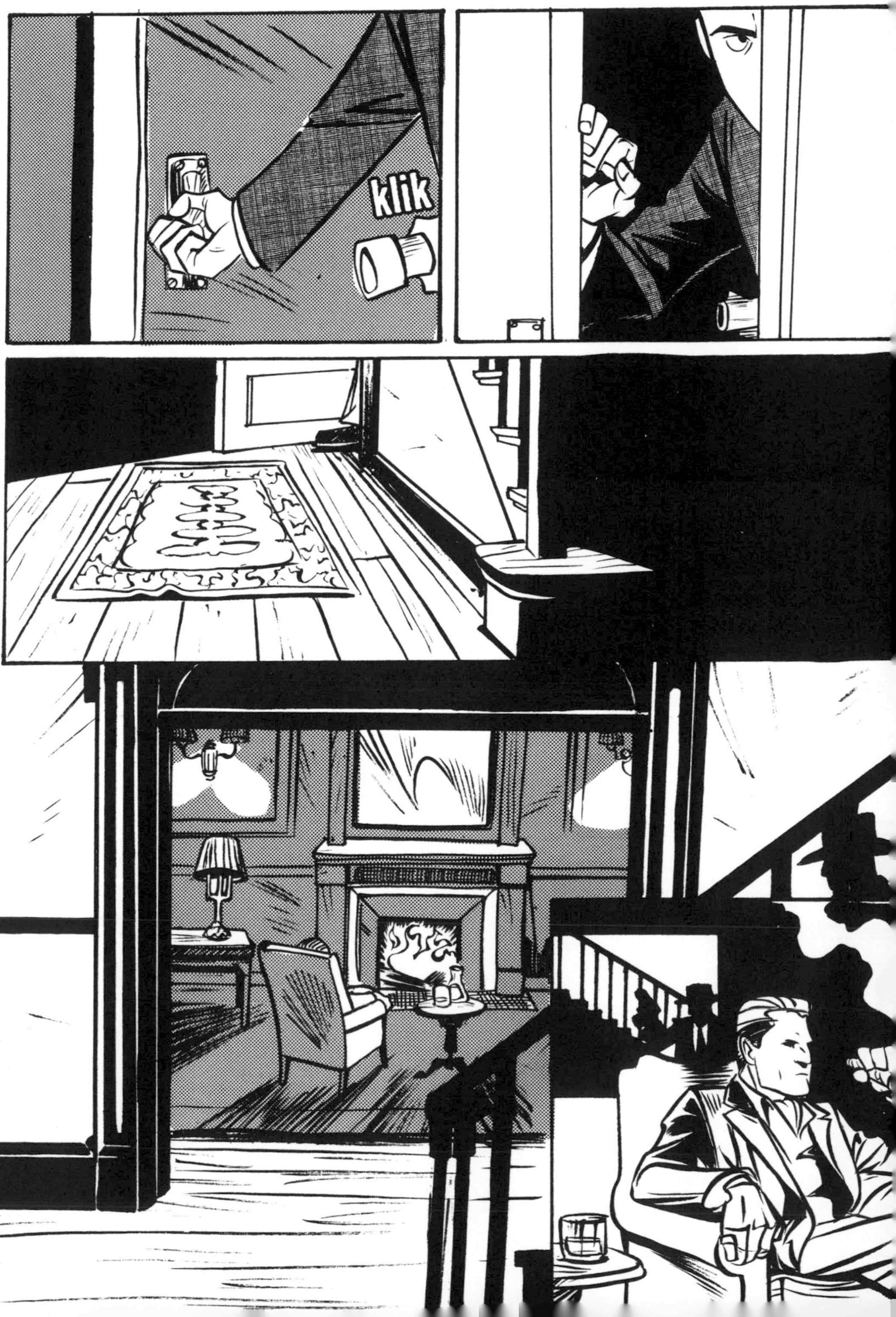
klik

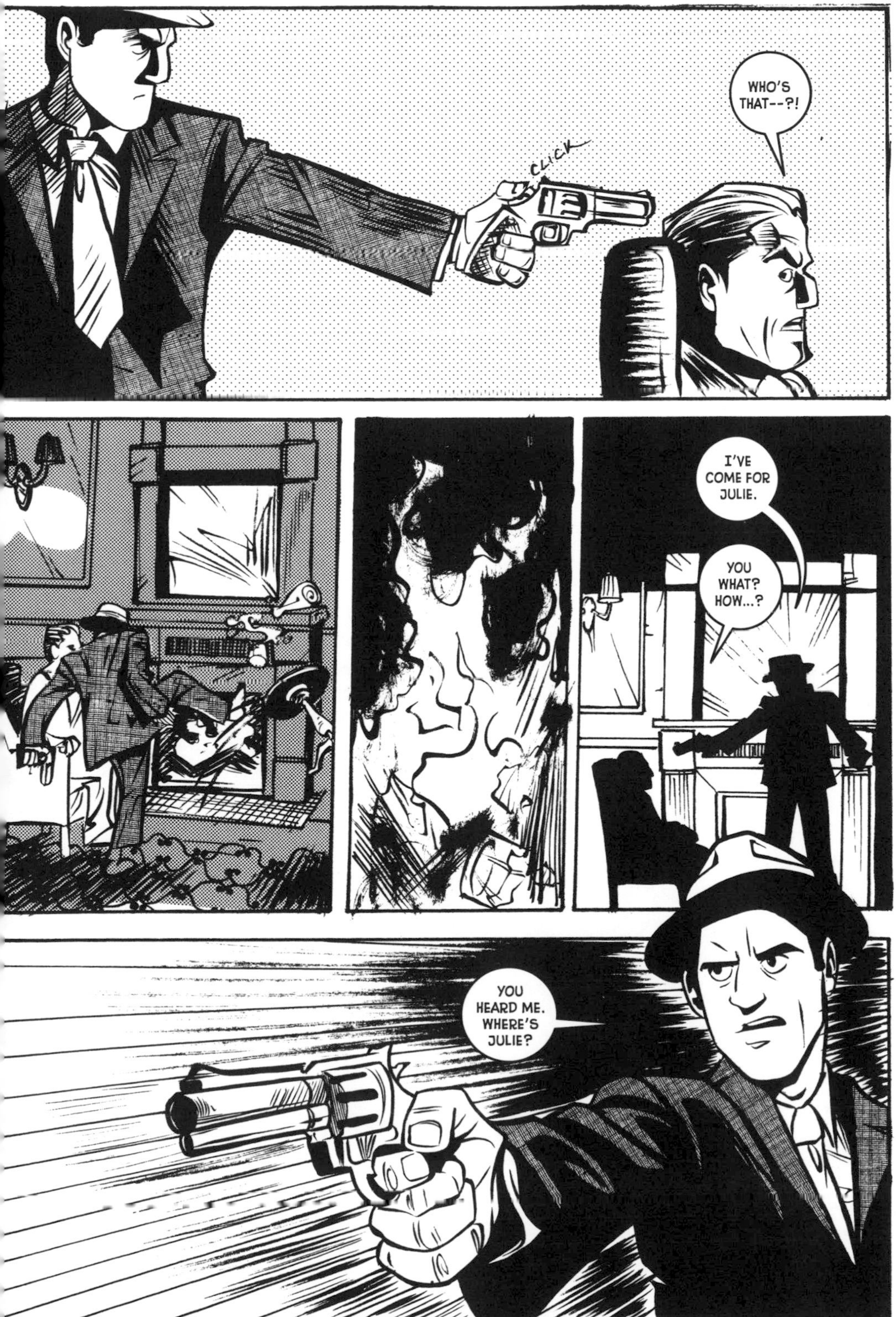
CLICK
WHO'S THAT--?!
I'VE COME FOR JULIE.
YOU WHAT? HOW...?
YOU HEARD ME. WHERE'S JULIE?

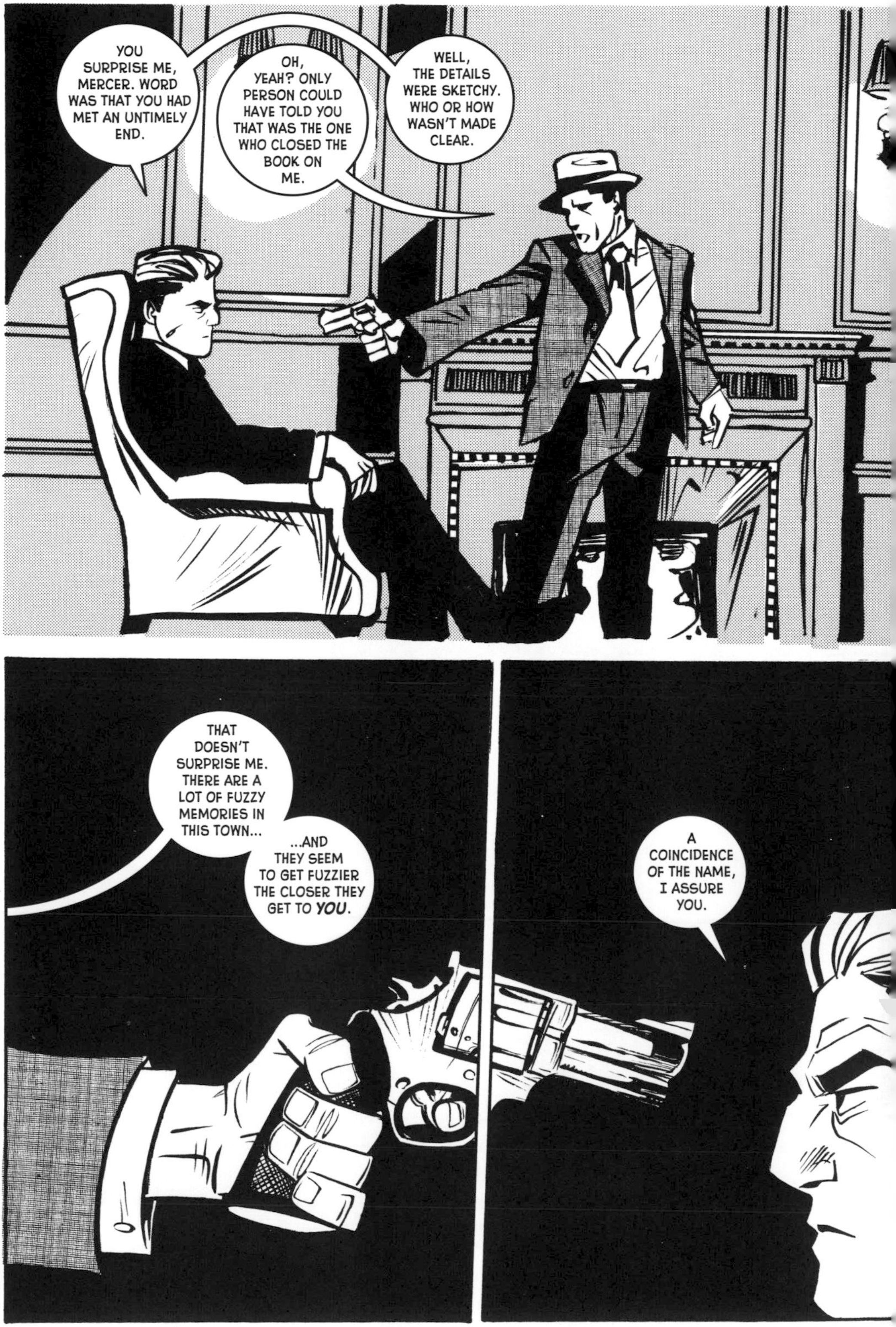
YOU SURPRISE ME, MERCER. WORD WAS THAT YOU HAD MET AN UNTIMELY END.
OH, YEAH? ONLY PERSON COULD HAVE TOLD YOU THAT WAS THE ONE WHO CLOSED THE BOOK ON ME.
WELL, THE DETAILS WERE SKETCHY. WHO OR HOW WASN'T MADE CLEAR.
THAT DOESN'T SURPRISE ME. THERE ARE A LOT OF FUZZY MEMORIES IN THIS TOWN...
...AND THEY SEEM TO GET FUZZIER THE CLOSER THEY GET TO *YOU*.
A COINCIDENCE OF THE NAME, I ASSURE YOU.

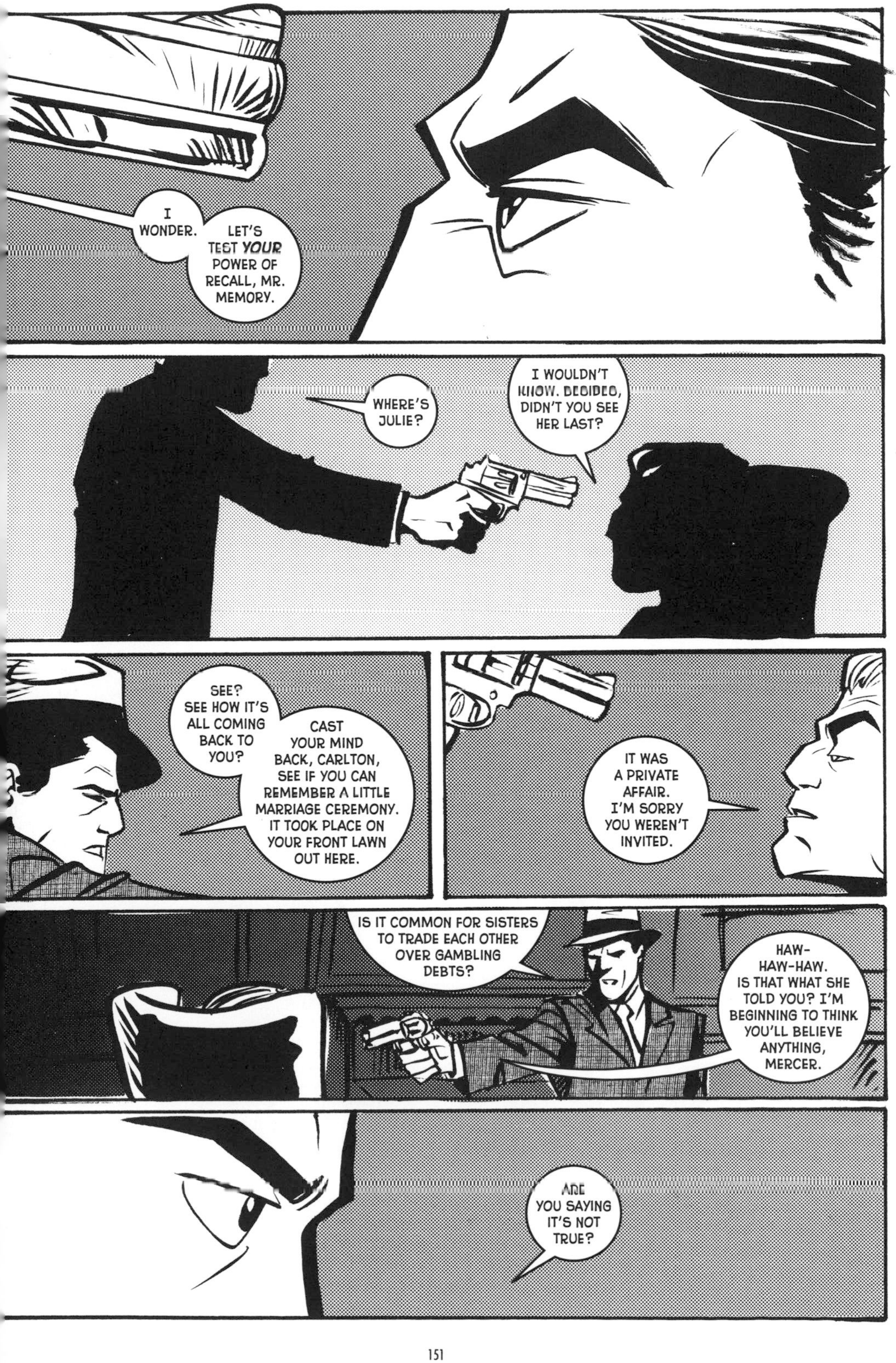
I WONDER.
LET'S TEST YOUR POWER OF RECALL, MR. MEMORY.
WHERE'S JULIE?
I WOULDN'T KNOW. BESIDES, DIDN'T YOU SEE HER LAST?
SEE? SEE HOW IT'S ALL COMING BACK TO YOU?
CAST YOUR MIND BACK, CARLTON, SEE IF YOU CAN REMEMBER A LITTLE MARRIAGE CEREMONY. IT TOOK PLACE ON YOUR FRONT LAWN OUT HERE.
IT WAS A PRIVATE AFFAIR. I'M SORRY YOU WEREN'T INVITED.
IS IT COMMON FOR SISTERS TO TRADE EACH OTHER OVER GAMBLING DEBTS?
HAW-HAW-HAW. IS THAT WHAT SHE TOLD YOU? I'M BEGINNING TO THINK YOU'LL BELIEVE ANYTHING, MERCER.
ARE YOU SAYING IT'S NOT TRUE?

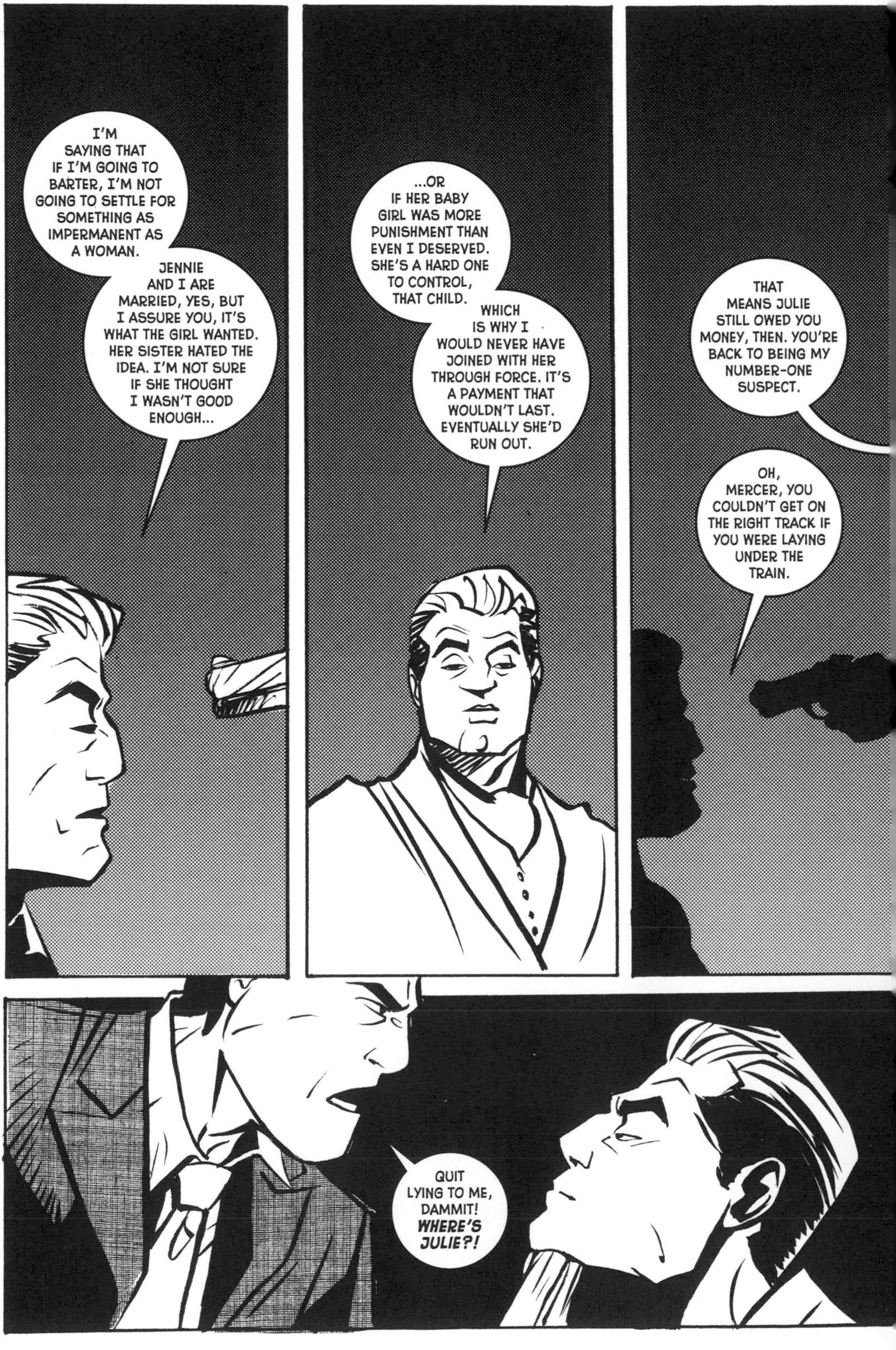
I'M SAYING THAT IF I'M GOING TO BARTER, I'M NOT GOING TO SETTLE FOR SOMETHING AS IMPERMANENT AS A WOMAN.
JENNIE AND I ARE MARRIED, YES, BUT I ASSURE YOU, IT'S WHAT THE GIRL WANTED. HER SISTER HATED THE IDEA. I'M NOT SURE IF SHE THOUGHT I WASN'T GOOD ENOUGH...
...OR IF HER BABY GIRL WAS MORE PUNISHMENT THAN EVEN I DESERVED. SHE'S A HARD ONE TO CONTROL, THAT CHILD.
WHICH IS WHY I WOULD NEVER HAVE JOINED WITH HER THROUGH FORCE. IT'S A PAYMENT THAT WOULDN'T LAST. EVENTUALLY SHE'D RUN OUT.
THAT MEANS JULIE STILL OWED YOU MONEY, THEN. YOU'RE BACK TO BEING MY NUMBER-ONE SUSPECT.
OH, MERCER, YOU COULDN'T GET ON THE RIGHT TRACK IF YOU WERE LAYING UNDER THE TRAIN.
QUIT LYING TO ME, DAMMIT! ***WHERE'S JULIE?!***

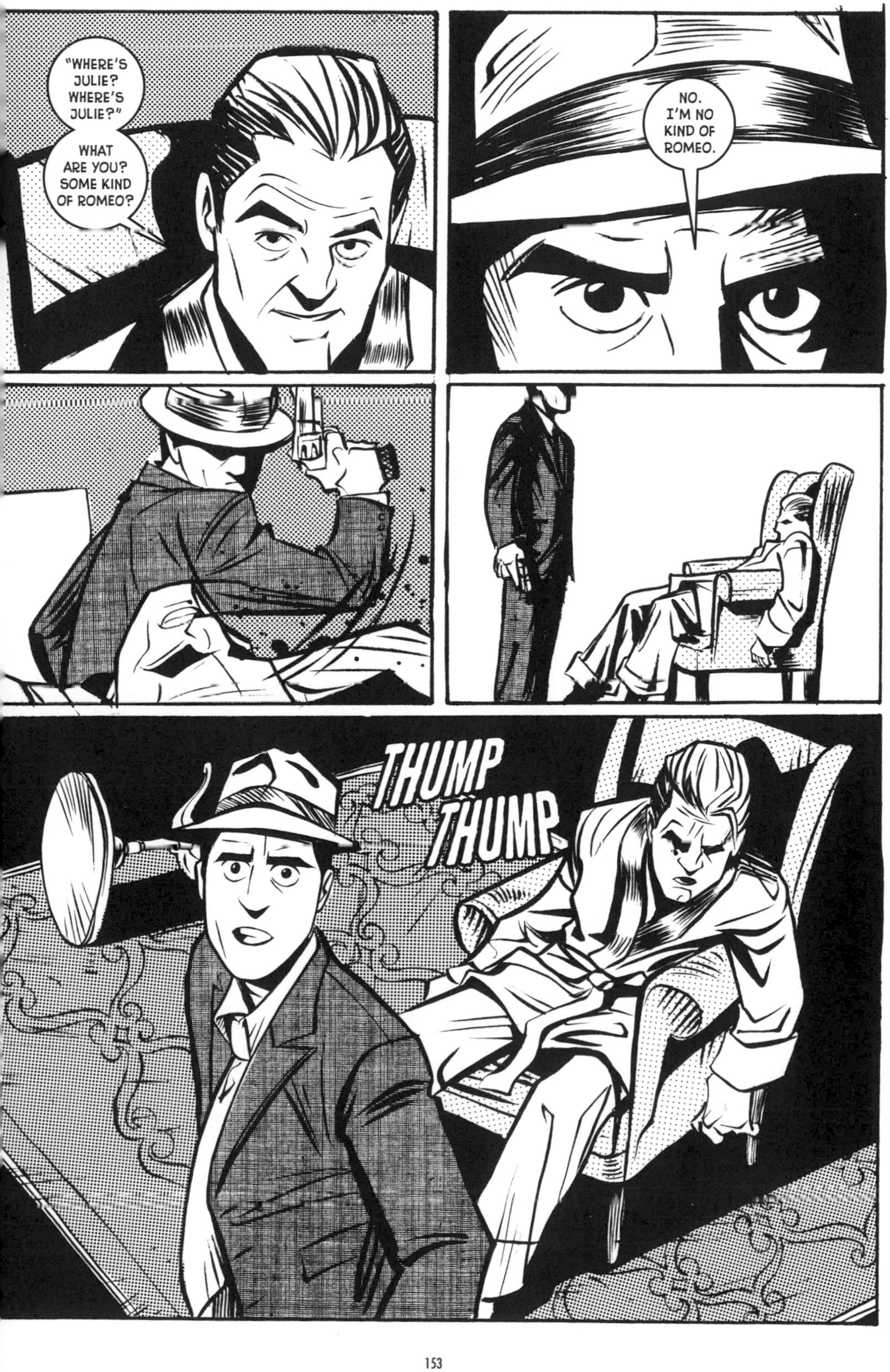
"WHERE'S JULIE? WHERE'S JULIE?"
WHAT ARE YOU? SOME KIND OF ROMEO?
NO. I'M NO KIND OF ROMEO.
THUMP
THUMP

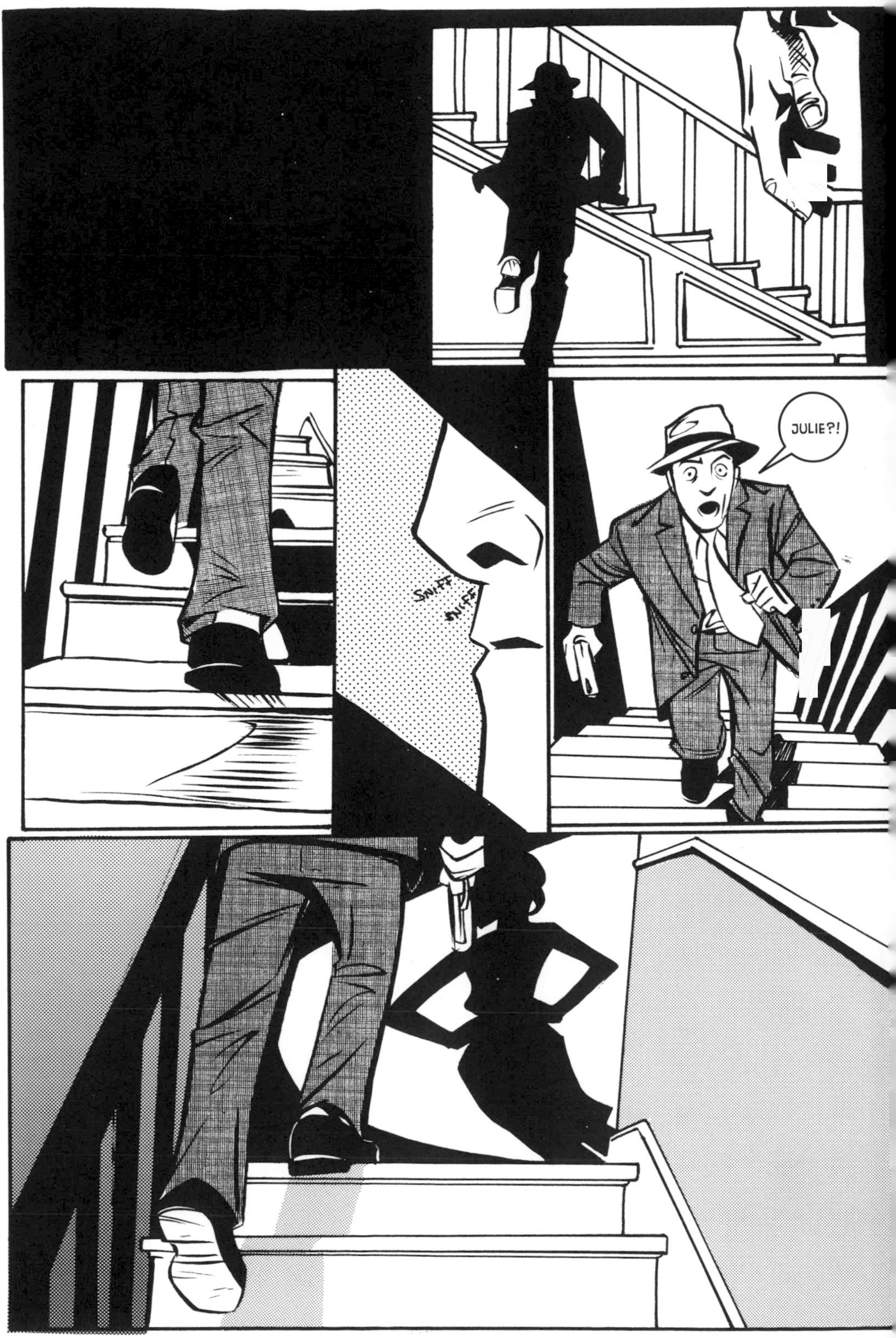
SNIFF
SNIFF
JULIE?!

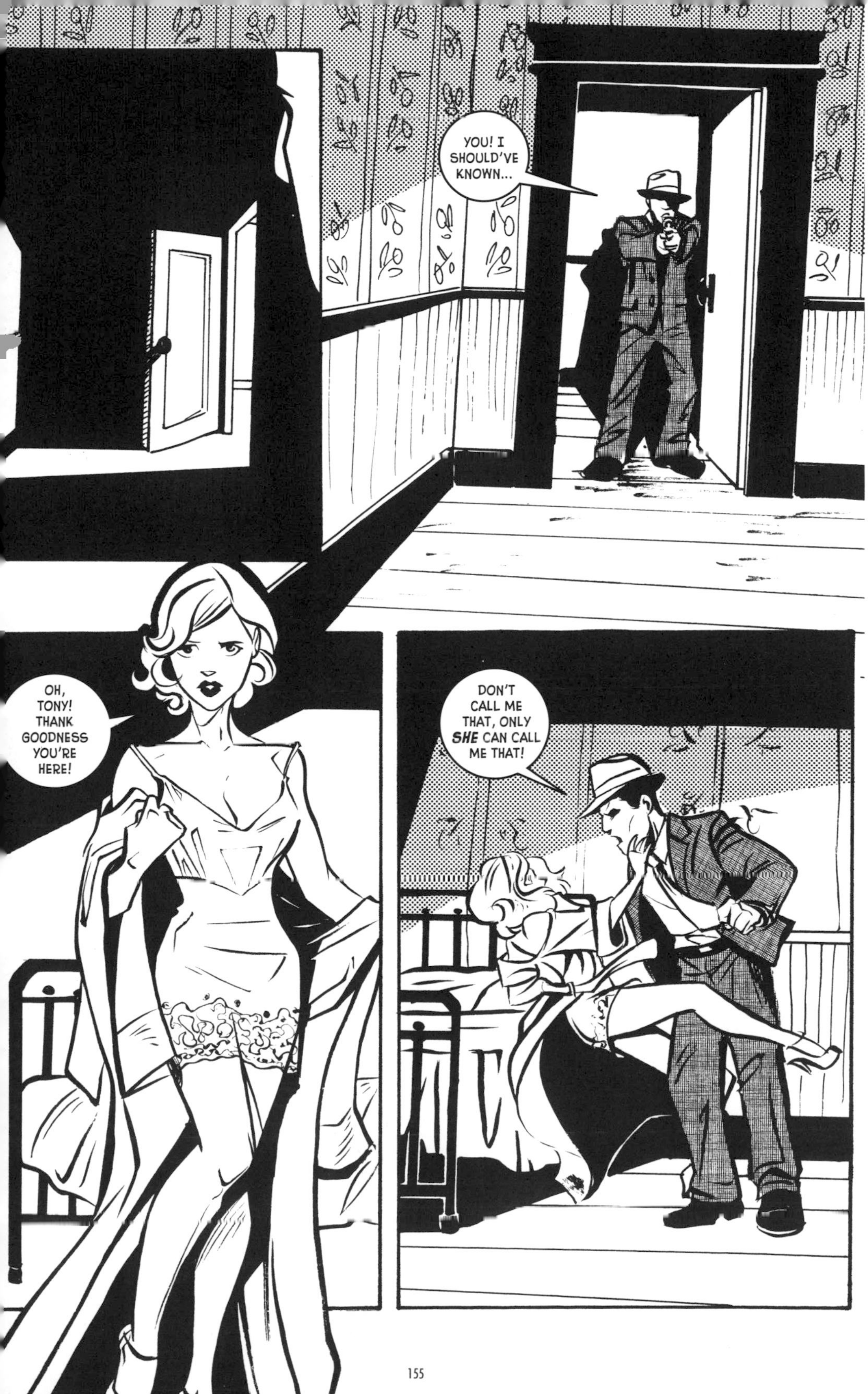
YOU! I SHOULD'VE KNOWN...
OH, TONY! THANK GOODNESS YOU'RE HERE!
DON'T CALL ME THAT, ONLY SHE CAN CALL ME THAT!

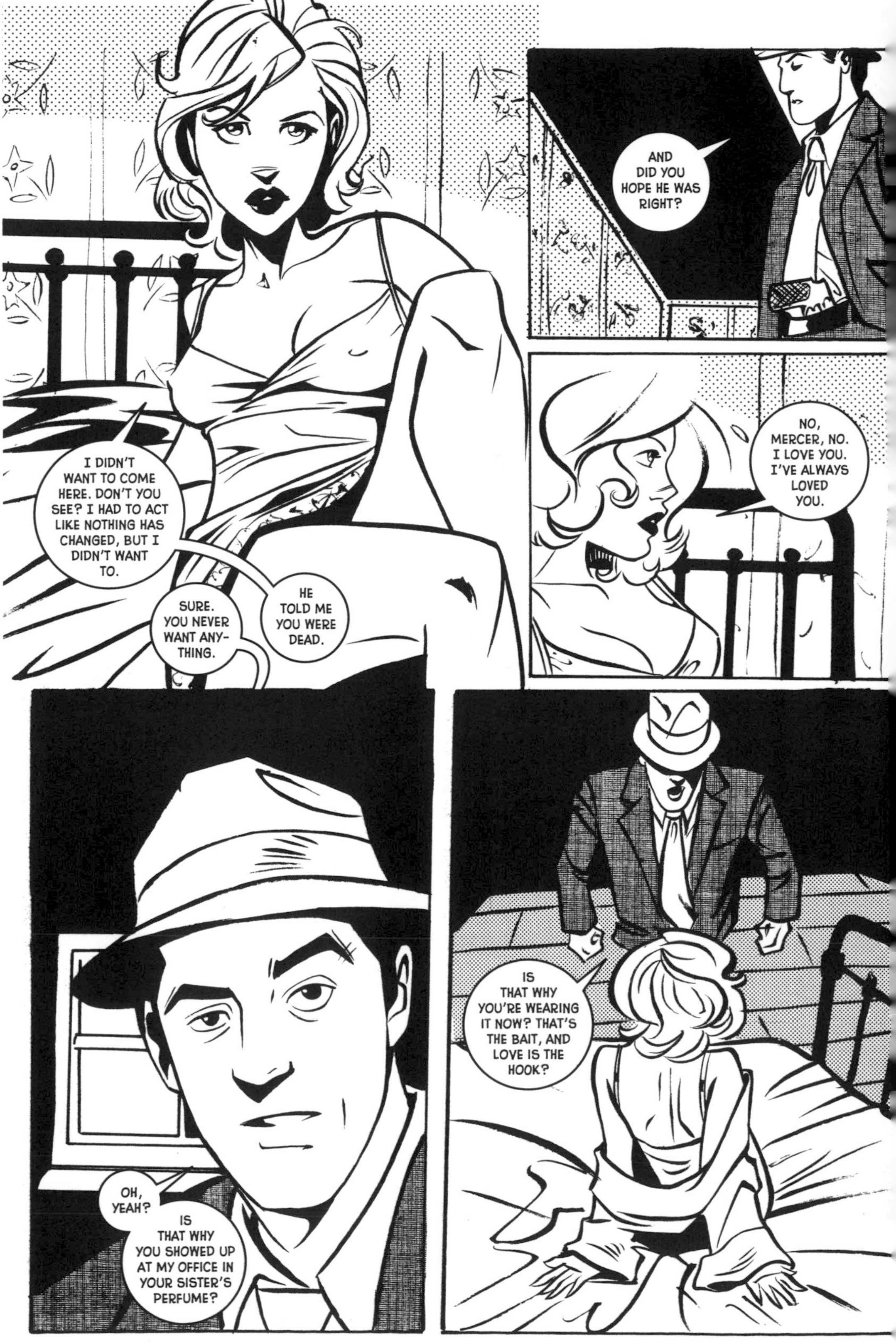
AND DID YOU HOPE HE WAS RIGHT?
I DIDN'T WANT TO COME HERE. DON'T YOU SEE? I HAD TO ACT LIKE NOTHING HAS CHANGED, BUT I DIDN'T WANT TO.
HE TOLD ME YOU WERE DEAD.
SURE. YOU NEVER WANT ANY-THING.
NO, MERCER, NO. I LOVE YOU. I'VE ALWAYS LOVED YOU.
OH, YEAH?
IS THAT WHY YOU SHOWED UP AT MY OFFICE IN YOUR SISTER'S PERFUME?
IS THAT WHY YOU'RE WEARING IT NOW? THAT'S THE BAIT, AND LOVE IS THE HOOK?

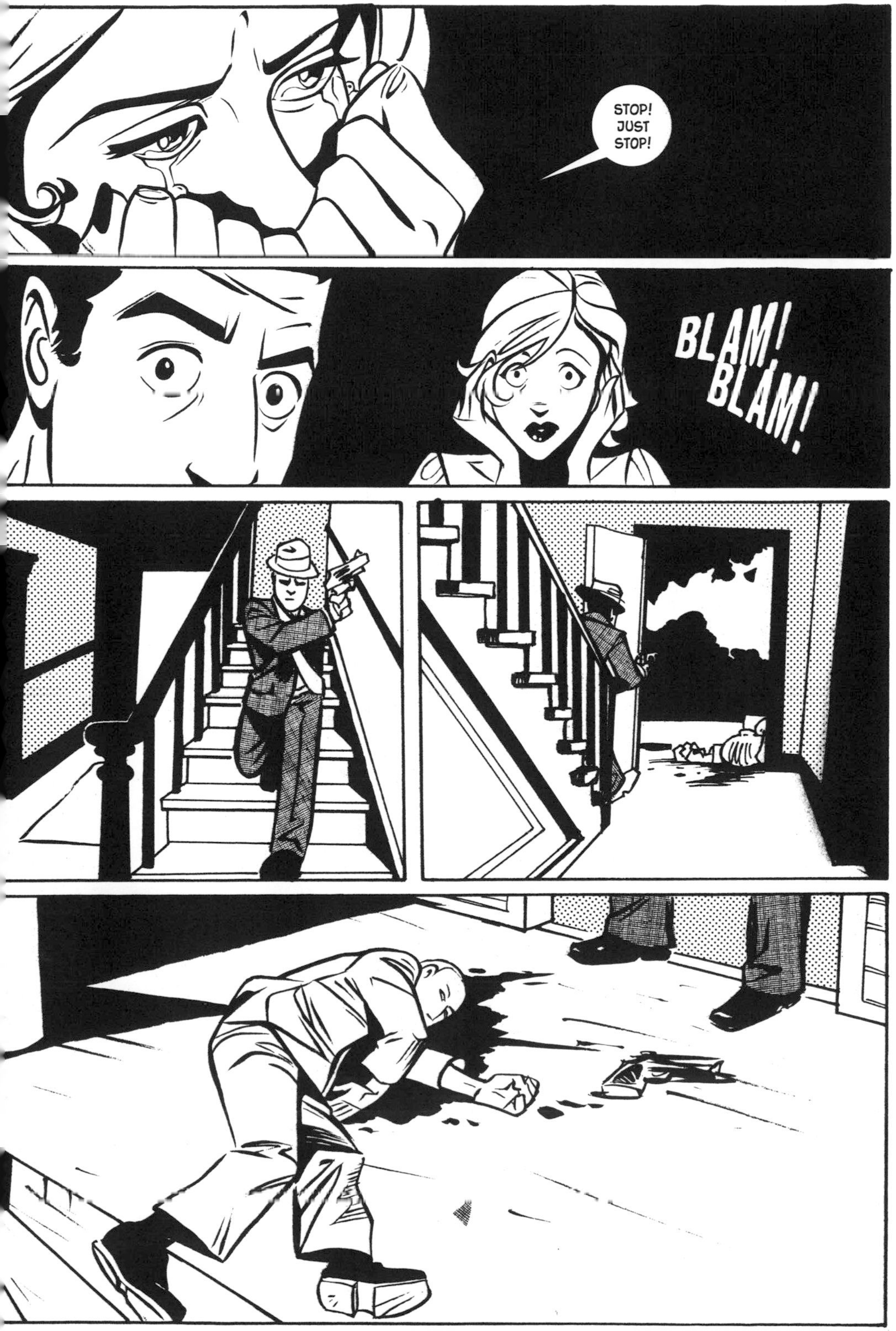
STOP!
JUST
STOP!
BLAM!
BLAM!

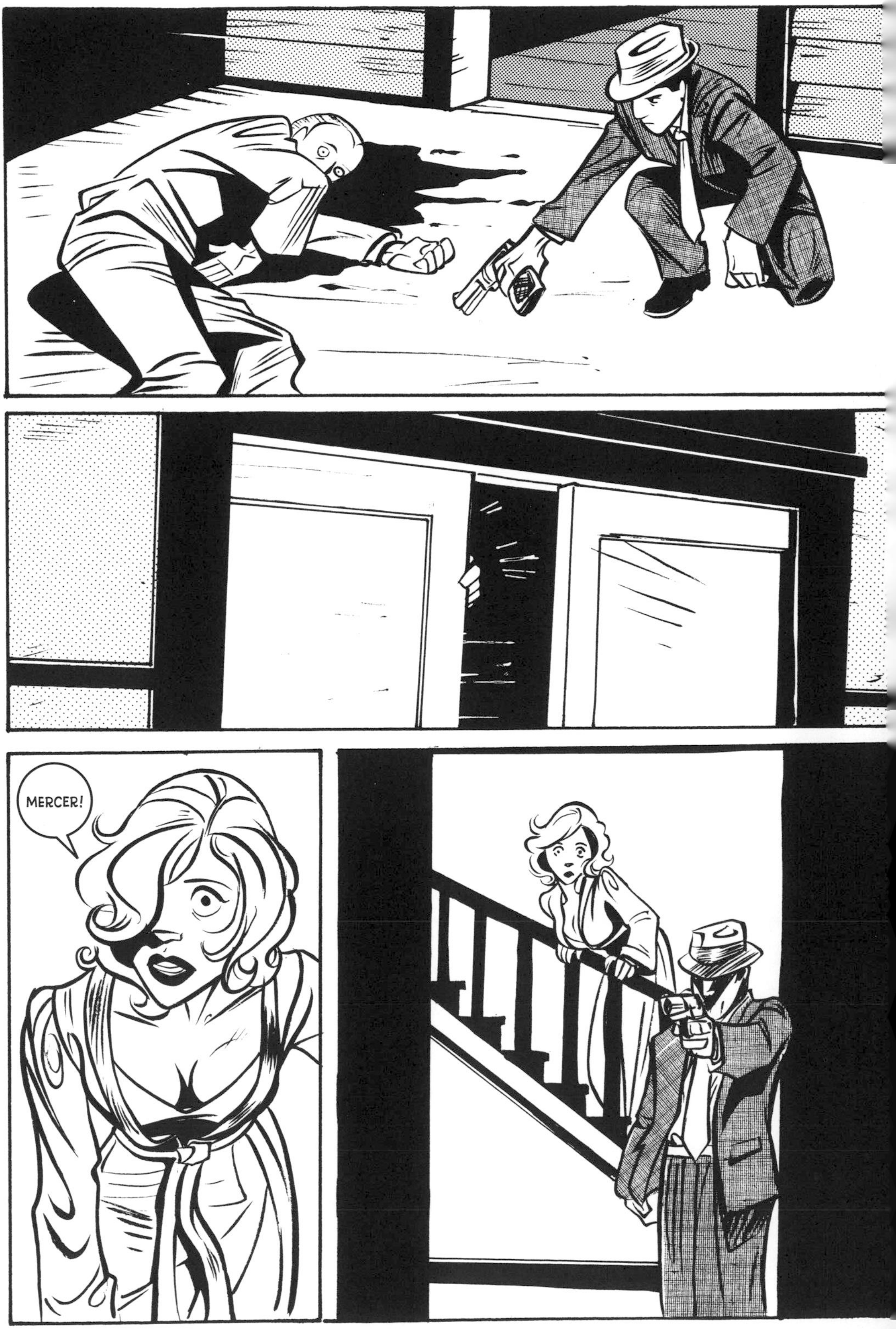
MERCER!

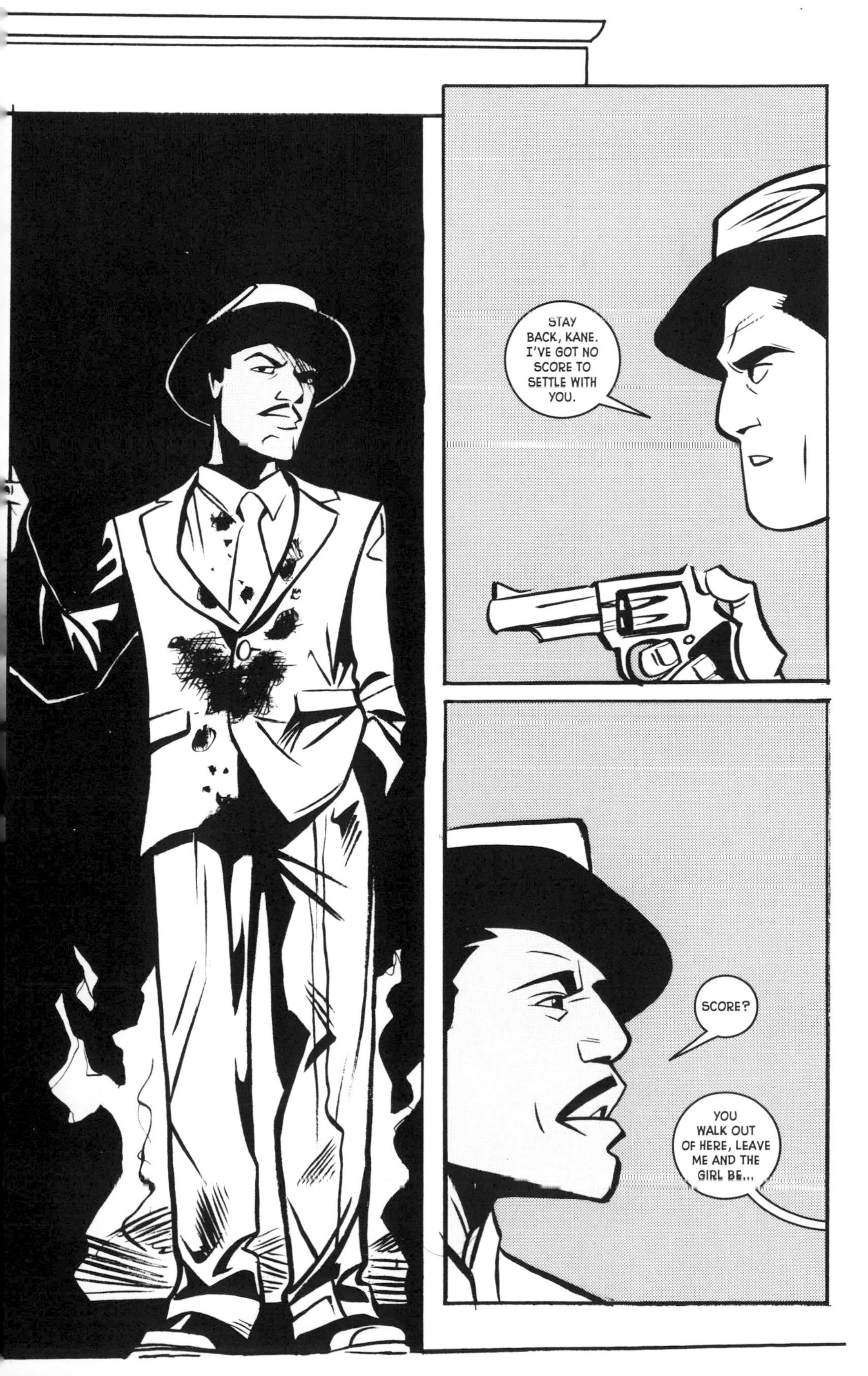
STAY BACK, KANE. I'VE GOT NO SCORE TO SETTLE WITH YOU.
SCORE?
YOU WALK OUT OF HERE, LEAVE ME AND THE GIRL BE...

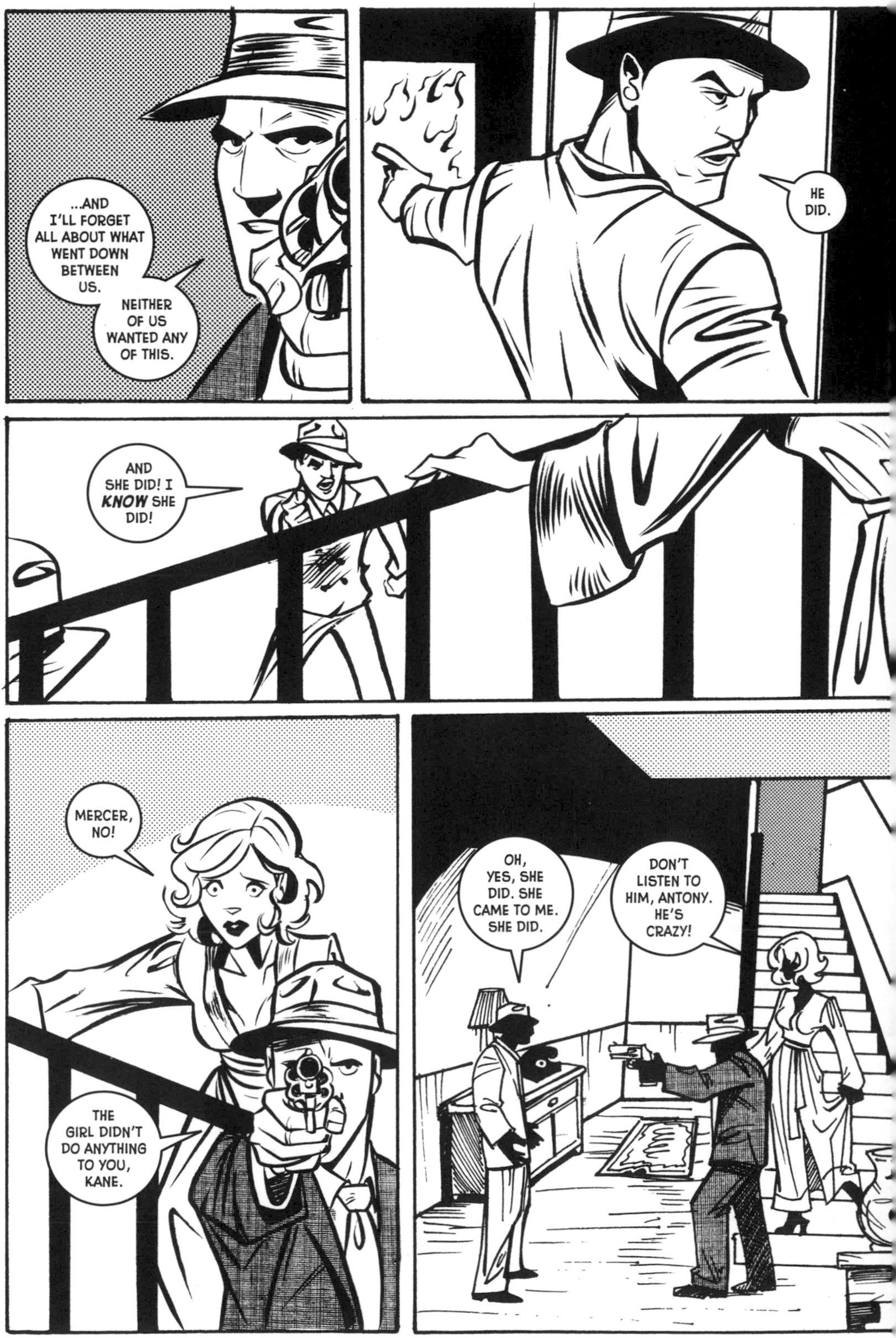
...AND I'LL FORGET ALL ABOUT WHAT WENT DOWN BETWEEN US.
NEITHER OF US WANTED ANY OF THIS.
HE DID.
AND SHE DID! I KNOW SHE DID!
MERCER, NO!
THE GIRL DIDN'T DO ANYTHING TO YOU, KANE.
OH, YES, SHE DID. SHE CAME TO ME. SHE DID.
DON'T LISTEN TO HIM, ANTONY. HE'S CRAZY!

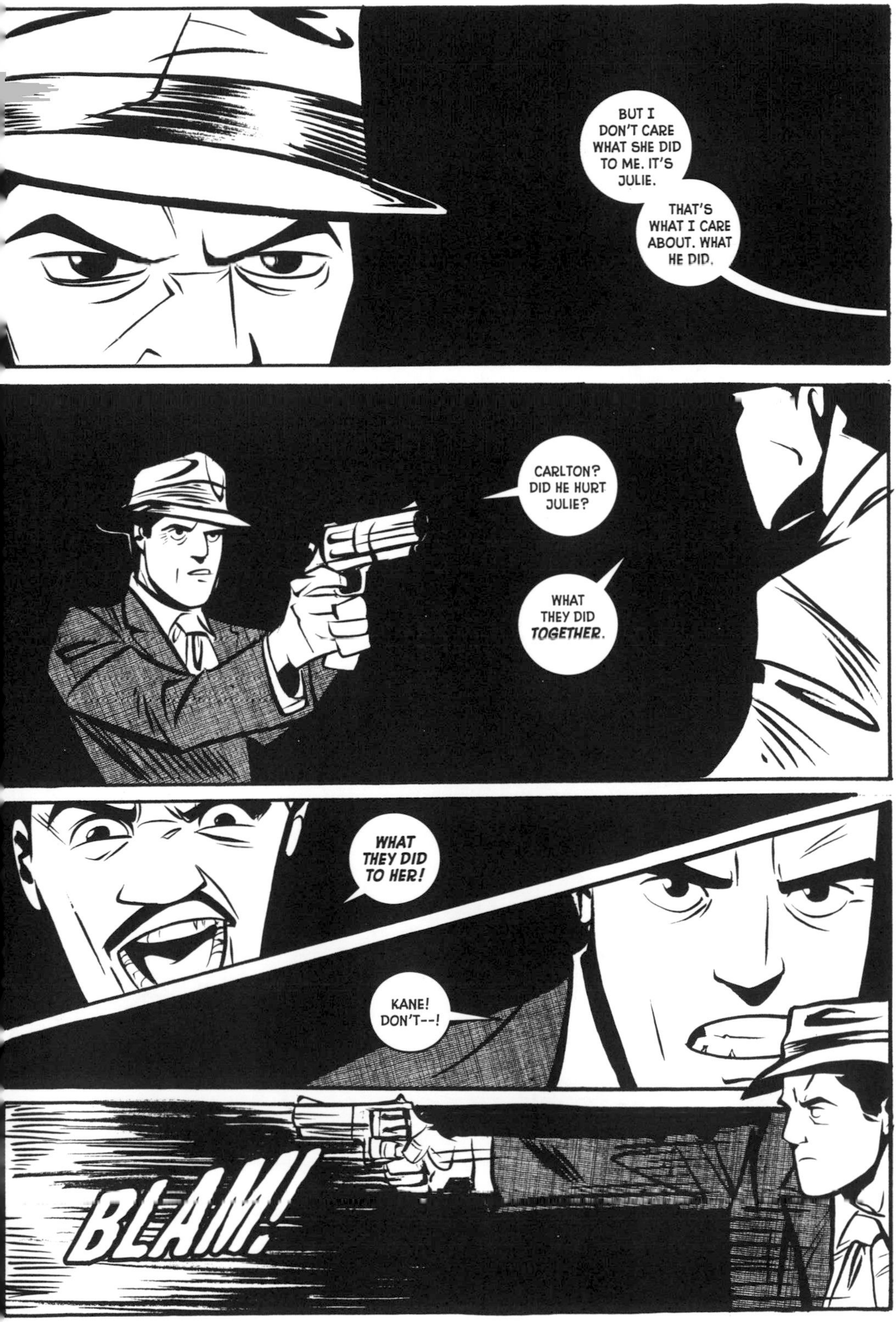
BUT I DON'T CARE WHAT SHE DID TO ME. IT'S JULIE.
THAT'S WHAT I CARE ABOUT. WHAT HE DID.
CARLTON? DID HE HURT JULIE?
WHAT THEY DID *TOGETHER*.
WHAT THEY DID TO HER!
KANE! DON'T--!
BLAM!

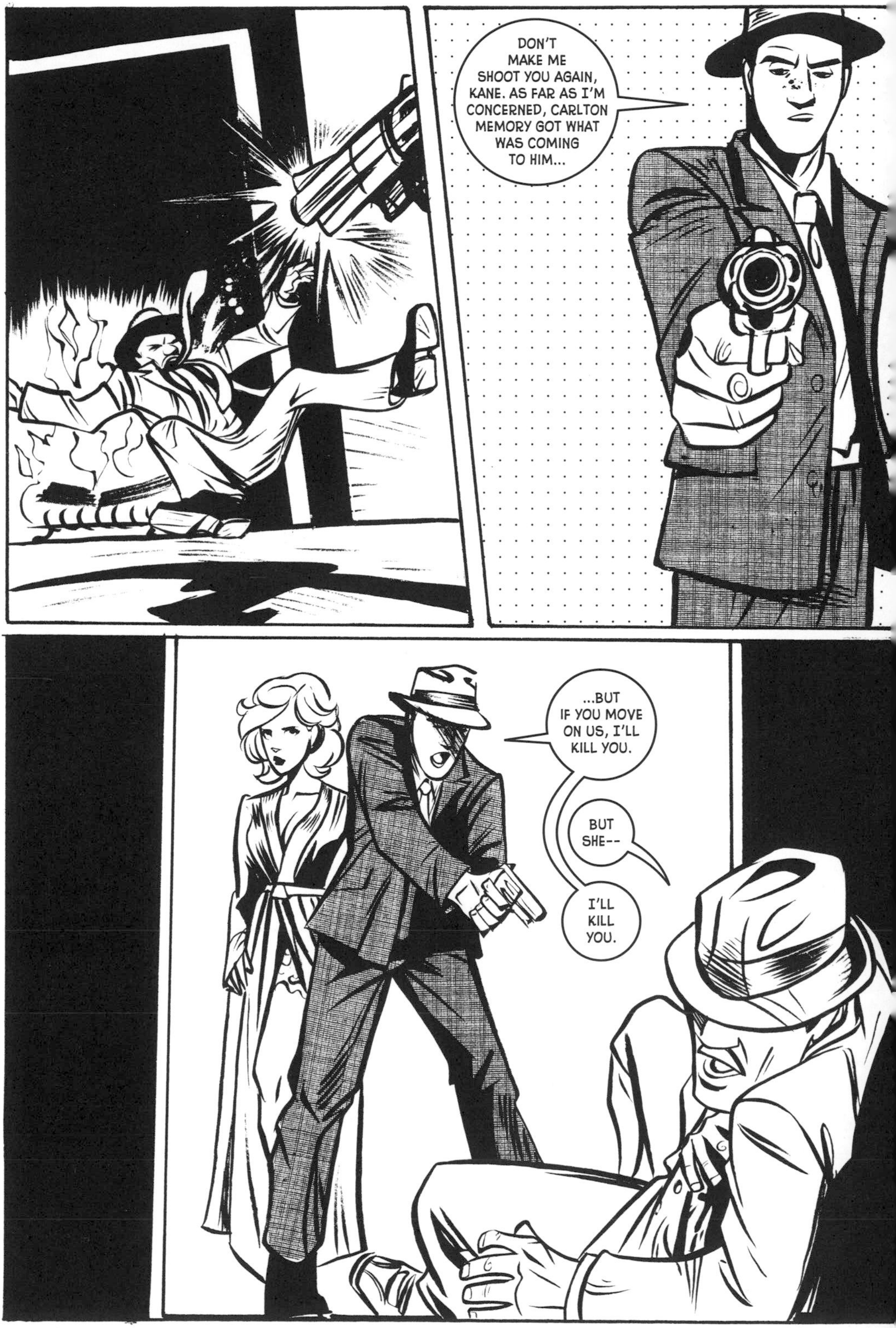
DON'T MAKE ME SHOOT YOU AGAIN, KANE. AS FAR AS I'M CONCERNED, CARLTON MEMORY GOT WHAT WAS COMING TO HIM...
...BUT IF YOU MOVE ON US, I'LL KILL YOU.
BUT SHE--
I'LL KILL YOU.

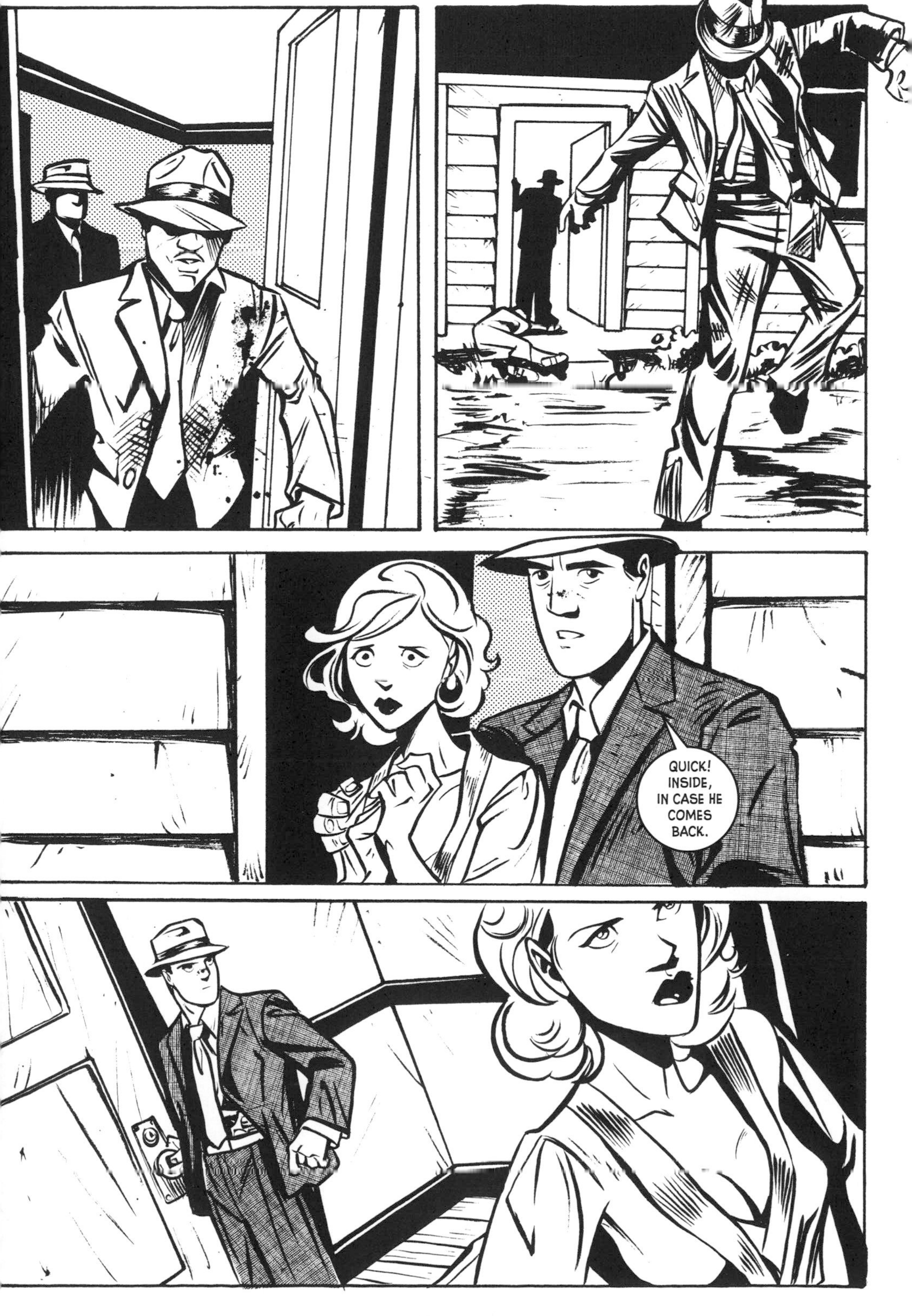
QUICK! INSIDE, IN CASE HE COMES BACK.

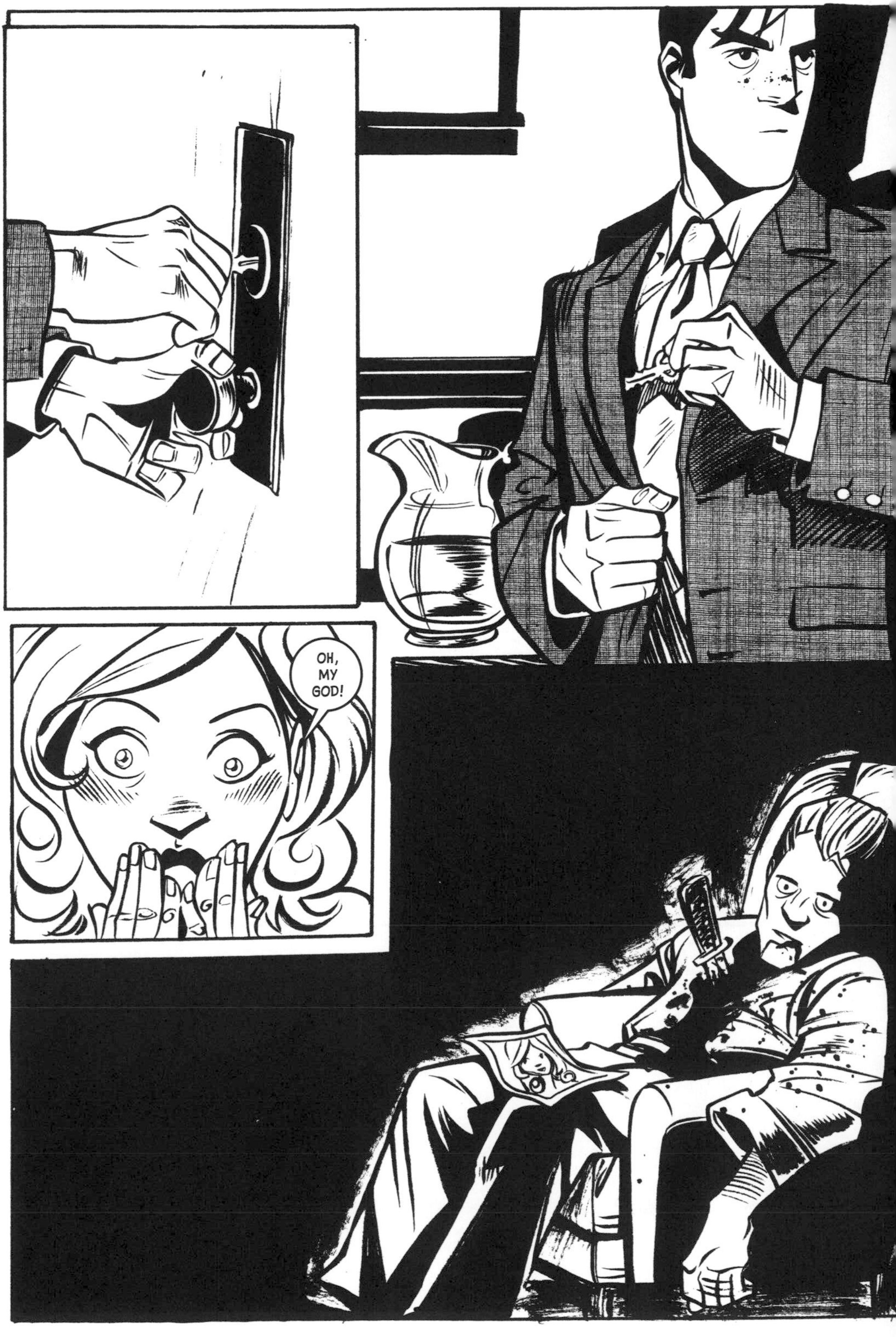
OH, MY GOD!

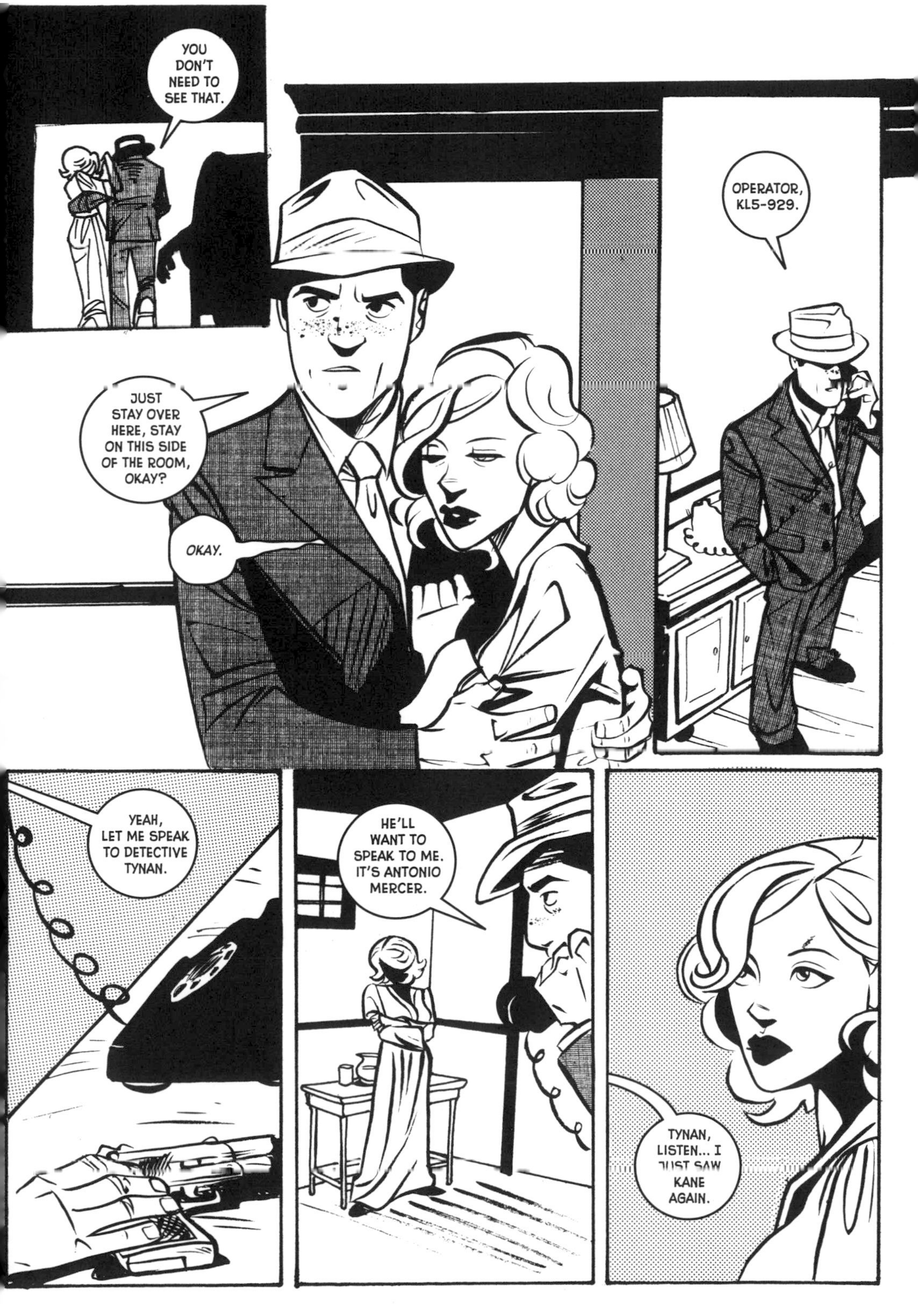

YOU DON'T NEED TO SEE THAT.
OPERATOR, KL5-929.
JUST STAY OVER HERE, STAY ON THIS SIDE OF THE ROOM, OKAY?
OKAY.
YEAH, LET ME SPEAK TO DETECTIVE TYNAN.
HE'LL WANT TO SPEAK TO ME. IT'S ANTONIO MERCER.
TYNAN, LISTEN... I JUST SAW KANE AGAIN.

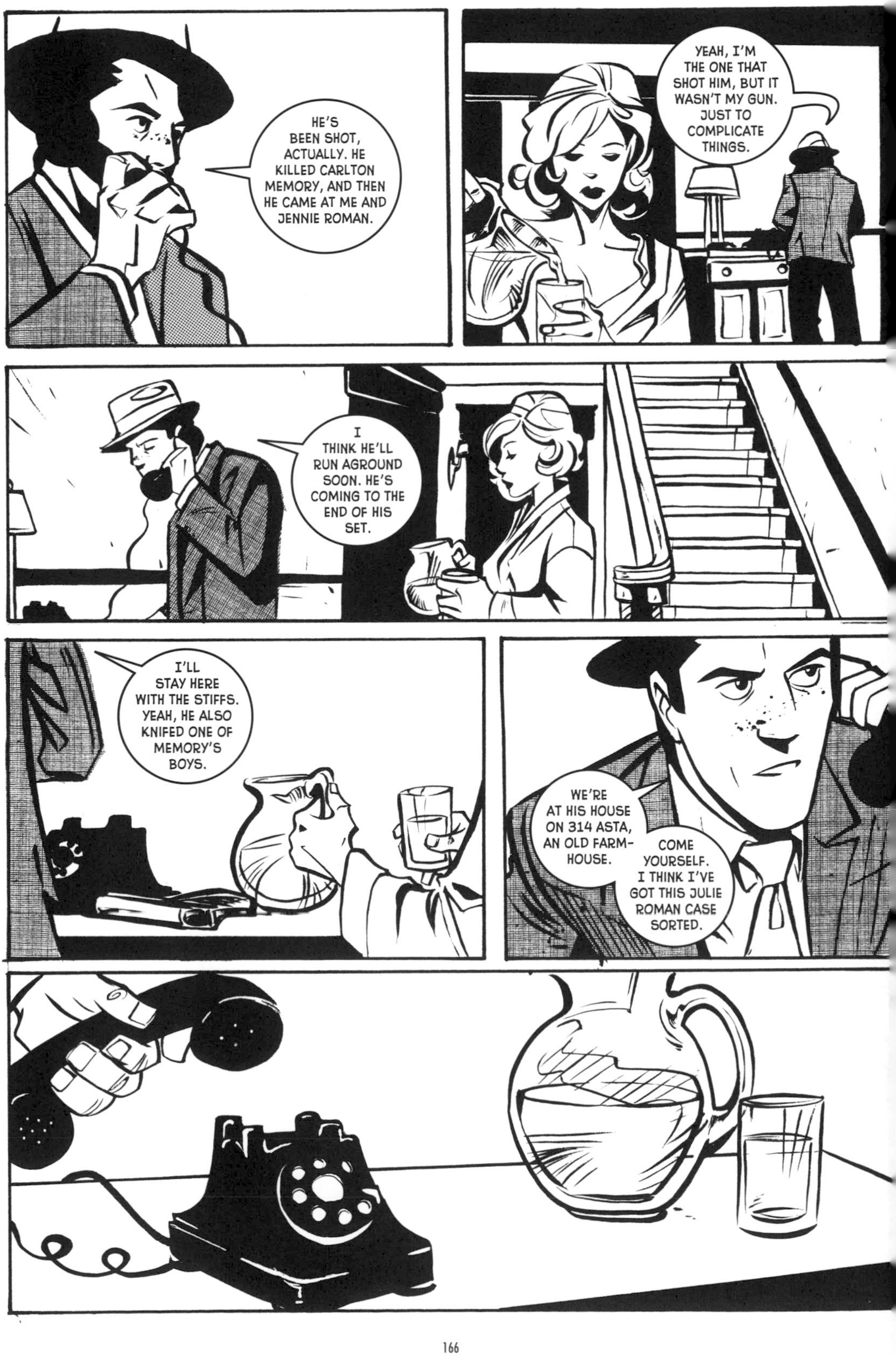
HE'S BEEN SHOT, ACTUALLY. HE KILLED CARLTON MEMORY, AND THEN HE CAME AT ME AND JENNIE ROMAN.
YEAH, I'M THE ONE THAT SHOT HIM, BUT IT WASN'T MY GUN. JUST TO COMPLICATE THINGS.
I THINK HE'LL RUN AGROUND SOON. HE'S COMING TO THE END OF HIS SET.
I'LL STAY HERE WITH THE STIFFS. YEAH, HE ALSO KNIFED ONE OF MEMORY'S BOYS.
WE'RE AT HIS HOUSE ON 314 ASTA, AN OLD FARM-HOUSE.
COME YOURSELF. I THINK I'VE GOT THIS JULIE ROMAN CASE SORTED.

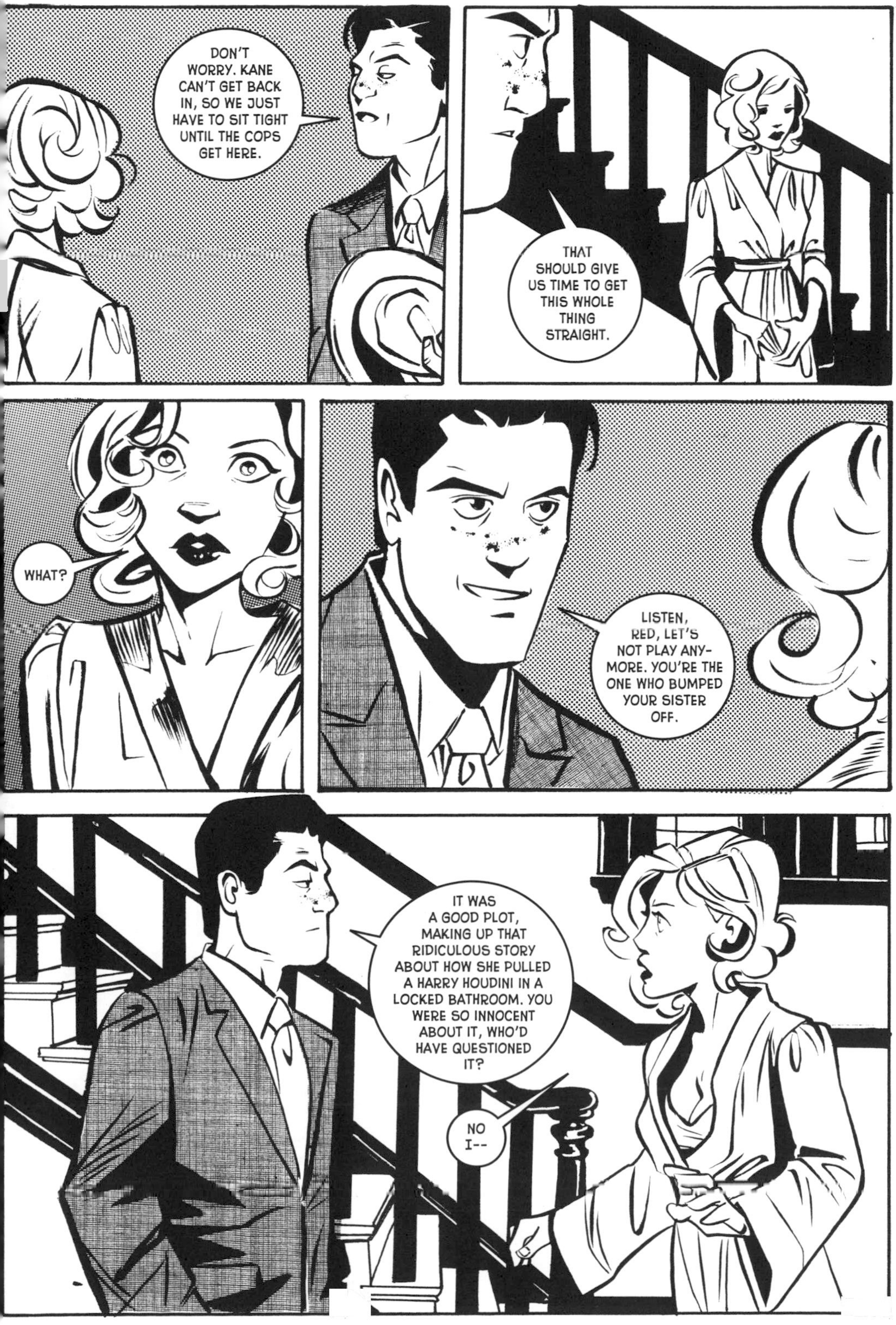
DON'T WORRY. KANE CAN'T GET BACK IN, SO WE JUST HAVE TO SIT TIGHT UNTIL THE COPS GET HERE.
THAT SHOULD GIVE US TIME TO GET THIS WHOLE THING STRAIGHT.
WHAT?
LISTEN, RED, LET'S NOT PLAY ANY-MORE. YOU'RE THE ONE WHO BUMPED YOUR SISTER OFF.
IT WAS A GOOD PLOT, MAKING UP THAT RIDICULOUS STORY ABOUT HOW SHE PULLED A HARRY HOUDINI IN A LOCKED BATHROOM. YOU WERE SO INNOCENT ABOUT IT, WHO'D HAVE QUESTIONED IT?
NO I--

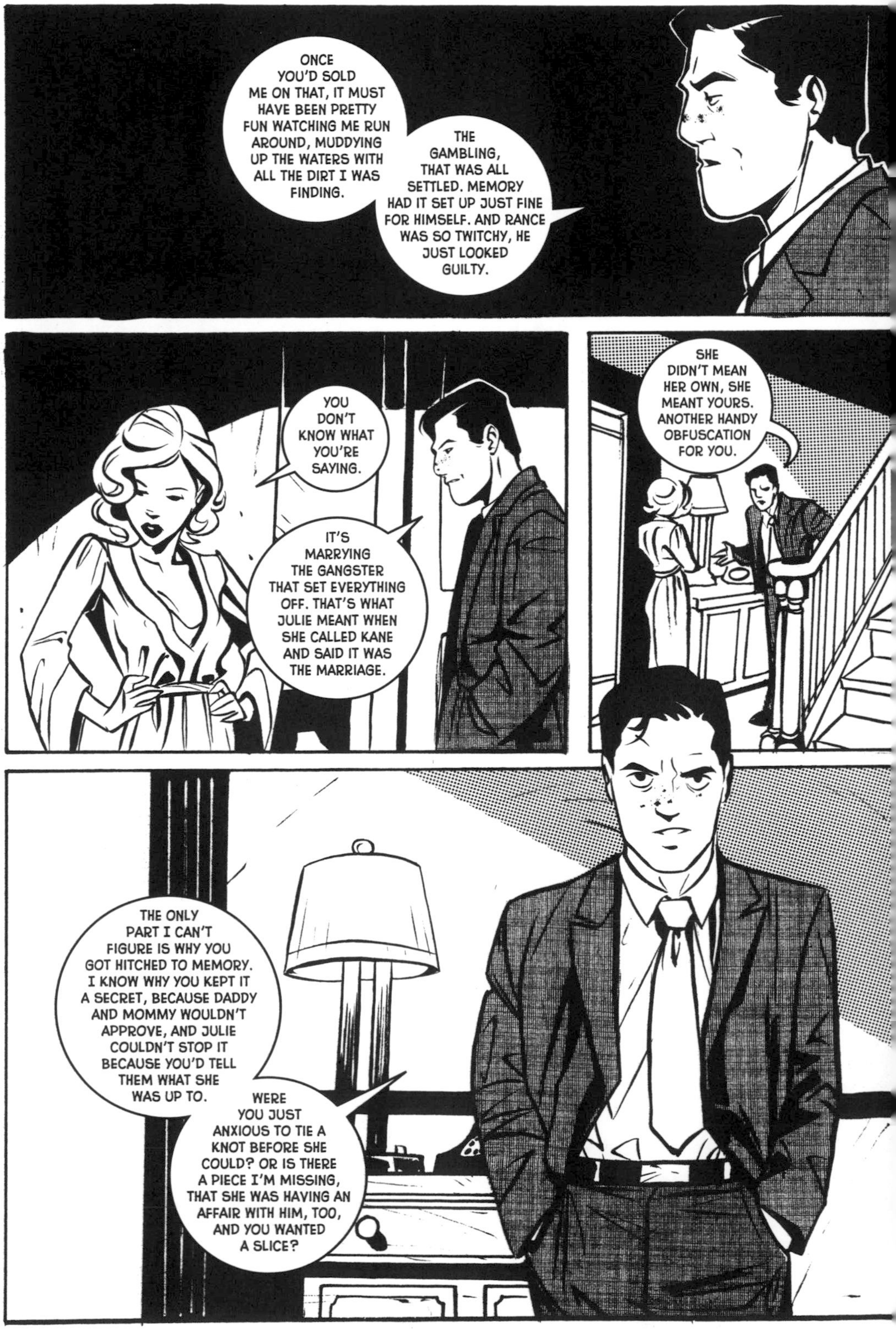
ONCE YOU'D SOLD ME ON THAT, IT MUST HAVE BEEN PRETTY FUN WATCHING ME RUN AROUND, MUDDYING UP THE WATERS WITH ALL THE DIRT I WAS FINDING.
THE GAMBLING, THAT WAS ALL SETTLED. MEMORY HAD IT SET UP JUST FINE FOR HIMSELF. AND RANCE WAS SO TWITCHY, HE JUST LOOKED GUILTY.
YOU DON'T KNOW WHAT YOU'RE SAYING.
IT'S MARRYING THE GANGSTER THAT SET EVERYTHING OFF. THAT'S WHAT JULIE MEANT WHEN SHE CALLED KANE AND SAID IT WAS THE MARRIAGE.
SHE DIDN'T MEAN HER OWN, SHE MEANT YOURS. ANOTHER HANDY OBFUSCATION FOR YOU.
THE ONLY PART I CAN'T FIGURE IS WHY YOU GOT HITCHED TO MEMORY. I KNOW WHY YOU KEPT IT A SECRET, BECAUSE DADDY AND MOMMY WOULDN'T APPROVE, AND JULIE COULDN'T STOP IT BECAUSE YOU'D TELL THEM WHAT SHE WAS UP TO.
WERE YOU JUST ANXIOUS TO TIE A KNOT BEFORE SHE COULD? OR IS THERE A PIECE I'M MISSING, THAT SHE WAS HAVING AN AFFAIR WITH HIM, TOO, AND YOU WANTED A SLICE?

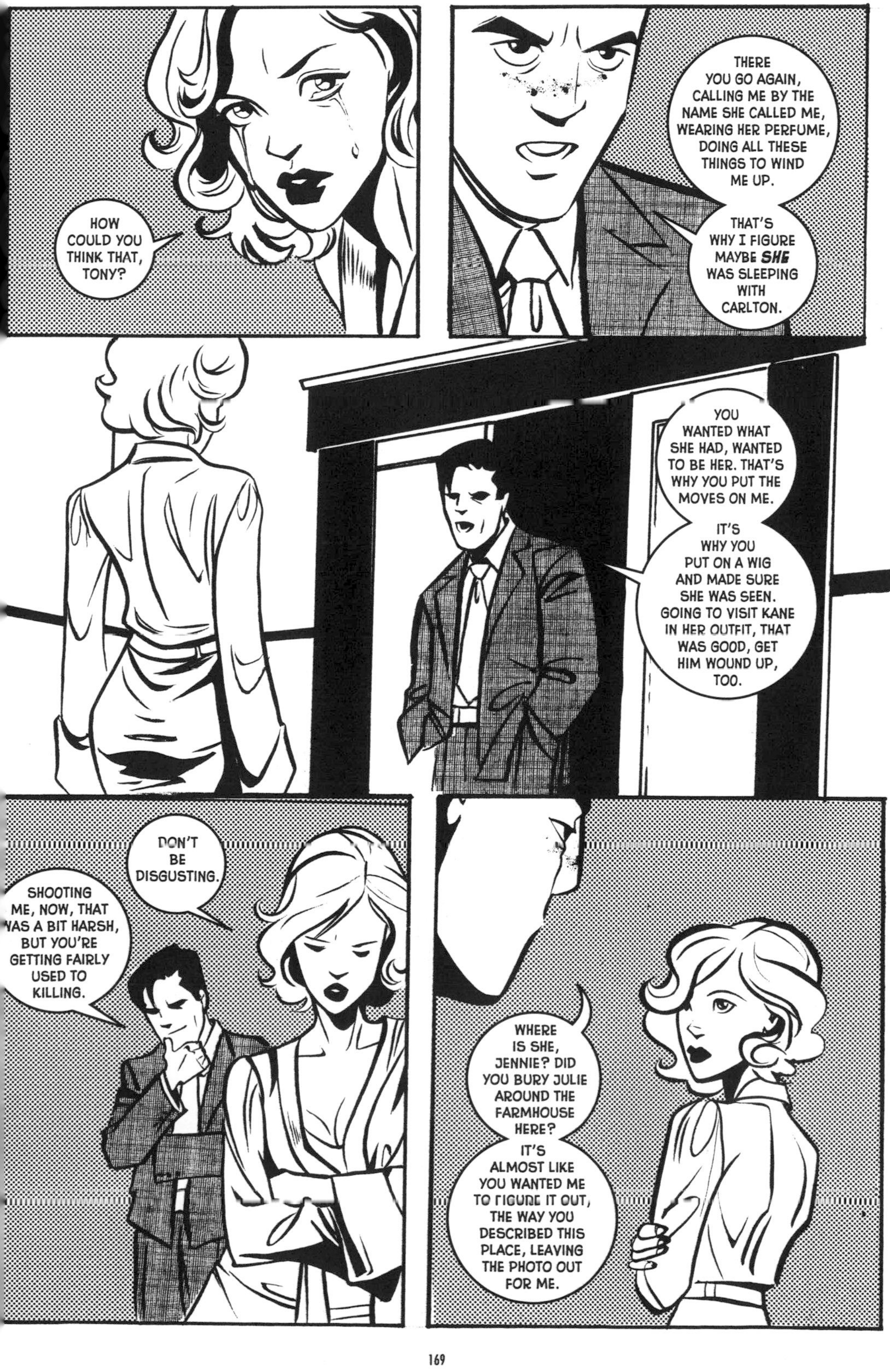
HOW COULD YOU THINK THAT, TONY?
THERE YOU GO AGAIN, CALLING ME BY THE NAME SHE CALLED ME, WEARING HER PERFUME, DOING ALL THESE THINGS TO WIND ME UP.
THAT'S WHY I FIGURE MAYBE SHE WAS SLEEPING WITH CARLTON.
YOU WANTED WHAT SHE HAD, WANTED TO BE HER. THAT'S WHY YOU PUT THE MOVES ON ME.
IT'S WHY YOU PUT ON A WIG AND MADE SURE SHE WAS SEEN. GOING TO VISIT KANE IN HER OUTFIT, THAT WAS GOOD, GET HIM WOUND UP, TOO.
SHOOTING ME, NOW, THAT WAS A BIT HARSH, BUT YOU'RE GETTING FAIRLY USED TO KILLING.
DON'T BE DISGUSTING.
WHERE IS SHE, JENNIE? DID YOU BURY JULIE AROUND THE FARMHOUSE HERE?
IT'S ALMOST LIKE YOU WANTED ME TO FIGURE IT OUT, THE WAY YOU DESCRIBED THIS PLACE, LEAVING THE PHOTO OUT FOR ME.

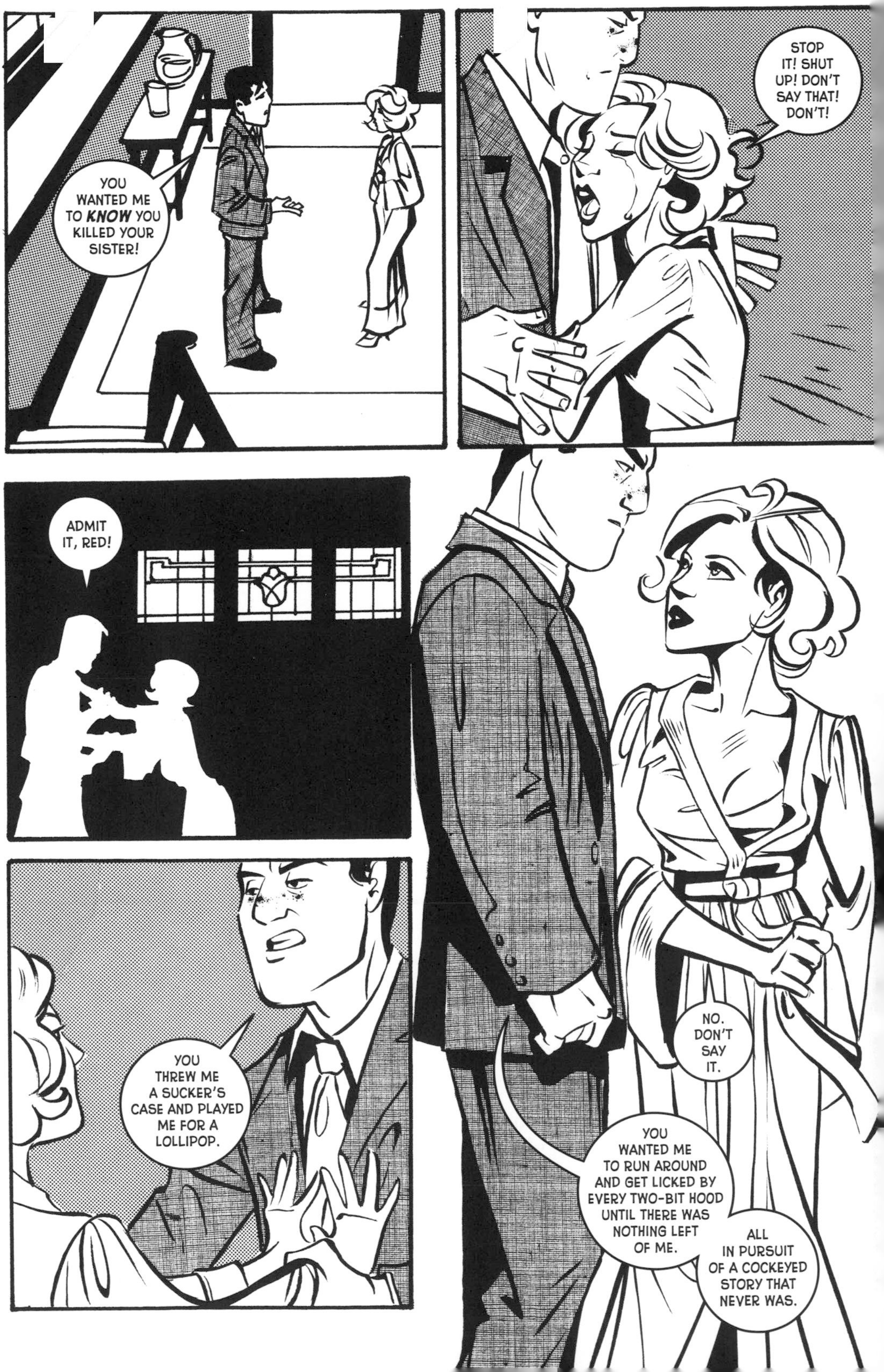
YOU WANTED ME TO **KNOW** YOU KILLED YOUR SISTER!
STOP IT! SHUT UP! DON'T SAY THAT! DON'T!
ADMIT IT, RED!
YOU THREW ME A SUCKER'S CASE AND PLAYED ME FOR A LOLLIPOP.
NO. DON'T SAY IT.
YOU WANTED ME TO RUN AROUND AND GET LICKED BY EVERY TWO-BIT HOOD UNTIL THERE WAS NOTHING LEFT OF ME.
ALL IN PURSUIT OF A COCKEYED STORY THAT NEVER WAS.

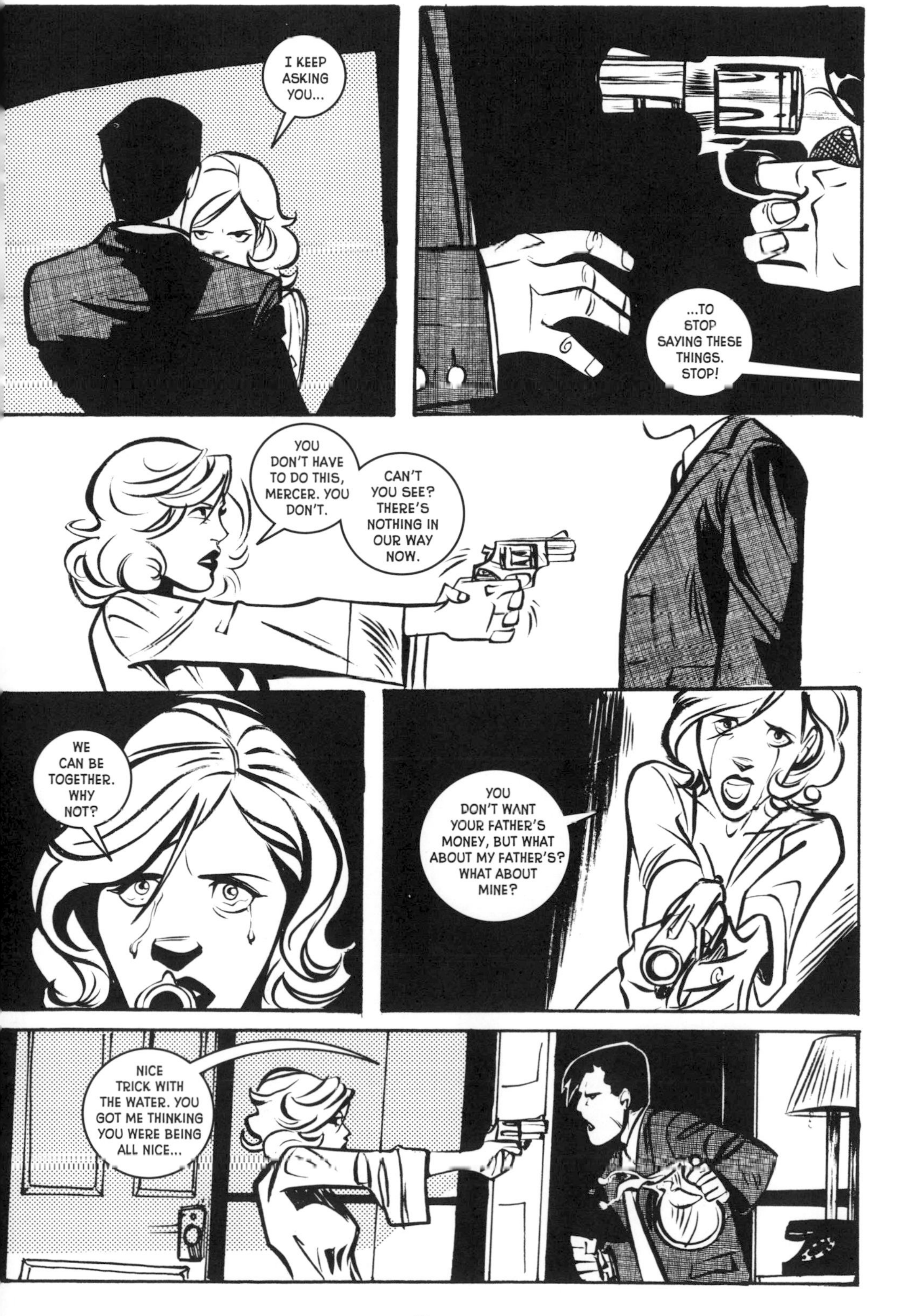
I KEEP ASKING YOU...
...TO STOP SAYING THESE THINGS. STOP!
YOU DON'T HAVE TO DO THIS, MERCER. YOU DON'T.
CAN'T YOU SEE? THERE'S NOTHING IN OUR WAY NOW.
WE CAN BE TOGETHER. WHY NOT?
YOU DON'T WANT YOUR FATHER'S MONEY, BUT WHAT ABOUT MY FATHER'S? WHAT ABOUT MINE?
NICE TRICK WITH THE WATER. YOU GOT ME THINKING YOU WERE BEING ALL NICE...

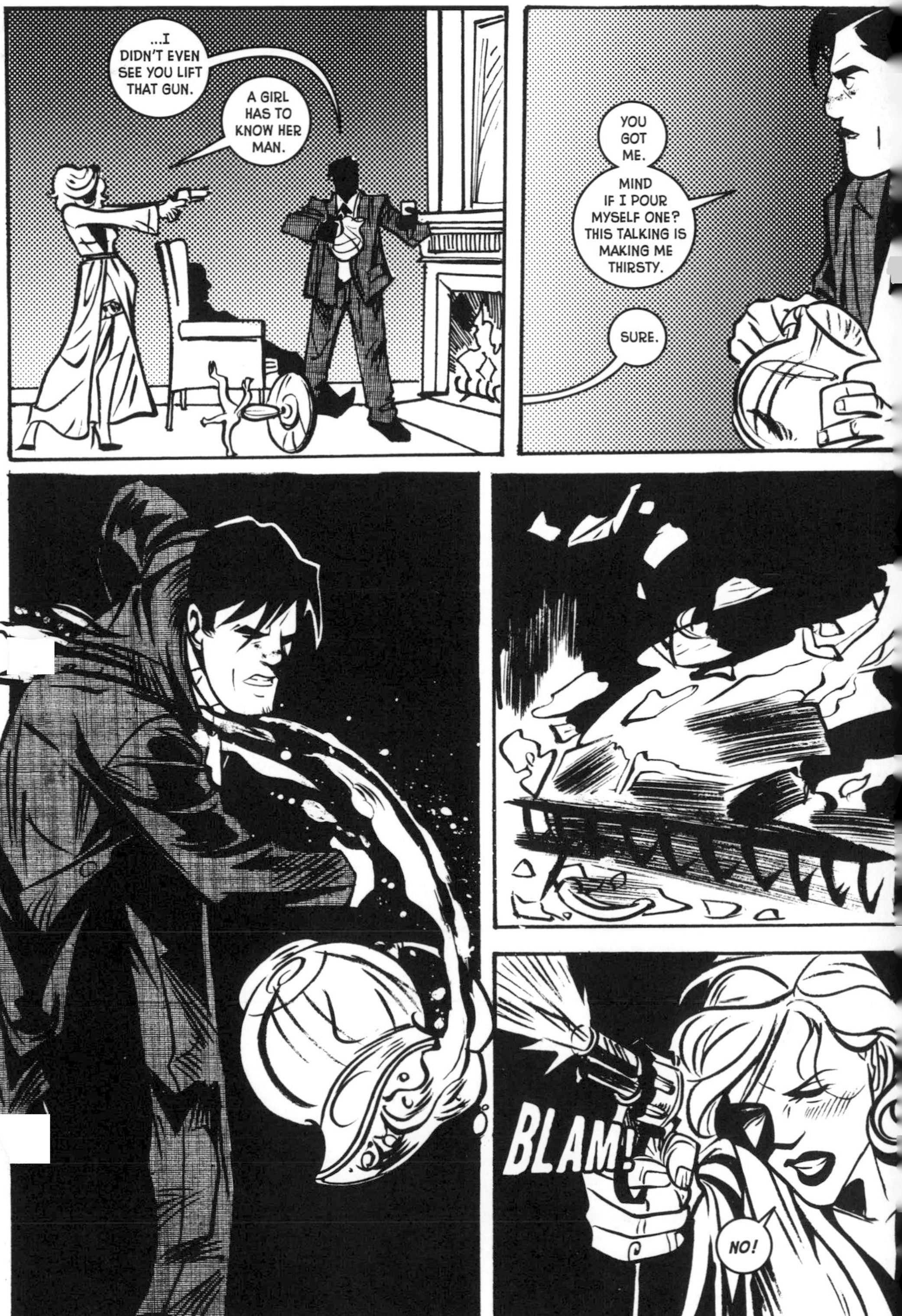
...I DIDN'T EVEN SEE YOU LIFT THAT GUN.
A GIRL HAS TO KNOW HER MAN.
YOU GOT ME.
MIND IF I POUR MYSELF ONE? THIS TALKING IS MAKING ME THIRSTY.
SURE.
BLAM!
NO!

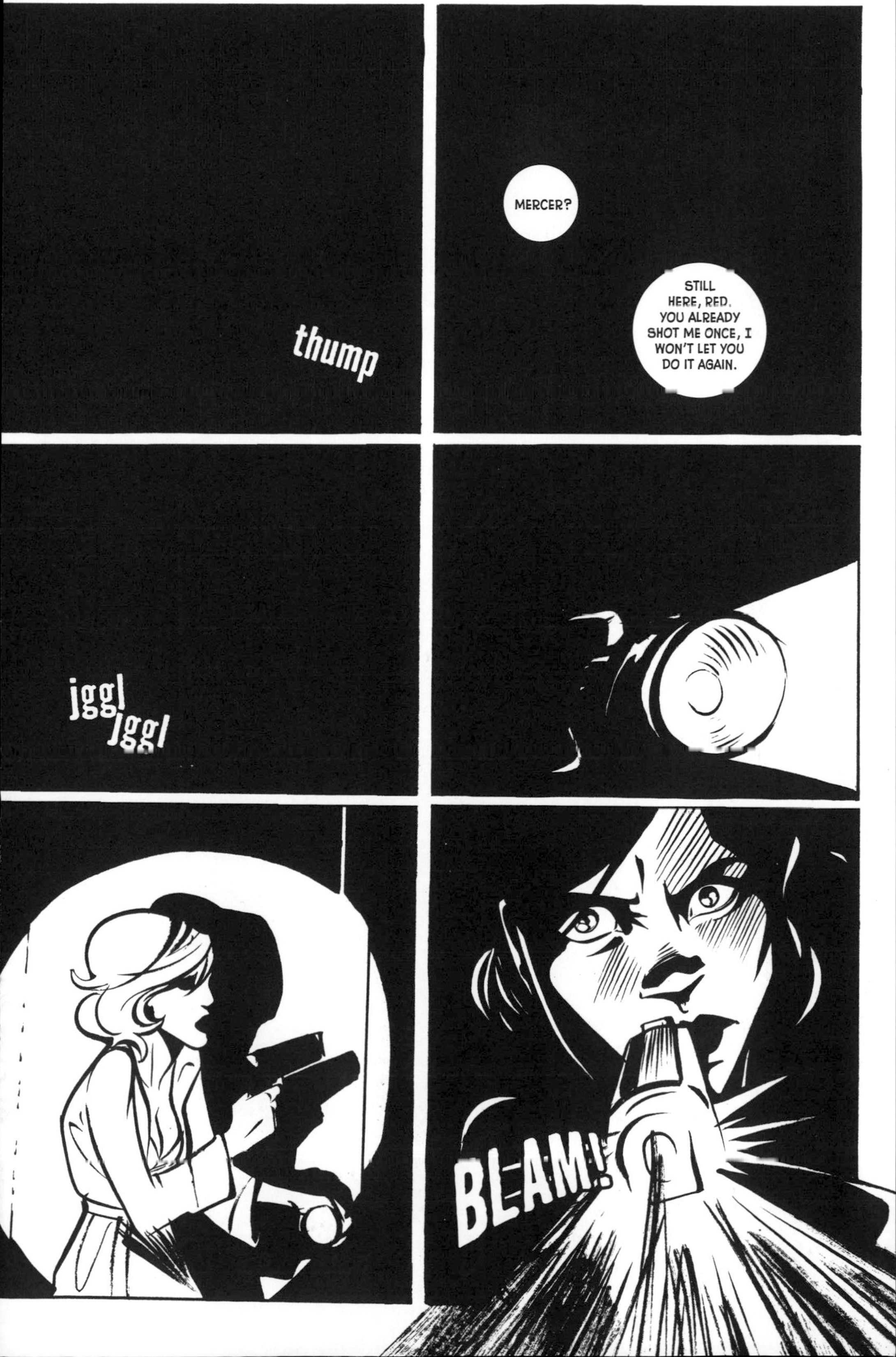
thump
MERCER?
STILL HERE, RED. YOU ALREADY SHOT ME ONCE, I WON'T LET YOU DO IT AGAIN.
jggl
jggl
BLAM!

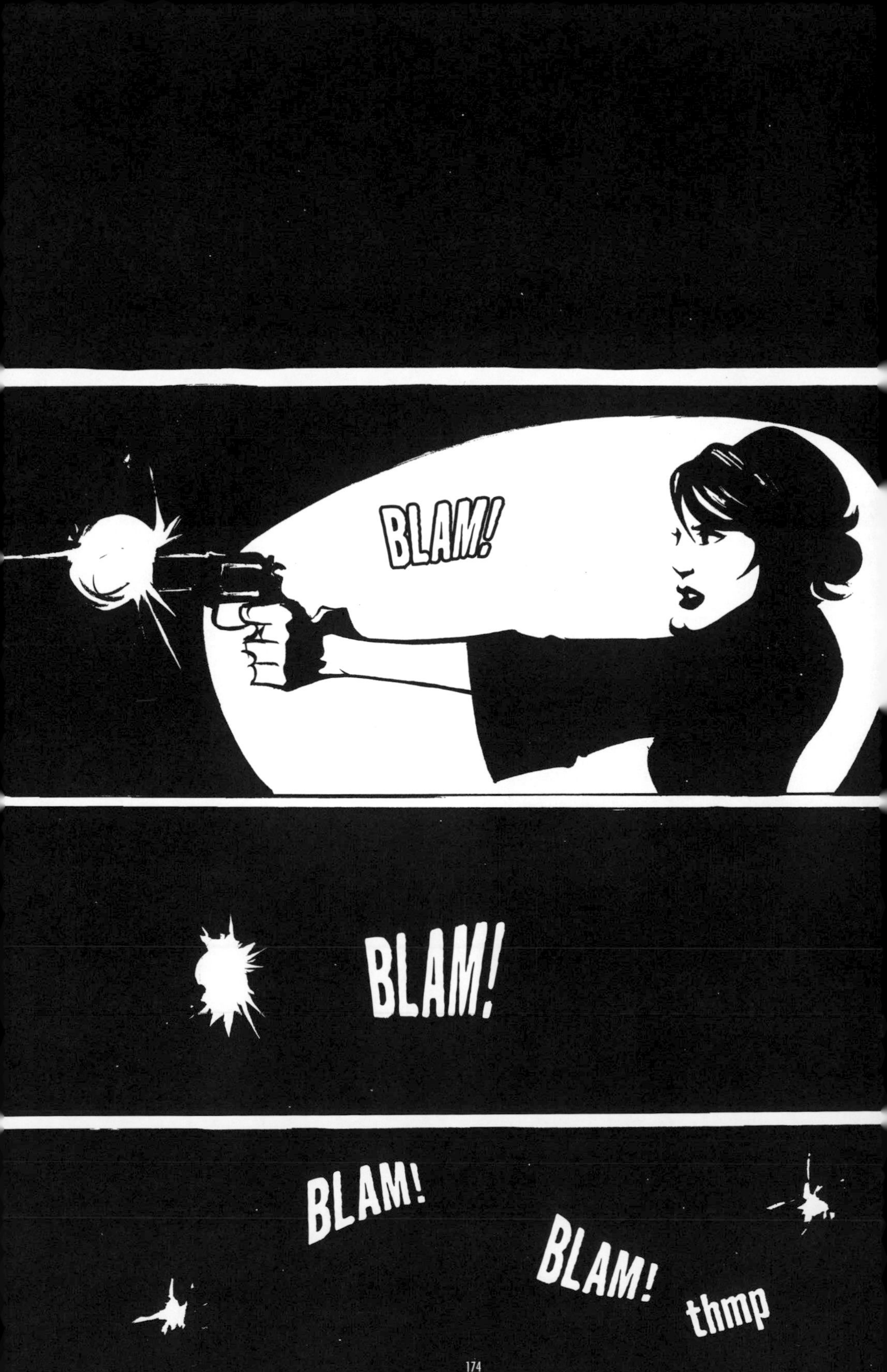
BLAM!
BLAM!
BLAM!
BLAM!
thmp

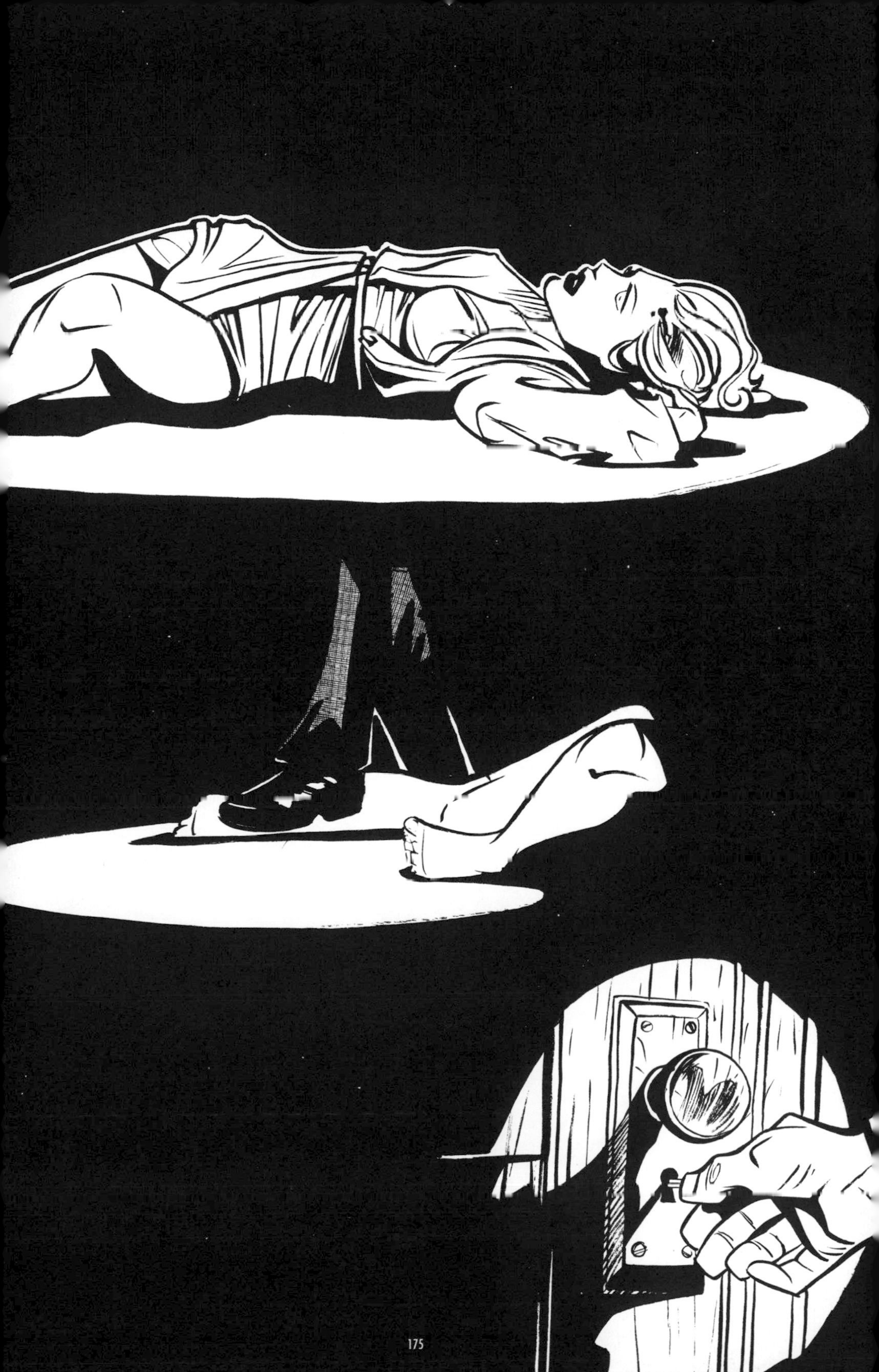

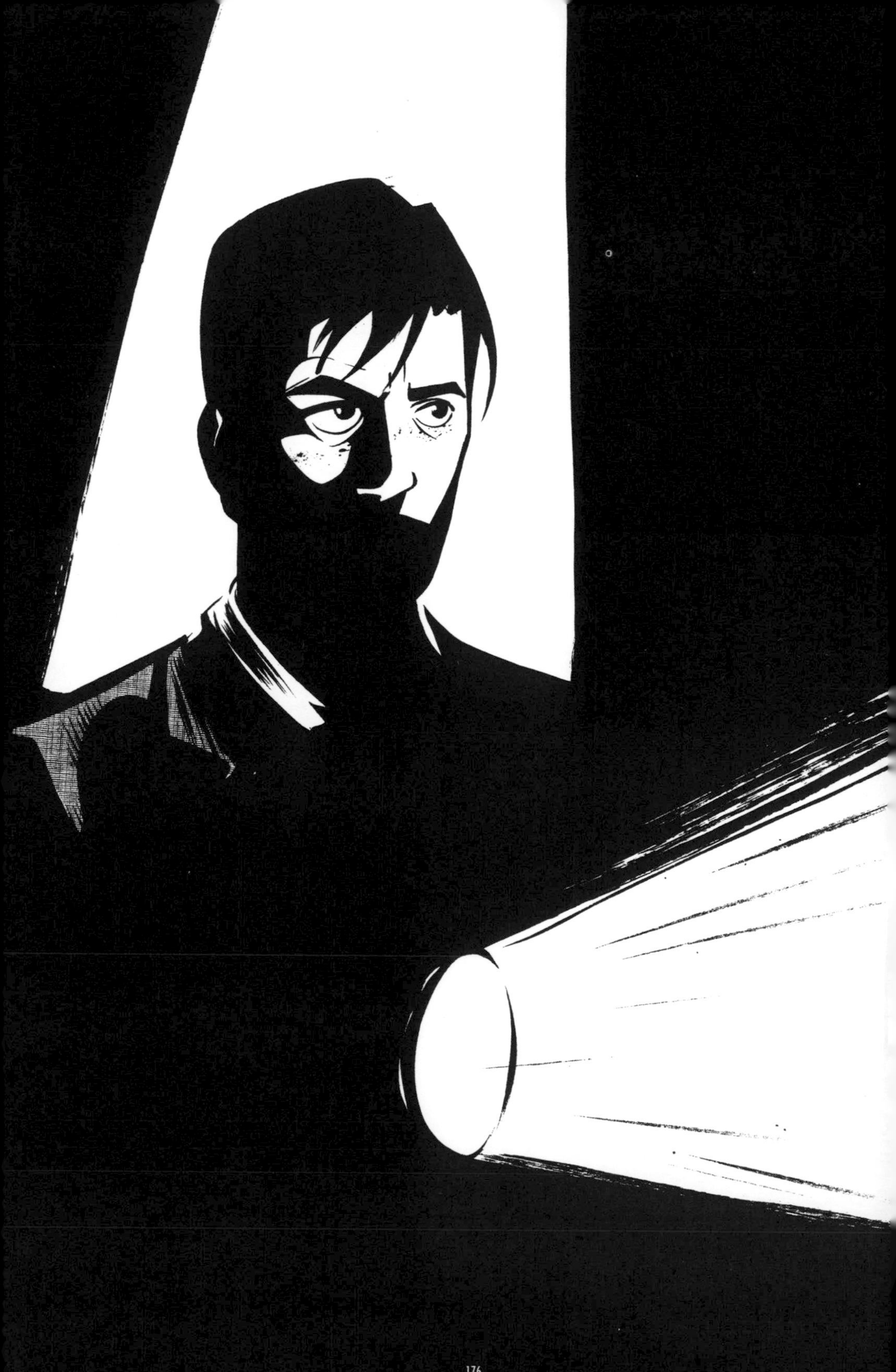

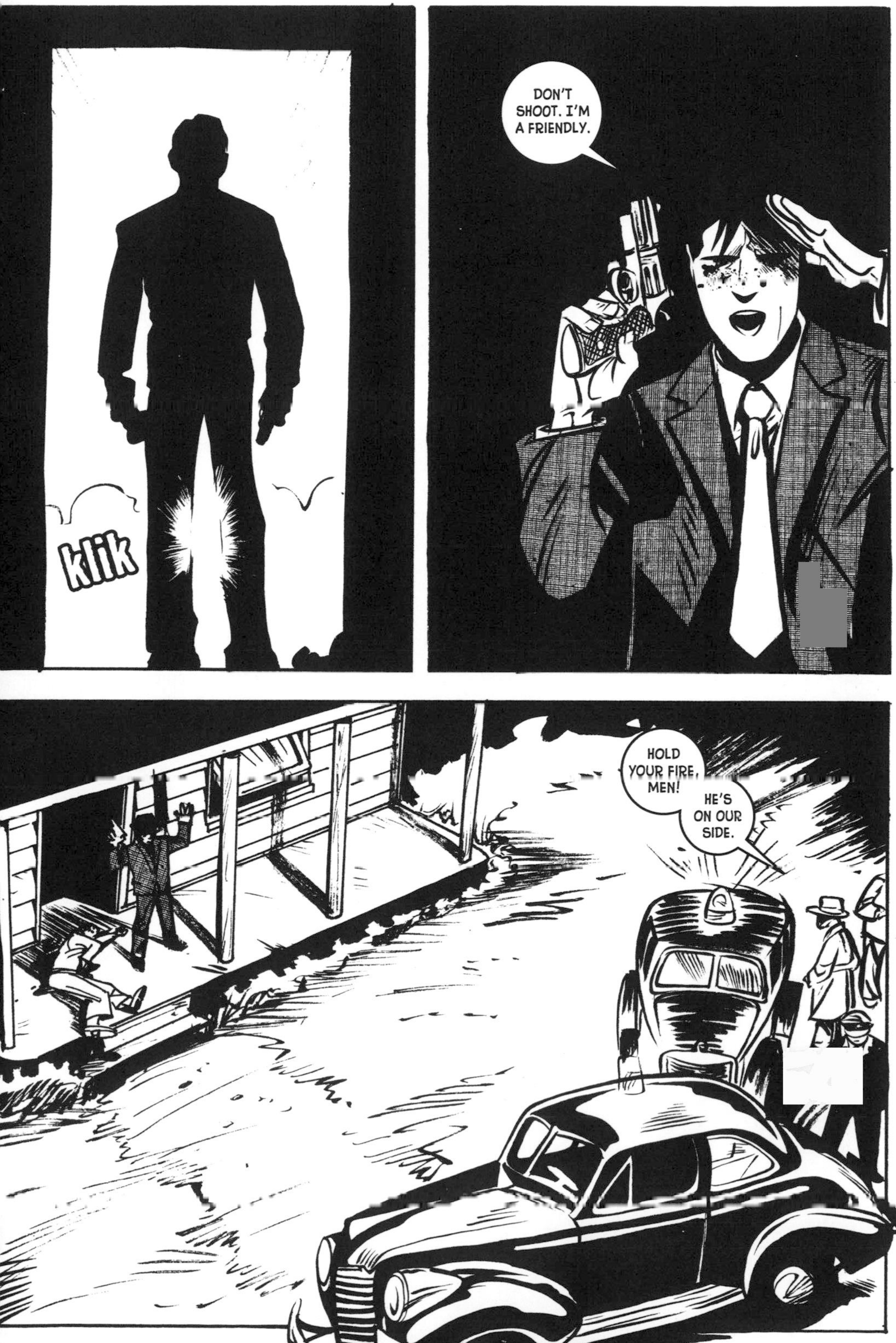
klik
DON'T SHOOT. I'M A FRIENDLY.
HOLD YOUR FIRE, MEN!
HE'S ON OUR SIDE.

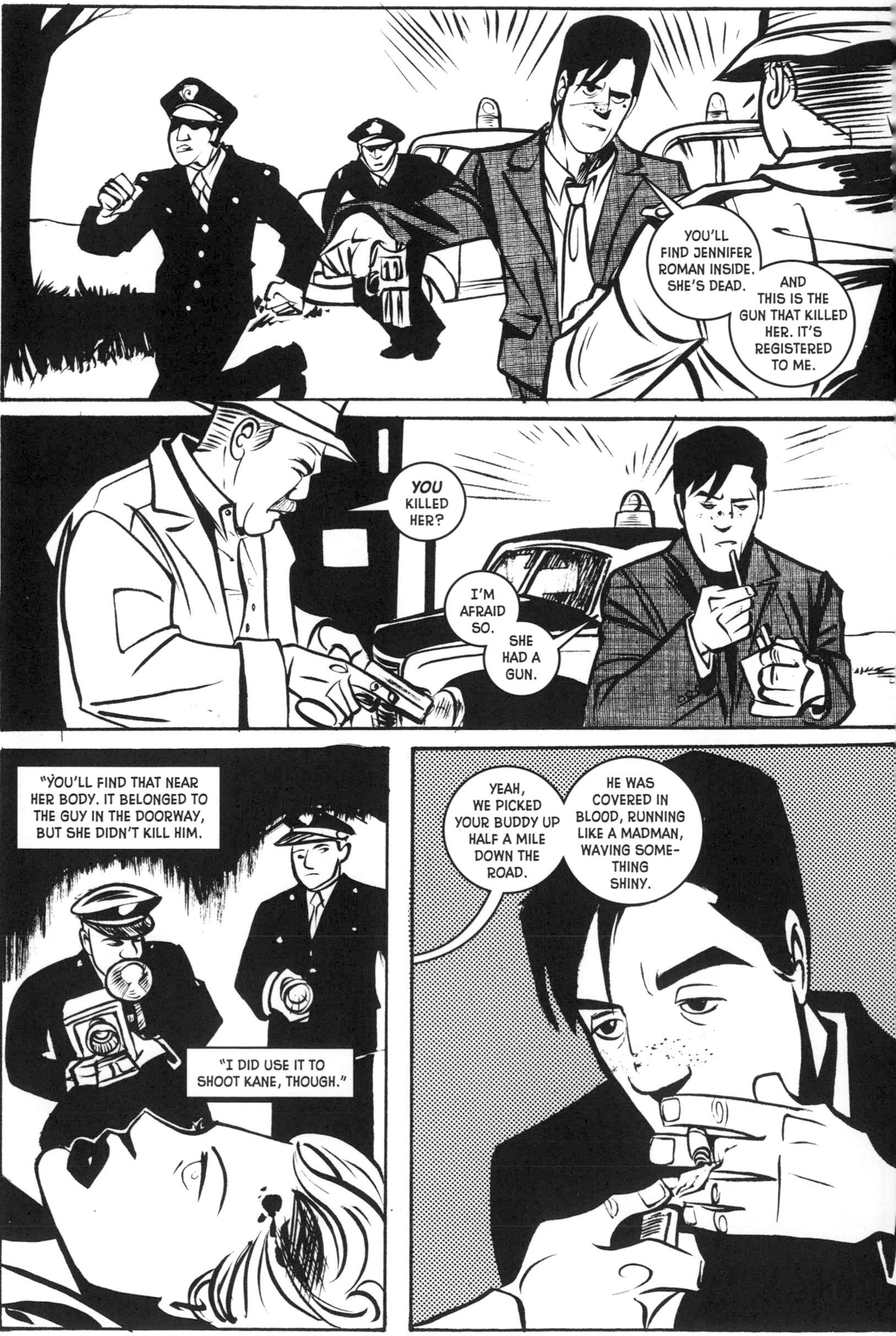
YOU'LL FIND JENNIFER ROMAN INSIDE. SHE'S DEAD.
AND THIS IS THE GUN THAT KILLED HER. IT'S REGISTERED TO ME.
YOU KILLED HER?
I'M AFRAID SO.
SHE HAD A GUN.
"YOU'LL FIND THAT NEAR HER BODY. IT BELONGED TO THE GUY IN THE DOORWAY, BUT SHE DIDN'T KILL HIM.
"I DID USE IT TO SHOOT KANE, THOUGH."
YEAH, WE PICKED YOUR BUDDY UP HALF A MILE DOWN THE ROAD.
HE WAS COVERED IN BLOOD, RUNNING LIKE A MADMAN, WAVING SOME-THING SHINY.

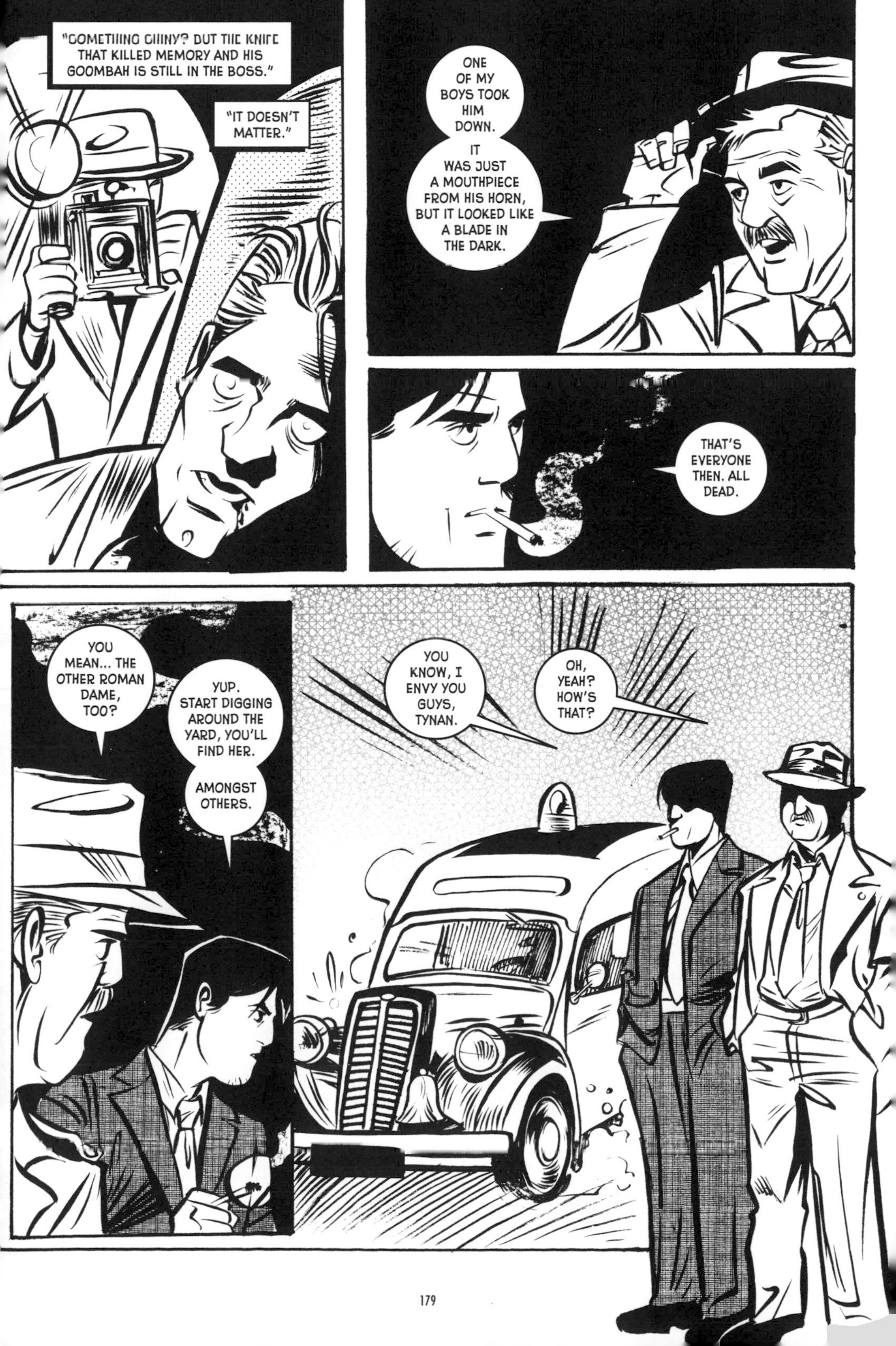
"SOMETHING SHINY? BUT THE KNIFE THAT KILLED MEMORY AND HIS GOOMBAH IS STILL IN THE BOSS."
"IT DOESN'T MATTER."
ONE OF MY BOYS TOOK HIM DOWN.
IT WAS JUST A MOUTHPIECE FROM HIS HORN, BUT IT LOOKED LIKE A BLADE IN THE DARK.
THAT'S EVERYONE THEN. ALL DEAD.
YOU MEAN... THE OTHER ROMAN DAME, TOO?
YUP. START DIGGING AROUND THE YARD, YOU'LL FIND HER.
AMONGST OTHERS.
YOU KNOW, I ENVY YOU GUYS, TYNAN.
OH, YEAH? HOW'S THAT?

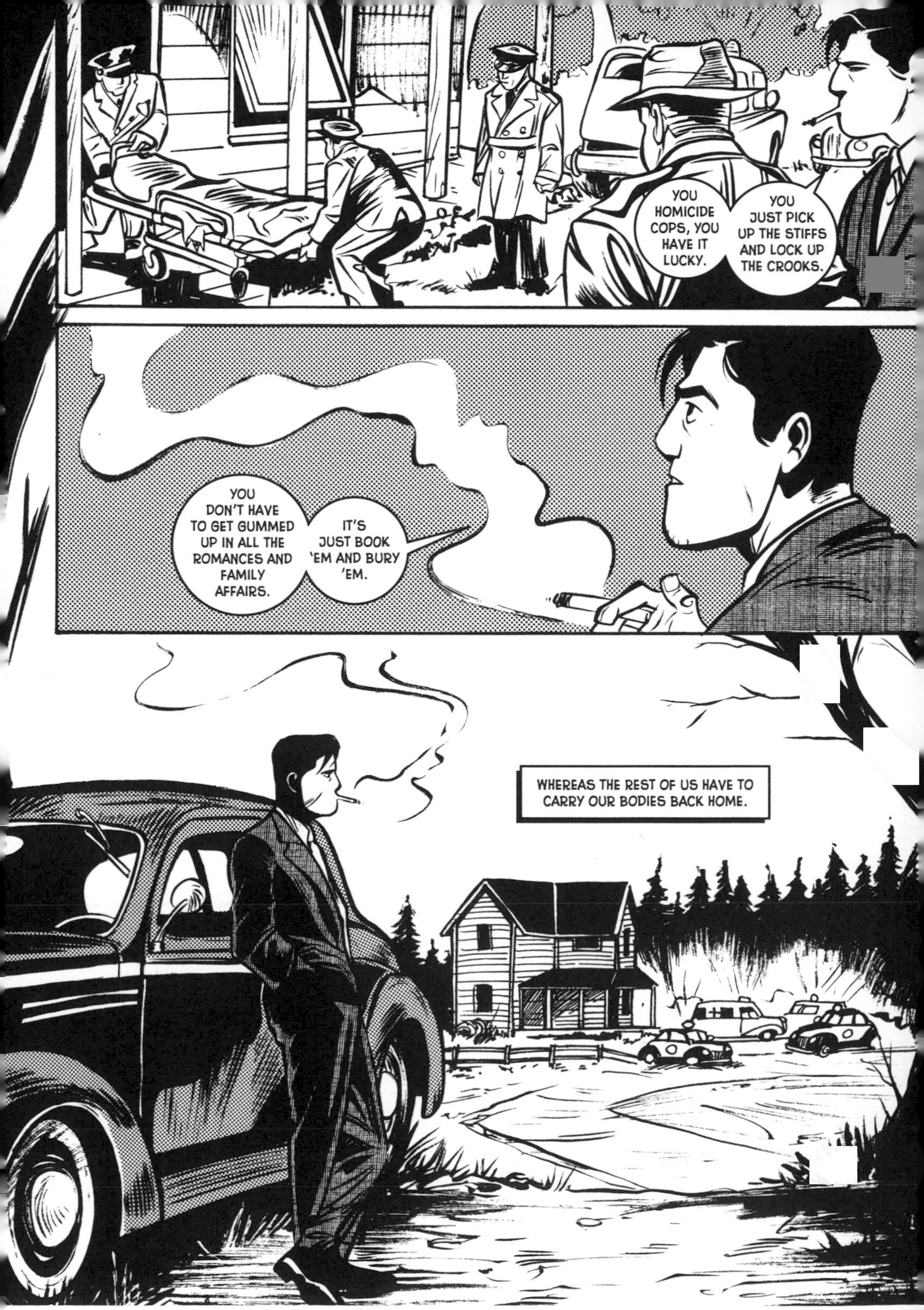
YOU HOMICIDE COPS, YOU HAVE IT LUCKY.
YOU JUST PICK UP THE STIFFS AND LOCK UP THE CROOKS.
YOU DON'T HAVE TO GET GUMMED UP IN ALL THE ROMANCES AND FAMILY AFFAIRS.
IT'S JUST BOOK 'EM AND BURY 'EM.
WHEREAS THE REST OF US HAVE TO CARRY OUR BODIES BACK HOME.

THE END

An Oni Press Production

JOËLLE JONES & **JAMIE S. RICH** first collaborated on the acclaimed comic book *12 Reasons Why I Love Her*, and have since shown up as a team in the pages of *Popgun*, *Portland Noir*, and *Madman Atomic Comics*. Joëlle also did the cover and interior illustrations for Jamie's novel *Have You Seen the Horizon Lately?*

Separately, they have multiple creative works between them. Joëlle has contributed to the long-running comics series *Fables* at DC/Vertigo, and she drew the Minx young adult graphic novel *Token*, written by Alisa Kwitney. Her next longform project is called *The Starving Artist*, also from Vertigo.

Jamie has published four prose novels, including *Cut My Hair*, *I Was Someone Dead*, and *The Everlasting*. He wrote the comics series *Love the Way You Love*, which was illustrated by Marc Ellerby. Additionally, he has had short stories in *Four-Letter Worlds*, *Buffy the Vampire Slayer: Food Chain*, *Put the Book Back on the Shelf*, *The Dark Horse Book of the Dead*, and *This is a Souvenir*, teaming him with artists as diverse as Andi Watson, Chynna Clugston, Guy Davis, Natalie Nourigat, and Kelley Seda.

Both Rich and Jones currently reside in separate locations in Portland, OR, U.S.A. They will next be seen on the printed page as a team working with Nicolas Hitori de on the Oni Press series *Spell Checkers*.

www.confessions123.com • *www.joellejones.com*

Other books by JAMIE S. RICH *& Oni Press*

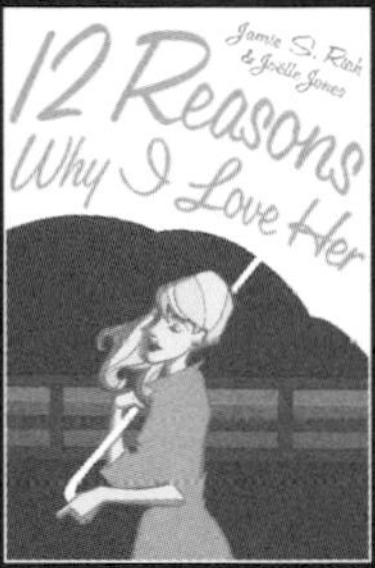
Jamie S. Rich & Joëlle Jones
12 Reasons Why I Love Her

12 REASONS WHY I LOVE HER
By Jamie S. Rich & Joëlle Jones
144 pages, 6x9 trade paperback
black and white interiors
$14.95
ISBN 978-1-932664-51-5

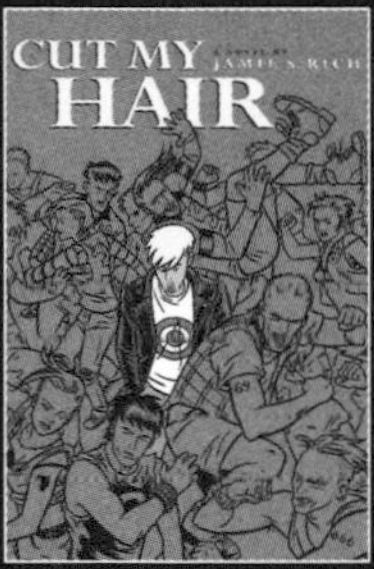
CUT MY HAIR

CUT MY HAIR
By Jamie S. Rich
236 pages, 6x9 trade paperback
black and white interiors
$15.95
ISBN 978-0-9700387-0-8

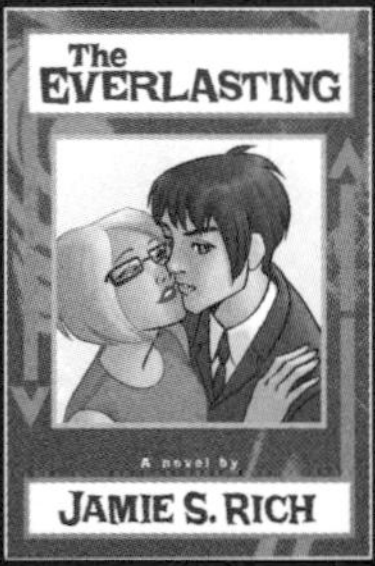
The EVERLASTING
A novel by
JAMIE S. RICH

THE EVERLASTING
By Jamie S. Rich
496 pages, 6x9 trade paperback, novel
$19.95
ISBN 978-1-932664-54-6

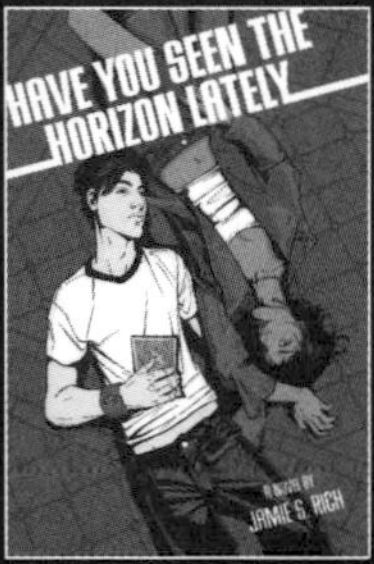
HAVE YOU SEEN THE HORIZON LATELY
JAMIE S. RICH

HAVE YOU SEEN THE HORIZON LATELY?
By Jamie S. Rich
380 pages, 6x9 trade paperback, novel
$19.95 US
ISBN 978-1-932664-73-7

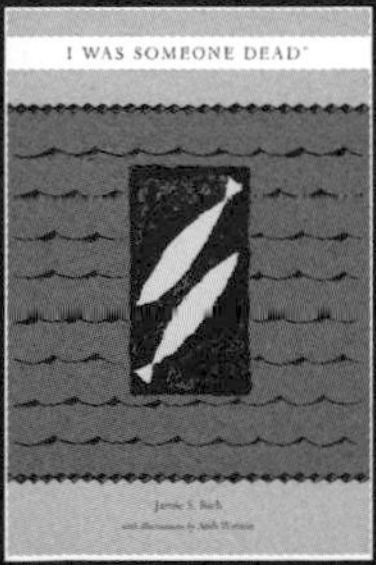
I WAS SOMEONE DEAD

I WAS SOMEONE DEAD
By Jamie S. Rich & Andi Watson
136 pages, digest
black and white interiors
$9.95
ISBN 978-1-932664-26-3

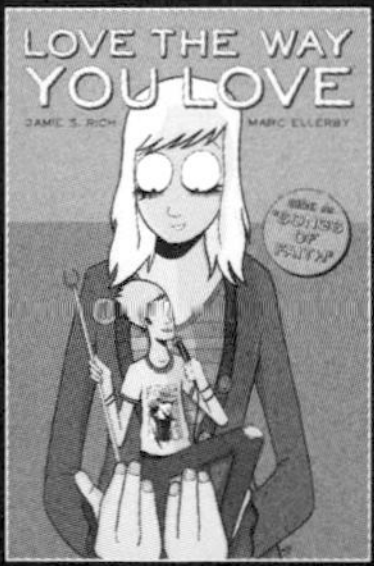
LOVE THE WAY YOU LOVE
JAMIE S. RICH
MARC ELLERBY

LOVE THE WAY YOU LOVE: SIDE A
By Jamie S. Rich & Marc Ellerby
200 pages, digest
black and white interiors
$11.95 US
ISBN 978-1-932664-66-9

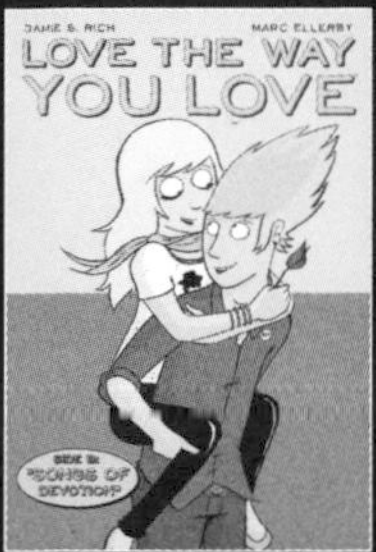
JAMIE S. RICH
MARC ELLERBY
LOVE THE WAY YOU LOVE

LOVE THE WAY YOU LOVE: SIDE B
By Jamie S. Rich & Marc Ellerby
200 pages, digest
black and white interiors
$11.95 US
ISBN 978-1-932664-95-9

For more information on these and other fine Oni Press comic books and graphic novels, visit www.onipress.com.
To find a comic specialty store in your area, call 1-888-COMICBOOK or visit www.comicshops.us.

OTHER THRILLERS FROM ONI PRESS

CAPOTE IN KANSAS
A DRAWN NOVEL
ANDE PARKS
CHRIS SAMNEE

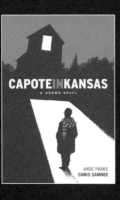

CAPOTE IN KANSAS
By Ande Parks & Chris Samnee
128 pages, 6x9 trade paperback
black and white interiors
$11.95
ISBN 978-1-932664-29-4

THE DAMNED
VOLUME ONE
"THREE DAYS DEAD"

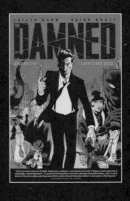

DAMNED, VOLUME 1: THREE DAYS DEAD
By Cullen Bunn and Brian Hurtt
160 pages, 6x9 trade paperback
black and white interiors
$14.95 US
ISBN 978-1-932664-6-38

ANTONY JOHNSTON & BRETT WELDELE
JULIUS

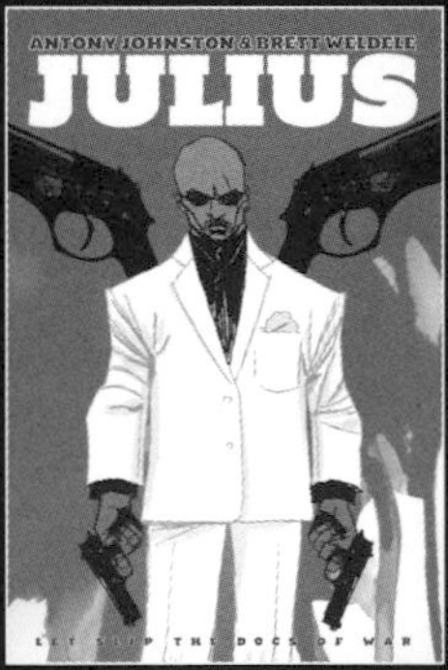

JULIUS
By Antony Johnston & Brett Weldele
160 pages, digest
black and white interiors
$14.95
ISBN 978-1-929998-80-7

PAST LIES
CHRISTINA WEIR NUNZIO DEFILIPPIS CHRISTOPHER MITTEN

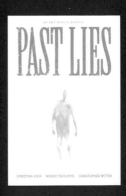

PAST LIES
By Nunzio DeFilippis, Christina Weir & Christopher Mitten
168 pages, digest
black and white interiors
$14.95
ISBN 978-1-932664-34-8

SCANDALOUS
J. TORRES | SCOTT CHANTLER

SCANDALOUS
By J. Torres & Scott Chantler
104 pages, digest
black and white interiors
$9.95
ISBN 978-1-929998-98-2

UNION STATION
ANDE PARKS

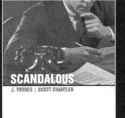

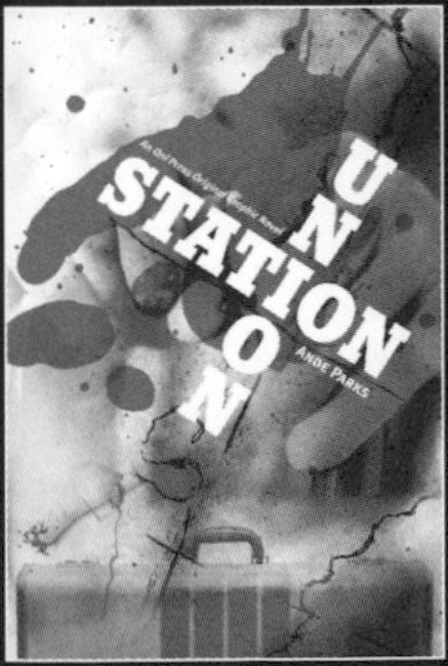

UNION STATION
By Ande Parks & Eduardo Barreto
128 pages, 6x9 trade paperback
black and white interiors
$11.95
ISBN 978-1-929998-69-2

oni PRESS

www.onipress.com

For more information on these and other fine Oni Press comic books and graphic novels, visit www.onipress.com.
To find a comic specialty store in your area, call 1-888-COMICBOOK or visit www.comicshops.us.